Outsider Within

Outsider Within

Reworking Anthropology in the Global Age

FAYE V. HARRISON

University of Illinois Press

URBANA AND CHICAGO

Library of Congress Cataloging-in-Publication Data
Harrison, Faye Venetia.
Outsider within : reworking anthropology
in the global age / Faye V. Harrison.
p. cm.
Includes bibliographical references and index.
ISBN-13: 978-0-252-03261-5 (cloth : alk. paper)
ISBN-10: 0-252-03261-6 (cloth : alk. paper)
ISBN-13: 978-0-252-07490-5 (pbk. : alk. paper)
ISBN-10: 0-252-07490-4 (pbk. : alk. paper)
1. Ethnology—Philosophy.
2. Applied anthropology.
I. Title.
GN345.H43   2008
306—dc22   2007044080

Contents

Acknowledgments

I am indebted to a long list of colleagues, friends, and relatives without whom I could not have completed this book. I was introduced to many of the components of a critical anthropology of anthropology by the late St. Clair Drake. On the very first day I met him, he addressed aspects of anthropology's racial politics that stimulated me to begin thinking about the ways in which ideas and academic careers are concretely related to the world. His encyclopedic knowledge of Africa, the African diaspora, and the history of blacks in anthropology made a deep impression that inspires me to this day. In many respects, my project in reworking anthropology as an "outsider within" is meant to extend his legacy as a teacher and role model.

Before I studied with Drake and other professors who influenced me at Stanford, mainly Bridget O'Laughlin, Sylvia Yanagisako, Bernard Siegel, and Michelle Rosaldo, I studied with Louise Lamphere while I was an undergraduate at Brown. Louise may have been more responsible than anyone for convincing me that becoming an anthropologist was something I could actually do. I truly appreciate her interest and moral support, which have been sustained over the years. The late George Houston Bass was another Brown professor whose belief in my abilities made an important difference at a formative phase. His vision for the black performing arts was expansively interdisciplinary and included a historical appreciation for the role that the anthropologists Zora Neale Hurston and Katherine Dunham played in translating ethnographic and folkloric material into performative and literary praxis. He encouraged me to cultivate a wide repertoire of skills that would bring together the performer, writer, and anthropologist into a single integrated whole. In a challenging course on multiracial societies in the Americas,

Rhett Jones taught me some important lessons about the usefulness of social theory in interpreting history and asking historical questions. Years later at his invitation, I returned to Brown to give a colloquium on anthropology, dramatic performance, and dramaturgic metaphors in social analysis. Upon hearing about the Association of Black Anthropologists' (ABA's) plan to publish *Decolonizing Anthropology,* he encouraged me to submit a proposal to the Center for the Study of Race and Ethnicity in America. Funds from the Center made it possible for the ABA to publish the book through the American Anthropological Association (AAA). The impact of the book has been considerable. I thank Rhett Jones for his foresight in understanding the book's significance.

A number of colleagues have given me immeasurable support over the many years it has taken to complete this book. Gina Athena Ulysse, Pem Davidson Buck, Anne Francis Okongwu, Ann Kingsolver, Yvonne Jones, Lee D. Baker, Layli Phillips, Willie Baber, Tony Whitehead, Audrey Smedley, Arthur Spears, Deborah D'Amico, Lanita Jacobs-Huey, Karla Slocum, Deborah Thomas, and Marilyn Thomas-Houston, an inspirational cheerleader, have been in my amen corner, patiently awaiting the outcome of my protracted labors. A number of years ago, Gina gave me a beautiful unfinished poncho made from fabric painted by a talented Haitian artist, Joseph Eddy Pierre. The colors and symbols are simply awe inspiring. She made me promise not to wear the beautiful garment until I finished the book. Since then, I have happily looked forward to adorning myself with that work of art, which will always remind me of the importance of good friends who give gifts as well as tough love when you need them most.

I deeply appreciate Constance Sutton's moral support for my Caribbeanist work. The colloquia and symposia she invited me to were invaluable forums for presenting and getting useful feedback on research I undertook while employed in institutional settings where there were few, if any, colleagues and students who shared my interests. Arlene Torres and Kevin A. Yelvington are also colleagues whose interest in my work in Jamaica and on the history of African American and African diaspora anthropology raised my morale at moments when I doubted whether my scholarship was having an impact. The International Union of Anthropological and Ethnological Sciences (IUAES) has given me the chance to extend my kindred-thinking network to include a number of individuals whose everyday practice of anthropology takes place in universities and applied research settings all over the world. I especially value the opportunity to get to know and work with Jan Delacourt, Esther Njiro, Subhadra Mitra Channa, and Wu Ga. Through our concerted activities in the IUAES Commission on the Anthropology of Women, we have contributed important new perspectives to several conferences and forums, both academic and activist, in different parts of the world. Those experiences have contributed an important dimension to my identity as an anthropologist.

I would like to acknowledge the influence that my former Stanford class-mate, Glenn Jordan, has had on my thinking. My approach to the critical anthropology of anthropology owes a great deal to what I learned from him as a graduate student and later as a young professional. His methodology for "reading St. Clair Drake," which he developed in a 1982 working paper, and his role in co-organizing with me a 1985 AAA session to honor Drake's career made a deep and lasting impression on my thinking about "outsid-ers within" anthropology. Glenn's enthusiastic feedback on the first essay in which I confronted the problem and possibilities of anthropology's intel-lectual peripheries signaled that I was heading in a promising direction. In many respects, that essay paved the way for this book.

Two subsequent intellectual history projects were also instrumental in setting the stage and preparing me for this book. I am thankful to Donald Nonini, another Stanford alumnus, for initiating our exchanges on W. E. B. Du Bois's significance for anthropology. Out of them came a special issue of *Critique of Anthropology*. Ira E. Harrison, a colleague at the University of Tennessee–Knoxville, planted the seeds for the intellectual biographies com-piled in the book we coedited, *African-American Pioneers in Anthropology*. The original plan was for Glenn Jordan to coedit the book with Ira. When Glenn realized that he had to shift his attention to his dissertation research in Cardiff, Wales, where he eventually settled, he suggested that I take his place in collaborating with Ira. Ira welcomed the idea, and the rest is history. Willie L. Baber, who contributed the chapter on Drake to *African-American Pioneers* as well as an essay to the Du Bois collection, has been someone with whom I have shared long-standing interests and, like Glenn, the mid- to late 1970s Stanford experience of working with common professors, principally Drake and O'Laughlin. I appreciate Willie's patient listening and encourage-ment, especially that afternoon when I stopped by his home in Greensboro on my way back to Knoxville from Duke. I had just participated in a 2002 summer institute on "Globalization, Women, and Development" and was excited about that as well as my book project. I talked his ears off about the essay that was to become the final chapter of this book. Within a couple of years, we both had the opportunity to move even farther south to Gainesville, Florida, where we are colleagues in the Department of Anthropology and the African American Studies Program.

Paule Cruz Takash has shared my interest in remapping anthropolo-gy's center. I thank her for being willing to work with me on the "Critical

Center(s)" session for the 1999 AAA meeting. Although that Presidential Session emerged from our shared brainstorming about "anthropology at the millennium," she assumed the responsibility for doing most of the organizational work communicating with the panelists and sending them suggested readings to stimulate their thinking along convergent lines. I appreciate her commitment to building alliances and to helping her colleagues move productively beyond bipolar conversations about race.

I give my sincerest heartfelt thanks to Cheryl Rodriguez and Maria Vesperi for reading the entire manuscript and making helpful suggestions for revising it. Elizabeth "Liz" Dulany, my editor, has had the patience of Job for longer than I care to admit. She was the "midwife" for *African-American Pioneers in Anthropology*. Based on that experience, I knew that her vision was compatible with mine and that she would caringly guide me through the stages of publishing this book. Her remarkable track record as an acquisition editor includes the publication of the late Beatrice Medicine's book, *Learning to Be an Anthropologist and Remaining "Native,"* and the reprinting of the English translation of Haitian ethnologist Anténor Firmin's 1885 *The Equality of the Human Races*. I wanted my work to be in the good company of titles such as these. Rebecca Crist and John Hulse were instrumental in the final phases of book production. I really appreciate their contributions.

I also must acknowledge the institutions and departments that have given me the time, space, and funding to work on this book and the research that informs it. Support from all the universities that have employed me over the years, from the University of Louisville to the University of Florida, has contributed to my ability to accomplish the multiple phases and facets of this work. I wrote the prospectus for the book while working in the Women's Studies Program at the University of South Carolina. Jan Simek, former head of the Department of Anthropology at the University of Tennessee–Knoxville, played a major role in recruiting me back to Tennessee and in supporting this and all of my other projects. He arranged for me to have time release from teaching so I could focus on my writing. His successor as department head, Andrew Kramer, Mariana Ferreira (who is now at San Francisco State), Murray Marks, and Charles Faulkner were also sources of encouragement and collegiality. The highlight of my thirteen years at the University of Tennessee was my experiences with students, especially those who enrolled in my graduate courses on social inequality, human rights, and urban problems. Too numerous to list, they stimulated my thinking and renewed my sense of purpose as an educator. Support from the University of Florida's African American Studies Program made it possible for me to complete the book. I especially thank my colleague and friend Marilyn

Thomas-Houston, a former interim director of African American studies, and Neil Sullivan, former dean of the College of Liberal Arts, for their confidence in my work and for making it possible for me to join them at the University of Florida.

Over the years, William L. Conwill and our sons Giles, Mondlane, and Justin Harrison-Conwill have had to live with me as I have struggled to find just the right balance between family, career, and community engagement. I cannot imagine a more supportive partner than William. I hope he understood what he was getting into back then when our campus coffeehouse conversations about social scientists' misunderstanding of black family dynamics eventually led us to a more intimate collaboration. The ideas expressed in this book are in many ways consistent with his thinking on the philosophy and politics of social science, specifically psychology. His critique and alternative to Eurocentric and class-biased approaches to African American households and families set the basic parameters for the work in mental health, counseling, and education that he has undertaken in clinical, community, and academic settings.

Giles Burgess, named after forefathers from both sides of our family, is an inspiration as I watch him explore the possibilities for his future. I cannot adequately express in words how gratifying it is to witness his becoming a second-generation anthropologist. I hope that my generation has made it more possible for his to enjoy the benefits of an anthropology that is receptive to the challenges of their diversity.

* * *

Some of the chapters in this book were originally published elsewhere, in somewhat different form. Permission to reprint this material is acknowledged here:

Chapter 3: "Remapping Routes, Unearthing Roots: Rethinking Caribbean Connections with the U.S. South," originally titled "From the Chesapeake Bay to the Caribbean Sea and Back: Remapping Routes, Unearthing Roots," reprinted with permission from *Caribbean and Southern: Transnational Perspectives on the U.S. South,* volume 38 of the Southern Anthropological Society Proceedings, edited by Helen Regis (Athens: University of Georgia Press, 2006).

Chapter 4: "Writing against the Grain: The Cultural Politics of Difference in Alice Walker's Fiction," originally titled "Writing from the Grain: The Cultural Politics of Difference in Alice Walker's Work," reprinted by permission of Sage Publications Ltd. from *Critique of Anthropology* 13, no. 4 (1993): 401–27.

Chapter 6: "Gangs, Politics, and Dilemmas of Global Restructuring," originally titled "Gangs, Grassroots Politics, and the Crisis of Dependent Capitalism in Jamaica," reprinted with permission of coeditors David Hakken and Hanna Lessinger from *Perspectives in U.S. Marxist Anthropology* (Boulder, CO: Westview, 1987), 186–210.

Chapter 7: "The Gendered Violence of Structural Adjustment," originally published as "The Gendered Politics and Violence of Structural Adjustment: A View from Jamaica," reprinted with permission from *Situated Lives: Gender and Culture in Everyday Life,* edited by Louise Lamphere, Helen Ragoné, and Patricia Zavella (New York: Routledge, 1997), 451–78.

Chapter 12: "Academia, the Free Market, and Diversity," originally published as "New Voices of Diversity, Academic Relations of Production, and the Free Market," reprinted with permission from *Transforming Academia: Challenges and Opportunities for an Engaged Anthropology,* AES Monograph Series Number 8, edited by Linda G. Basch, Lucie Wood Saunders, Jagna Sharff, and James Peacock (Arlington, VA: American Anthropological Association, 1999), 72–85.

Introduction

Since the mid-1970s, when I began my graduate studies, I have been a part of a number of overlapping conversations concerning anthropology's past, present, and future. In these dialogues, the discipline's accomplishments, limitations, and new possibilities have been viewed from diverse perspectives, including those fashioned and articulated by feminists, native and minoritized intellectuals, postcolonial theorists, poststructuralists, postmodernists, and proponents of other projects for critically reconstructing the ways in which anthropological knowledge is produced and applied.

Many anthropologists and students of anthropology are eager to gain a deeper understanding of how anthropology is interpreting and theorizing the dynamics that are making the world's societies increasingly multicultural, postcolonial, and global. They are also interested in how anthropology itself—both as an intellectual discipline and as a professional culture—is changing in response to the demands and potential of the current historical context. Of course, contemporary anthropology has unfolded from earlier periods in which the field's contradictory relationship to European colonialism was the focus of intense debate.

In this book, I seek to explore anthropology's potential for transformation and the role that critical anthropologists and interlocutors can play in liberating the discipline from the constraints of its colonial legacy and post- or neocolonial predicament. Building upon earlier writings (e.g., Harrison 1991 [1997]), I elaborate on what I think "reinventing" and "decolonizing" anthropology entail. My intention is to offer a multidimensional strategy or model for transformation based on the notion of "reworking" the field. My idea of reworking anthropology underscores the importance of holism, reintegration, and synthesis—*weaving*, as Josep Llobera underscored in his approach to developing a "proper history of anthropology" (1976, 19). Weaving, in my view, is also integral to a robust perspective on anthropology today and in the future. Based on my sense of the discipline's trajectory over time, I have attempted to weave a synthesis from elements of anthropology's best practices. This synthesis informs the way I think about the overall project, whose ultimate goal is to create conditions for a more enriching and enabling analysis and understanding of the human experience.

Toward that laudable end, a critical project for reworking anthropology must find creative ways to achieve a number of interrelated objectives and eventual outcomes, which, to a considerable extent, must be grounded in a critical anthropology of anthropology. These objectives can best be described as a call for: (1) rehistoricizing anthropology (both the researchers and those whom they research), (2) rethinking theory (what it entails and who is authorized to do it), (3) rethinking the cross-pollinating intellectual potential of both intradisciplinarity and interdisciplinarity, (4) rising to the growing challenges of ethically and politically responsible research, and (5) mapping the mediated connections among local and supralocal spheres of culture, power, and political economy as they are being realigned and restructured in the age of neoliberal globalization. Other important objectives that also must be met if we are to pursue the critical reconstruction strategy I have in mind are (6) interrogating the ways anthropology is practiced in academia and beyond, (7) promoting greater diversity and deepening the democratization of participation and decision making in the profession, (8) finding more effective ways to link our academic pursuits to urgent issues of public engagement, and, finally, (9) developing a commitment to decentering Western epistemologies and to promoting a genuine multicultural dialogue in the study of humanity. The rationale and details of this multipronged strategy are discussed more fully in chapter 1.

Clearly, an ambitious project of this magnitude must be a collective effort. Reworking anthropology along all of these dimensions depends upon the cooperative labor of a critical mass of kindred-thinking people. In chapter 1, I identify potential sites of cooperation, coordination, and collaboration for anthropologists who are already pursuing parallel and potentially convergent interests. My wish is to offer a coherent vision that may facilitate and inspire work toward integrating and unifying disparate approaches that could conceivably work together to build an alternative mode of anthropological praxis (Buck 2001, 7–8).

Autoethnographic reflections on my own anthropological praxis over the past two decades have stimulated me to undertake a wide-ranging meta-analysis that spans several scholarly areas: the history of anthropology, historical anthropology, political anthropology, and anthropological political economy; African American, women's, southern, and Caribbean studies; intensive ethnographic fieldwork in Jamaica and more exploratory field trips to other parts of the Caribbean, including Cuba; and critical race studies, global studies, human rights research, and the anthropology of anthropological theory and practice. This book, then, is about reworking anthropology as I have come to think about it based on my experiences as a racially marked woman socially positioned to view anthropology and the world that anthropologists study from a particular set of angles—one that I believe is insightful and thought provoking in a constructively nuanced and illuminating way. My vantage point is grounded in the complex social facts that condition my struggle to "live in the West with 'other-than-Western' eyes," as Zillah Eisenstein describes how "W. E. B. Du Bois, Ida B. Wells, Paul Robeson, Malcolm X, and Martin Luther King" have offered "more inclusive and non-racist . . . theory . . . [and] re-visionings of democracy" (Eisenstein 2004, 114). As she goes on to say, "racialized and gendered bodies matter enormously" in how we make sense of and write about the world. The more we come to understand the multiple axes of identity that shape who we are as individuals who are raced, gendered, and classed, "the greater the vision of inclusiveness" we bring into our praxis (Eisenstein 2004, 115).

The following thirteen chapters, whose specific contents will be described in the historical and theoretical overview and frame provided in chapter 1, illuminate the ideas and experiences that led me to build the conceptual framework and holistic model that I have tried to apply to my own research, social analysis, theorizing, and activism as a sociocultural anthropologist. Insofar as this book is based on my work as an African Americanist and Caribbeanist, it is my hope that it advances anthropological and interdisciplinary studies of African Americans and the wider African diaspora. I must underscore, however, that I also want my analysis to contribute, more generally, to anthropology on a whole. I use African diaspora situations and contexts as points of entry into an interrogation of a much wider terrain: that of global capitalism with its shifting dynamics of racial, gender, class, and national differentiation, and that of human resilience in struggles for survival, dignity, and rights. Contrary to the tendency of some people to view studies of black folk as well as black scholars through myopic, "ghettoizing" lenses, I argue that understanding black experiences is important because they speak to the universal human condition just as much as any other people's experience. This, of course, includes the experiences of the most powerful Westerners, whose historically contingent, culturally bounded, and politically enforced regime of truth has long usurped the power to define mainstream Western attributes as normative and even universal. This discursive ploy converts the most idealized versions of these features into emblems of social identity reserved for those assigned to the high ranks of superiority, dominance, and privilege. It is my hope that readers will learn from my analysis of anthropology's limits and possibilities and find ways to apply the lessons to a wide variety of ethnographic contexts, in which, despite sociocultural differences, the peoples under study share a basic psychic unity and a general human family resemblance with the racially subordinated and economically challenged African-descendant communities that I describe in this book.

This project represents my attempt to make a claim for an alternative space for critical anthropological praxis, not a margin or periphery, not even what has been the contemporary "outsider within" location that African American feminist sociologist Patricia Hill Collins (1990) describes in her epistemological mapping of African American women social scientists. Similar to the "third space" that working-class British photographer and cultural critic Frances Angela (1990) envisions, the more democratized and decolonized space that I envision would permit a diversity of anthropologists—diverse in terms of intellectual perspectives as well as sociocultural, geographic, and national origins—to meet and productively engage each other at the "crossroads of knowledge" (di Leonardo 1991). Within that sort of radically reconfigured intercultural and cross-fertilizing context, anthropology as Édison Carneiro, Allison Davis, Ella Deloria, St. Clair Drake, Zora Neale Hurston, Rómulo Lachatañeré, Ruth Landes, Américo Paredes, and Eslanda Goode Robeson once knew it—laden with stark gender, racial, and national hierarchies—will no longer exist.[1] The challenge before us is to rework anthropology toward that ambitious vision and goal.

PART I

Toward a Critical Anthropology
of Anthropology

1. Reworking Anthropology from the "Outside Within"

Critiques, Reinventions, and Competing Historical Memories

A few years ago, a visit to http://sites.netscape.net/Harrisof/homepage would have taken you to a newly constructed homepage—that no longer exists today. Had you visited it then (before Netscape eliminated its free service of providing space and a user-friendly menu for constructing homepages), you would have found a simple graphic of a globe with the following narrative:

WELCOME TO FAYE V. HARRISON'S HOME PAGE!
REMAKING ANTHROPOLOGY FOR TODAY'S WORLD

Anthropology is the study of humankind and its societies and cultures across time and space. As a discipline it's come a long way since the good old days when European males (and they WERE primarily men) traveled deep into the bush of distant lands to investigate exotic, "primitive" peoples in the non-Western—and colonially dominated—world. Today anthropologists work everywhere, studying Europeans as well as Africans, elites as well as peasants and working classes, and kinship as well as the new modalities of association being formed in cyberspace. Today, anthropologists are less likely to think of "culture" in terms of bounded, fully integrated, and static systems, and they are more inclined to ponder cultural processes, dynamics, and conflicts grounded in uneven fields of power that cross the contested boundaries of nation-states and peoples. In an age of heightened globalism and transnationalism, many of the peoples with whom anthropologists work are repositioning and re-identifying themselves as agents of continuity and discontinuity within diasporas, borderlands, and other contexts of interculturality. Among those contexts are the same sites where ethnographers once claimed to have "discovered" isolated and functionally structured bands, tribes, chiefdoms, and kingdoms. Now we realize that even fifty or a hundred years ago, those ethnographically demarcated societies were elements within the wider fields of cultural contact, power, and economic articulation constitutive of the colonial spheres of a larger world system. Today more anthropologists find themselves on the same critical plane with the people they investigate, and increasingly they see their studies as collaborations and partnerships that problematize the traditional dichotomies between researcher and researched, subject and object, self and other. No longer are the foci of inquiry as amenable to being cast as ethnographic characters in a drama about the fossilized tribal remnants of an evolutionary past. Anthropology's reinvention is now well under way, in part because the subjects of Empire are striking back.

In the past forty years, anthropology has undergone considerable change in response to the volatile world outside of academia as well as in response to debates and pressures that have been internal to the discipline in its operations across a number of interrelated institutional contexts—university departments, professional associations, editorial boards, museums, and private and government funding sources. As someone who was introduced to anthropology in the early 1970s at a moment when reinventions, including feminist and various native anthropologies, were on the rise, I have witnessed much of this change and have to some degree participated in efforts that, both intellectually and organizationally, made some of the transformation possible. Throughout my career, I have undertaken both scholarly work and professional activist service that I conceptualize as part of a larger project for decolonizing and democratizing anthropology, enhancing the discipline's ability to produce knowledge uncompromisingly aligned with the promotion of social justice and human liberation. Although I am acutely aware of the shifts and related struggles that have helped constitute anthropology's present challenges and wish to underscore them as a foundation and source of inspiration for my anthropological praxis, there are those in the profession who are more inclined to take this history for granted, playing it down or misrecognizing the power dynamics that have driven it and remained alive, although in a more tempered form.

Not long ago, I was invited to give a colloquium at a major northeastern university. I decided to address various approaches to "reinventing anthropology," from Dell Hymes's (1969) and Talal Asad's (1975) seminal interventions to an array of more recent projects whose objectives are, more or less, consistent with the general aim of remaking and rewriting anthropology (e.g., Abu-Lughod 1991; Harrison 1991a, 1991b; Rosaldo 1989; Ulin 1991).

One of the comments made after my presentation was that no one in that department talked about the idea of remaking anthropology, at least not anymore. Perhaps this was so because so many of the trends I identified in my presentation have been accepted into the discipline's more diverse and multivocal mainstream. Consequently, very little thought was being given to the controversies and conflicts that made those trends possible as authorized modes of producing anthropological knowledge. Those struggles had become part of a past infrequently invoked. The politically charged impulse toward radical critique and reconstruction, which had been so prominent during the 1960s and 1970s, has been tempered, if not altogether lost. The new status quo, made up of liberal/left-leaning scholarship in that particular program, is no longer *reinventing* anthropology; it is *doing* anthropology and enjoying the rewards for having achieved recognition in the field. My very sense of professional identity and my critical vantage, however, are informed by a historical consciousness of one who belongs to a people, both in the immediate ethnoracial and wider diasporic senses, still underrepresented in anthropology, and academia generally, and subjected to ideological othering and nativization. Given this subaltern positionality, I cannot just *do* anthropology without being concerned with how the discipline is changing, what these changes mean now, and what they will mean in the long range.

The relatively limited sense of the continued need for a critical anthropological project and for linking current trends to an ongoing struggle for anthropology's reinvention is also evident in other situations. For instance, in a provocative essay, Herbert Lewis (1999) has written that the so-called new anthropology born of post-1960s critiques and the later postmodern turn has seriously misrepresented anthropology and its history. He organizes his counterargument around three major components of this purported misrepresentation, arguing against what he sees as the postmodernist fallacy that conventional inquiry has fallen into the trap of ahistoricism, valorized notions of cultural boundedness, and specialized in the study of radical alterity or difference. Although many of Lewis's points are convincing, others are not.

In his absolutely correct claim that anthropologists have not only studied people radically different from themselves and constructed ethnographic exoticism in terms of a radical alterity or otherness, he cites the work of W. Lloyd Warner and his African American associates, Allison Davis, and St. Clair Drake, about whom my colleagues and I have written (I. Harrison and F. Harrison 1999; Harrison 1988b, 1992). During the 1930s and 1940s, these scholars studied U.S. culture and social structure, particularly as they related to social class and race (conceptualized in terms of caste) as major organizing principles in U.S. society. Warner (1941, 1942; Warner and Srole

1945) was the principal investigator for the classic "Yankee City" studies, and he mentored Davis and his main collaborators and coauthors, Burleigh and Mary Gardner, in their investigation of the social organization and political economy of Jim Crow segregation in Natchez, Mississippi (Davis, Gardner, and Gardner 1941). That study, along with Warner's work, was one of the earliest to apply anthropological methods to urban U.S. society. It resulted in the publication of *Deep South* (1941), a classic ethnography that Davis's protégé, St. Clair Drake, to whom he had taught English literature at the historically black Hampton Institute (now Hampton University), helped make possible through his assistance with data collection.

Although Lewis clearly establishes his claim that anthropology has been much more variegated and inclusive than overly simplified critiques allow, he fails to acknowledge the power dynamics and politics of reception that relegated much of that diverse scholarship to minor-stream or, in many cases, downright peripheral status. The 1930s research on racial repression in Mississippi and the later study Drake and sociologist Horace Cayton (1945) undertook of African American migration and adaptation to Chicago made more of an impact in sociology than in the anthropology current at that time. The canon—the exemplars of conventional anthropology—that has determined the boundaries of the most valued modes of anthropological inquiry has not included these texts Lewis cites in his provocative rehistoricization of the field. I applaud him for underscoring the unwitting tendency of the new anthropology to replicate this pattern of erasure by having only a partial and incomplete understanding of the discipline's history and by treating anthropology simply in terms of the trends that have been most visible and emblematic. My major concern, however, is that Lewis maps anthropology's diverse schools of thought on a relatively leveled playing field, ignoring the unevenness and differential visibilities built upon the academic terrain. Lewis writes of Warner, Davis, and Drake's work as though postmodernists have been the major culprits in erasing these scholars from what is recognized as anthropology and its history. Erasure, however, well preceded the rise of postmodernism in anthropology (Harrison 1988b, 1991a, 1993b; F. Harrison and I. Harrison 1999). The specific subjugation of knowledge leading to the marginalization of Davis and Drake (and of African American anthropologists more generally) has been exposed in the writings of critical anthropologists (Baker 1998; Harrison 1988b, 1992, 1999, 2006b), who have constructively drawn upon insights from Marxist-leaning as well as postmodern critiques. Lewis's intervention fails to recognize this aspect of the discipline's more recent history when he reclaims neglected scholarship without acknowledging earlier reclamations and the exclusionary dynamics those studies revealed. Lewis, hence, is not the first anthropologist to insist upon a revisionist history of anthropology, one more encompassing than the scope of the field surveyed in postmodern critiques as well as in standard canonical projects.

I see myself as one among those who are producing an "alternative anthropology" (Buck 2001, 7–8), an anthropology critically reconstructed and reworked to correct and transcend the most problematic aspects of the discipline's colonial history and legacy. The transformed anthropology I envision would not fail to incorporate Warner, Davis, and Drake into its historical memory, as Lewis and others have urged. Nor would it erase indigenous and Latino anthropologists such as Ella Deloria (1941, 1988) and Américo Paredes (1958, 1978) or limit itself to the history of anthropologists in the United States and Western Europe. It would recognize that although the profession's institutional centers have been dominated by British, American, and French axes of authority, the intellectual life of the discipline has extended well beyond the North's major metropolitan centers to a variety of sites, typically devalued as peripheral zones of theory (Appadurai 1986) around the world. India, for instance, has a rich anthropological tradition, one that has historical ties, of course, to British social anthropology (Srinivas 1997); however, Indian anthropology has developed an impetus of its own. Besides India, which—as reflected in the *Annual Review of Anthropology*'s recent contents—is beginning to be recognized as an important locus for social anthropology, other national and regional anthropologies merit greater international exposure and study. Given my interest in the African diaspora, I am particularly intrigued by the various anthropologies that have developed around the study of African descendants and their cultural life and history (Harrison 2006a).

As one example, Haiti's school of *ethnologie* helped define the parameters of Haitian national identity and culture by documenting the first black republic's African heritage and the lifeways of the small-scale agrarian producers who have constituted the majority of the nation. More than twenty years ago, Drake (1980) alerted us to the significance of this particular school in his seminal writing on the black experience in the history of anthropology. More recently, Carolyn Fluehr-Lobban (2002) and her colleague Asselin Charles have brought to light the significance of the Haitian statesman Anténor Firmin's treatise, *The Equality of the Human Races* (1885 [2002]). This long-neglected work presented an elaborate counterargument to Count Arthur de Gobineau's racist tome on the natural heritability of human differences. It also delineated the parameters for an alternative anthropology, referred to as an *anthropologie positive*, a "scientific inquiry guided by factual evidence . . . not simply philosophical rebuttal" (Fluehr-Lobban 2002, xvii). Jean Price-Mars, a physician and politician who wrote a biography of Firmin (1978), was Haiti's leading ethnologist during the first half of the twentieth century. As Kevin A. Yelvington (2006b) shows in his study of the international intellectual social formation to which Melville Herskovits belonged, Jean Price-Mars's (1928) writings on African syncretisms in the folk culture and religion of Haitian peasants paralleled and perhaps even had some influence on Herskovits's research and programmatic directives for developing Afro-American anthropology. Price-Mars's work stimulated literary imagination as well as the production of scientific inquiry. Particularly in the writings of Jacques Roumain, founder of the Bureau d'Ethnologie, these two trends were pursued both in tandem and in the fused genre of ethnographic fiction (Roumain 1944; Dash 1978; Harrison 2006a).

Yelvington's (2006b) mapping of Herskovits's intellectual social network also points to Fernando Ortiz's Afro-Cuban studies (Ortiz 1906, 1940 [1995]) and the school of Afro-Brazilian scholarship that revolved around Arthur Ramos (1935). If we closely examine the networks of these focal figures, we find Afro-Latin American anthropologists, frequently independent vernacular intellectuals (Farred 2003) without prestigious institutional affiliations or academic security. Probably the most prominent African diasporic ethnographers were Rómulo Lachatañeré (1938 [2005]), a pharmacist and photojournalist who worked closely with Ortiz, and Édison Carneiro (1936, 1937), a journalist perhaps best known in the United States for his controversial collaboration and intimate relationship with Ruth Landes (1947; Cole 2003). In his own right, however, Carneiro wrote articles and books on Candomblé and other aspects of black folklife, such as capoeira, a dance-martial arts genre that has recently attracted an international following.

I have gone into some detail on African diaspora specialists in other parts of the hemisphere, because a decolonized anthropology (Harrison 1991b [1997]) must be internationalized. This alternative anthropology would be organized around not only culturally diverse research subjects but also culturally and nationally diverse researchers, analysts, and theorists. This kind of intellectual community would bring varied epistemological, theoretical, and methodological concerns into a difference-friendly synergetic space characterized by neither a conventional center nor a margin. I shall further explore the implications of these and other spatial metaphors for interpreting anthropology's knowledge/power dynamics as I proceed with my reflections.

Exploring the Politics of Race and Space in Academia

For more than twenty years, I have played the role of an outsider within anthropology rather than that of an academic comfortably incorporated into the mainstream (Collins 1990, 1998). As I see it, my professional role is shaped by my positionality as a racially marked woman, particularly as one of African descent. Despite the privilege of having been trained in a leading graduate program and the opportunities I have had over the years to participate in gate-opening activities by serving on important editorial boards and review panels for research funding institutions and on the executive committees of national and international professional associations, I remain an outsider within anthropology. I am an heir to an intellectual estate that can be traced to one of the discipline's earlier peripheries, particularly those sites where African American scholarship was undertaken and subjected to a politics of reception that devalued it, relegating it to the ranks of virtual invisibility. I see the work that I do as part of the living legacy of that scholarship as well as that of some mainstream intellectual lineages that bequeathed some of the important tools I include in my conceptual, theoretical, and methodological repertoire. I am not, then, an ethnic absolutist in the sense of refusing to recognize the intellectual and cultural pluralism, hybridity if you will, that has shaped my very existence. It is also important to point out that the reclamation of my most neglected intellectual ancestors does not mean that I celebrate everything they did without subjecting their work to constructive criticism (Baker 1998; F. Harrison and I. Harrison 1999). It is through honest, constructive criticism that my colleagues and I are reworking anthropology, building upon best practices from the past to create at least some of the conditions necessary for transformations that will take us beyond the limits of the discipline's colonial legacy.

For more than fifteen years now, I have written about processes that have led (and still lead) to the hierarchical ordering of anthropological knowledge, center–periphery relations, and specifically the peripheralization of African American scholarship despite its substantive, theoretical, and methodological significance (Harrison 1988b, 1992, 1993b, 2006b; F. Harrison and I. Harrison 1999). Although the periphery has certainly been a site of subordination and devaluation, often driven by racial and gender discrimination, it has also been a creatively variegated space in which scholars—among them racial minorities, women, Third World, and left-wing activists—have pursued important new developments, some of which have come to be recognized and appropriated, albeit belatedly, by the center. Allison Davis, whom I discussed in my earlier assessment of Lewis's critique of recent anthropological trends, was one such scholar. He believed in the power of social scientific applications for solving social problems (Drake 1974). He especially wanted to dismantle racism and saw anthropology as a source of potentially useful weapons in that struggle for justice-seeking change. Influenced by the way many Depression-era activists drew upon Marxism, he brought Marxist insights into an analysis primarily driven by structural functionalism. He was the senior researcher in a number of biracial collaborations that studied blacks as well as whites, never reducing the study of race to the study of racial subordinates (Harrison 1992, 1997a). In 1994, a Black Heritage stamp was issued to commemorate Davis's contributions to public policy. *Anthropology Newsletter* published a front-page article, "Stamp of Approval," that summarized his career (*Anthropology Newsletter* 1994). Despite his prominence in matters of educational policy during the civil rights and early post–civil rights era, Davis had been a rather peripheral figure in anthropology. Because he worked in education (in the University of Chicago's former Department of Education), it was often assumed that he was an educational psychologist. His published work is rarely included in anthropology curricula or cited in anthropological writings. (I made these observations in a letter to the *Anthropology Newsletter* editor [Harrison 1994b]).

Allison Davis mentored St. Clair Drake, who was one of my most inspiring professors in graduate school (Harrison 1997a, 1997c). He taught me the basics of a noncanonical intellectual history and of applying an anthropological lens to anthropology itself. From those lessons I have fashioned my own version of "an anthropology of knowledge" informed by the more established sociology of knowledge upon which Drake often drew. Drake became an anthropologist because of Davis's influence and example. Davis invited Drake to join the research team that resulted in *Deep South* (Davis, Gardner, and Gardner 1941 [1988]). From that formative experience, both the fieldwork and the activism in which he engaged while in Depression-era Mississippi, Drake went on to the University of Chicago, where he earned his PhD in social anthropology. Before completing his doctorate, he coauthored the now classic *Black Metropolis* (1945) with sociologist Horace Cayton. He did his dissertation research (Drake 1954) on race relations in Cardiff, Wales, a topic more consistent with interests in sociology than in the anthropology of that time. That project, however, was his plan B after having plan A, a proposal to work in West Africa, rejected for funding because of the major gatekeeper in African studies Melville Herskovits's skepticism concerning African Americans' ability to do objective research on politically charged matters related to race and Africa (Drake, personal communication, 1975; Yelvington 2003, 2006b). He subsequently worked as an Africanist (e.g., Drake 1959, 1960) before returning to the study of race, power, and urban unrest in the United States (Drake 1966). After many years at Chicago's Roosevelt University, he spent the last years of his career at Stanford and, after his retirement, at his home in Palo Alto, California, writing a historical anthropology of the precolonial and colonial African diaspora (Drake 1987/1990, n.d.). His impressive oeuvre was situated on the margins of mainstream anthropology but at the very center of debates in Africana studies, especially the scholarship that activist intellectuals from Africa and the African diaspora produced. Toward the end of his life (thanks to the nomination and lobbying of Africanist George Bond), he was given the belated recognition of a Bronislav Malinowski Award for his contributions as an applied anthropologist. He accepted the award from the Society for Applied Anthropology (SfAA) with some mixed feelings. He claimed that his goal had not been to advance anthropology per se but to use its tools to promote the understanding and liberation of Africans and African descendants throughout the world. He thought it ironically reflective of anthropology's contradictions that the prestigious award was named in honor of a man whose posthumously published diaries explicitly revealed his racist feelings toward the Melanesians he represented in ethnographies that became exemplars. Of course, this is not to say that those exemplars and the canonical standards they set were at all bias free (Thomas-Houston, personal communication, 2005).

The lives and careers of anthropologists like Davis and Drake attest to the vitality, creativity, and critical edge of the margins, which have been rich borderlands adjoining anthropology to other fields. These sites of interface and convergence have been important cross-fertilizing grounds in which provocative new ideas have been produced. As I am using them, the concepts of margin and periphery do not signify negation or an absence of merit; instead, they denote spaces in which resilience and resistance may engender the articulation of alternative perspectives.

Race, Gender, and Class on the "Outside Within"

The power dynamics associated with what sociologist Patricia Hill Collins (1990) calls "outsider within locations" persist even in the midst of considerable change—positive change. My experience in academia and professional anthropology has been racially marked. In much of my everyday work life, many, if not most, of my values and behaviors are much the same as those of my white colleagues and students. Yet the behaviors of many of these colleagues and students communicate to me that difference rather than sameness is perceived—and in some instances imagined. My visibility as a racially different person too often blinds them to characteristics that should be much more important. Attributes valued within academia are sometimes construed in racially distorted ways. For example, intellectual competence, normally expected of professors, may become a problem when it clashes with the belief still too commonly held that blacks are less intelligent than whites. An intelligent black professor may be viewed as an exception to the rule and/or as a target for student—and collegial—resentment and recalcitrance. Her authority in the classroom may be resisted or rejected. This problem is most pronounced when the professor's teaching is critical of the students' commonsense views of the world.

Whether in the classroom or in service activities, racialization is rampant. I have written earlier (Harrison 1999) about a racializing experience with a national funding agency. The minutes recording the highlights of an all-day meeting attributed one or two minority-related statements to me while crediting other issues, the core substance of the meeting, to white males who had frequently followed up on points I had initiated and spoken about eloquently. The minutes summarized the whole day's meeting in a way that made it clear that an African American woman had been present—and hence the diversity requirement had been met. Although I understand the importance of ensuring minority involvement by institutionalizing set asides, I deeply regret that once gates are opened through this mechanism, our work is not more often evaluated according to color-blind criteria. Even when we want to be treated like persons whose most visible characteristics—intelligence, professional competence, and ability to articulate convincingly—have nothing to do with race, that rarely seems to happen. Whether we like it or not, race is an enduring principle of classification and organization within academe, relegating some people to outsides within. Putting colored people in their place through racially marked circumscription, often layered with meanings related to gender and class, may be subtle, but it is, nonetheless, real. In order to negotiate, resist, and adjust to its most humiliating and hurtful forms, racially marked intellectuals often find themselves deploying energy that might otherwise be invested in furthering their scholarship.

Beyond my own writings on the racial and gender politics of intellectual centers and peripheries, spatial metaphors are commonly used to elucidate the relational dynamics and divisions of labor that influence the production and circulation of knowledge in race, class, and gender-cognizant contexts. Consider the following examples. African American feminist theorist and cultural critic bell hooks titled one of her early books *Feminist Theory: From Margin to Center* (1984). Lowery Stokes Sims's (2002) study of the Afro-Chinese Cuban artist Wifredo Lam argues that the "significance of Lam and his work will come to light . . . [when he is] judged by criteria generated from his own center rather than on the margins of modernism" (B15). In the latter context, Lam is usually relegated to the status of an "authentic primitive," "trained in conventions of primitivism" attributed to the innovations of Pablo Picasso. Frances Angela, a working-class English photographer, has characterized her work as "a place of resistance . . . neither the old margin nor the co-optation of the center but a third space where new subjectivities, new politics and new identities are articulated. [Her] new location has the resources of the center but remains outside to disrupt and resist, continually threatening the center with the contradictions of the margins" (Angela 1990, 73).

This third space that Angela claims to occupy is similar to the outside within in which I locate myself and the particular "minoritized" (Dominguez 1994) intellectuals about whom I have written—such as W. E. B. Du Bois, Allison Davis, St. Clair Drake, Manet Fowler, Eslanda Robeson, and Beatrice Medicine (Harrison 1988b, 1992, 1999, 2001). I recognize, however, that today's outside within provides greater access to mainstream resources than was typically the case in past generations. In underscoring connections and continuities across time, I do not wish to suggest that the quality of academic life has not changed and, in some meaningful respects, improved. My emphasis on continuity and legacy, however, is intended to highlight the enduring, albeit more subtle, forms of subjection that racially marked intellectuals continue to confront all across academia and its disciplines.

The Knowledge/Power of "Outsiders Within"

My thinking on the critically creative scholarship that has emerged in anthropology's outside within is rooted in my earliest writings on peripheralization (Harrison 1988b) and the decolonization of anthropological knowledge (Harrison 1991a [1997]). In more recent years, these ideas have been further distilled in view of my exposure to Patricia Hill Collins, a sociologist who has written on black feminist epistemology (1990, 1998). Her concepts of "outsiders within" and "outsider within locations" and my notion of peripheralized scholars point to many of the same issues.

Collins has written compellingly that African American women, whether social scientists or domestic workers, travel across boundaries of race, class, and gender to "move into and through" various outsider within locations. These spaces link communities of differential power and are commonly fertile grounds for the formulation of oppositional knowledge and critical social theory. She admits that the occupants of outsider within locations (which, beyond African Americans, include "other similarly situated groups" as well as "White 'race traitors', feminist men, and other individuals critical of their own privilege" [Collins 1998, 234]) do not always produce theory critical of social injustice. There is no homogeneity in their identities and politics (Collins 1998, 235); however, some outsiders within manage to become critically creative within spaces of disjuncture in which conflicting perspectives and interests meet and clash and where critical social theory may come to be aligned with concrete opposition to social injustice.

Influenced by Robert K. Merton's writing (1972) on the roles of outsiders and insiders within domains of knowledge, Collins initially coined the term to "describe the location of people who no longer belong to any one group . . . who [find] themselves in marginal locations between groups of varying power." Reducing the concept to an identity category, however, was a limitation (Collins 1998, 5). In later turns in her thinking, she moved to an understanding that "outsider within location describes a *particular knowledge/power relationship*, one of gaining knowledge about or of a dominant group without gaining the full power accorded to members of that group" (6; emphasis mine). She applied this concept to both black women intellectuals, in their relationships to their disciplines/professions, and black domestic workers, who have historically traveled back and forth between their own families and those of their employers with whom they often become intimately familiar. This contradictory and stratified intimacy is reflected in the not uncommon way that a typical black domestic has been described as being "like one of the family." Despite the insider knowledge gained about white middle-class families, domestics never become full-fledged members. The special angle of vision gained from their work experience has engendered distinctive knowledge of the so-called hidden transcripts of whiteness, a knowledge that is shaped by their knowledge of African American family life. The insights and understandings that emerge from this expanded field of observation and interaction are not readily available to whites and blacks whose lives are largely confined to monoracial domains. Collins argues that black female social scientists also have a unique angle of vision or—in light of the heterogeneity among black women—angles of vision that inform the role they play in producing new knowledge and effecting change within academia.

I find it significant that Collins's outsider within epistemology, the grounding from which she elaborates black feminist social theory, is informed by her understanding of black domestic workers and the vernacular knowledge they have historically developed and deployed in their everyday lives and struggles. I also make a connection between intellectuals—intellectual workers—and ordinary working people, and, as a consequence, I envision my work as part of a dual legacy. There is the legacy of W. E. B. Du Bois's foundational interdisciplinary scholarship, which in many respects set the stage for the first cohorts of African American anthropologists and for much of the critical anthropology of race and racism being revitalized today (Harrison 1992; Baker 1998). I have been part of a collective endeavor to bring an awareness of Du Bois's significance into present-day anthropology (Harrison and Nonini 1992; Baker 1998). I wish to acknowledge formally yet another legacy, however, and that is the living legacy produced from the family values, hard (often oppressive) work, and selfless sacrifices of my foreparents, especially my fore*mothers,* who enabled their descendants to realize, or move toward realizing, some of their/our dreams. One dream, among others, is that we become educated, full-fledged citizens of the nation (and the world), without forgetting our ancestors' old-school lessons as we make our way forward.

My research on my own family reunion tradition and the values it transmits concerning family, work, education, spiritual well-being, civic responsibility, and political participation (Harrison 1995a) compelled me to reflect on one particular foremother: an emancipated woman named Susan Brown. The life of Grandma Susie, my great-great grandmother, has been an important source of inspiration for me. Having the occasion to think about her, who she was, and how she helped set the stage for my extended family's inter-generational saga has prompted me to think about the relationship between her experience as a formerly enslaved, nonliterate woman and the knowledge I labor to produce as a professional anthropologist. In the final chapter of this book, I elaborate my thinking on this connection. Here, however, I only sketch an outline of those ideas and the sentiment that helps bind the relationship between the personal, professional, and political that I embody, represent, and enact in my everyday life.

"How on Earth Did You Become an Anthropologist?"

Commonly, when I tell nonacademic people what I do for a living, they respond with puzzled looks on their faces and ask me: "How on earth did *you* get into *that*?" Their question is not a trivial one, because anthropology still has a popular image of being exotic, Indiana Jones style. Among people of color, in the United States and in some other parts of the world, it has a reputation for being racist and colonial. They tend to associate it with the privilege of white people, males mainly, going to far-off places to study Africans and Pacific Islanders and later displaying souvenirs—that is, artifacts—in natural history museums alongside exhibits of flora and fauna. Those more learned laypeople may be aware of the history of ethnographic exhibits that bordered on circus freak shows, subjecting natives to the demeaning gazes of both popular consumption and scientific racism. "Can't imagine many of *us* going into that field. Why did *you* get into it?"

When I was an undergraduate student majoring in anthropology at Brown University, a young African American woman enrolled in the anthropology graduate program. I was eager to get to know her, but she left within months of her arrival in Providence. I remember the disgust she expressed for the racist literature she was assigned to read. She quickly reached the conclusion that anthropology was not for her after all. When I decided to go on to graduate school, I sometimes had to defend myself against students in other disciplines who dismissed anthropology as a racist, colonial field that no longer had a meaningful place in the world at a time when there were armed struggles throughout southern Africa. They insisted that it was liberation time and anthropology was, or certainly should be, obsolete. Most of my critics had never got beyond a single introductory course, if they had taken any anthropology at all. They had not stayed around the Anthropology Department long enough to be exposed to the material the more progressive professors covered in class and discussed during their office hours.

Louise Lamphere's classes especially opened my eyes to the possibilities of the anthropological method. She introduced me to the works of black sociologist Joyce Ladner, anthropologist Elliot Liebow, and a number of emergent feminist anthropologists. Her classes gave me an inspiring glimpse into the then current trends in the critical reconstruction of anthropology. I will never forget her handing me a paperback copy of Dell Hymes's (1969 [1974]) *Reinventing Anthropology*. I do not remember what we were talking about or what she said about the book, but I do remember her giving it to me to read. The significance of reinventing anthropology did not really click in my head until later on, and even then it took a while longer for me to realize that my own agenda, as I came to define it, was consistent with that directive.

The anthropology I learned at Brown did not seem to present any major problems to me. Admittedly, there was a conspicuous absence of texts by anthropologists of color. It was not until I began to read more anthropology, historical as well as contemporary works, that I realized that Lamphere and the anthropologists she assigned were not necessarily standard fare; they represented more recent politically engaged trends. My understanding of those trends and my exposure to African American social scientists, including the anthropologists Zora Neale Hurston and Katherine Dunham, in African American studies courses convinced me to pursue further studies in anthropology. Thanks to a Samuel T. Arnold Fellowship that Brown awarded every year to a graduating senior (actually, three fellowships were conferred annually), I spent the year after my graduation in London, England, examining the situation of black, largely Caribbean, immigrants, who were being politically defined as a major social problem for the English nation (Harrison 1975a, 1975b, 1976a, 1976b). My exploratory fieldwork focused my attention on the problems black youths confronted: in their homes, where their parents frequently could not understand why they were not thankful to be in Britain; on the streets, particularly Brixton's streets, where they were susceptible to being harassed by the police; in schools, where they were apt to be labeled uneducable and tracked accordingly; and in the job market, where they were assigned to what they considered to be demeaning "shit work," which the more radical, against their parents' advice, refused to accept. I was in Brixton at the height of the mid-1970s "moral panic" over mugging that Stuart Hall and his cultural studies colleagues (Hall et al. 1978) examined in *Policing the Crisis,* an important study that theorized the role of the state and media in manufacturing mainstream consent for the authoritarianized law-and-order regime imposed to keep black immigrants and the white British citizenry in their places.

Following my fieldwork initiation in Britain, I entered the graduate program at Stanford University with a clearer idea of what I wanted to accomplish. I knew I needed the conceptual, methodological, and ethical skills to be better able to negotiate the demands of difficult fieldwork situations. I had learned from my experience in London that social research is often seen as comparable to intelligence gathering in support of state surveillance and containment. I quickly found out that so-called natives can be quite uncooperative, that they have ideas of their own about the merits or demerits of research, and that my textbook education had not adequately prepared me for what I encountered in the real world. I needed graduate studies to help me understand and be able to negotiate the kinds of ethical and political quandaries I was likely to face again in Britain as well as in Africa, the Caribbean, or at home in the United States, were I to work in those settings.

My experience in England gave me a strong sense of conviction about becoming an anthropologist; however, I was not at all immune from having doubts and second thoughts. In fact, during my very first quarter at Stanford, I took a class with a professor who, in the middle of a heated exchange between us, told me that I should study political philosophy rather than anthropology. My ideas for making sense of what I had observed in London, which were the focus of papers I wrote for his class as well as for a core course in applied anthropology (Harrison 1975a, 1975b), were not consistent with his idea of what ethnographers should do. Influenced by ethnomethodological trends, he thought that we should produce cultural analysis largely from an emic point of view.

I panicked. *My God, was I in the wrong field?* Should I be in political science or philosophy, as he had claimed? Which point of view qualifies as emic when members of the same society and community disagree over, and vigorously contest, cultural meanings and political ideologies? Was it philosophy and not anthropology to rework a Marxist concept of class struggle in order to explain black immigrant youths' contestations of "shit work"? There were Caribbean immigrants who drew upon Marxist ideology to make sense of their experiences, just as there were others who saw in England the chance to enjoy an improved life in the mother country. In time, I realized that everyone in the department, faculty and students, did not agree with this professor's assessment of my thinking. My approach to anthropology turned out not to be off base after all. St. Clair Drake, Bridget O'Laughlin, Sylvia Yanagisako, Michelle Rosaldo, and Bernard Siegel helped convince me that I had made the right decision to pursue a PhD in anthropology. I came to see that there was enough space in the field for people who thought like I did. But that first quarter was such a close call! I almost turned my back on anthropology for an alternative career path.

I think I made the right choice when I selected anthropology as a major and later as a profession. In a relatively recent essay (Harrison 2002b, 146–47), I suggested that my childhood experiences in Virginia may have inclined me toward becoming an anthropologist. I grew up in the segregated South in the midst of the civil rights movement. My curiosity about race and racism—a curiosity borne not only from an intellectual exercise but from the social suffering and outrage of a people subjected to oppression—prompted me to raise serious questions that in later years I would realize were most amenable to anthropological inquiry with its comparative ethnographic lens. Anthropological analysis played an important role in offering me the concepts, vocabulary, and comparative perspective for articulating a critique of racism and the culture of race in which I have lived. That critique has been an invaluable resource in helping me gain an enabling and affirmative sense of my full humanity.

Which Way Forward against Current Dangers of Marginalization?

I came of age during the time that the late William Roseberry (1996) characterized as the post–World War II era's second generation and its particular set of crises, namely, those associated with what Del Hymes (1969 [1974]) referred to in his advocacy for a reinvented anthropology. During that generation, whose beginnings were marked by the Vietnam War and the antiwar movement's response to it, anthropology was challenged and reconfigured by an array of critiques and debates, among them a radical project of reconstruction that underscored the usefulness of political economy and historicized studies of power, two interrelated trends that have had a profound influence on my work (Roseberry 1996, 15). This was an exciting time, when the discipline was being rethought and intellectual genealogies redrawn to include lines of thought (e.g., Marxist theory) that otherwise would have been earmarked for canonical erasure (16–17). Then came the climate of the mid- to late 1980s, when a newer generation of graduates found more interest and excitement in the postmodernist project of rewriting anthropology, whose currency remains strong today. Much of the work within this project fails to be anchored in political engagements grounded in concrete struggles outside of the politics that prevail within an elitist academy.

In the midst of a period of neoconservative reaction when academic unemployment reached crisis proportions, Roseberry voiced his fear that the restructuring of higher education (as well as of anthropology departments) that characterized the 1990s would result in the radical restriction of the range of anthropological practices, closing in on the spaces in which politically engaged anthropology and history can be practiced (Roseberry 1996, 20). He claimed that during that late twentieth-century and early twenty-first-century moment, work that "develops the cultural history tradition . . . and most of the work that develops the . . . materialist tradition" has fallen out of favor and is vulnerable to being purged (21). He acknowledged that his claim was rather extreme and that he himself hoped he was wrong (22). In my view, he correctly pointed to the danger, but not the historical inevitability, of certain once more popular modes of inquiry—the very modes I was trained to employ—being airbrushed from the contemporary scene. He went on to argue that "[m]ore broadly, it is the very attempt to analyze and understand the relations and structures of power in, through, and against which people live, which serves as a basis for such an anthropology. For such analysis and understanding, histories of colonialism or capitalism are never sufficient, but they remain necessary. Class analysis is never sufficient, but it remains necessary. Processual analysis, scientific and otherwise, is never sufficient, but it remains necessary. Ethnographic analysis of local fields of power is never sufficient, but it remains necessary. Grand narratives (I am willing to let "master narratives," whatever they are, go) are never sufficient, but they remain necessary" (Roseberry 1996, 22). Roseberry clarified that he was not advocating the "mechanical reproduction of decades-old traditions." Instead, he urged their "active development . . . criticism, incorporation of new perspectives, or of ways of being political. Otherwise, we end up with anthropology-lite, which might fit rather well in a restructured, defunded academy" (22).

Building Conceptual/Analytical Bridges

Roseberry's directive was that we not allow the strengths of the reinventing anthropology period to be purged from the discipline's early twenty-first-century agenda. Although his political economy of professional anthropology is insightful, he may have overstated the unpopularity of political economy and politically engaged forms of anthropological practice. Eric Wolf's influence has been considerable over the past two decades. Also the work of June Nash, Joan Vincent, Michel-Rolph Trouillot, and others has been quite visible although perhaps not as popular as that of anthropologists working along more poststructural lines. One response to Roseberry's fear could be informed by Robert Ulin's (1991) call for bridging and synthesizing elements from political economy and postmodernism (see chapter 4). In Ulin's view, this is a promising way to advance "the critical anthropological project." Along similar lines a few years earlier, Marcus and Fischer (1986) had espoused the value of interpretive political economies.

A bridging of sorts, achieved through the blurring of boundaries between competing theoretical camps, is also reflected in Karen Brodkin's work (e.g., Brodkin Sacks 1989). Brodkin has long been committed to socialist feminism. She is a Marxist working in the postmodern era, and her social analysis has been influenced by some of the ideas that have taken form because of the postmodern turn. She has reworked the concept and meaning of class along nonessentialist lines. She decenters masculine industrial work and includes unwaged work, particularly women's domestic and community work. She places considerable emphasis on the multiple identities and experiences of working-class people and on intersecting axes of race, class, and gender. Some concerns Brodkin articulates are consistent with Carolyn Martin Shaw's (1995) approach to race and sexuality in Kenya; yet Shaw identifies herself as a postmodernist. Her particular brand of postmodernism, however, is critical of Foucault's philosophy for its loss of individual agency in abstract concepts and cumulative historical processes. She claims that her approach is post-Marxist in that it situates class alongside race and gender and considers not only organized workers but interest groups and social movements as important agents of cultural production and social change. Even though labels and self-definitions do not always point to substantive synthesis, a considerable amount of intellectual creolization has already occurred along the lines of Ulin's argument.

I think there is more theoretical diversity than Roseberry painted in his picture of contemporary anthropology. Anthropology has become more multicentered and multivocal. Although the process of transformation is certainly not complete (and will probably never be, with our notions of what constitutes transformation shifting as we move along), anthropology is more democratized, with its gates opened wide enough for at least some former outsiders to find space in the center and on the outside within it. Whether we will achieve more than a token presence of outsiders within is a question we will have to continue asking, seeking responses through both intellectual and organizational means. Substantive democratization is not accomplished by only writing multivocal texts; it requires active organizing within and across communities to build new forms of inclusion, association, alliance, and decision making.

Building Organizational Bridges

Roseberry's depiction of a climate of purging fails to provide a view of anthropology's wider landscape, some of whose dimensions reflect promising alternative trends. Despite—and probably in response to—the wider political climate and the shift toward less politically engaged modes of inquiry, projects for remaking anthropology, inspired by the debates and struggles of earlier times, were not at all dead in the 1980s and 1990s. Older journals like *Critique of Anthropology* and newer ones like *Identities* and *Transforming Anthropology* attracted work that was committed to anthropology's critical reconstruction. *Critique*'s identity was clearly that of "a journal for the critical reconstruction of anthropology." In its recent redesigned format, that description, which used to appear in a subtitle, has been omitted, but the journal continues to publish the results of critical, radical research. The Association of Black Anthropologists (ABA) has also been an important base for outsiders within. Its critical vision is reflected in its journal, *Transforming Anthropology*, and in *Decolonizing Anthropology* (Harrison 1991b [1997]), a book that has gone through three editions in response to market demand. The ABA along with the Association of Latina and Latino Anthropologists (ALLA), the Society for the Anthropology of North America (SANA), and a number of other units within the American Anthropological Association (AAA) mobilized, both individually and in coalition, to have a voice in the governance and reorganization of the AAA. Having the organizational means to express collective dissent and make proactive interventions allows small organizations like the ABA and ALLA to resist and combat the politics of purging about which Roseberry warned us. Still-existing reinvention projects are part of this mobilization.

Reinvention strategies have been varied but rarely have they fully acknowledged their common or overlapping objectives and the significance of forging a "web of connection" (Haraway 1988), a coalition of knowledges (Harrison 2000), to offset the negative effects of fragmentation, overspecialization, and the "more critical than thou" syndrome that is sometimes implicit in writings that fail to acknowledge affinity with similar projects. Fortunately, a few anthropologists have started to redress this serious limitation. For example, the late Beatrice Medicine, a prominent American Indian anthropologist, collaborated with feminist and applied anthropologist Sue-Ellen Jacobs to reprint thirty of Medicine's previously published articles in *Learning to Be an Anthropologist and Remaining "Native": Selected Writings* (Medicine 2001). The book is unusual in that it has two forewords, one by Medicine's son, sculptor Ted Sitting Crow Garner, and the second written by an African American anthropologist who situates Medicine's career within the context of the discipline's not uncomplicated historical relationship with Native Americans. You may not be surprised that I am that anthropologist (Harrison 2001). I had the privilege of chairing the Society for Applied Anthropology's Malinowski Award Committee the year Medicine was conferred the prestigious honor. I was happy that Bea wanted to use my award ceremony introduction, which I began with a simple poem written in her honor, as a foreword to her book. In my view, that was an expression of solidarity between women who recognize a common bond, a shared struggle, and interlocking projects for anthropology's present and future.

Modeling a Coalition of Knowledges

In 1999, a Presidential Symposium at the AAA meeting also made this kind of an acknowledgment. Latina anthropologist Paule Cruz Takash and I co-organized "Anthropology at the Millennium: Retrospectives from the Discipline's Critical Center(s)," which brought a plurality of critical projects together in a single conversation. Black anthropology, Latina/Latino anthropology, Native American anthropology, applied anthropology, gay/lesbian/transgendered anthropology, feminist anthropology, women in archaeology, and progressive anthropologists focusing on North America were represented in that united front, which, in many ways, was perhaps more performative than substantive. I say this because in the everyday intellectual practices of critical anthropologists, they do not necessarily read, teach, and cite each other's work, taking it as seriously as Foucault, Bourdieu, or other major figures with which many anthropologists are now framing their analyses. For instance, although anthropology and feminist anthropology in particular have "come a long way, baby," black feminists still feel alienated from and marginalized within feminist anthropology, as reflected in the perspectives included in *Black Feminist Anthropology* (McClaurin 2001) and in A. Lynn Bolles earlier call for decolonizing feminist anthropology (Bolles 1995). In the AAA session Cruz Takash and I co-organized, various critical anthropologies claimed space in the discipline's center, which we remapped as multicultural, multitheoretical, and multifocal; in other words, a space where there is ample room for diversity and less exclusive forms of authority. As the abstract Cruz Takash and I wrote stated:

[T]he disciplinary "center" that [we] claim is much more democratic and accommodating of multiple and diverse perspectives than the received center that excluded, hierarchized, and peripheralized knowledges and groups that challenged hegemony. This session marks a timely and important conceptual shift in that its more inclusive mapping of disparate reconstructive projects surveys the anthropological terrain in a way that any particular project cannot effectively accomplish alone from its partial perspective. The web of connections that the panelists seek to construct may clear the way for a more grounded, more enabling form of anthropological theorizing and praxis. (Cruz Takash and Harrison 1999, 32)

Our goal was to reterritorialize anthropology in terms that are no longer translatable as a center-periphery dichotomy. We hoped to destabilize that conventional power relation by exposing the shifting patterns of peripheralization and counterperipheralization that have been integral to anthropology's development, past and present. By bringing together several partial perspectives and being open about their situatedness (Haraway 1988), we aimed to construct a cooperative model for the coordinated reorganizing and reworking of anthropology. This intellectual project was undertaken around the same time a number of associations within the AAA (ABA, ALLA, SANA among them) were building a coalition to mobilize for needed changes within the AAA's governance. The critical reintegration of anthropology requires both intellectual and organizational work as well as an engagement with wider public interests.

Making Sense of, and Negotiating, Anthropology's Pluralities

Anthropology is a diverse field in which progressive, politically engaged inquiry exists alongside projects that eschew politics beyond that found in texts or that aligned with neoconservative, neoliberal agendas. How do we reconcile the tension between the discipline's different faces? There is the face of an anthropology marked by a progressive praxis sensitive to and, in some cases, actually organically grounded in real-life struggles, and there is also an anthropology of co-optation, expressed, for example, in radically deconstructionist texts informed by the particular stream of postmodernism that Carolyn Martin Shaw (1995) has described as the skeptical variety, pessimistic about all meaning and politics. Anthropology's politically problematic face, however, is not solely postmodern. There is also the angle that rejects all forms of postmodernism and favors the strengthening of science. Frequently, the ideas of scientific anthropology that are advanced are those that advocate a hegemonic science free from values, politics, and subjectivity. I characterize the most rigid of those approaches as ideologies of scientificity or scientism, some of which have been amenable to the revival of biological determinism and sociobiological perspectives consistent with that line of thought. These approaches should not be confused with more critical biocultural syntheses open to dialogue with sociocultural perspectives that recognize the significance of power, political economy, and political ecology in understanding cultural dynamics (Leatherman and Goodman 1998).

Anthropology's political and ideological heterogeneity has led to the articulation of conflicting accounts of the discipline's politics. Despite Roseberry's concern about the dangers of purging, he acknowledged that anthropology, particularly during its earlier periods, was receptive and conducive to the work of liberals and progressives. Consistent with this view, a number of recently published works, arguing for anthropology's continued relevance and authority, have highlighted anthropologists' roles, historically, as critics, advocates, and subversives. Jeremy MacClancy's *Exotic No More: Anthropology on the Front Lines* (2002) is probably the most notable example. This view of anthropologists as disproportionately liberal and leftist, of course, contrasts with earlier characterizations of the field that criticized anthropology for its colonial and imperial underpinnings. In *Decolonizing Anthropology* (Harrison 1991a [1997], 1991b [1997], 1991c [1997]), my colleagues and I zoomed in on the discipline's most politically compromising contradictions to develop an argument for an anthropology for social justice and liberation. I recognize, however, that anthropology is variegated and multidimensional. It encompasses contradictory and conflicting trends. It is a site of contestation and debate, both intellectual and political. It is a "battlefield for competing theories" and histories (Llobera 1976, 19). Before we can rework the field, we must understand what we have before us—the good, the bad, the ugly. What have the major arguments been in the debates over the sort of discipline anthropology has been, is, and ought to be? I will reexamine some of the major critiques and commendations before I discuss my own vision of the strategies necessary, if not sufficient, for reworking anthropology and transforming it into the sort of humanity-affirming inquiry that better meets my goals as an outsider within, particularly one who is socially positioned as a racially marked and gendered subject and agent of change.

Revisiting the Critiques

In some, perhaps many, parts of the world, anthropology is still perceived to be a demeaning and objectifying discourse that remains part of the legacy of colonialism and a vehicle for legitimating current policies of global, neocolonial capitalism. In *Indians and Anthropologists* (Biolsi and Zimmerman 1997), a collection of essays on Vine Deloria Jr.'s influence on the critique of anthropology, the discipline is characterized as a "quintessentially Western project [that] does not ask questions native peoples ask or need answers to" (*Chronicle of Higher Education* 1997, A17; see also Michaelsen 1999 for a discussion on Amerindian antianthropologies and autoanthropologies).

Are these negative reactions a response to the persistence of problematic trends, or are they based on an enduring reputation or stereotype that conflicts with how current anthropologists actually go about their work and with the textual outcomes of that work? At a SfAA meeting a few years ago, a roundtable on globalization led to a lively exchange on the reactions against anthropological research in various parts of the world. One anthropologist who worked in New Zealand recounted how she had confronted Maori resistance against being studied. I discussed the problem anthropologists still have in parts of Africa, where anthropology is dismissed as an obsolete colonial discipline, whereas sociology, despite its problems, is more accepted. In Africa and India, it is not uncommon for anthropologists to work as and identify themselves as sociologists. On one hand, the boundaries between the two disciplines are artificial, and they have merged into a single social science, especially as they are practiced in many postcolonial contexts. On the other hand, the adoption of a professional persona as a sociologist may be a strategy for passing, a rational approach to professional survival in situations in which anthropology has a bad reputation.

A few years ago, the esteemed Bernard Magubane, a formerly exiled South African who worked in the University of Connecticut's Department of Anthropology for many years, published a compilation of essays in a book published by Africa World Press, a small independent press that distributes its publications internationally, particularly on the continent and in the diaspora. Magubane's book is entitled *African Sociology* (2000). Magubane may indeed identify as and may *be,* among other things, a sociologist. Before coming to the United States, he studied under sociologist Leo Kuper at the University of Natal. Beyond that background in sociology, I suspect that an editorial decision was made to market the book to an African and African diasporic audience. Moreover, Magubane, as reflected in the contents of some of the essays reprinted in the book, has serious problems with anthropology, claiming that it should "cease to exist." If one takes this strong position, does one then identify as an anthropologist? Magubane, I believe, is committed to building a social science that does justice to Africa and the world's social realities. He uses the term *sociology* not to denote a distinct discipline housed in departments and articulated through specific journals.

For him, the sociology of Africa is the study of African societies and the depth of the problems that thwart their development. Hence, an essay that offers an uncompromising critique of social anthropological treatments of social change is entitled "Crisis in African Sociology." Most of the content is focused on the crisis of anthropological work that refused to deal with the colonial context. Magubane also refused to accept the traditional separation between societies subjected to an anthropological lens and those studied by sociologists. He defines the study of the world's societies as sociology. Social anthropology has been a problematic subset that has nativized and decontextualized the African experience. It is from this African sociological vantage that he confronts anthropology's problems.

More than twenty years ago, Magubane and Faris (1985 [2000]) critically reflected on anthropology's political relevance to the history of modern capitalist expansion. In their view, anthropology "was born of Western imperialism to bring to the West information and artifacts as a consequence (and sometimes in support of) imperialist exploitation of the peoples of Asia, Africa, and the Americas" (499). They went on to suggest that anthropology's problems as a body of discourse and practice extend beyond the discipline's "instrumental activity" (502). The very nature of the discipline with its triumphalist, rationalist and liberal foundations needs to be deconstructed. Even radical anthropological projects are often suspect in the Southern Hemisphere, where many people associate anthropological research with a degrading tradition of objectification and othering (502). As a consequence, anthropology is often eschewed in universities within postcolonial countries. Magubane and Faris argue that the future of anthropology is to cease to be "the anthropology we know" and to become a mode of inquiry that can articulate a sense of political objection.

Another South African anthropologist, Archie Mafeje, offered a frontal attack against the anthropology institutionalized and mobilized within metropolitan contexts (1997). In a damning critique of Sally Falk Moore's (1994) book, *Anthropology and Africa,* Mafeje castigates the author for neglecting the role that African intellectuals have played in social science debates and paradigm shifts in African studies, particularly the anthropological study of Africa (Mafeje 1997, 6–12). He was particularly troubled by Moore's "contemptuous tone regarding . . . scholars that . . . deconstruct the 'colonial mentality' of Anthropology" (3). The final paragraph of his review punctuated his concern: "Mudimbe's hostility to colonial anthropology is shared by many African scholars. To harbour such feelings an African scholar does not have to be a trained anthropologist. . . . What is important is the images of Africa they conjure up and their association with the colonial past. Sally Moore mistakenly thinks that this does not matter any longer in the post-colonial era and pours scorn on the 'colonial period mentality' critique. These issues are still very much alive among African intellectuals, to whom she seems to pay no attention, as is reflected in her references in which Africans are conspicuous only by their absence" (Mafeje 1997, 11).

In her reply, Moore (1998) failed, or perhaps refused, to respond to Mafeje's major contention concerning Western scholars' tendency to ignore African intellectuals. Instead, she focused on Mafeje's lack of familiarity with the latest trends in anthropology and his overestimation of his own role as well as the role of Africans in influencing paradigm shifts in anthropology. This heated exchange sheds light on "the absence of a sense of a common project between African scholars of Africa and American Africanists" (Mwangi and Forgey 1996, 4). Also at issue here is a conflict over authority and authenticity in the epistemology of Africa. Moore refuses to give credence to Mafeje and other Africans' assertion of "interpretive rights . . . variously founded on cultural fluency, political engagement, lived experience, and immersion in daily Africa, a specifically African epistemological heritage, and so forth. [We can also speak] of a much less recognized authenticity, what we call the 'the new authenticity,' one that is forged from the inverted double of the older form. This form no longer bases its claims on the universalism or truth of its categories of analysis, but precisely on their contingency and fragmentation, and which by leveling the justification for any one authoritative voice, or authorizing condition, admits them all into an indeterminate discursive arena wherein they jostle and overlap, producing 'hybridity,' 'polyvocal exchange,' and 'bricolage'" (Mwangi and Forgey 1996, 4).

Mafeje is not alone in his view of Western anthropology. Many other African scholars have criticized their "structured exclusion . . . from elite institutional practice in the United States [which is] based on the dubious propositions that (1) empirical work is a- or pre-theoretical, (2) that theory enjoys some sort of ontological supremacy over empiricism, and (3) that Africans do not in fact produce what can be called 'theory'" (Mwangi and Forgey 1996, 3). This does not mean, however, that a small elite of African intellectuals has not been embraced by Western academia. Mamphela Ramphele, for instance, was successful in having her voice heard and in positioning herself at the World Bank. But most Africans working in African institutional contexts remain rather invisible and disadvantaged. Mafeje's critique has significant parallels with those that minoritized anthropologists in the United States have made.

Optimistic Views of Anthropology's Future Possibilities

Although Magubane and Mafeje envision and advocate for a postanthropological era in which African scholars deconstruct and displace all forms of dominating knowledge, there are other African anthropologists who take a more positive stance toward the discipline. Two in particular offer interesting insights. Another South African anthropologist, the medical doctor, former comrade, and self-acknowledged paramour of Black Consciousness Movement leader Steve Biko, Mamphela Ramphele acknowledges the discipline's baggage, but she underscores that it can be "much more than the handmaiden of colonialism [or neocolonialism]" (1995 [1999], 166). In her poignant memoir, she writes of anthropology's role in South Africa during the apartheid era: "[A]s I learned of the discipline . . . I learned to distinguish between the prostitution of Anthropology by racists and colonialists to serve their own ends, and Anthropology as a social science. Although a particularly vicious form of Anthropology operated in some Afrikaans-speaking universities, which provided ethnological justification for segregation, there was also another tradition which had earned South African Anthropology a place of honour internationally [and] . . . had led to a greater and more sophisticated understanding of South African society" (Ramphele 1995 [1999], 166).

Ramphele goes further, making the following important observation on the anthropological method: "I also noticed that the method of Anthropology—participant observation—was not very different from what I had used as an activist in community development work. I had to live among the people I worked with, observe what they did, why certain things made sense to them, and what motivated them. Participant observation is a prerequisite of any action which would try to change people's life circumstances" (Ramphele 1995 [1999], 166–67).

Kwesi Prah, a Dutch-trained Ghanaian anthropologist working in South Africa, also takes an optimistic view of anthropology's possibilities in Africa and elsewhere around the world. In his more epistemologically oriented view, an alternative universalism is possible. He claims that anthropology "as a universal idea cannot live without [Africans] as either subjects or objects" (Prah 1997, 444). He argues that "[i]n order to achieve a universalism of all voices, and not a universalism under restrictive Western hegemony, African anthropological endeavors must realize and accept the fact that ultimately the centre of gravity of anthropological knowledge production must be situated in Africa so that the 'otherness' of the subject of anthropological study which the history of Western anthropology has imposed on Africa is removed" (444).

Prah ends his commentary with the following remarks: "[I]n order to achieve true universalism in the production and reproduction of anthropological knowledge, we must all, North and South, learn to look at ourselves, hear others about ourselves and themselves, and above all allow others to speak for themselves" (Prah 1997, 445). Although Prah offers an optimistic view of anthropology's potential future, Roseberry provides a complimentary characterization of the discipline's past. He states that

> [A]nthropology has never provided a congenial home for conservatives or those who serve power. Intellectually, its (often competing) relativistic and evolutionary emphases are *potentially* unsettling to western or "American" or "British" chauvinisms. Practically, anthropology's emphasis on fieldwork has taken its practitioners to the fringes of empire, placing them in a virtually unique position among social scientists to report *substantively* on empire's effects and victims. Of course, it has also placed anthropologists in position to *serve* empire, as in British Africa, or among Native Americans, or the U.S.'s growing informal empire after World War II. But the numbers of anthropologists who so served were never so great, nor was anthropology ever so central to the imperial project, as its critics . . . proclaimed. (Roseberry 1996, 14)

Along similar lines, British anthropologist Jeremy MacClancy challenges critics' view of anthropology as tarnished by an "imperialist" brush. He writes that although "[i]t is true that in colonial times many anthropologists were funded by colonial agencies . . . that does not necessarily mean that their work assisted the colonial process." Many British anthropologists who worked in Africa in the postwar period "acted as liberal critics of the colonial regime, not as its handservants" (MacClancy 2002, 13). Alex de Waal continues this line of argument with his claim that despite their assigned role as adjuncts to military intelligence, anthropologists working in "Sudan during its Anglo-Egyptian days . . . frequently ended up with more sympathy and understanding for the subjects of their research and wrote up their reports accordingly" (MacClancy 2002, 13, citing de Waal). These writers underscore how anthropology "helps to empower the alienated and give voice to the otherwise unvoiced," and how "anthropology can humanize institutional process, the effects of politics, and the work of nations" (MacClancy 2002, 13). MacClancy insists that anthropologists are "on the side of 'the people', the subalterns" (13).

Revising the Revisions

These revised accounts of anthropology's history provide important insights into a discipline that was never as intellectually or politically monolithic as earlier critiques suggested. Anthropology has long been a locus for struggle over the discipline's relationship to colonial and now post- or neocolonial domination—whether to rationalize or apologize for it or work toward subverting it. Although this may be true, I think it is also important for us to interrogate these revisionist accounts for what they omit and silence concerning power dynamics; racial, class, and gender politics; and the extent to which liberal and radical anthropologists have, nonetheless, benefited from their privilege as, for the most part, middle- and upper-middle-class whites. We should question whether this privilege, usually unrecognized, and the hegemonic cultural orientation that makes it unrecognizable by naturalizing it are unwittingly expressed in ethnographic praxis and the resulting texts. It is important to be especially attentive to the more subtle mechanisms by which power disparities are reproduced in spite of the best intentions and progressive politics.

If so many anthropologists have been progressive advocates of the world's people, as the revised histories assert, then how do we explain the crisis of representation and authority, the resentment felt by so many anthropological subjects, the marginalization of racially and nationally subordinated anthropologists, and the erasure of women's scholarship through prevalent patterns of citation, as Lutz (1990) has documented? These are serious issues that should not be airbrushed even when we recognize and celebrate our successes and best practices, when we acknowledge that important precedents have been set in deploying anthropological tools according to an ethic of social responsibility and political engagement.

Zooming in on the demographics of race, Robert Alvarez (1994), based on data from the early 1990s, has written that U.S. anthropology is statistically whiter than sociology and the other social sciences. Since then, anthropology seems to have grown more diverse and open to diversity, both demographically and intellectually. I infer this from the number of women, nonwhites, and non-Westerners represented among the leading anthropologists whose work appears to be substantively engaged and frequently cited. As Dominguez has explained, the hypervisibility of minoritized and postcolonial immigrant intellectuals has something to do with the particular brand of racial politics enacted in the U.S. academy.

Despite the contradictions of constructing and managing diversity in academia, the scholarly interventions, for instance, of Lila Abu-Lughod, Arjun Appadurai, Ruth Behar, the late John Ogbu, Michel-Rolph Trouillot, Brackette F. Williams, Sylvia Yanagisako, Aihwa Ong, Akhil Gupta, David Scott, Renato Rosaldo, Kamala Visweswaran, Lee D. Baker, Patricia Zavella, and others are making significant impacts. These individuals have published in visible venues on issues setting the terms for important new trends. To what extent, however, is this diversity reflected in the contents of proseminars in graduate programs around the country? Will the diversification we have managed to achieve be sustained and even expanded over new generations of anthropologists? Scrutinizing this trend more closely, we must ask a series of important questions: What form has anthropology's diversity assumed? Will transnationals (especially from middle and elite backgrounds) be privileged at the expense of domestic minorities? In other words, will anthropology follow Harvard's example? Lani Guinier and Henry Louis "Skip" Gates have gone public with a report on the demographics of black students at the nation's leading university: Most have Caribbean and African backgrounds. Is diversity being restructured and managed to exclude native African Americans—or in the "Hispanic" context, the historically underrepresented and still excluded Latinos? Will the trend toward internationalization produce an academic elite of colored intellectuals who are effectively divorced from the experiences and concerns of rank-and-file minorities? Within the rank and file I include academics who, both here and abroad, are vulnerable to peripheralization at a moment when academia is being restructured to create conditions for an increasingly bifurcated labor market made up of those with and those without job security and those with the means for research productivity and those with oppressive teaching loads. These are among the problems we need to address before we can truly assess anthropology's progressiveness and openness to equality and change.

Moving toward a Multidimensional Strategy for Reworking Anthropology

As I have said before, there are multiple projects for critically reconstructing anthropology. All of them do not express their rationales in exactly these terms, but my reading of the anthropological literature and my participant observation in the activities of the AAA and SfAA suggest to me that there are a number of projects with similar aims. Unfortunately, they often compete against one another rather than build upon their commonalities and complementarities.

The symposium that Paule Cruz Takash and I co-organized back in 1999 attempted to offset this fractionalizing tendency and create an alternative model for reintegrating the best practices. Most of the projects or approaches are unidimensional, focusing on a single issue. For instance, Lila Abu-Lughod (1991) focuses on writing against culture. Reconceptualizing culture has been a key focus for a number of other anthropologists (Keesing 1994; Gupta and Ferguson 1999) interested in taking anthropological analysis in more satisfactory directions.

As I have already pointed out, Ulin (1991) focuses on bridging political economy and the interpretive techniques of postmodernism. Behar and Gordon (1995) are concerned with increasing the visibility and recognition of "women writing culture," the innovative, experimental ethnographic writing that Clifford and Marcus (1986) neglected to include in their *Writing Culture*. Socialist feminist Karen Brodkin Sacks (1989) has placed the building of a unified theory of race, gender, and class on the agenda. Aihwa Ong (1999) and Don Robotham (1997) have addressed the need to study alternative modernities. Marcus (1999) and his colleagues have been interested in making methodological innovations for working in the more complex, unexpected locations for ethnographic research—namely the contemporary domains of corporations, philanthropic organizations, research labs, cyberspace, and academic presses. Mary J. Weismantel (1995) reconstructs theory by following the implications of the indigenous theory and knowledge she grew to understand through her fieldwork among the Zumbagua. She shares theoretical authority with her research consultants, whose non-Western epistemology is fertile ground for the elements of theory that are useful for anthropological understanding. The emphasis on developing dialogues with and reconciling Western anthropological perspectives with non-Western intellectual traditions is found in my own writing (Harrison 1991a [1997]), which underscores the importance of decentering Western ethnographic authority. Along similar lines, Glenn Jordan's (1991 [1997]) notion of a new cultural anthropology revolves around dispersing ethnographic authority through collaborative research with communities under the lens of research. The rethinking of gender and sexuality, bringing attention to transgendered subjectivities, has also been a key approach to making anthropology more accountable for the whole range of social realities that constitute the human cultural variation on which it claims to have expert knowledge (Moore 1999).

My approach to reworking anthropology highlights the importance of holism, reintegration, and synthesis, which might be characterized as a kind of weaving. Josep Llobera emphasizes the significance and usefulness of weaving in his perspective on developing a "proper history of anthropology" (1976, 19). In my view, the method of weaving is central to developing a proper anthropology in the postcolonial world. The framework that I advocate delineates several objectives. The ultimate goal is to create conditions for a more compelling and enriching analysis of the human experience. Toward that end, this critical project, which demands a great deal of cooperative work, depends on our finding creative ways to achieve nine interrelated objectives and eventual outcomes.

First, this critical anthropological project must be grounded in a historical consciousness of where the discipline has been, where it is now, and where it is going or can potentially go. In other words, it must be committed to *rehistoricizing anthropology,* rethinking and reconstructing our historical understanding of both the researchers and those who have been researched—the peoples subjected to anthropological investigation through the ethnographic gaze, which in too many instances has denied them history and agency (Wolf 1982). A rehistoricized anthropology should be attuned to the diverse institutional settings, both academic and nonacademic, as well as the geopolitical or national contexts within which multiple modalities of anthropological knowledge have been produced. Through rehistoricization, we are able to situate and move toward decentering dominant Eurocentric and Northern axes of ethnographic authority within wider fields, networks, and regimes of disciplinary and interdisciplinary power. As a mode of critical analysis, rehistoricization enables us to unbury and reclaim neglected knowledges (e.g., women's [Cole 2003; Gacs et al. 1988; Lamphere 2004], African American [Baker 1998; I. Harrison and F. Harrison 1999], Latina and Latino [Dominguez 2000], and American Indian [Medicine 1988; Michaelsen 1999]), exposing the power dynamics that have shaped the relationship between canonical and noncanonical aspects of intellectual production. In other words, rehistoricization makes us attentive to the "modes, means, and relations of intellectual production" as they shift over time and space (Harrison 2006b, 392). Within this strategy, the approach to texts, those deemed to be worthy of being included in the disciplinary canon and those excluded from it, is predicated on the assumption that ethnographies, archaeological reports, theoretical essays, journalistic accounts, and ethnographically inspired fiction are all "discursively constructed, historical[ly contingent] phenomena situated in the material circumstances of both the institutionalized profession and the vagaries and trends of the wider world. We must recognize that once [these accounts] are written, the biases and evaluations of readers, particularly those with gate-keeping power, determine their reception. Reader-text-context interactions, which are integral to the politics of reception, 'govern whether texts are incorporated into the canon, whose disciplinary significance is reproduced over time'" (Harrison 2006b).

Another dimension of analysis and deconstruction that rehistoricization entails is the careful scrutiny of the concepts, interpretive metaphors, and analogies that have been employed in sociocultural analysis and theorizing. It is also important to interrogate the models and methodologies utilized, including the procedures for achieving some measure of validity and reliability, as they have been defined within the context of the various research designs that are explicit or implicit in anthropological writing. Yet another concern is the extent to which intradisciplinary and interdisciplinary border crossings have had an impact on anthropology's development. This is a question that I will address again later, but here I wish to zoom in on the historical implications of how interdisciplinary research has been differentially evaluated and incorporated into the discipline. Following up on points made earlier, I want to point to the interdisciplinary significance of St. Clair Drake's research, which drew a great deal from urban sociology and history. During the 1940s, his scholarship was deemed to be more sociological than anthropological and was virtually ignored within anthropology as a consequence. Drake is often identified as a sociologist even in anthropological and history of anthropology literature, such as Jerry Gershenhorn's (2004, 127, 231) intellectual biography of Melville Herskovits. The insights from psychology that were integrated into the culture and personality and national character school to which Ruth Benedict and Margaret Mead contributed, however, were evaluated in more positive terms (e.g., Erickson 1999, 79–83). Even though, in time, they came to be criticized and replaced by less essentialist approaches to culture and identity, those earlier psychological anthropologies remain on record as a significant chapter in the history of anthropology. They are typically covered in introductory textbooks and in more advanced histories. How many conventional histories of anthropology include a discussion—or even a footnote—on the early anthropological studies, often drawing on urban sociology, conducted in U.S. cities? As I discussed earlier, Lewis's (1999) well-meaning attempt to compensate for this neglect was compromised by his failure to admit the uneven and unequal terms of incorporation. Thomas Patterson's (2003) social history of the discipline represents a more critical alternative, as does Karen Brodkin's historical sketch of the perspectives that have theorized the diversity of U.S. society (2001). The most important work that rehistoricizes anthropology's contribution to the intellectual and social construction of race has been done by Audrey Smedley (1993 [1999]) and Lee D. Baker (1998), who provides an excellent history of the earliest generations of African American anthropologists, especially those aligned with the Boasian school and a slightly wider group of researchers whose anthropological work was folkloric in orientation and focus.

The second major objective of the critical anthropological project that I am pursuing along with kindred-thinking anthropologists (e.g., Mc-Claurin 2001) is to *rethink, rework, and reassess what constitutes theory and theorizing and who is authorized to do it.* Theory is an important site of struggle, because it has an important influence over the directions and scope of anthropological inquiry. Historically, the authority to construct and validate theory has been "differentially structured, with race, gender, class, and national origins as salient conditioning factors" (Harrison 1993b, 402). Anthropologists truly interested in critically reconstructing anthropology should be committed to leveling the discursive playing field so that all interested parties can have a genuine (rather than token) say in how to theorize the past and present sociocultural terrain. We also need to recognize that theory—the concepts, metaphors, models, and propositions that provide interpretive and explanatory frames—can assume multiple forms and levels—not only densely articulated, abstruse prose that requires a doctorate to decode (Harrison 1993b, 1999, 2000). This sort of inaccessible writing may be only passing for theory if, upon close interrogation, it is defective in its claim to provide tenable explanations.

My approach to theory questions the dichotomous and hierarchical relationship that is conventionally assumed to exist between theory and practice. In my view, theory is itself a kind of practice—hence, the tendency among some contemporary writers to use the process-centered term *theorizing*. But what kind of practice can or should theorizing be? What kinds of practices have been represented in anthropology's history over the past century and within the recent past? To what extent are the discourses touted as theoretical gendered masculine or raced white? Catherine Lutz (1995) has provocatively claimed that social theory is gendered, and drawing upon her argument, I have pointed out how gender and race work together to produce dynamics that strongly influence which intellectuals become recognized as producers of theoretically significant work and which ones, regardless of how theoretically rich their writings may in fact be, are evaluated largely for the descriptive data that their scholarship yields—if they receive any attention at all. The project that I envision is critical of the biased mechanisms of evaluation that result in a gendered, racialized division of intellectual labor that nearly categorically assigns, for instance, most black intellectuals to social locations in which the publicly recognized legitimacy to formulate and validate theory is largely unavailable. Although there are certainly a few minoritized and postcolonial anthropologists whose work is respected for its theoretical import (e.g., the MacArthur Award recipient Brackette F. Williams [1997–2001]), there is still the need to create a more inclusive space that welcomes a diversity of culturally inflected perspectives, from the everyday theory of indigenous peoples, domestic workers, immigrants, and refugees to the theorizing in which native anthropologists—particularly the historically underprivileged varieties—engage (Jones 1970). We need to work against commonly believed myths such as "blacks don't do theory" and be more willing to rethink the definitions and boundaries that are often accepted uncritically. The project I have in mind promotes this kind of rethinking and also recognizes that theory is formulated, reworked, and refined in the contexts of both basic and applied research. The history of the Afro-Atlantic points to many cases of intellectual production in which making a stark distinction between basic and applied, or theoretically driven versus practical, research is problematic and disrespectful of the ontological and epistemological orientation common within the culturally and politically specific milieus within which racially marked intellectuals have traditionally worked to produce socially relevant and enabling knowledge (F. Harrison and I. Harrison 1999; Medicine 2001).

The critical project that I envision must also pursue a third objective: *rethinking the implications and possibilities of both intradisciplinarity and interdisciplinarity* for anthropological inquiry and analysis. It must recognize that the interfaces and bridges between disciplines as well as between anthropology's subdisciplines may be potentially fertile grounds for cultivating promising new directions. Intradisciplinarity does not result automatically from a four-field approach to organizing anthropology departments and professional organizations. The mere juxtaposition of the subfields does not necessarily lead to meaningful and sustained cross-field dialogues that influence the kinds of questions anthropologists take into their research. In fact, in many cases, the juxtapositioning approach is fraught with tensions and conflicts that preclude building the kinds of critical learning communities necessary for sustaining a culture of intradisciplinary engagement.

Robert Borofsky's (2002) historical survey of the first hundred years of the *American Anthropologist* revealed that despite the prevalent lip service given to a commitment to a four-field discipline, only 9.5 percent of the articles were based on cross-subfield collaborations or syntheses. Contrary to the claims implied by our mission statement and charter myth, most anthropologists work within their subdisciplines, in rapidly proliferating areas of specialization. Anthropology is often characterized as the most interdisciplinary of all the social sciences and humanities. A study of intra- and interdisciplinary exchanges, however, measured through citation practices in "influential journals . . . with 'high impact scores' in the *Social Science Citation Index*" revealed an overall pattern of insularity. Disappointingly, anthropology had the smallest percentage of interdisciplinary citations (0.3 percent) compared with psychology (6 percent) and economics (10 percent) (*Chronicle of Higher Education* 2002, A18). Of course, citations do not necessarily reflect the extent to which ideas from other disciplines have been reworked and assimilated. According to Richard Swedberg, the editor of *Economics and Sociology,* "[q]uite a few economists today are talking about norms and institutions, which suggests that they've developed their own versions of sociological concepts, even if they haven't read much sociological literature itself" (A18). I would hope that critical anthropologists would be more aware of the genealogy of the concepts and methods integrated into their tool kits and able to map them on the multi- and interdisciplinary landscapes within which they work.

The strategic and fruitful cross-fertilization of ideas and methods is sometimes visible in the work of anthropologists who situate themselves in the context of area studies (e.g., African or Caribbean studies) or in that of topical areas that may be particularly amenable to intradisciplinary and interdisciplinary dialogue and debate. For example, the study of race, health, the environment, and economic development can be framed and pursued to engage cross-subfield and interdisciplinary pursuits. Critical biological anthropologists interested in understanding the power dynamics and the political ecology of human biological functioning in historical and/or contemporary contexts of economic development and global restructuring draw upon the work that sociocultural anthropologists, frequently medical anthropologists, have done on similar questions. A critical biological synthesis that brings adaptation and ecology together with culture, power, and history in an integrated analysis is being developed to advance this approach (Goodman and Leatherman 1999).

For the past several years, since the AAA presidency of Yolanda T. Moses (Mukhopadhyay and Moses 1997)—the first African American to hold that office and an educational leader who put the problem of race among the issues at the top of the profession's agenda—I have been involved with a group of anthropologists working to bridge the gap between biological anthropologists and cultural anthropologists in the study of race and racism. We have made an effort to facilitate and frame a dialogue that engages the perspectives of archaeologists and anthropological linguists as well as cultural and biological anthropologists. A publication that came out of this effort also included nonanthropologists, a geneticist and ethnic studies scholar, to underscore the interdisciplinary significance of our endeavor (Harrison 1998). The conceptual overview that I contributed to "Contemporary Forum: Race and Racism," published in *American Anthropologist,* the flagship journal in the United States, allowed me to stretch beyond my earlier limits (Harrison 1995b), as I thought seriously about the implications of, and possibilities for, intra- as well as interdisciplinary interfaces and intersections. There are interesting and innovative possibilities for raising research questions from such interstitial and hybrid locations, which can foster constructive dialogue if not synthesis and fusion. This is the direction in which critical intra- and interdisciplinarity can potentially lead us. The intradisciplinary interfaces that are the most promising depend on the kinds of questions we ask. Consequently, the biological-cultural intersection is not necessarily a productive site for scholarly advancement for many inquiries. There are indeed cultural anthropologists with legitimate scholarly agendas that lie far outside of this particular space of intradisciplinary engagement. Coming to this conclusion has led some sociocultural and biological anthropologists (as well as archaeologists who identify with anthropological science) to organize themselves into separate departments. Stanford and Duke are two examples of this trend, which goes against the grain of the dominant four-field approach. They represent programmatic alternatives to the traditional four-field approach, which they see as a "sacred bundle" that warrants being "unwrapped," exposed for its epistemological limitations, and dislodged from its hegemonic position (Segal and Yanagisako 2005).

The seeds of my thinking about the implications of working across the boundaries of subfields and disciplines were probably planted five years before publishing "Contemporary Forum," when I was invited to write a foreword for the 1993 reprint of a 703-page anthology, a benchmark as Arthur Tuden (1993, vii) described it. Originally published in 1977 as a volume of *Annals of the New York Academy of Sciences, Comparative Perspectives on Slavery in New World Plantation Societies* (Rubin and Tuden 1993 [1977]) embodied the proceedings of a megasymposium that Vera Rubin and Arthur Tuden organized to respond to the ideological and political implications of *Time on the Cross* (Fogel and Engerman 1974). Fogel and Engerman's controversial study of slavery in the U.S. South was based on the highly mathematical and computerized methods of cliometrics. The picture of slavery they portrayed made slavery appear humane and beneficial to both the plantocracy and the enslaved workforce. Rubin and Tuden organized the conference to make the comparative research record more publicly known. An impressive international cast of prominent cultural anthropologists, sociologists, geographers, economists, political scientists, and, of course, historians were invited to present papers, most of which were later published in what may still be one of the most extensive compilations on New World slavery.

The foreword I was privileged to write for the 1993 edition gave me the opportunity to fashion an interdisciplinary synthesis that reframed the volume in light of where the literature had gone since the late 1970s. I was also intrigued by the implications of revisiting the 1970s symposium in the wake of the 1992 quincentenary of Columbus's "discovery" of what was from his perspective a New World. Writing from the vantage point of the descendants of the conquered and enslaved, I highlighted the volume's significant contributions as well as exposed some of the silences and gaps that more recent trends in historical archaeology, biohistory and biological anthropology, gender studies, and Africana studies had filled. The sections of the essay that I included on trends in the historical archaeology of plantation slavery and the analysis of human remains were areas that I had only begun to explore, largely due to the influence of a few graduate students who helped me think about the connections and mutual interests between anthropology's subdisciplines. Unfortunately, productive cross-subfield exchanges, particularly with cultural anthropology, were few and far between in my department; hence, I went against the grain by attempting to follow a pandisciplinary approach whenever it seemed appropriate or informative in my courses on the Caribbean, the African diaspora, social inequality, and human rights. In these topical areas, material on archaeological and human biological perspectives (particularly related to health) could easily be integrated to demonstrate the potential complementarity of the subdisciplines—which is not usually realized—and the ways in which they may extend anthropological knowledge.

When I was asked to guest edit the *American Anthropologist* Contemporary Issues Forum in the late 1990s, I was more than prepared to do so because of my previous experiences studying, teaching, and editing publications about race, engaging the dynamics of interdisciplinarity in women's studies during a brief tenure working in a women's studies program, and exploring the contours and politics of intradisciplinarity within anthropology (as I had experienced them in two different departmental cultures). I had also rehearsed my ideas in a short essay I was invited to write for *Brown Alumni Monthly,* which in 1994 published a series of essays on the university's most distinguished teachers, including Rhett Jones, who had been my history professor as an undergrad. Two of his former students were asked to reflect on the influence of his teaching. Those essays accompanied a longer essay that Jones himself wrote on his career at Brown teaching African American studies and history. His application of sociological concepts and theory in interpreting historiographical evidence made a lasting impression on me, inspiring both my teaching and scholarship. I wrote in honor of my former professor, who introduced me to the history of New World Maroons—runaway slaves—and their struggles to escape slavery for freedom:

> In a sense, [Rhett Jones and I, as well as others who think like us] are academic maroons, escaping the colonizing confinement of overly-compartmentalized thinking, mapping new terrain, and laying new foundations in the quest for

academic freedom. In the West, most knowledge [has been] approached in a piecemeal way, through separate disciplines, which can fragment the way we . . . perceive the truth and the world. I work from the borderlands of intersecting disciplines, weaving together fragments often assumed to be incompatible or marginal. For example, much of the work done in women's studies and ethnic studies has been considered marginal to the mainline disciplines, yet we are seeing within anthropology and the social sciences that they are among the most fertile grounds for understanding the structure of society in general. . . . Rhett Jones' example impressed upon me that my life and work need not be structured along stark lines of either/or. [Hence, for the past] twenty years I've migrated across extremely blurred boundaries from ethnography to fiction, from classroom to boardroom, from teacher to performer, from analyst to activist, and from career woman to mother. (Harrison 1994a)

The fourth objective for the holistic critical anthropological project I am describing is *the pursuit of a socially responsible ethics and politics of ethnographic research for producing ethnography and ethnographically informed social analysis* that, among other things, illuminates the interlocking dynamics of culture, power, and political economy within a framework nuanced by historical depth, local-global linkages, and the dialectics between structure and agency. Consistent with or as a corollary to this objective is the imperative that ethnographic analysis elucidate the multiple modalities of violence, including the long-neglected problem of structural violence—systemically induced violations—and its relationship with other forms of violence, which range from symbolic to political and domestic violence (Farmer 2003, 2004; Harrison 1997b). In varying ways, these multiple and interrelated violences are manifested in the diverse sociocultural contexts that ethnographers study, particularly those in which abject poverty, social suffering, and human rights abuse prevail. Throughout much of the African diaspora, economic marginalization is rampant, as Whitten and Szwed pointed out in their overview of Afro-American anthropology more than thirty years ago (Whitten and Szwed 1970). Pervasive marginalization is not produced and reproduced over extended spans of time without the abuse of power in its performative and structural modalities. These dynamics implicate unjust political systems that range from authoritarian to bourgeois democratic. Contrary to neoconservatives' and the complacent silent majority's commonsense thinking, the contradictions within the highly touted democratic polities, from Jamaica to the United States, warrant critical scrutiny. Such investigations can illuminate these polities' track record in respecting or disrespecting human rights—civil and political as well as the barely recognized social and economic rights delineated in international covenants and conventions that have extended international standards of human rights beyond the parameters of the Western liberal tradition.

The relationships between "violence, suffering, and power" too often remain unrecognized and undertheorized in anthropological and other social analyses (Bourgois and Scheper-Hughes 2004, 318). As Paul Farmer's public anthropology demonstrates to us, in the real world of everyday life and status quos, "most violent acts are not deviant. They are defined as moral in the service of conventional norms and material interest" (Bourgois and Scheper-Hughes 2004, 318). The critical ethnographic enterprise is designed to work toward "more truthful accounting" and to fight social censorship and "amnesia" (Farmer 2004, 317). Much along the lines of Roseberry's thinking, Farmer points out that contemporary anthropology's trend toward greater "specialization and subspecialization" has, unfortunately, been accompanied by an "erasure of history and political economy"; however, we cannot produce a "robust anthropology of structural violence" without these "broad bodies of knowledge" (308).

A cornerstone in sociocultural anthropology, ethnographic methodology is based on a conceptualization and theory of knowledge production in which personal participation and immersion are key conditions for data collection in the real-life settings for research that we call "the field." The specific techniques and methods for ethnographic data gathering are varied and may include a mix (or a triangulation) of qualitative and quantitative approaches, depending on the nature of the research questions. Ethnography's practice in the field, its textual products after fieldwork has been completed, and its analytical substance, theoretical frames, and worldly applications have all received a great deal of attention. The crisis of representation has occupied considerable focus with the postmodern turn's privileging of texts and their literary devices, notably their rhetorical expression of poetics and politics. Ultimately, the crisis of representation is rooted in the wider crisis of legitimacy that implicates the forces of neocolonial structural power (Wolf 1990). Structural power and related structural violence within neoliberal capitalism have engendered patterns of geopolitical and economic development that set the stage for many of the tensions between ethnographers and the ethnographic subjects who have often been represented as radically different others, exotics. The ethnography of neoliberal capitalist landscapes and the violence-laden social dramas (e.g., Harrison 1997b) they engender must balance anthropologists' interests in writing experiments, to the extent that they are deemed important, against a commitment to speaking truth to power. That language of truth must convey a historicized social analysis attentive to political economy as well as the "racial, ethnic, class, and national differences that condition gendered experience" (Harrison 1993b, 402). At a historical moment when disparities of wealth, health, life expectancy, and military control are widening, there is an urgent need for critical ethnographic research that can expose worldly problems as well as point the way to interpretive frames that contribute to the formulation of theory bold enough to envision "an alternative to established political-economic configurations" (Harrison 2000, 62). Jamaican anthropologist Don Robotham argues that such an "alternative should inspire people to mobilize" (Harrison 2000, 62–63).

The fifth project objective follows logically from the fourth. It involves using critical ethnographic insights along with other kinds of evidence to *map the mediated connections between the local and supralocal—the national, regional, and "glocal"—sphere.* My emphasis here is on the need to make extrapolations and weave syntheses from ethnographic cases in order to *theorize the sociocultural and political-economic terrain of the contemporary global order* as it is manifest in the contexts and practices of ethnographically observable everyday life. The global is also manifest in the "webs of living power" (Farmer 2004, 309) within institutions and structures operating at various levels and in diverse settings around the world. My hope is that ethnographic analysis of the caliber described will inspire more anthropologists to intervene in interdisciplinary debates on the workings and contradictions of global capitalism, late modernity, or postmodernity; the manifestations, dilemmas, and embodiments of structural violence; and the spaces and modalities of agency. Anthropological interjections can address issues of global-scale concerns without losing sight of experience-near dynamics, including the admirable resilience as well as the culpability of local actors.

The final four objectives extend the parameters for building a critical anthropology of anthropology. The sixth objective is to *interrogate the ways in which anthropology is organized and practiced in both academic and nonacademic contexts here in the United States and abroad.* I am insisting that we not restrict our critiques, interrogations, and analyses of anthropology to the study of the texts and discourses that are windows onto the values, knowledges, and ideologies of the intellectual discipline with its mainstreams and minor streams. We also need to examine the profession's social organization, its multiple stratifications, its informal power dynamics and formal modes of governance, and its economic organization—the segmented labor market, workplace conditions, the status and experience of women and minorities, the structure of philanthropy and contracts, and the publishing enterprise, from the evaluation of publishability to marketing. Anthropology is an institutional complex amenable to investigation in much the same way that social scientists study the social institutions of ethnographic others. Over the past decade-and-a-half, the gendered and racial economy of anthropology has received increasing attention (Alvarez 1994; Baker 1998; Harrison 1991a [1997], 1999); however, there is still a need for more systematically collected data, particularly on racial minorities and the racism they confront within their profession (Whitehead, personal communication, 2005). This was one of the conclusions of the 1973 *Report of the Committee on Minorities and Anthropology*, which recommended that the AAA investigate the "problem of racism and discrimination . . . especially in its own midst" (American Anthropological Association 1973, 93). Unless anthropologists find ways to dismantle this persistent problem, the material context for epistemological racism is sustained, adversely affecting the ways in which anthropological knowledge is produced (Scheurich and Young 1997).

The seventh directive is that *anthropology as an intellectual community must undergo further democratization*. This can be accomplished in good measure through activism—political organizing—within and in between the various institutions of the profession, expanding the space for diversity at all levels of participation and decision making, subverting core-periphery relations by reshaping the politics of reception that determines the kinds of work supported and rewarded. The eighth objective and call to action is for anthropologists to find more effective ways to *mobilize knowledge and professional resources for forms of democratic engagement that link our academic pursuits to public interests*. It is to the advantage of various publics that we use professional service as a launching ground for meaningful public engagement in areas such as popular education, social policy, and human rights. Although anthropologists are active in many local contexts working with varied constituencies, we are rarely in the eye of the wider public, especially on the national level. In public discourses to which we could contribute considerable knowledge and insight, we are typically absent. We need to come up with strategies to change this so that anthropologists are among the leading social critics, advisors to progressive political leaders, and leaders in their own right. There are also other ways to have an impact without necessarily being featured in *The New York Times* op-eds or on PBS, CNN, or the BBC. For instance, practitioners of activist anthropology (e.g., Charles Hale and Edmund Gordon of the University of Texas at Austin) depart from conventional models of public intellectualism, which rarely question the epistemological and political underpinnings of knowledge production and dissemination. The activist model advocates building long-term alliances with grassroots organizations and social movements, deploying anthropological skills and pragmatic solidarity to support people who mobilize for change outside of established political entities. Physician and critical medical anthropologist

Paul Farmer, who works in Haiti, is a major proponent of doing research that is linked to social justice struggles. He is adamant that "[t]the divorce of research and analysis from pragmatic efforts to remediate inequalities of access is a tactical and moral error—it may be an error that constitutes, in and of itself, a human rights abuse" (2003, 22).

The ninth and final objective entails *decentering Western dominance* by creating conditions for leveling Northern and Southern anthropologies and for restructuring their grossly asymmetrical relationship with each other. This is the only way that currently existing anthropology with its dominant spheres of influence can be freed of its overwhelming Eurocentrism and underpinnings of white supremacy. Jacob Pandian's *Anthropology and the Western Tradition* (1985) argues that anthropology, as we know it, is largely a Western discourse to make sense of otherness and its relationship to the West. I am intrigued by the prospects of expanding the terms for anthropology so that the possibility exists for an alternative and thoroughly decolonized anthropology (Buck 2001; Harrison 1991a [1997], 1991b [1997]), one critically reconstructed by having its most useful tools reworked and reassembled into a better-honed repertoire.

The applied anthropology of anthropology that I envision is informed by my experiences over the past twenty years as an activist in a variety of professional and community contexts. I have organized scientific sessions and special events for AAA meetings and for congresses and intercongresses of the International Union of Anthropological and Ethnological Sciences (IUAES); networked across several sections to build coalitions; edited news-letters, special issues of journals, and books; served on numerous editorial committees and executive boards; organized delegations to international conferences such as the United Nation's NGO Forum for the World Conference against Racism; and led an international women's organization (namely, the IUAES Commission on the Anthropology of Women). In university and university-community settings, I have worked with student activists in teach-ins to provide extracurricular education on South African apartheid and U.S. foreign policy in Latin America and the Caribbean. I have been part of a AAA-sponsored work group implementing a public education initiative on race and human variation that is designed to translate anthropologi-cal knowledge for wider publics. In these activities, my professional service overlaps with my scholarly pursuits and politics. As I pointed out earlier, or-ganizational work affects the intellectual climate and contents of professional meetings and journals. It builds new constituencies for new perspectives. It brings people together who might not otherwise have a common cause. It refashions the politics of reception for new trends in knowledge and new voices for an expanded, democratized disciplinary diversity.

Thematic and Topical Foci

I have organized the twelve essays that comprise the main body of this book around five themes, which summarize my vision of anthropology's possibilities as a critical project: (1) rehistoricizing anthropology, (2) interdisciplinary dialogues with interlocutors, (3) the power of ethnography and the ethnography of power, (4) structural violence here and there in an era of global restructuring, and (5) blurring boundaries between academia and beyond. These themes are obviously drawn from similarly labeled objectives and calls for action; however, the five I have selected are meant to represent wider umbrellas under which other closely related objectives can also be addressed in the chapters tied to particular themes. This fusion and consolidation of selected objectives into major organizing themes reflect the extent to which the nine issues I have enumerated overlap and grade into each other. For example, although rethinking theory is not one of the five thematic foci around which chapters are organized, a critical reconstructive approach to theoretical practice is certainly relevant for much of the scholarship that rehistoricizes anthropology. Rethinking theoretical practices is also germane to interdisciplinary engagements, analyzing globalization and structural violence, and investigating the culture, sociopolitical organization, and political economy of professional anthropology. Moreover, theory informs and makes a difference in determining the strategies for community organizing; it influences the models of activism and social change that we deploy. As I understand it, intersections of theory, race, gender, and power are integral to this critical project.

All of the objectives I have enumerated in this chapter are not expounded on in the chapters that follow. For instance, in order to economize space, I have not included any essays that directly address the significance of anthropology's intradisciplinarity. I have, however, dealt with this matter in other writings, particularly in my contributions to expanding the discourse on race and New World slavery along more interdisciplinary and intradisciplinary lines (Harrison 1993a, 1998). Indeed, in one way or another, I have addressed and worked toward achieving all of this holistic project's objectives in different aspects of my career as an anthropologist. Most of the twelve chapters that make up the main body of this book were written over the past fifteen years; a third of the chapters are based on work I have done in the past five years. Five chapters have been published before but are reprinted here because of their relevance to my argument. In the case of one of the previously published pieces (chapter 5), I have made substantial revisions to update it in light of more recent changes. These chapters show the development of my thinking over time, and they demonstrate the versatility of my interests as an anthropologist interested in political ethnography, intellectual and social history, social theory, interdisciplinary studies, Africana and Caribbean studies, feminism, and the art and science of creating syntheses and solving jigsaw puzzles.

Rehistoricizing Anthropology—Both the Researchers and the Researched

Two chapters address the challenges and implications of rehistoricization. The first is derived from the reclamation research I have done on earlier cohorts of African American anthropologists and sociologists who addressed problems that have been particularly relevant to anthropological analysis. In the mid-1980s I co-organized two AAA sessions in honor of St. Clair Drake's life and career, in recognition of the fortieth anniversary of *Black Metropolis: A Study of Negro Life in a Northern City,* the classic sociological/ anthropological study that Drake coauthored with Horace Cayton (Drake and Cayton 1945). One of the sessions, co-organized with Glenn Jordan, focused on Drake's career as an applied anthropologist working mainly in Africa and the United States; the other, co-organized with Dallas Browne, was organized as a Festschrift in honor of Drake's contributions to urban anthropology. The latter eventually led to the publication of a special issue of *Urban Anthropology and Studies of Cultural Systems and World Economic Development* entitled "Black Folks in Cities Here and There: Changing Patterns of Domination and Response" (Harrison 1988a). In the introduction that I wrote to conceptually frame and situate the articles as well as Drake's significance for contemporary urban anthropology, I introduced my thinking on a diasporic analytical frame and on the racialized power relations that led to the peripheralization of black scholars such as Drake and before him W. E. B. Du Bois, Oliver Cox, and Drake's mentor, Allison Davis, in urban anthropology (Harrison 1988b). That essay, and later essays on Du Bois's influence on early African American anthropologists, drew upon, synthesized, and, I hope, extended earlier arguments presented by Council Taylor (1971), E. Irene Diggs (n.d.), and sociologists Dan Green and Edwin Driver (1976) on Du Bois's too often negated contributions. Over the next several years, I collaborated with a colleague, Ira E. Harrison, to compile a group of intellectual biographies of African American pioneers in U.S. anthropology (I. Harrison and F. Harrison 1999). During the 1990s I also wrote about the politics of anthropology, particularly as it relates to the need to decolonize the discipline (Harrison 1991a [1997]) and to dismantle a racialized, gendered division of labor that often refuses to validate women of color's writing and knowledge claims "against the grain" (Harrison 1993b).

"Unburying Theory, Repositioning Practice: Anthropological Praxis in Peripheral Predicaments" was written in the mid-1990s in the midst of this rehistoricization and decolonization work. Rejecting the conventional theory and practice dichotomy, it examines the praxis of two African American anthropologists whose careers began in the period between the 1930s to the 1950s, Allison Davis and Manet Fowler, the first black woman to earn a PhD in anthropology from a U.S. university. Both undertook research projects that brought a social justice perspective to urban ethnography. Both produced social analysis rich in its potential for both practical applications and theoretical construction. The theoretical significance of applied anthropology is highlighted by examining Davis's and Fowler's work. Nonetheless, neither became readily recognized names in mainstream anthropology. The essay addresses what we can learn from them and others who have been in similar predicaments.

The second chapter in the first part of the book, "Remapping Routes, Unearthing Roots: Rethinking Caribbean Connections with the U.S. South," reflects my thinking on the neglected historical and contemporary connections between the U.S. South and the Caribbean. The essay was originally written as a keynote address for the Southern Anthropological Society's 2003 annual meeting, whose Key Symposium focused on transnational connections between the South and Caribbean. The invitation to be the keynote speaker gave me the opportunity to write up ideas I had been mulling over for many years. I was given the platform to publicly address some of the questions I had begun asking as a graduate student whose approach to studying Caribbean anthropology included a consideration of the region's family resemblance to the plantation societies in the U.S. South along with those along the Atlantic and Caribbean coasts of the Central American and South American mainland. The chapter pushes us to consider the implications of rethinking the histories and remapping the cultural geographies of both the South and the Caribbean. At a moment when anthropologists are crisscrossing and blurring the boundaries of culture, nation, and identity, we need to take the implications of unboundedness and transterritorialization into our thinking about the historical development of our own assumptions and concepts as well as about the histories of the peoples and societies we study. It was possible to write this essay because I found an interesting way to apply principles from recent studies of transnationalism and globalization. I also built upon insights from my personal history and autoethnographic awareness as a native of the Chesapeake Bay region.

Interdisciplinary Dialogues with Strategic Interlocutors

The next two papers address anthropology's relationship to, or place within, the concerns of interdisciplinarity by focusing on two interlocutors, Alice Walker and Gordon K. Lewis, whose writings in African American women's fiction and Caribbean politics, respectively, resonate strongly with many anthropological perspectives. These concerns include writing against conventional conceptions of culture and engaging in modes of cultural criticism and sociopolitical analysis informed by the knowledges and lived experiences of ordinary folk. It is noteworthy that both of these nonanthropologists had aligned themselves or acknowledged an affinity with particular black anthropologists. Walker was responsible for helping to revive interest in the largely forgotten novelist, folklorist, and ethnographer Zora Neale Hurston. Lewis acknowledged St. Clair Drake for having given him insights into the workings of racially stratified societies in the Americas.

"Writing against the Grain: Cultural Politics of Difference in Alice Walker's Fiction" was written as a black feminist response to the biases and silences in *Writing Culture* (Clifford and Marcus 1986), which in many respects displaced the innovative ethnographic writing of feminist and minoritized anthropologists outside the boundaries of the textual experiments associated with anthropology's postmodern turn. "Writing against the Grain" was one of several essays compiled in two volumes on "Women Writing Culture": the first was a special issue of *Critique of Anthropology* (Behar 1993) and the other a book, *Women Writing Culture* (Behar and Gordon 1995), which comprised a more extensive collection of essays and featured a diverse group of established feminist anthropologists. The first volume provided an outlet for several of Ruth Behar's University of Michigan graduate students, who had written seminar papers that were later presented in a 1991 public symposium ("Women Writing Culture: Anthropology's Other Voices") to which Catherine Lutz, Kamala Visweswaran, and I were invited. My essay was included in both volumes, although the chapter published in the book was much condensed. The version that appears here is a slight revision of the original *Critique* article, which, unlike the compressed book chapter, offers a substantive theoretical rationale for an anthropological engagement of Walker's writing. "Writing against the Grain" is not only a counterargument to Clifford, it is also an affirmative dialogue with Michael Fischer's chapter in *Writing Culture*. Fischer makes some provocative claims about ethnic literary genres, namely autobiography and autobiographical fiction, which I wish to extend to ethnic fiction generally. He argues that these genres represent a model for "a fully reflexive ethnography" (Clifford and Marcus 1986, 23).

"Probing the Legacy of Empire: Reflexive Notes on Caribbeanist Gordon K. Lewis" was written to be presented in a symposium that New York University anthropologist Constance Sutton organized in memory of Lewis, a Welshman who lived and worked most of his adult life in the Caribbean. A professor of political science at the University of Puerto Rico, Lewis wrote about the entire region, from the Anglophone islands and mainland territories to the Spanish-speaking societies. The topics he addressed also ranged widely from colonial and postcolonial state development to Caribbean intellectual history. His qualitative approach to problems of power and culture made his scholarship resonate with the work of anthropologists. In a sense, he built a bridge between anthropology and political science.

The invitation to participate in the memorial symposium gave me a chance to extend my knowledge of Lewis. His works (especially Lewis 1968) were must-reads in graduate school. Nonetheless, I did not really know that much about him—that he had married and raised a family with a black Barbadian (Bajan) woman; that he had spent time in Tiger Bay, the colored and multiracial community in Cardiff where St. Clair Drake had done his doctoral research; or that he had spent time in Chicago and come to see that city and perhaps the United States through a race-cognizant lens that St. Clair Drake and Horace Cayton had crafted. In many ways, that lens had prepared him for what he would find in the Caribbean, where the politics of pigmentocracy pervaded so much of the logic of societal organization.

My reflexive reading of Gordon Lewis, particularly the essays and lectures Sutton made available to me, helped me rethink the significance my own trajectory as an anthropologist who had begun her serious ethnographic explorations among black and colored immigrants in England and later found her way to the Caribbean, namely an urban Jamaican political hotbed, a garrison constituency where the concerns of political scientists and anthropologists like me could be wedded.

The Power of Ethnography, the Ethnography of Power

Most sociocultural anthropologists understand that ethnographic research and representation at its best can powerfully portray and humanize the problems that preoccupy social scientists, many of whom deal with these issues in ways distant from the actual lived experiences that are translated into the language of independent and dependent variables. Ethnographers tend to treat those problems through the lens of an experience-near analysis that zooms in on the everyday lives of ordinary people and the dilemmas they negotiate. In much of the global south and the African diaspora, poverty and other kinds of structurally mediated social suffering, what my Jamaican friends call "sufferation," are prevalent. Critical anthropologists are aware of the importance of producing ethnographic description and analysis that clearly exposes and explains the effects and sources of the many forms and expressions of violence and power—which are the stuff that contributes to the persistence of the social inequities that characterize much of diasporic experience.

I have done fieldwork in an impoverished and politically subjugated locality where these problems are rampant. Fieldwork was difficult, full of ethical and political dilemmas I had to learn to negotiate. I have examined the politics of my research in downtown Kingston, Jamaica, elsewhere, placing it in the context of the island's political challenges during the 1970s and 1980s as well as in that of my personal political orientation and identity (Harrison 1991c [1997]). Part III of this book features two essays based on the fieldwork I conducted intermittently from 1978 to the mid-1990s. They examine the interplay among politics, violence, crime, class, and gender in a context shaped by neoliberal economic policies (e.g., the International Monetary Fund's (IMF's) once-mandated structural adjustment) and the constraints and possibilities of globalization. Much of my research focused on the urban informal sector, including the illicit sphere of drug trafficking that situates many local residents within transnational circuits of exchange. Those circuits are often mediated by Jamaican diasporic fields, which connect the place I call Oceanview to the market demand of consumers in cities and even rural towns in the United States, Canada, the United Kingdom, and beyond. Street gangs (also called posses) are at once local and transnational units of social and economic organization that, despite their illegality, play a central role in the survival of economically challenged households and communities, whose human rights are undermined by Jamaican democracy's authoritarian face. Indeed, human rights are thwarted by sufferers finding themselves caught between a rock and a hard place—between the state's authoritarian face and the excesses posses perpetrate while attempting to secure their footing on a terrain upon which the options for subsistence security and social mobility are limited and, to a considerable extent, illegal.

"Gangs, Politics, and Dilemmas of Global Restructuring in Jamaica" is an updated version of one of the first pieces I published on my Kingston work. It provides an explanation of Jamaica's crime problem as well as a historical perspective on the prominent role of gangs in Jamaican society, politics, and economy. Especially since the 1980s, Jamaican gangs or posses have been characterized as a nation within a nation, powerful enough to elude and expose the limits of the social controls exerted by the state's policing and military apparatuses. The essay also argues that Jamaica's policing strategy is a problem that has led to a human rights crisis, especially in the eyes of international human rights organizations such as Human Rights Watch and Amnesty International.

"The Gendered Violence of Structural Adjustment" takes the analysis of Oceanview's adverse circumstances in the direction of an exposé of the local impact of the IMF's structural adjustment program (SAP), from the late 1970s until 1992, when the SAP officially ended. Although IMF loans had ended, the government's policies were consistent with earlier IMF mandates. The government had bought into the ideology and the practice of neoliberal globalization, as economist Michael Witter pointed out in the informative and provocative film, *Life and Debt*. This chapter illuminates the SAP's gendered and classed ramifications in Oceanview, a downtown neighborhood and political garrison constituency where power is contested and claimed through paramilitarized means. This mode of political enforcement valorizes expressions of ghetto masculinity that glorify physical violence against other men and against women. Violent contests over gender identities became more intense when Oceanview's economic conditions, which had long been depressed, declined even further because of the negative effects of structural adjustment and export-led development strategies. In this context, some local women activated their social networks in ways more conducive to truce making, nonpartisanism, and the organization of sanctuary spaces as an alternative to gang and political party turfs. These mobilizations seemed to challenge the established construction of manhood and womanhood and suggest an alternative view based on regenerating the community, reconciliation, and peace.

Structural Violence Here and There in the Global Era

The three chapters in this fourth part of the book (whose theme is inspired by Drake's 1987 book title, *Black Folk Here and There*) build on insights from ethnographic research in the Caribbean and the United States to interrogate some of the ways that structural violence is manifested across numerous settings that are being dramatically reconfigured by the forces of global restructuring. These chapters put a number of disparate sites and problems together on the same page: poverty in urban Jamaica and rural Appalachia; structural adjustment in Jamaica and the U.S. embargo against Cuba; global apartheid as a multiaxial, intersectional concept for grappling with the deepening disparities among the world's peoples, the most impoverished being disproportionately women of color; human rights as a focus for political mobilization in the U.S. South as well as elsewhere in the post–Cold War era; and the role of advocacy in research.

"Everyday Neoliberalism in Cuba: A Glimpse from Jamaica" deals with how two Caribbean neighbors are adapting to the constraints of global restructuring, the U.S. hemispheric and global hegemony, and how and why those adaptations, both at the household and national levels, intersect. The chapter underscores the importance of resisting and overcoming the linguistic gerrymandering that too often separates or distances research done in the Anglophone Caribbean from that done in Cuba and the rest of the Spanish-speaking Caribbean, which is often mapped as part of Latin America as though Cuba, the Dominican Republic, and Puerto Rico are not both Caribbean *and* Latin American.

"Global Apartheid at Home and Abroad" was originally written as part of the 1997 Society for Applied Anthropology keynote session organized in response to Philippe Bourgois's provocative commentary on anthropologists' responsibility to confront inner-city apartheid in the United States (Bourgois 1996). In this chapter, I elaborate my thinking on the concept of global apartheid and map it across a global terrain that includes white Appalachians who are also victims of a political economy of classed and gendered racialization in which regionally marked, impoverished whites have been relegated to problematic predicaments. I argue that this kind of racial regime, which is typically unmarked, is partly responsible for the continued underdevelopment of Appalachia. The chapter also offers a critical race-feminist analysis of the growing inequalities of wealth, health, and life expectancy that the global restructuring of capitalism engenders. I explore the role that applied and activist anthropologists can play in advocating social, economic, and political justice. In later essays, ironically published before the first exploration of global apartheid that appears here, I examine the human rights ramifications of U.S. foreign policy and politically complicated environmental crises. My overall conceptualization of global apartheid as a condition exacerbated by globalization and as a major source of structural violence is developed in these interrelated essays, which, together with the chapter included here, constitute a trilogy (Harrison 2002a, 2004).

"Justice for All: The Challenges of Advocacy Research in the Global Age" was presented as the pubic lecture component of my contribution to a visiting scholar program organized in memory of Delmos Jones (1970, 1971, 1997) at the City University of New York's Graduate Center in 2003. In this essay, I revisit Jones's vision of an anthropology dedicated to exposing the consequences of social inequalities and the possibilities for social change that community organizations can potentially represent. Building on his foundations, I examine an organizing trend currently being pursued in the southern region of the United States: a coalition, with transnational linkages, revolving around advocacy for political, social/cultural, and economic human rights in the South, understood to be part of the "Global South. "

Academia and Beyond

Three chapters address the book's final theme on blurring the boundary between anthropology's academic and public expressions. "Teaching Philosophy" is a short piece written originally as a statement included in a teaching award nomination. So much of what academic anthropologists actually do is teach, prepare for classes, and advise students that I think it is important to include a chapter underscoring our role as educators and mentors who raise consciousness and inspire thoughtful and thought-provoking action. Effective teaching is not just about preparing students to pass tests and earn credentials; it is about preparing them to assume roles as citizens of the world, flexible enough in their outlook and skills to be able to adapt intelligently and responsibly to the ways in which the world is rapidly changing.

"Academia, the Free Market, and New Voices of Diversity" demonstrates my critical anthropology of anthropology perspective. A cultural critique of recent trends in the restructuring of higher education and the managing of diversity, the chapter illuminates the racial and racialized gendered politics involved in accommodating difference in postsecondary education institutions. The chapter exposes the unequal relations of intellectual production—the power disparities—and the racial and gendered economy of universities wherein women of color, as faculty, administrators, and students, are compelled to negotiate difference and their outsider-within statuses in particularly challenging ways. It is within this context that I situate the everyday work lives of minoritized anthropologists whose experiences I have come to know and share.

The final chapter, "A Labor of Love: An Emancipated Woman's Legacy," is a particularly poignant piece written in response to a provocative and inspiring essay that Virginia Dominguez (2000) published in *Cultural Anthropology*. Dominguez urges us to read between the lines and beyond the text of published works. She interprets the photographs included in a number of ethnographic and other social scientific books. Those photographs sometimes tell a different story from what the texts seem to say. Dominguez is especially concerned with realist, modernist texts that espouse a view of social science that excludes emotions like love.

Dominguez's reflections on the politics of love underlying the research projects her article features stimulated me to think about the labors of love that have informed the praxis of my favorite anthropologists—former teachers and ancestors I have sought to reclaim. And then there is also my own labor of love driving my choice of research questions and analytical foci. As an anthropologist who sees herself as an intellectual *worker* rather than as a member of a privileged elite, "the talented tenth" (Du Bois 1903; James 1997), I see my project in reworking anthropology as a labor of love.

The labor motif prompted me to revisit an experience of mine in which I was in protracted labor, giving birth to my first son. An analysis of that highly personal situation exposes a number of layers of meaning and provocation germane to this book and to my life and career as a black woman who struggles to achieve a social balance between personal development, family responsibility, career building, intellectual integrity, and political engagement. In this book, I have tried to give a glimpse of a three-dimensional life of an intellectual with a long-term agenda driven by heartfelt convictions about what anthropology means and can be made to mean. This project is more than an intellectual exercise, for it has become integral to my life, social being, and identity. It is, as you will see, a labor of love.

Acknowledgments

This chapter was difficult to write, but several colleagues and friends were generous with their encouragement and moral support. Thanks to Gina Athena Ulysse, who pushed me to finish it; Ann E. Kingsolver, who sent me useful references and germane essays; Pem Davidson Buck, who patiently listened to me rehearse many of the ideas over many years; and Marilyn Miller Thomas-Houston, whose confidence in me exceeds my own. Marilyn has been my number one cheerleader and promoter and a sister-colleague in two of the institutions where I have worked. Our respective journeys are truly parallel and convergent. There are many others who have fed me nourishing food for thought, inspired me, and helped me believe that this project was worthwhile. Among them were Lee D. Baker, Arthur Spears, Tony Whitehead, Willie Baber, Audrey Smedley, Lanita Jacobs-Huey, Carolyn Fluehr-Lobban, Yolanda T. Moses, and Louise Lamphere, who was the teacher-mentor who helped convince me that I was graduate school material. The intellectual and activist dimensions of her career have been an important role model for many younger women in academia. The class-action suit she filed against Brown University in the mid-1970s exposed a pattern of discrimination that the university was mandated to redress under a court order. In some respects, her courage back then helped create conditions that eventually resulted in an African American woman, Ruth J. Simmons, becoming president of that Ivy League institution. Yvonne V. Jones, then chair of the Department of Anthropology and the Department of Pan-African Studies, helped convince the University of Louisville to give me my first tenure-track job. Conversations we began in the early 1980s inspired me to begin exploring the history and politics of African American anthropology. Without the intellectual friendship I have enjoyed with her and with so many others, I might have been tempted to leave academia for some other kind of work.

PART II

Rehistoricizing Anthropology

2. Unburying Theory, Repositioning Practice

Anthropological Praxis
in Peripheral Predicaments

Projects to Critically Reconstruct Anthropology

According to many social analysts, the anthropology of the postcolonial and postmodern era is in the midst of a serious identity crisis. To resolve this critical state of affairs, a number of projects are being undertaken to reintegrate (Stocking 1992), recapture (Fox 1991), decolonize (Harrison 1991), or transform (*Transforming Anthropology* 1990–present) the anthropology that has lost some, and perhaps much, of its mystique and authority in a climate in which the certainty of cultural truths and knowledge claims has been destabilized. As philosopher and cultural critic Cornel West has expressed the problem, much of the construction and "deconstruction" of knowledge today is marked by epistemic skepticism and explanatory nihilism (1991, xxii). No longer is there widespread confidence in "master narratives" and global theories (Foucault 1980, 80). What has emerged as "theory" has relinquished the goal of asking and answering the larger questions concerning social change—whether positive or negative—and the realignments of global political economy. It has also undermined the ontological status of the subject while ironically confirming the privileged standing of Western masculinist thought (Christian 1987; Harrison 1991, 5; Mascia-Lees, Sharpe, and Cohen 1989; Singer 1994, 1995). Paradoxically, this privileging of male-centered perspective is disguised by the feminine clothing and transvestite-style presentation that Catherine Lutz (1995) claims for postmodernism, whose characteristics are, to a large extent, consistent with the dominant gender ideology's construction of the feminine.

In response to the heightened vulnerability to the intellectual cynicism and political impotence so characteristic of this late twentieth-century period, a number of critical social analysts have argued in favor of more enabling explanatory accounts of both local and global sociocultural phenomena. These accounts, they point out, need to be "wedded in a nuanced manner to concrete historical analyses" (West 1991, xxii) as well as to sociopolitical engagement in one form or another (Leacock 1987). According to this impulse, then, the conceptual dualism that separates, dichotomizes, and hierarchically orders "theory" and "practice" (especially the overtly politicized variety) must undergo radical "unthinking" (Wallerstein 1991) to give way to a more organic and dialectical view of the relationship between what are, in fact, interrelated and mutually reinforcing modes of social practice. The dialectical unity of theory and practice within the matrix of worldly praxis is, hence, necessary for reconstituting knowledge and the social relations for producing and applying it.

Anthropology's discomfited place within this postmodern and postcolonial predicament is being negotiated and repositioned by a number of competing projects. The historian of anthropology, George Stocking Jr., in what he titles the "postscriptive prospective reflections" concluding the essays in *The Ethnographer's Magic* (1992), elucidates what he understands to be the major models for anthropology's paradigmatic reintegration: (1) a variety of postmodern turns (Marcus and Fischer 1986; Clifford and Marcus 1986); (2) feminist anthropology, which situates "gender at the crossroads of knowledge" (di Leonardo 1991); (3) attempts to synthesize postmodernism and historicized political economy (Ulin 1991); and—citing my work—(4) the call to decolonize anthropology by synthesizing four reinventive streams—neo-Marxist political economy, interpretive and reflexive ethnography, a multiracial and class-cognizant feminism, and radical traditions of subaltern scholarship (Stocking 1992, 370, citing Harrison 1991, 2).

Of these contenders in the contest over anthropology's future directions, all except certain variants of postmodernism are committed to working against the received tradition of dualism and its attendant value-free and politics-free mystification of knowledge by grounding social inquiry in some form of practical, worldly politics. According to applied anthropologist Merrill Singer (1994), postmodernism has a fundamental aversion to political engagement and anthropological praxis, despite its rhetorical emphasis on power, authority, and multivocal dialogue. Carolyn Martin Shaw (1995, 16), however, has a more nuanced position from which she describes at least two postmodernisms: skeptical postmodernism (e.g., Jean Baudrillard), which presents a pessimistic and negative view of the world as fragmented, chaotic, and meaningless; and affirmative postmodernism (e.g., Gayatri Spivak), with its openness to struggle and resistance and its recognition of visionary, nondog-matic political projects and social movements. In Singer's view, the former variety has counterproductively pervaded much of anthropological inquiry and ethnography, which, as Joan Vincent reminds us, is "the one vehicle above all others through which anthropologists represent and transform theory" (1991, 47). Because of the influence of this brand of postmodernism, the power and authority of writing and authorship have been privileged over the wider circumstances of organizational and structural power (Wolf 1990), which condition the unequal relations of material and intellectual production.

Echoing West's critiques (1991), literary scholar Barbara Christian (1987), and many others, Singer underscores that anthropology's postmodern turn tends to express an acute skepticism of cultural truths and assumes a pessi-mistic epistemological relativism positioning all perspectives as equally self-interested and contestable. Consequently, radical critique from positions of political engagement is, in effect, neutralized or, at worst, invalidated (Jordan 1991). In light of this jettisoning of theory in praxis, postmodern anthropolo-gists, therefore, have no valid basis upon which to take sides in sociopolitical conflict (Singer 1994). Ironically, a discourse claiming to be fundamentally dialogic and committed to decentering ethnographic authority may have as a subtext the hegemonic recentering of academic anthropology in a disci-pline that is increasingly based on work and other forms of practice outside the academy (Singer 1994, 340). Another of postmodernist anthropology's paradoxes is that the preoccupation with multivocality has not rendered the discourse any less Eurocentric or masculinist than the positivist and realist anthropology it seeks to displace (Harrison 1991, 1993). The most widely read and cited sacred texts of the new postmodern canon have largely erased the writing of feminists, social analysts of color, and intellectuals from the southern hemisphere (Harrison 1991, 1993; Behar and Gordon 1995). Yet many of the ideas and critiques from these positions have been appropriated and incorporated into postmodernism's vision of postpositivist anthropology.

Repositioning Praxis

The reinvention of anthropology that has been pursued in one form or an-other over the past three decades cannot be achieved without repositioning *praxis* as legitimate, desirable, and necessary for the vitality and advancement of anthropological inquiry and knowledge. The valorization of anthropologi-cal praxis entails a redefinition and reconstruction of what we understand to be theory and theorizing. In the decolonization project many of my colleagues and I have been pursuing, we envision theory not as a discrete, bounded set of ideas or the sterile reification of intellectual mastery that is positioned at the apex of a hierarchy of knowledge and power, but as a social process integral to producing the kinds of validated knowledge that can influence the redirection and scope of social inquiry as well as the application of its results. The construction, testing, elaboration, and refinement of theory depend on the cross-fertilizing and diversely landscaped grounds of practice, in which theory's utility and validity are ultimately assessed. In turn, applications of theoretical knowledge are evaluated in the dual terms of practical efficacy and theoretical enrichment. Rather than being atheoretical, as assumed by the received convention, applied research is potentially rich in some of the necessary materials and conditions for building theory. With this promise in mind, both Wayne Warry (1992) and Merrill Singer (1994) define theory as the process of explaining the problems that are of central concern to communities in need of change. In the community-centered research that they conduct, theory is collectively formulated and applied to strategies of intervention. This mode of knowledge production entails a participatory methodology based on the multiperspective and polyphonic discourse that Donna Haraway (1991) envisions as an alternative to the elitist objectivism that universalizes the "partial perspective" of the Euromasculine subject, which is situated in a discursive field marked by differential sociopolitical stakes and an inequality of positioning (cf. Trinh Minh-ha 1989).

Warry's and Singer's view, along with that of many other scholars of radical political persuasion and of color, is that theory is not the private property or academic capital of the privileged few but an integral part of the everyday life and struggle of "living thinkers" (James 1993) who theorize "to save lives" (Christian 1987). Consequently, theory is located not only in formal statements of abstract logic or in convoluted deconstructive hermeneutics (in which it is often privileged nowadays), but it is also embedded in oral and scribal traditions of storytelling, social criticism, and autobiography as well (Christian 1987; James 1993). In my earlier work, I have explored the alternative mode of theorizing embedded in black women's fiction, particularly the variety inspired by Zora Neale Hurston's ethnographic representation of black folklife (Harrison 1993). I argued that fiction can offer a sanctuary from the constraints positivism imposes on subjectivity and verification. Concerning the limits of positivist epistemology, I stated that "the ideology of science as Eurocentrically and androcentrically defined objectivity has to a considerable extent denied Black women the legitimacy to make reliable truth claims that White males [as symbols of universality] can replicate" (410).

In this chapter, I shift my focus to ethnography and place my emphasis on the theorizing in praxis that underpins and informs it. Theory is envisaged as a practice among others performed and enacted by anthropologists as well as by the subjects we study or study collaboratively *with* in research ventures. I am most concerned with the anthropological praxis of feminist and African American predicaments. Here I will focus on two persons who were among the first cohorts of African Americans to earn PhDs in anthropology: Allison Davis, the former University of Chicago professor of education and posthumous honoree of the 1994 Black Heritage stamp (*Anthropology Newsletter* 1994), and Manet Fowler, a largely unknown entity who in 1952 was the first black woman to receive a doctoral degree in anthropology from a U.S. university. Both of these anthropologists' research was related to racial inequality in U.S. society, and in later work they both touched on questions of gender inequality as well. My interest in this early cohort stems from my individual and cooperative attempts to rehistoricize the politics of anthropology's past and present in line with Joan Vincent's historicist strategy for recapturing anthropology's credibility and authority (Vincent 1991). She advocates repossessing and repositioning the discipline's past, both its exposed and hidden dimensions. Even the eminent steward of anthropology's canonical history, George W. Stocking Jr. (1992), has acknowledged the fruitfulness and necessity of "[rescuing] neglected precursors of paradigmatic alternatives . . . [and examining] anthropology . . . from the perspective of those who have been its subject 'others'" (8). As Renato Rosaldo (1993 [1989]) clarifies, making anthropology work for us in the present requires creating space for subaltern analyses that, as he demonstrates in *Culture and Truth,* enrich as well as complicate anthropological practice (189). To repossess and reposition subaltern subjects, hidden intellectual lineages must be traced so that dusty old skeletons can be removed from the closet. This process is a necessary phase in a larger struggle to emancipate subjugated knowledges that have been either appropriated, disguised, and buried within bodies of systematizing theory or altogether disqualified and discarded in the garbage dump of historical memory (Foucault 1980, 82–85).

Like all other hegemonic disciplines, anthropology is produced and reproduced in a nexus of institutional and discursive power that differentially incorporates multiple knowledges by valorizing some and subjugating others. Davis and Fowler represent instructive examples of how a racial and gendered economy of anthropological science (cf. Harding 1993) has operated to position praxis in peripheral space and, consequently, bury certain modes of theoretical and political expression. Before anthropology can be decolonized and reinvented, it has to confront the hierarchy-producing practices that have rendered and still render the Davises and Fowlers of the profession largely invisible and irrelevant.

It is my view that theory must be claimed and captured and then redefined and repositioned in an organic interrelationship with the various practices that make up the routine life and work of anthropologists: research design, acquisition of support and sponsorship, fieldwork, data analysis and inter- pretation, writing different kinds of texts (ethnographies, essays, cultural critiques) to address different audiences, publishing, peer reviewing pro- posals and manuscripts for their fundability and publishability, reading and evaluating the quality and significance of published works (i.e., engaging the politics of reception; Vincent 1991), teaching (which involves selecting texts that have canonical import or potential), applied work, partisan activism, and so forth. Theorizing is conventionally elevated to a distinct suprapractice invested with the symbolic capital that only an elite can accumulate in view of the unequal social relations of intellectual production that have histori- cally disadvantaged women and subjugated peoples. Within the domain of theory construction, especially in the social sciences, there has historically been an internal hierarchy that privileges nomothetic or grand theory, sub- ordinates middle-range theory beneath it, and virtually displaces lower-level explanations of particular, local problems from the theoretical realm. The latter accounts, it has been reasoned, are much too close to the raw data of indigenous cognition to be considered theory. The authority of conventional theory is contingent upon the power-mediated differentiation between the observer and the observed as well as between "abstract observer" and "practi- cal observer." My vision of theory operates against this elitist division of intel- lectual labor. It is my view that theory and theory making assume multiple forms and that those varied forms and contents should all have a place in a more democratized anthropology marked by more leveled role relationships. Although I admit that I think that the most elitist versions of theory should be decentered and displaced from highest authority, my position is to deny privilege but not academic freedom to those theorists.

I am particularly interested in claiming theory now because what the late Barbara Christian (1987) called the current "race for theory" is having in- sidious results: It is neutralizing the voices of women and people of color by relativizing our work, reducing its import, and minimizing the significance of our subject positions. This subjugation of oppositional knowledges is being accomplished through both the masculinization and the whitening of theory, which generally downgrades and devalues feminist and subaltern discourse (Lutz 1995; Harrison 1991, 1993; Trinh Minh-ha 1989) for its partisan "special interests," its failure to "denude" itself of references to concrete experience and historically specific contexts (Lutz 1995), and often its critically ambivalent relationship to the canon.

Repossessing the History of Anthropology's Black Praxis

I am attempting to clear the grounds for an archaeology of knowledge from which to unbury the theoretical shards of the life stories, ethnographic analyses, and applied work of U.S. anthropology's black pioneers. My project to "unbury" these "gifts of black folk" has been inspired, in part, by my work on the biography of Manet Fowler as a piece of the larger, collective effort to make public the lives and contributions of black ancestors and elders (Harrison and Harrison 1999). Over the course of six years of correspondence, telephone conversations, and occasional face-to-face encounters, I reconstructed the skeleton of a "subaltern anthropology" that, unfortunately, has not left many traces in the published record (Harrison 1993). Explaining to me why she did not publish most of her work, Dr. Fowler related that her work had been "buried" by organizational clients who repudiated and discarded her analyses and recommendations for confronting problems of social welfare and public health and by publishers who made radical rewrites, depoliticization, and dilution of arguments a condition of publication.[1]

Although Fowler has certainly been an inspiration to this project, even before I started her biography, I had already begun thinking and writing about African Americans' ambivalent relationship to anthropology. Those beginnings led me to think more seriously about excavating the buried knowledges that one of my former Stanford professors, St. Clair Drake, and his mentor, Allison Davis, helped produce from their antiracist stands. In Davis's case, there is an extensive trail to follow, for he did publish and, generally, in easily accessible outlets; nonetheless, his work (on racial caste, personality development and childhood socialization, and the cultural and class biases of IQ) has not, however, figured prominently in mainstream anthropology. Hence, he, too, was figuratively buried by the prevailing politics of reception. For the most part, his work was not received by an anthropological audience, and even many African American intellectuals assumed that he was an educational or child psychologist because of his later work and its policy and programmatic applications within education and social welfare.

Allison Davis: Fighting Racism and Other Inequalities

Like most early black anthropologists, Davis, who began his career as an English professor, was attracted to anthropology because of the antiracist promise expressed in Boasianism. William Willis (1974, 1975) argued that Boasian antiracism was limited by its assimilationism and its focus on Euroracism; that is, the racist assaults that targeted southern and eastern Europeans, Jews, Gypsies, and other so-called subraces of European origin. The Boasian attack against Jim Crow oppression in the United States was more oblique. The research Boas supervised on southern black folklife reveals the limitations of his approach to the black racial predicament. Willis argued that Boas's view of black folklore was so narrowly conceived that white supremacy and black people's struggle for survival and citizenship rights were not dealt with as salient factors in the sociocultural environment (Willis 1975, 327). Consequently, an opportunity to study black folk's accommodation and resistance to the U.S. variant of apartheid was lost.

Under Lloyd Warner's guidance, Davis helped fill that gap. During the 1930s, when Malinowski-trained Hortense Powdermaker also worked in Mississippi, Davis, his wife, Elizabeth, the husband and wife team of Burleigh and Mary Gardner, and St. Clair Drake conducted an extensive, nearly two-year biracial research project in Natchez. Davis was the senior researcher who, according to Drake, took the lead in conceptualization and data interpretation. He was "responsible for the basic theoretical contributions" (Drake 1974, 47). That ethnographic investigation of caste and class in a southern town was designed to extend the body of evidence Warner had collected in the New England–based "Yankee City" studies of the integrative function of social class in (ethnically plural) industrial society. In the South, class operated in conjunction with and was subordinated by caste. The caste construct was used to underscore the rigidly enforced rank ascription and endogamy that marked segregated society and made it similar to caste-stratified societies elsewhere. Conceptualizing race as caste was a means of working against the biodeterminist and essentialist thinking that was so prevalent during that time that even the otherwise sympathetic work of liberal antiracists such as Powdermaker was affected. According to Gertrude Fraser's reading of *After Freedom,* Powdermaker's (1939) analysis subtly betrayed implicitly assimilationist and essentialist assumptions concerning race (Fraser 1991, 412).

The caste construct allowed Davis and his colleagues to underscore the social and historical forces that constructed bounded social entities defined as mutually exclusive "races" destined to live in perpetual inequality in spite of the intimate proximity that sometimes existed across caste boundaries. In some respects, *Deep South* (Davis, Gardner, and Gardner 1941) foreshadowed current analyses of race's social construction. Even the current work concerning the cultural terrain of whiteness and white dominance owes a debt to this watershed study that probed the everyday life social organization and political economy of whites as well as blacks. The book's treatment of family and sexuality in some ways anticipated R. T. Smith's model of the dual marriage system in the plantation and postplantation societies of the West Indies

(1987). *Deep South* suggests that this model, or a revised version of it, could be extended to the plantation South. The model situates lower-class black families in relationship to more privileged black, brown, and white families, with whom some of them have consanguineous, if not so-called family ties (cf. Douglass 1992). In both the South and the Caribbean, privileged white men historically have had the social license to mate polygynously (both legally and extralegally) and to cross class and color lines. Whereas in the West Indies, the progeny of such color crossings have been recognized as outside children and have occupied some intermediate status, in Mississippi and elsewhere in the United States, no real middle ground was recognized. Strict rules of hypodescent and endogamy precluded the public recognition of racially mixed relatives of white families. Caste, then, was rigid and permanent—unless a black person was phenotypically white enough to pass and willing to migrate northward away from family and the public visibility of its caste status.

Deep South's analytic framework combined a Marxist-influenced political economy with structural functionalism to elucidate the cultural politics and terror of Jim Crow in a way that no other work published in the 1930s and early 1940s did. Offering an alternative to the city centeredness of much of the later research in urban anthropology, the ethnography probed the wider context of agrarian land tenure, property relations, and plantation production within which southern urban life was embedded. Davis and his colleagues and, later, Davis himself in more distilled writing (i.e., his dissertation and a publication; Davis 1945) revealed in uncompromising terms and imagery the role of intimidation and violence in reinforcing labor control and enforcing caste proscriptions, especially in the economic sphere in which race was not completely organized on caste lines (Davis 1945). Davis explicitly stated his intention as that of providing "a *theory* of violence as a reaction to the breakdown of caste in the economic sphere" in which resource competition and class mobility sometimes contradicted and destabilized the hegemony of caste (1945, 7; emphasis mine).

Davis's social class concept was informed by Max Weber as much as Karl Marx. Davis's emphasis on social status groups or cliques as one indicator of class positioning allowed him to transcend economism in favor of a more multidimensional approach that took into account the influence of family, peers, and lifestyle in shaping social identity and consciousness of kind. His concern with class stratification within the two castes also worked against the tendency in much of mainstream scholarship to treat race categorically and monolithically. Davis and colleagues' representation of caste underscored the heterogeneity of both blacks and whites in light of the homogenization of racial status imposed by the laws of segregation. Although *Deep South's* theoretical framework has its inconsistencies and contradictions, it offered a novel and relatively uncompromising explanatory account of racial oppression and repression.

The fertile quality and analytical power of Davis's theoretical practice cannot be discerned simply by evaluating *Deep South* and the few other publications it spawned. Did the work engage other researchers in the practice of testing, revising, and refining the theory of racial inequality? This question pertains to what Vincent calls the politics of reception, which determines whether texts and intercollegial conversations are acknowledged and reproduced beyond the limits of their authors' immediate lives. In Davis's case, the answer is "yes, but only to a point." *Deep South*'s treatment of caste stimulated considerable debate, but more so among sociologists than among anthropologists. Key among the latter, however, was Davis's protégé, St. Clair Drake, who, after Natchez, went on to graduate school at the University of Chicago. While still a student, he became part of a major research project focused on the black South Side of Chicago. That investigation, the first to involve anthropology in a major metropolitan setting, resulted in *Black Metropolis* (1945), coauthored by Drake and sociologist Horace Cayton. This sociological and ethnographic hybrid, among other things, put Davis's notion of caste to the test and concluded that the concept had limited heuristic value for the study of race in competitive industrial settings in which interlocking hierarchies of class and ethnicity were highly salient in the dynamics of, for example, trade unionization and machine politics. Although in Chicago race was not as rigid as southern caste, neither was it equivalent to the ethnicity that European immigrants experienced. Drake and Cayton were among the earliest social scientists to question the usefulness of Robert Park's Euro-immigrant model that still dominated scholarly and public discourses on race during the early post–World War II period (Drake and Cayton 1945; 1993 edition, xlviii, 757). The persistent structural and ideological barriers constitutive of racism precluded black assimilation into mainstream society.

Drake and Cayton's friendly critiques had a constructive effect on Davis's later work, most of which was conducted in Chicago. The revised notion of race along with theoretical insights from his earlier research in Mississippi and Louisiana informed his investigations of childhood personality development across class and racial lines and his studies of the cultural and class biases of IQ testing. As we shall see, this second phase of his career (or third, if we include his early work in English literature) had some important practical applications.

Theorizing is always undertaken in webs of intercollegiality and intertextuality. It is important to note that these webs and networks are differentially located on the institutional topography. It made a difference that Davis and Drake were affiliated with Chicago and were able to benefit from the academic capital that Chicago networks could confer. Yet, despite this advantage, their racial status as well as their status as anthropologists working in the United States on racism and the most stigmatized racial minority—social problems that were not considered exotic—contributed to their relative invisibility and irrelevance within mainstream anthropology. Unfortunately, there was no readily available place for black anthropologists or for those not working in conventional areas for the study of otherness. A consequence of this was that for most of their long and quite productive academic careers neither Davis nor Drake was in the position to train graduate students in anthropology who could carry on and extend their struggle to bring anthropological praxis to bear on U.S. racism.

Despite this, Davis's contribution did have some discernable worldly impact, and this praxis was honored in February 1994 by the issue of a Black Heritage stamp in his name and image. In a front-page article published in *Anthropology Newsletter* (1994), it is indicated that his "pioneering work in education and the social sciences . . . helped to [de]legalize racial segregation" (1, 6; no Freudian slip intended, I assume). Another article published in *The Journal of Blacks in Higher Education* (1994) underscored that he "was one of the first critics of . . . intelligence tests. . . . His thesis that social class, rather than race [as a so-called biological phenomenon], was the determining factor in black educational inequality, formed the basis for the federal antipoverty program's Operation Head Start, a major and durable achievement that seeks to get disadvantaged children started off on the right educational foot" (23). It is also noteworthy that Davis's earliest personality-development research in the deep South (e.g., *Children of Bondage;* Davis and Dollard 1940), along with that of many other black and white social scientists, informed the litigation for school desegregation. Historian Richard Kluger (1976) has pointed out that Davis was among thirty-five or so who filed an amicus brief included as an appendix to the 1954 *Brown v. Board of Education* case material. A few years before that, Thurgood Marshall hired political scientist John A. Davis—Allison Davis's brother—to lead a research task force to substantiate the NAACP Legal Defense Fund's case against segregated schooling with social science research. I think I can safely surmise from this that *Children of Bondage,* which Davis coauthored with John Dollard, as well as Davis's other work, was an integral component of the assembled evidence.

Davis carried his concern with issues of social change to the very end of his career and life. His last publication, a book titled *Leadership, Love, and Aggression* (Davis 1983), explored the lives of four African American leaders:

Frederick Douglass, W. E. B. Du Bois, Richard Wright, and Martin Luther King Jr. Davis's objective was to uncover the psychological mechanisms that could account for these men's ability to channel and convert their anger and aggression into constructive social and political action for effecting change. Obviously, Davis himself had converted the indignation he felt toward racism into his particular version of anthropological praxis.

Manet Fowler: Negotiating Industrial Conflict and University-Community Relations

Somewhat in contrast to Davis, Manet Fowler did not benefit from having a stable or permanent institutional home from which to build and extend her anthropological praxis. She claimed that she never intended to have an academic career. Rather, her goal was to work as a practitioner—"to put anthropology to [practical] use to improve conditions in U.S. society" (personal communication). A practitioner she certainly was; however, her career trajectory did not embed her work in a supportive network of kindred spirits that would stimulate and be stimulated by her. I do not mean to suggest that she had no colleagues or friends, but my biographical research does indicate a conspicuous "burying" pattern, as I suggested when initially introducing her to the themes of this chapter.

Because of her interest in applying anthropology, in 1950, with Ralph Linton's blessings, Fowler transferred (with several years worth of credit hours) from Columbia to Cornell, where a combined program in applied anthropology and sociology had recently been established by Alexander Leighton, who had been trained in psychiatry as well as anthropology. In two-and-a-half years, she completed requirements for a PhD in cultural and applied anthropology in the Department of Sociology-Anthropology and in the New York State School of Industrial and Labor Relations. Her specialized training drew on the methodological and theoretical frameworks of sociology, social psychology, and what was then the emergent field of human relations in industry. What is remarkable about Fowler's graduate experience, and that influenced her dissertation research, is her reconciliation and synthesis of her department's two competing yet, as her work demonstrated, complementary approaches to doing applied social research. On one hand, there was Leighton's personality and culture approach and, on the other, William Foote Whyte's individual in society, social interaction brand of industrial and organizational sociology. Rather than joining either faction, she stood her ground in between.

Fowler's 1952 dissertation, "The Case of Chef A: An Inquiry into and Analysis of a Human Relations Situation," the only full-fledged piece of research that is easily accessible to scrutiny, focused on a 1950 service workers' strike against their university employer, "Atherton University," a pseudonym for Cornell. Combining and demonstrating the utility and complementarity of the personality study, life history, or dynamic equilibrium approach with the social interaction/social situation framework, she reconstructed and explained the *multiple* causes and consequences of the strike, which she viewed as a human relations problem rich with implications for the development of more effective labor management and conflict resolution policies.

Her main vantage point for tracing the course of action was from her scrutiny of a middle-aged black kitchen worker, Chef A. It was largely through his perceptions, experiences, and decisions that she came to see and understand the psychological and interpersonal dynamics that gave rise to the labor conflict as well as to the chef's involvement in it. Fowler's analysis illuminated the multifaceted and multilayered context and content of the chef's personal decision to join the service workers' union and participate in strike action, after having resisted even nominal membership for four years. She justified her methodological emphasis on a single social actor and personality in terms of its being "a tool for theoretical inquiry" that would be used for "relating observations [on] the nature of individually-centered experience to general theoretical and technical principles . . . applicable to . . . comparable situations" (1952, xxxi). One of her study's specific contributions was to demonstrate the usefulness of the personal document or life history narrative to human relations in industry and, thereby, bring that field in line with anthropology and psychology, two disciplines that had already developed the means to collect and make analytical use of such data.

Although the dissertation was organized around Chef A's life, Fowler's ethnography examined the causes and effects of the strike from multiple views. She built her analysis around the multiple voices and divergent perspectives of striking and nonstriking workers, students, university administrators, community people, and the various newspapers that contributed to the intensely lively public debate over the details of why and how the strike occurred; over whether the workers had the legal, civic, or moral right to organize against a university, which was a nonprofit institution that legislation differentiated from industry and business enterprise; and over whether the university as an institution supposedly embodying the highly valued principles of democracy should recognize the union and permit its workers to engage in collective bargaining around issues of wages, work conditions, job security, and fringe benefits. Fowler characterized Atherton University as an industrial organization marked by increasingly centralized, depersonalized control, and hierarchical relations between administrators and subordinate employees. She demonstrated how the industrial life of the university with its formal and informal dimensions was conducive to a stressful climate that vitiated work conditions and morale and exacerbated conflict.

Fowler argued that economistic concerns were not alone in prompting the strike. Low wages and inadequate benefits were necessary but insufficient conditions. The quality of interpersonal communication and interaction between supervisors and employees was also a significant motivating factor and perhaps even a catalyst. This appears to be especially the case for Chef A, whose high informal status had eroded when a southern white woman who was impersonal and hostile toward the black kitchen staff assumed the duties of dietitian in his work setting. Fowler argued that the quality of informal organization within the workplace is particularly important in dead-end jobs for which material rewards and security are minimal. Explaining Chef A's motivation for joining the union, then, Fowler observed that the changes imposed from a higher centralized authority, personified by the bigoted southern dietitian, made the social relations of work more stressful, unpredictable, and insecure. Chef A's personality led him to compensate for the insecurities and liabilities that work imposed by seeking security and assets elsewhere—namely in the union, in which his sense of self-worth and his status needs as a working-class black man were more adequately met. Accordingly, his personality regained a more balanced state of dynamic equilibrium, and he found an alternative place for more satisfactory and satisfying social interaction. The chef's commitment to the union and to the strike was the result of multiple causes—cultural, social, economic, as well as psychological. Fowler's position was that a theoretical framework that neglects personality variables, or one that foregrounds them to the neglect of social relational factors, is incomplete and inadequate. She sought a more comprehensive approach from a critical synthesis of complementary strategies of inquiry.

Fowler's ethnography is an excellent example of thick description that has the effect of taking the reader into the three-dimensional social space of Atherton's town-and-gown environment. Her detailed descriptions and virtually unedited dialogues nearly replicate her field experience. The dissertation is as much an exercise in synthesizing theory for the purpose of conflict resolution in labor negotiations as it is a life story of a transformed worker and an ethnography of town-and-gown relations in a university town. Her approach to theoretical construction is particularly instructive in that she situated the two competing strategies of inquiry in the "partial perspectives" (Haraway 1991) of the two theorists. Fowler applied the life history and social situation approaches to her professors' intellectual development as well as to the key informant Chef A. This indicates the extent to which she was able to deconstruct the etic-emic dichotomy, level the observer-observed hierarchy, and implicate the cultural context and social positioning of theorists in analyses their work informs.

It is perhaps noteworthy that the University of Chicago had an important impact on Whyte's intellectual development. Before joining Cornell's faculty, he had been a colleague of Warner, Davis, and others with whom Davis was to collaborate over the course of his career. Indirectly, then, Fowler's web of connections was linked to Davis, with whom she also shared a commitment to furthering an applied anthropology of racially stratified industrial society—whether by an ex post facto situation of applying the results from basic research or by pursuing applied research with anticipated interventions built intrinsically into the methodological design.

To underscore Fowler's commitment to praxis research and academia's (past) reception to it, let me briefly relate a later chapter of her life story in which her approach to research was very much at issue in an affirmative-action dispute over a job contract. In the late 1960s and early 1970s, she worked at Syracuse University as director of the Family Service Center in the School of Social Work. She left that position, perhaps the only full-time university position she ever held, because the university terminated her contract. In her view, Syracuse refused to support the research she was doing on racial and gendered aspects of aging in the local community. The research was organized to include the active participation of community members. To this end, she organized a local board to advise and provide regular input into the management of the project. It was Dr. Fowler's view that the university was threatened by her attempt to do a kind of participatory research that redistributed control and shared authority with the local community, which, as a result, resisted conventional means of objectifying studied populations by asserting itself as a collective intellectual agent. This approach to social research and to restructuring the university's relationship to surrounding communities was probably considered too political and disruptive for the School of Social Work and the wider university. Consequently, Fowler was seen as a troublemaker who was leading the community against the university.

According to Fowler's vision, an applied anthropologist is a "professional helper" who facilitates the development of new modes of research that empower ordinary people by building into the research design more equalized relations of ethnographic investigation. She claimed that her views were misrepresented in the transcripts of her case against Syracuse. Although she had stated during the hearing that she wanted to be "a professional helper, not a leader," she was misquoted as having said she wanted "to be a leader."

This error offended her deeply, for it negated the very intentions and goals that defined her professional integrity.

To a considerable extent, Fowler's praxis is embedded in the various informational and public relations brochures, consultancy reports, grant proposals, scripts for radio programs (e.g., *Voice of America*), book reviews (Fowler 1942, 1953), and newspaper and magazine articles that she produced over the course of her multifaceted career as an independent anthropologist working in her own home, which she designated as "Research House." She lacks a publication record commensurate with her talents, proficiency, and brilliance in good measure due to the nature of contract-based consultancy work, in which the agency or company owns the data and documents the consultant generates, unless an alternative arrangement is negotiated. In many cases, Fowler's reports shed light on aspects of reality that her clients preferred to ignore. Such controversial and unsatisfactory documents were often buried.

Fowler claimed that the biggest obstacle she encountered was not overt racial or gender discrimination but the "discrimination" or unfair treatment exercised by those easily threatened by a person who "works like a dog" to do her best to achieve excellence. Manet Helen Fowler chose to go against the grain and "to go it the hard way" to expose critical areas in need of remediation and substantive change. And change *is* threatening to those heavily invested in an established status quo.

Conclusions

In Eleanor Leacock's posthumously published essay, she stated that an adequate theory of society and social change "must take into account: first, economic and historical processes and their interrelations at a specifically societal level; second, social-psychological processes and their functioning at the level of the individual; and third, the interrelationships between the two" (1987, 333).

She went on to argue that sociopolitical commitment and engagement can set the stage for formulating new theory adequate to the task of dealing with social complexity and social change (Leacock 1987, 332). Contrary to positivist assumptions, she claimed that personal involvement can enhance the rigor and scientific validity of research, reminding us that "scientific rigor—conscientious attention to detail, careful consideration of the unexpected or seemingly contradictory, deliberate weighting of alternative explanations . . . is not by itself a matter of politics. People on all sides of political fences can be either careful or sloppy in collecting and organizing data, and either intently thoughtful or casually superficial in drawing conclusions from them" (332).

In her view, "the more serious a person's commitment is to helping some group obtain the information or skills it needs to improve its situation, the greater the care and accuracy devoted to research and support service *should be.*" Belying received ideas of validity and theory, she underscored that "given an able and conscientious researcher, advocacy leads to fuller and more accurate understanding than attempted neutrality. To attempt neutrality . . . means to align oneself, by default, with the institutional structures that discriminate against and exploit poor and non-white people . . . one can ignore the realities of power and skirt the touchy question of conflict, and thereby fail to deal with the total structure of relationships in which people are involved" (Leacock 1987, 323). Moreover, "[f]ar from leading to the avoidance of theoretical problems, [personal involvement] forces researchers who are serious and conscientious about their work to give the most careful attention to theory" (332).

Leacock's understanding of engagement and theoretical adequacy is, more or less, borne out in the Davis and Fowler cases. Whether in a single study or over the course of several, both Fowler and Davis built conceptual frameworks and accumulated a repertoire of analytical skills that allowed them to make sense of the interaction between multiple aspects and levels of racially and class stratified society. Both understood research, whether basic or applied, as a vehicle for improving social conditions and promoting meaningful social change.

The research paradigm I am proposing, one that embeds knowledge production in contexts of social action and political engagement, is not new. It is one that has been a virtual tradition for those communities of scholars who have had to respond to the urgency of worldly oppression and conflict and who have pursued activist-oriented social research *to save lives.* Paraphrasing the words of literary critic Barbara Christian, many feminist and racially subordinated researchers—and I see myself in this light—seek knowledge, write, teach, and theorize *to save our own lives.* Political engagement assumes a diversity of forms, and can be defined in both narrow and broad terms. I am not suggesting that all researchers necessarily have to be connected to studied communities in the way that, for instance, Merrill Singer obviously is to his. What is important is for the Singers of the profession to be better integrated into the strategic webs of intercollegiality and communicative action that influence the kinds of research and theorizing that come to be valorized by anthropologists.

Because the legacy of the past is still with us in the present, I advocate that more of us revisit what anthropologists of social conscience and consciousness have already done, that we unbury the intellectual skeletons from their unmarked graves and breathe new life into them. Let us take very seriously the theoretical and political lessons that can be learned from individuals like Allison Davis and Manet Fowler. I am not at all urging us to deify them, for they were not without sin or analytical limitations that perhaps some of us could conceivably redress. I would, however, like to see more anthropologists engaging these scholars' work as seriously as we have engaged the canon of the Great Fathers—and of course a few token Great Mothers—of classical, modern, and now postmodern anthropology. The growing numbers of anthropologists interested, for instance, in the socially constructed workings of race—and research on this issue has indeed expanded—would certainly benefit from a close reading and constructive critique of Davis and Fowler, the significance of whose work persists today (Harrison 1995).

The legacy of the past is in the present in more ways than in the racial or gendered economy of anthropological knowledge. As a set of commentaries in *Practicing Anthropology* (1995) argues, the consequences of discriminatory elitism pervade the profession in the artificial divide between pure and applied research, in the segmentation of the academic labor market, and, in general, the diffuse politics of intellectual production, distribution, and consumption. In this age of diversity and difference, anthropology has an opportunity to become more inclusive and whole, to become the study of the world's peoples by any women and men willing to commit themselves to the challenges, dilemmas, predicaments, and rewards of anthropological praxis.

Anthropology has an opportunity to listen to, and learn from, a rich diversity of voices. When I first rehearsed the ideas presented in this chapter several years ago at Michigan State University, in the symposium "Beyond Basic and Applied: New Research Paradigms in Anthropology and the Other Social Sciences," I illustrated this point about our being able to listen and understand what diversity can teach us by using Sojourner Truth, specifically her famous "Ain't I a Woman" speech, as an analogy. I attempted to echo the sentiments expressed by Truth's famous words of wisdom, in which she laid claim to an oppositional and transformative subjectivity as an African American woman. Taking the liberty of paraphrasing and extending her poignant words with insights from Barbara Christian (1987) and bell hooks (1989), I closed my talk by asking the audience to imagine a powerful but unexpectedly articulate Sojourner Truth–like figure—a historically quintessential "outsider within," talking back to the received conventions of anthropology in much the same way that Truth spoke up at that 1851 women's rights conference in Akron, Ohio. If you recall, that meeting was disrupted by a group of jeering white men—whom social critic and humorist Roger Moore (2001) would undoubtedly label "stupid white men." Those men attended the meeting to express their outrage against the women's agenda. Truth courageously challenged the antagonists by "speaking truth to power." What would a Truth-like voice have to say about emancipating anthropological theory and practice from its subjugated, peripheral spaces, particularly those places in which women of color find their scholarship ignored—even by other women? Perhaps she would say something like this:

> Ain't I a woman with a mind to think for myself? Look at me! I have plowed and planted the fields of knowledge and gathered it into the barns, and no man could head me—and ain't I a woman? I can work as hard as any man . . . and bear the lash of no rewards as well—and ain't I a woman? Ain't I a woman with a mind and heart to save my people's lives?

3. Remapping Routes, Unearthing Roots

Rethinking Caribbean Connections with the U.S. South

Beyond Boundedness

Finding ways to think and raise researchable questions about international and transnational relations between the U.S. South and the Caribbean region is a significant and timely project. The discreteness and boundedness of culture, society, and nation have been criticized in the conversations anthropologists have been having about writing and theorizing against these received notions. During the current era when anthropologists are examining the multiple processes shaping global restructuring, integration, and disjuncture and when anthropology itself is being reworked and transformed as a discipline, it is more than appropriate to reconceptualize and reimagine the South and the Caribbean by deterritorializing the sociocultural and structural features typically associated with them and then reterritorializing and remapping them across the coordinates of interlocking transnational fields of identity, sociocultural dynamics, power, and political economy.

This line of rethinking emerges logically from current trends in anthropological interrogations. For me, it also emerges organically from my lived experience as a Southerner born and raised in Norfolk, Virginia, as a Caribbeanist and African diaspora scholar, and as a minoritized intellectual who draws upon both her intellect and her intuition, who respects both the power of rigorous empirical observation and the bold license of the imagination and who acknowledges a place for a politics of love in the social production of knowledge (Dominguez 2000). Long before I was inspired by the writings of Lila Abu-Lughod (1991); Linda Basch, Nina Glick-Schiller, and Cristina Szanton Blanc (1994); Akhil Gupta and James Ferguson (1992); or Jamaican-born

Black British cultural studies theorist Stuart Hall (1995, 1999), just to name a few, I had already begun a journey to understand the relationships between culture, power, political economy, and history and the connections, convergences, and parallels that exist between the South and the Caribbean.

Rethinking with Intuition and Imagination

I was moved to wonder about Southern-Caribbean connections for a number of reasons. One was purely personal and intuitive. My earliest travel experiences in the Caribbean and Caribbean diaspora, beginning as a high school student in Puerto Rico for a language program, made me intensely aware of a general family resemblance with which I felt at home and connected, even when there were language barriers. When I first visited Jamaica, where I have worked intermittently since the late 1970s, I felt an uncanny déjà vu, perhaps based on all I had read and the diasporic consciousness I had cultivated over many years. The feelings Jamaica evoked in me inspired me to wonder whether the Middle Passage ordeal of any of my ancestors had taken them to the Caribbean and, at some later point, transported them to the English colony of Virginia. Virginia, the birthplace of my paternal family, was the plantation society from whose plantocracy emerged presidents who helped shape the parameters and identity of what was to become the United States of America. George Washington, Thomas Jefferson, and others climbed into national and international prominence on the backs, the bellies, and even the bosoms of enslaved human beings. Was my uncanny sense of having been in Jamaica before like the journey that independent filmmaker Haile Gerima charted for Mona/Shola in *Sankofa*? In that powerful film, the international fashion model Mona, despite her initial resistance, was returned to her forgotten and silenced past in order to be freed from the chains of mental slavery, the neoslavery of a market-centered world, a Babylon that commodifies everything, including black women's bodies and the globally circulated mass-mediated images of those bodies as seductive objects of consumer desire.

Remapping Space across Time

Beyond the intuitive dimension of my motivation to build a conceptual bridge from the South to the Caribbean, I was also inspired by one of my teachers, the late St. Clair Drake, who was both Southern and Caribbean. Dr. Drake was born in Suffolk, Virginia, of a Virginian mother and a Barbadian father. His father found his way to the southeastern coast of Virginia on one of the many merchant ships that landed there from all over the world. The senior Drake later became a prominent minister and advocate of the Garvey movement. He made a deep impression on his son, who became a Pan-Africanist neo-Marxist activist scholar. Before his death in 1990, Drake was an Africanist and African diaspora scholar who laid the groundwork for diaspora studies long before diaspora was a buzzword (Drake 1987, 1990). His example and influence have profoundly inspired my work in ways that I never expected when I was his student.

During my graduate school years, Drake encouraged me to draw a heuristic map of the Caribbean so that the U.S. South and the littoral areas of Central and South America were included in how I approached the region as a variegated sociocultural and political-economic entity. That mapping of the circum-Caribbean was enhanced by my consideration of the even more encompassing plantation America, which extended my examination to Latin American regions such as the plantation zones of Colombia and Brazil. With these overlapping maps, I was able to frame my thinking about Southern and Caribbean connections and commonalities in terms of both parallel adaptations to "common structural and ecological situations" (Goody 2003) and multidirectional flows of people, culture, knowledge, and commodities across the space of those portions of the Atlantic world. As a graduate student, I was particularly interested in the parallel political-economic structures that set the parameters for varying histories and developments of socioeconomic organization, kinship, racial identities, and cultural resistance. It is within this conceptual frame that I continue to approach the interrelations that the Caribbean has and has long had with the South, specifically the Chesapeake, Carolina (and Georgia) low country, the Gulf Coast, and Florida, which basically represent the U.S. South's littoral zone. Because the Chesapeake Bay area is probably less known for its connections to the Caribbean, I will consider them after highlighting some of the links characterized by the three other subregions.

South Carolina's Caribbean Connections

These interrelations are integral to understanding the multidimensional social and cultural history of the South, as historians, historical archaeologists, and cultural anthropologists are making clearer. For instance, South Carolina was settled by colonists from Britain and Barbados. Later during the Revolutionary War era, South Carolinian black loyalists who fought with the British, either because their masters were pro-British or because they sought their freedom from their pronational independence patriot masters, were evacuated along with other loyalists from all over the thirteen colonies to other parts of the British Empire and to Great Britain itself. African Americans went to Canada (especially Nova Scotia, where my colleague Marilyn Thomas-Houston is conducting ethnohistorical and ethnographic research on this South Carolina diaspora); they also went to Africa, particularly Sierra Leone; and, finally, some made their way to the West Indies, especially to the Bahamas and Jamaica.

Following in the footsteps of historian Monica Schuler (1979), anthropologist John Pulis (1999c) has traced the trajectory of black loyalists in Jamaica. Pulis (1999a) is also known for his work on the ethnohistory and theology of Rastafari. Thanks to Jamaican anthropologist Barry Chevannes (1994), we know that Rastafari's cultural genealogy includes influences from the mid-nineteenth-century Great Revival and the cultural resistance of an even earlier generation of syncretic Myalists. Pulis (1999b) presents evidence showing that most of the black loyalists who made their way to Jamaica were from South Carolina and Georgia rather than from the North. That migration had a significant cultural and political impact, most notably the development of the Native Baptist movement. Pulis scrutinizes the life trajectories of two itinerant ministers, Moses Baker and George Liele, and their participation in the Native Baptist movement, which laid the foundations for Revival or Revivalism, a major vehicle for cultural resistance and political contestation. The Native Baptist leadership, in which African Americans figured prominently, "galvanized support against slavery, the slave trade, and the passage of colonial legislation that violated English law" (Pulis 1999b, 12). Native Baptist preachers transmitted a "message of freedom and emancipation" and over time "provided the infrastructure for the 'Baptist War' (1830–32), the single largest slave rebellion to occur in Jamaica" (31). Messages of freedom and emancipation were also transmitted from the Caribbean to the South. The most powerful instance of this lies in the influence of the slave rebellions that culminated in the Haitian Revolution. Word of the revolution and its commitment to the ideas of equality and liberty traveled far and wide through the idioms of people, both enslaved and free, who cherished freedom.

Louisiana and the Gulf Coast–Caribbean Creole Zone

Of course, South Carolina is only one of many points of departure—or entry—for illuminating the South's historical relationship with the Caribbean. There are other cases that we can reflect on. Two in particular readily come to mind: southern Louisiana and Florida. I call the case of southern Louisiana and the wider Gulf Coast region the French Creole cultural zone.[1] This region has a history of cultural, economic, and demographic commonalities, connections, and exchanges with the French Caribbean. Indeed, "[f]rom

1718 to 1768, Louisiana was in the hands of the French. [It was in many ways] [l]ike its vastly more prosperous sister colony of St. Domingue (now Haiti)" (Dominguez 1986, 23). Because of economic difficulties the colony presented to France, Louis XV passed it on to Spain, whose king was his cousin, in 1768. In 1803, the territory was sold to the United States. During this period of transition, a major transition was also going on in St. Domingue, soon to become the independent black republic of Haiti. Between 1789 and 1810, major waves of refugees streamed into Louisiana from Haiti. Their presence made a marked influence, because, as Dominguez states, "[t]hey came from an island that excelled in sugar production, had long had large labor-intensive plantations, had been settled much longer than Louisiana, and hence boasted a socially established Creole sector" (102).

But those established Creoles of Haitian and later Louisiana society were not the only Caribbean people whose presence had an impact on the socio-cultural landscapes of Louisiana and the wider Gulf Coast. Let us not forget all the enslaved Africans and African Caribbeans who had no choice but to accompany their masters in their great escape from St. Domingue. Those forced immigrants, according to my anthropological understanding, were also cultural and linguistic Creoles, in the etic sense of the term if not in their ethnic identity, whose sensibilities and experiences would lead them to make significant contributions to Louisiana cultural life—most visibly in the realms of cuisine, language, religion, music, and festival arts—such as the culture and art of Mardi Gras. Helen Regis (1999, 2001) has done some interesting and significant work on the cultural politics of festivals, parades, and processions among working-class African Americans in New Orleans. These Afro-Creole performances, which include the black Indian masking that folklorist and ethnomusicologist Joyce Jackson studies, have tremendous potential for further study. The comparative study of how Indians are represented can potentially illuminate the multiple meanings of these stylized figurations in a variety of Caribbean festivals, including Trinidadian Carnival and the Jonkonnu traditions in Jamaica, a number of other English-speaking islands, and, as I shall demonstrate later, the eastern low country or tidewater region of North Carolina.

Because of the racial and cultural politics of identity, speaking what used to be called Negro Creole was a marker that made it impossible to claim a Creole identity (Dominguez 1986, 211). This speaks to the contested nature of cultural categories and meanings and to the importance of not thinking of culture or cultural areas in homogeneous and power-evasive terms. The morphology and lexicon of Louisiana Creole resembles those of Haitian Kreyòl and is derived in good part from "the language spoken by the [enslaved workers who were forced to accompany the refugees] from St. Domingue who came to Louisiana at the beginning of the 19th century. For years it was predominantly a language of rural blacks in southern Louisiana" (210). The public language of white and colored Creoles was French; however, we should distinguish public linguistic performances and personae from actual linguistic practice in the hidden transcripts of closed quarters. There is ample evidence that the most class-privileged Creoles, especially those of color who were adamant about distinguishing themselves from blacks, regularly engaged in code switching from perfect French in public to Creole in private (211). Code switching of a sort also occurred in the realm of religious expression and practice in which some Louisianians shift from Roman Catholicism to the mysteries of Voodoo/Hoodoo.

From Florida to the Bahamas

Another important point of embarkation from the South to the Caribbean is Florida's connections to the region through its Spanish colonial ties with the Hispanic Caribbean and the struggles for freedom of its African-descended inhabitants. Historians (Landers 1990, 1999), historical archaeologists (Deagan and MacMahon 1995), and anthropological ethnohistorians (Howard 2002) have documented Florida's borderland significance as a site of refuge, marronage, and military defense against Anglo-American expansion and racial slavery. The social and cultural history of Gracia Real de Santa Teresa de Mosé or, more simply, Fort Mosé and other important sites offers important clues about the lived experience of Maroons, many of them escapees from South Carolina and Georgia plantations, and about the nature of their alliances with the Spanish and with indigenous peoples, especially those Lower Creeks who came to be identified as Seminoles.

Rosalind Howard's (2002) important research on the Bahamas-bound journey of the Black Seminoles revives an interest that whetted the intellectual curiosity of an earlier generation of researchers. I was introduced to some of them when as an undergraduate I did a history research paper on the Red/ Black alliance that was a central feature of the Seminole Wars, which spanned from 1817 to 1855, across thirty-eight years of intermittent armed struggle. At that time, I was unaware that two early African American anthropologists, Laurence Foster (1931) and William Willis Jr. (1971), had investigated the nature of African and Amerindian contact in the colonial Southeast. In the 1920s and 1930s, Foster studied the Black Seminoles, focusing on three of the migratory paths that they took from Florida to defend and affirm their freedom in the face of being reinslaved by Anglo-Americans in the wake of the Seminole Wars. The Black Seminoles migrated to Oklahoma, where the majority of conquered aboriginals and their black allies were relocated, Texas, Mexico, and the Caribbean. It took nearly seventy years before an anthropologist followed the fourth path that led Black Seminoles to the Caribbean, specifically Andros Island in the Bahamas chain. It took this long in good part because the careers of anthropologists like Foster and Willis were limited by what philosopher of science Sandra Harding (1993) would call the racial economy of anthropological science. They did not have teaching positions in institutions where PhD students likely to be interested in black–Indian contact—or anything black—were trained. Consequently, their projects were erased from the discipline's canon by a regime of knowledge that defined the parameters for research. That regime has obviously undergone considerable change, opening the gate to new ideas as well as to old ideas that were for too long silenced.

Currently, the Caribbean's connections to Florida are highly visible, especially in southern Florida, which has become the gateway to Latin America and the Caribbean. I will have more to say about this later, but now I wish to discuss at some length the routes and roots that have tied the port city of Norfolk and its tidewater hinterland in Virginia and eastern North Carolina to the Caribbean, largely the former British West Indies.

Traveling from Kingston, Jamaica, to Norfolk, Virginia, and Back

There is one historical embarkation that has led me on a particularly intriguing journey to and from the Caribbean. As I suggested at the outset, this journey has been driven by intuitive, imaginative, and intellectual streams of reflection, particularly those that came together in a 1992 experience in Kingston, Jamaica. That experience was responsible for launching me into a more systematic search for hidden and silenced connections embedded in the narratives and archives of history.

I spent an afternoon with an old friend who had taken me under her wing when I initiated my dissertation research in 1978. She had been one of my key informants or research consultants, but she became much more than that. She was my teacher and fictive kinswoman. In many respects, a family resemblance united us, and that afternoon yet another dimension of our common experience and past became more apparent. That afternoon, fourteen years after we had first met, we walked along the Kingston waterfront, which is walking distance from the impoverished neighborhood where I had met my friend. We walked and talked, reminiscing about years past when she and her sisters, all of whom had emigrated from Jamaica, used to take the ferry from Kingston to Port Royal. Her father had spent many years fishing in Port Royal, which became his second home. The waterfront, beautified by redevelopment, brought back memories of her prematurely shortened childhood, which somehow seemed happier in light of the many trials and tribulations she had endured as an adult.

The waterfront beautification, the result of 1980s development efforts to boost the Jamaican economy, contrasted sharply with the rough, tough, and eroding topography of Oceanview, the garrison constituency about which I have written over the years. As I sat and felt the cool breeze from the sea, I thought about the locality's blight and how the already poor community had suffered under the fifteen-year regime of structural adjustment and export-led development. I had made it my job to help document Oceanview residents' "sufferation" and to instantiate the claim that "capitalism gone mad," as Calypsonian social criticism had so aptly put it, resonating with Rastafarian-inspired commentary about Babylon's wicked "downpression."

For a moment, though, the refreshing sea breeze distracted my thoughts from Oceanview's problems, the mere thought of which made me feel profoundly sad and angry. As we gazed out at the sea, I began to think aloud about another waterfront in the town along the southeastern coast of Virginia where I was born. I showed my friend a postcard I kept in a miniature photo album I carried in my bag. The basic layout and design of the two sites were strikingly similar, as though both Norfolk's and Kingston's redevelopment had followed the same architectural and spatial blueprint and were variations on the same theme.

That is highly likely to have been the case. Downtown waterfront development is imagined in the context of a common set of discursive practices among urban planners, who define and limit what is imaginable and amenable to implementation within and across urban spaces (Cooper 1999). North American models of beautification and revitalization have defined standards operative across a transnational field of application in which a shared discourse is practiced and enforced through vertical relations of planning and writing prescriptions for urban development. Hence, the waterfront projects in both Norfolk and Kingston share a resemblance owing to convergent developments in two different parts of the hemisphere where a common vision and blueprint have been adapted in two different places. That convergent pattern duplicated a landscape design that was noticeable not only to me. The striking similarities between Kingston and Norfolk had also been observed by a Jamaican acquaintance who had spent time in Hampton Roads, the cities, towns, and counties of southeastern Virginia. When she found out that Norfolk was my hometown, the first thing she said to me was how much Norfolk's waterfront had reminded her of Kingston.

The similar downtown landscapes stimulated me to think more about parallels and convergences that place the Chesapeake region of Virginia on the same critical plane with Jamaica and the rest of the Caribbean. Despite my inability to recall any of the Virginia history textbooks I read in school ever mentioning anything about Virginia's relationship to the West Indies, I eventually came upon information that expanded my understanding of that relationship. Interestingly, in a 1986 encyclopedia set sold in the supermarket where I regularly shopped in Kentucky, the entry on Norfolk captured my attention, because it stated that the town's *"early growth was based on the West Indies trade and the shipping of products from the plantations of Virginia and North Carolina"* (*Funk and Wagnalls New Encyclopedia* 1986; emphasis mine).

A few years later, an aunt sent me her copy of *Norfolk: Historic Southern Port* (Wertenbaker 1962 [1931]). She knew that I would be was particularly interested in the book because of its detailed discussion on Norfolk's participation in the West Indian trade. Since then, I have come across other work on what Caribbean historian Franklin W. Knight and his colleague, Peggy Liss, have called Atlantic port cities (Knight and Liss 1991). For instance, historian Jacob Price's (1974, 1991) seminal scholarship on Chesapeake ports examined the place that Baltimore and Norfolk occupied in the development of the Atlantic world. He documented how the low country or tidewater regions of Virginia and Maryland (a state that is technically below the Mason-Dixon line and therefore Southern) were integrated in British colonial circuits of trade that linked them to the British West Indies. Norfolk in particular came to play a specialized role as a seaport town (1974, 169) that linked plantation societies in North America and the Caribbean.

Because the "mouth of the Chesapeake was considerably closer to the West Indies than was New England, . . . Norfolk schooners could go all the way to Barbados, or Nevis, or Antigua and back" in a more timely fashion than ships from the larger northern entrepôts or port cities, where the prices tended to be dearer also (Wertenbaker 1962, 35). In the West Indian provision trade, products from the Virginia and North Carolina hinterland (e.g., timber, pitch, tar, barrel staves, hides, tallow, candles, Indian corn, flour, bread, peas, pork, and beef) were sent to Caribbean islands stretching from Jamaica to Barbados in exchange for sugar, molasses, and rum; some pimento, ginger, coffee, and cocoa; and sometimes even slaves to satisfy regional and even national market demand.

Although firmly embedded in the British American political economy, Norfolk merchants did not restrict their commerce to the British West Indies. British mercantilist laws attempted to suppress trade with rival colonial territories; however, those restrictions were regularly circumvented in the interests of profit making—and when tensions between the English and French escalated, the profits were highest. Much of this illegal trade was undertaken with the help of neutral islands like St. Thomas and Curaçao, where Norfolk ships would dock long enough to exchange their cargoes for French sugar and molasses (Wertenbaker 1962, 41). Extensive relations with the French West Indies were developed, and opportunistic trade with Cuba occurred as well.

Historian Thomas Wertenbaker documents that, like Charleston, Norfolk's original settlers included people who had emigrated from the British West Indies during the late seventeenth century (1962, 14). By the late eighteenth century, the town's population "numbered among its prominent merchants not only native Virginians and recent Scotch immigrants but Englishmen, Irish, and French West Indians" (88). The latter had sought refuge from the slave uprisings that crystallized into the Haitian Revolution. As compared with northern locales, Virginia appealed to most of these refugees because they could "make use of the . . . slaves they had brought with them" (88). In time, most of the refugees, who numbered in the thousands, dispersed to other parts of the country. Baltimore was probably a popular destination, because it was a Catholic stronghold (Ina J. Fandrich, personal communication, February 27, 2003). Those French West Indians who remained attempted to restore their fortunes by becoming merchants (Ina J. Fandrich, personal communication, February 27, 2003).

Historian Tommy Bogger also writes of the French refugees who streamed into Norfolk. In his book *Free Blacks in Norfolk, Virginia: The Darker Side of Freedom* (1997), he points out that a fleet of 137 vessels sailed into Norfolk in July 1793 bringing free people of color as well as enslaved people, both of whom were initially welcomed along with the white refugees. In time, however, as more refugees streamed into the town, the presence of free French blacks became a problem in a place where policies and laws were designed to restrict the numbers of African descendants who were free. By 1795, the mayor complained to the governor that "the refugees 'generally bring them [slaves and free blacks] in and plead ignorance of the law'" (Bogger 1997, 25, 26). Complaints about French blacks from the islands grew because when they interacted with the local blacks the latter became "impertinent" and hard to control in a situation in which there was "an inadequately armed militia" (26). Haitian blacks were suspected of contributing to the general unrest that led to the Gabriel conspiracy of 1800. The participants in that rebellion "were strongly motivated by the ideals of the French [and Haitian] Revolution[s]"—Liberty, Equality, and Fraternity. The flow of these ideals from Haiti to the U.S. South, mediated by the migration of French Caribbean immigrants and refugees, had a significant impact on the culture of resistance among free and enslaved African Americans.

I present this historical information about Norfolk because the Chesapeake case is much less known for its incorporation of Haitian refugees. Louisiana is the best-known case, and certainly larger numbers of French Caribbean immigrants found their way to the shores and hinterlands of the Gulf Coast, which was geographically closer to the Caribbean and a site where a French and Spanish colonial presence had an established history on the mainland. That family resemblance and common cultural ties made Louisiana an obvious destination. Nonetheless, it is important to note that other parts of the southern region, the more Anglicized, Protestant zones, were also reception areas for flows of people, commodities, and ideas from the French Caribbean and from Haiti in particular.

Caribbean–Southern Cultural Ramifications in Jonkonnu/John Canoe Style

The ideas, commodities, and human beings who traveled back and forth between the Chesapeake and the Caribbean had impacts on the cultural history of the South and the Caribbean. Just as Revolutionary War–era black loyalists from South Carolina and Georgia influenced cultural transformations in Jamaica, the Caribbean immigrants who traveled to Southern ports or through them to various destinations beyond Norfolk, Charleston, and New Orleans brought rich cultural cargos with them as well. With those cargoes they provided important inputs into the many local and subregional varieties of Southern culture. We may never fully understand the complex sociocultural processes that influenced those cultural continuities and change, but there are clues that we might follow to expand our knowledge and deepen our understanding.

Eastern North Carolina's northernmost reaches were historically a part of the hinterland linked to Norfolk. Until the 1930s, a street festival known as Jonkonnu, John Canoe, or Coonering was a tradition in this part of the state. Jonkonnu is a Christmas and New Year's season festival more commonly found in the Caribbean. Varieties of this secular tradition of masked and parading Jonkonnu bands are found in British-influenced societies such as the Bahamas, Bermuda, Belize, Jamaica, Nevis, and Guyana. The Bahamas tradition appears to share only nomenclature with the Jamaican festival, which seems to have clearer connections with Belize's tradition, which has been influenced by the presence of Jamaican migrants in Central America.

Today, governments are preserving this festival art as a part of their national patrimonies and, in more economic terms, as part of the colorful cultural heritage component of tourism. In Jamaica, for instance, national festivals and competitions of folk arts that have featured Jonkonnu bands have been organized by either the government or other public institutions (e.g., the leading newspaper, *Daily Gleaner*), at least since the early 1950s, as part of the effort to mobilize a common national identity and appreciation of African Caribbean cultural heritage.

In Jamaica, as in eastern North Carolina in years past, Jonkonnu bands, made up of masked and costumed male dancers and musicians, traditionally performed in processions usually during Christmas. Now they are more likely to be staged during important state occasions, such as the annual National Festival or Independence Day celebrations in early August. Beginning in the early eighteenth century, these processions of Roots and Fancy Dress bands paraded down the streets, stopping house to house or at Great Houses, shops, and the offices of community dignitaries who were expected to give money or food to the performers (Bettelheim 1988, 39). The music performed is known as fife and drum music, and it consists of two drums, a fife, and a scraper/grater, sometimes a banjo, tambourine, or shaker added.

Roots masquerades include set characters (Cowhead, Horsehead, Pitchy Patchy, Devil, Warrior, Belly Woman, sometimes Bride, and Amerindian or Wild Indian), each with his own identifiable costume. Some folklorists hypothesize that the Pitchy Patchy costume with its layers of brightly colored strips of fabric has its origins in the vegetal clothing that Maroons wore for camouflage during guerrilla warfare. Jonkonnu bands of the Roots variety have been concentrated in the eastern parishes of the island where neo-African style predominates. Fancy Dress bands, on the other hand, were concentrated in western parishes. Their costumes show stronger European influences. Fancy Dress bands feature the courtly attire of kings, queens, and courtiers embellished by elements consistent with a creolized aesthetic. A specific John Canoe or Koo Koo character appears among masqueraders in Fancy Dress parades "dressed up in a mask with long flowing hair . . . carrying a model of a house on his head" (Bettelheim 1988, 48). In the Roots variety, the Canoe character wears a mask with ox horns or boar tusks.

Because of the high level of street violence in urban Jamaica, Jonkonnu performers are hesitant now to parade in public spaces. Consequently, there is no longer a living tradition of neighborhood-based festival participation. Moreover, this secular tradition has declined in popularity among younger generations, which have found alternative connections with Africa (e.g., through Rastafari) and have ambivalent feelings about a festival that originated as a slave celebration that, among other things, entertained the white masters. Performances now tend to be staged and sponsored by institutionalized patrons such as the Jamaican Cultural Development Commission.

In eastern North Carolina, the John Canoe or Coonering procession has been described as all male, with fiddles, banjos, and homemade instruments including lard-can drums. The procession would stop at the kitchen doors of big white-owned farms where John Cooners expected to be given money or food. One account by an uncle of an alumnus of the University of Tennessee's graduate program described waking up early Christmas or New Year's Day to the "raucous sound of music." The setting for that incident was fifteen miles southeast of Fayetteville (Brett Riggs, personal communication, February 3, 2003).

Accounts of similar Christmas season parades of masked revelers are found in the journal *North Carolina Folklore,* which documents the survival of a Pitchy Patchy style. According to an article written by Richard Walser (1971), "On Christmas Eve, John Kuners, Negroes, went about singing, dressed in tatters with strips of gay colors sewn to their garments. All were men, but some dressed as women. They wore masks. . . . They collected pennies at each house" (161). Descriptions of the John Canoe figure indicate that "he wears a mask. . . . He goes through a variety of pranks . . . and . . . is accompanied by a crowd of [Negroes] who make noise and music for 'his worship John Kooner'" (162). John Canoe is described as a ragman with two great ox horns or branching deer horns "attached to the skin of a raccoon" arranged over his head and face, leaving openings for his eyes and mouth. A second figure was described as the "best looking darkey of the place" who wears his Sunday best (162).

In some parts of eastern North Carolina, a reinterpreted form of "the custom survived for a while among whites who seem not to have been aware of its Negro origin" (Walser 1971, 169). Joncooners "were an established part of the Christmas observance" (169). Young men would dress up in "outlandish" costumes, often women's attire, and wear "scare-faces" (169). They would also, in minstrel style, blacken their faces or, if they preferred not to, would wear clown costumes and facial masks. Coonering would begin as early as five o'clock on Christmas morning, waking up residents with Christmas carols and other songs (170).

This past practice seems to have striking similarities with the recent blackface antics of white fraternities on college campuses in which white males parade around frat houses or the streets wearing blackface, sometimes Afro wigs, and pillow-stuffed bellies under women's dresses, making offensive statements about irresponsibly fertile welfare queens and African Americans in general. Are these instances of contemporary Coonering, especially when performed in the South? Was the Coonering of the past a mimetic expression that represented a form of minstrelsy? Are the present-day minstrel-like performances part of the legacy of Coonering? These are questions that I cannot answer at this time but are perhaps worthy of further exploration.

The origins of the Jonkonnu term are sometimes attributed to "the French phrase *gens inconnus* which means 'the unknown people,' a reference to the masking . . . of festival celebrants" (Howard 2004, 175). Sociologist Ira de A. Reid's 1942 *Phylon* article, "The John Canoe Festival: A New World Africanism," offered an alternate explanation. In his view, the origins of the East Carolinian festival are found in a retained Africanism traceable to West Africa. He claimed that there was an early eighteenth-century chief named John Connu. Supposedly, a festival he originated on the Guinea Coast was brought to the West Indies and later diffused to North Carolina, "whose more wealthy plantation owners had continuous commerce with the islands" (Walser 1971, 172). Some research suggests that commerce with Jamaica in particular gave rise to East Carolina's Jonkonnu tradition, a virtually forgotten tradition that is now being revived in limited contexts of public programming and cultural-heritage tourism.

The North Carolina Humanities Council has played an important role in promoting scholar–community collaborations for researching local histories of Jonkonnu. This research has fed into the revitalization of Jonkonnu as an element of cultural-heritage tourism. A couple of fairly recent examples of reviving or re-creating Jonkonnu are the following events advertised or reported on the Internet. Among the many Christmas festivities featured in New Bern, North Carolina, since 2000 is the Tryon Palace's reenactment. An advertisement published in 2001 stated the following:

> Making a return appearance for Christmas 2001 is Tryon Palace's Jonkonnu Celebration, the colorful African American holiday procession that was popular in eastern North Carolina during the 19th century but had disappeared by the start of the 20th century. When Tryon Palace Historic Sites & Gardens brought Jonkonnu back to life last Christmas, it proved to be such a crowd-pleaser that the Tryon Palace Jonkonnu troupe was later invited to reprise the celebration at Gov. Easley's inauguration in Raleigh. The Jonkonnu ceremony, a blend of West African and English traditions, features a festive parade of elaborately costumed singers, dancers and musicians. Free performances will take place between at 6 and 8 p.m. on each of the candlelight evenings, Dec. 14, 15, 21, and 22. (*Free Press, 2001*)

The celebration was also publicized with these words of invitation to the public:

> Elaborately costumed singers, dancers and musicians will re-create Jonkonnu, an African-American yuletide tradition unique to eastern North Carolina, along Pollock Street in New Bern at 6 p.m. and 8 p.m. today and Saturday. The festive procession will wind from house to house in the town's historic district, bringing to life a 19th-century blend of African, Caribbean and English customs. Free. (*Daily Reflector* 2001)

Twentieth- and Twenty-First-Century Configurations of Caribbean–Southern Connections

The continuous commerce between various parts of the South and the Caribbean constituted a transcolonial and later transnational sociocultural field that is a rich site for unburying and retrieving the silenced history that denies Southerners and Caribbean people the historical consciousness, memory, and knowledge that is part of their shared cultural heritage. The upper South has been especially neglected, and, for that reason, I feel motivated to fill that gap. Other gaps, however, need to be addressed as well, and a number of historians and anthropologists have been pursuing important research directions that give voice to silenced chapters of the convergent cultural and socioeconomic history of the South and the Caribbean.

Beyond questions of history, twentieth- and now twenty-first-century developments, both parallel adaptations to similar structural situations and direct interchanges between the two regions, encourage us to situate the Caribbean and the South within overlapping transnational fields. Anthropologists such as Tony Whitehead, Willie Baber, and myself—among others—are seeing to it that some of the concepts and theoretical discourses that were developed originally in the context of Caribbean studies and studies of plantation societies elsewhere are allowed to travel to the research agendas and social analysis being pursued in the South and the Southern diaspora. Tony Whitehead (1986, 1997) is an exemplary case of someone whose analysis of U.S. situations draws on tools honed through his earlier Caribbean research on family, fertility, and men. His approach to African American lower-class masculinity and its influence on health-related behaviors, particularly those affecting the incidence of HIV/AIDS, draws upon a model of masculinity he constructed through a constructive critique of Peter Wilson's (1973 [1995]) reputation–respectability typology. Whitehead has also used his model of socially balancing the values and practices of respectability and reputation in thinking in new ways about his own experiences as a black male from the rural tidewater region of Virginia. His Chesapeake subregional background may only be incidental to his work as an anthropologist, but I find it interesting that a fellow Virginian is drawing these kinds of connections and bringing interrogations of Caribbean life so close to home. He is an intellectual courier who has accepted the responsibility for fashioning and applying a repertoire of border-crossing, traveling theory.

Besides cultural constructs of manhood and womanhood and their embeddedness in intersecting hierarchies of race, class, and sexuality, other topics and themes that are amenable to this traveling theory approach include kinship, mating, household organization, and livelihood strategies; the social construction of race, especially in contexts such as New Orleans and Charleston, where tripartite classification systems have contested the Anglo-dominant bipolarity, and in the many areas of the South, parts of Virginia and North Carolina included, where triracial communities have defiantly claimed identities otherwise precluded by the "one drop rule"; the Caribbeanization of Southern places through new waves of immigration; the dual and conflicting politics of reception for various categories of Caribbean refugees, such as Haitians and Cubans, and the interplay between domestic and foreign policy concerns; the emergence of new Caribbean-inspired religious identities and the search for "Africa"; economic and environmental developments influenced by U.S. policy–induced conditions in the Caribbean; and threats to the viability of small farmers and considerations of the transnational relevance of the concepts crafted about agrocapitalism and reconstituted Caribbean peasants and proletarians. I will discuss four of these possibilities in greater detail in the sections that follow. Because debates concerning kinship, marriage, and sexual politics have been intense in both Caribbean and black American studies, I will treat this particular topic in some detail.

The Racial and Class Politics of Stratified Kinship and Marriage

Anthropological studies of kinship and social organization have elaborated parallel themes for Caribbean and African American studies. When I was a graduate student, I attempted to address these overlapping concerns by using the concept of plantation society as an analytical frame that allowed me to put the U.S. South and the English-speaking Caribbean in particular on the same page. The prevalence, for instance, of matrifocality in social organization, patterns of cooperative child raising within consanguineal groupings (most commonly organized around blood ties among maternal blood lines), and high rates of visiting relationships and consensual sexual unions were issues or problems that sociologists and anthropologists felt they had to explain. Were they pathological symptoms of attenuated families, part of the legacy of slavery that forced families apart, reducing them to mother-child dyads? Or was an alternative African-inspired cultural logic at work that organized primary relations around mothers and their kin, both female and male, and placed greater cultural emphasis on consanguineality than on conjugal ties (Sudarkasa 1996)? These adaptations emerged in different plantation and peasant society environments where migration from family land—be it peasant smallholdings barely capable of sustaining a household or sharecropper or tenant farming plots—was impelled to reproduce households, domestic networks, and families left back home in the country. Marked similarities, parallels, and instances of human agency were responding creatively yet restrictively to similar structures of power and political economy, structures with a shared history in many respects but also divergent histories marked by particularities specific to different social formations, different social orders.

R. T. Smith's (1987) and Lisa Douglass's (1992) analyses of the dual marriage system have a number of parallels with Allison Davis, Burleigh Gardner, and Mary Gardner's (1941 [1988]) analysis of kinship and mating across lines of caste and class in Natchez, Mississippi, in the 1930s. Anthropologists have not theorized openly and visibly about Southern kinship in terms of connections between whites and blacks. These have been neglected, taboo subjects since the publication of *Deep South*. My reading of that classic ethnography, which has been virtually erased from the canon of what we cite and what we teach our students, leads me to think that *Deep South*'s social analysis represented a kind of embedded theorizing about a system of stratified kinship and mating in which men of the privileged caste were granted the prerogative of marrying within their caste while having the license to have long- or short-term relationships with concubines from the lower caste. In other words, sociocultural principles operated that permitted white men to have their cake and eat it, too, in the midst of a repressive Jim Crow climate in which antimiscegenation was legally codified with a vengeance. The gender bias and sexual politics of this culture of racism was only a more hypocritical, contradictory, and repressive version of the variant that R. T. Smith characterized in his model of the Caribbean's dual marriage system. In this stratified but, in some significant ways, unified system, patriarchal prerogatives, constructs of masculinity, matrifocality, and interhousehold cooperation are manifested across social lines but in class-specific ways.

Thanks to Douglass's explanation, we have a better understanding of how interlocking hierarchies of gender, color, and class operate to constitute the shared cultural system that so many sociologists and anthropologists have failed to discern. R. T. Smith did us a real service by treating the double standard and masculine privilege as an issue worthy of theorizing. He explained how the de facto polygyny of upper-class men is informed by the same cultural system that informs the reputational behavior of lower-class African Caribbean men, who since Peter Wilson's intervention (1973) have been the focus of considerable debate in the literature. Masculine virility and strength exhibited in sexual conquests and managing multiple baby mothers simultaneously are valued so long as they are not taken too far, as Tony Whitehead tells us. Social balance is also valued, so when men end up not being able to contribute to the livelihood of their children, they are considered weak and perhaps wicked. This kind of demonstration of virility is also expected among middle-class and upper-class men, who in achieving social balance and some measure of respectability are expected to own up to their exploits and contribute to the livelihood and perhaps the social mobility of their outside children.

In the Caribbean, the climate has been rather promiscegenation, with ideologies of mixedness and *mestizaje* defining national identities. "Out of many, one people" is the national motto in Jamaica, emphasizing its multiracial heritage. But as many race-conscious Jamaicans point out, 95 percent of the population is black, so why overstate the presence of Chinese, Indians, Lebanese, Germans, and British-descended whites when, since the 1930s, the Rastafari have been insisting that Ethiopia—Africa—must be recognized as home?

The kinship and gender constructs that ethnographic research mapped in Mississippi and later in the Chesapeake city of Baltimore among lower-class black men (Whitehead 1997) are not limited to those sites. These constructs are relevant to studies of other parts of the South and its migration-mediated diasporas in northern, midwestern, and West Coast cities.

Besides kinship, marriage, and the cultural politics of masculine sexual prowess, there are other issues germane to the kind of research agenda I sketch here. I will raise some points about three of them before I conclude.

The Migration of African Caribbean Orishas and Loas

We should pay more attention to the newer migrations to the South and the consequent cultural and religious identities, such as those formed by Yoruba-inspired communities in South Carolina, Atlanta, and New Orleans. Cuban American anthropologist Beatriz Morales (1995) has written about the dispersion of the Yoruba religion in the United States and into the South.

This dispersion initially involved the migration of Cubans, particularly Afro-Cubans to the United States, where they continued their practice of Santería, and the more traditional Yoruba form of it called Lucumí.

In the midst of the 1960s and 1970s Black Movement, Santería underwent change with non-Cuban blacks being attracted to it as a purportedly more authentic, more African form of religiosity. In northern urban settings, a new syncretized Orisha-Voodoo emerged that placed greater emphasis on African cultural identity and less emphasis on the Roman Catholic saints that represented the Western framework. This Afrocentric negation of Santería's syncretic relationship to Christianity created tensions between Orisha-Voodoo and the followers of Santería.

That conflict led to the decision to establish a base in rural South Carolina. That base became the Oyotunji Village, a re-creation of an African village (see Clarke 2004). The Oyotunji settlers chose South Carolina rather than upstate New York because of their belief that the South was more conducive to building African culture. Religious specialists, initiated in Oyotunji, later established Yoruba centers elsewhere, such as the one in Atlanta. Morales (1995) shows how the Orisha-Voodoo religion is expanding to accommodate a shift back to a more Santería-oriented form because of Atlanta's growing multicultural population. As more Latinos joined, the temple established closer ties with the Santería community. As a consequence, the temple now initiates its adherents into either of the two traditions and both groups "treat each other as equals" (Morales 1995, 130).

The Cuban Embargo, NAFTA, and Sugar Politics in Florida

Anthropologist Max Kirsch (2003) has examined economic developments in the Florida Everglades zone that are influenced by conditions in the Caribbean and U.S. foreign policy, which are mutually constitutive. He demonstrates that the sugar industry based in the state of Florida has benefited from the U.S. embargo against Cuba, whose sugar cannot be imported here. The embargo created an opening for Cuban émigrés to build an enclave in Florida and lobby for protection from NAFTA's free trade regulations until 2008.

Sugar production, so central to the economic history of the Caribbean, expanded in Florida, however, to the detriment of Florida's wetlands, which have been drained. Sugar producers, especially the Cuban émigrés who restored their business interests with U.S. protection, became "a major force in national and Florida politics" (Kirsch 2003, 114–15), influencing foreign and domestic environmental policies. Until 2008, when the NAFTA exemption may be lifted, Cuban American–controlled sugar production will continue to be subsidized by the U.S. government. Both environmental and labor groups have taken the industry to court for polluting the environment and for mistreating and jeopardizing the health of migrant workers, some of whom are from the Caribbean (e.g., Haitians). Because of the vulnerable immigration status of the workforce and "the concern (and threats) about the possible loss of jobs," health conditions had not received the attention they deserved before the recent litigation (104). In response to the lawsuits, sugar companies have mechanized harvesting, relegating most workers to planting and to off-season migration to work on citrus farms in other areas.

The Everglades Agricultural Area is the locus not only of sugarcane production, it also is the fertile grounds for several other crops, among them "tomatoes, beans, lettuce, sugar beets, watermelons . . . and Chinese vegetables" (Kirsch 2003, 106). Beyond the production of these primary commodities, there is the presence of "strong fluid communities . . . [of African and Native Americans,] Mayan-speaking Guatemalans[, and] Caribbean immigrants . . . [that] exist beyond the realm of the production line" (107) or that of social service agencies whose conspicuousness and diversity belie their ability to meet basic needs and ameliorate local conditions. Through resilient ties of kinship and local organization, both American-born and immigrant workers negotiate the demands of their everyday lives in a nexus of culture, power, and identity that is situated where the local and transnational intersect.

Farmers and/or Peasants?

Some parallel problems might be better understood if we examine them with bifocal vision; that is, by asking questions that have relevance for both Caribbean and Southern contexts and that enable us to compare and contrast those cases. For instance, the work on the categorization, struggles, and negotiations of Caribbean peasants raises interesting questions that might fruitfully be applied to the daunting situation faced by the South's small farmers, particularly black farmers who represent an endangered species and are mobilizing to combat their plight. Being neither peasant nor proletarian (Frucht 1971 [1967]) seems to be the growing predicament for the variety of rural folk who might be categorized as farmers—from sharecroppers to tenants to landowners of varying scales.

Willie L. Baber has raised this question based on his work on the struggles of North Carolina farmers to survive agribusiness's encroachments on their land and degradation of their environment (Baber, personal communication with the author, November 15, 2000). His perspective on what he has observed in Halifax County in northeastern North Carolina has been influenced by his earlier work in rural Martinique on peasant production undergoing change in a globalizing economy (Baber 1988). Whether the concept of peasant, particularly how it has been formulated for Caribbean contexts, is appropriate for the South, situating the agricultural work of Southern smallholders alongside Caribbean peasants for the sake of comparison and contrast could add dimensions and nuances that otherwise would not be part of the discussion.

The importance of comparing and contrasting Southern and Caribbean cases is reflected in the parallel histories of the small farmers concerned. For instance, during the antebellum period, South Carolina and Georgia had protopeasant formations with concomitant systems of internal marketing similar to those developed in Jamaica and other parts of the Caribbean.

Peasant and proletarian are variable rather than categorical, essentialist realities. The boundary between these categories is ambiguous and conditioned by a hybrid experience. Richard Frucht's (1971 [1967]) writing on the rise and demise of peasants in Nevis presents a useful perspective on these matters. A reconstituted peasantry on the order of what emerged in the Greater Antilles and in certain Eastern Caribbean contexts did not develop in Nevis. The main reasons were the island's small size and the lack of open areas uncontrolled by plantations.

According to Frucht, "the word 'peasant' is not to be here understood as a categorical concept describing a subculture or kind of community. It is not to be so understood because the so-called peasantry of Nevis has always been inextricably bound to the plantation system or to some other system of wage labor in more than an occasional sense. This is an artifact of geography, of economic history, and of the economic and political predominance of the industrial, colonial power" (Frucht 1971 [1967], 99).

He went on to argue that "in Nevis, whereas there is a peasant-like means of production, which includes cultivation of small plots with the use of household labor and traditional manual technology, the relations of production are proletarian . . . based on the sale of labor for wages either paid in cash or in kind, and the latter through systems of sharecropping, farming out and under conditions of male labor emigration. Finally, the existence together and in alteration of seemingly disparate means and relations of production is an adaptation to the vicissitudes of a marginal economy" (Frucht 1971 [1967], 99).

He described how, over time, the predominance of sharecropping and farming out declined, and the big plantations were sold to speculators who, in turn, sold subdivided plots to smallholders. For a short while after World War II, a peasant adaptation was reconstituted; however, years later, emigration opportunities expanded as tourism and concomitant construction and service jobs emerged as a focus of economic life. By the 1960s and 1970s, dependence on remittances had replaced agricultural production as the livelihood strategy for roughly 70 percent of the adult population, whose peasant holdings were used for garden vegetables or as an asset to be used for "insuring bank loans for further emigration" (Frucht 1971 [1967], 102).

The declining viability of smallholdings as units of agricultural production and the growing dependence on alternative sources of income, primarily service jobs and remittances from transnational relatives, are also issues affecting many rural communities in the U.S. South. These communities are undergoing transformations influenced in part by their own specific histories of sharecropping, smallholdings, migration to the urban North, and now, in the context of the deindustrialization and economic restructuring, return migration, as Carol Stack's (1996) research documents.

Melissa Hargrove (2005) has shown how African Americans, specifically those with Gullah/Geechee identities, in South Carolina's Sea Islands are being circumscribed and in many instances altogether displaced by resort and tourism development. Similar to the situation in the Caribbean, tourism is capitalizing on the culturally distinctive heritage of sweetgrass basketmaking and Gullah language-based performances, while real estate developers are rapidly expanding the construction of hotels, golf courses, and wealthy gated communities that symbolically reinvent and romanticize the plantation. Local activist organizations are contesting the alienation of the Gullah from their traditional homes and means of livelihood. According to one grassroots organization, the Gullahs' human rights are at stake, and this grievance has been expressed in a United Nations forum (Hargrove 2000).

Traveling across Interlocking Transnational Fields: Concluding Remarks

In this chapter, I have related aspects of the history of my efforts to begin rethinking the transcolonial and transnational connections that have mutually constituted the two regions that we know as the South and the Caribbean. I have tried to give the reader a sense of how I am attempting to remap the cultural and structural space in which these two areas and zones of social analysis and theory conjoin and interpenetrate, using a cartography that is responsive to the passage of time. I have revealed aspects of my own personal journey to hear through and beyond the structured and enforced silences of the historical past and present so that more people of the South and the Caribbean might have the choice to claim the migrations, the evacuations, the commodity chains, the plantations, the smallholdings, the Maroon wars, the Baptist War, the systems of kinship stratified by color and class, the new religions, the Creole languages, the code switching, the Christmas and pre-Lenten festivals, the masks, and the musical revelry that have bound us together despite the big waters that appear to separate us. My listening beyond the silences has been aided not only by conventional intellectual tools but also by some measure of intuition and imagination, inspired by a politics of love.

Growing up in Norfolk, Virginia, may have predisposed me to study anthropology and to travel in search of, and later with, theoretical cargo whose value is transferable. This port city's relationship with major waterways, its openness to the Atlantic world, especially the Caribbean, made it an appropriate base of embarkation and disembarkation in my journey to and from, back and forth between the Chesapeake Bay and the Caribbean Sea, between my imagination and analytic intellect, between the temporal landscapes of ancestral presence and the cultural geography of present-day diasporas and their constituent diasporas. To and from, back and forth, remapping travel routes and unburying cultural roots as I go about my journey.

On the evening of February 22, 2003, as I was working on the original draft of this chapter, the Trumpet Awards ceremony, a program to celebrate African American heroes, sponsored by a number of major corporations (e.g., Delta Airlines, Coca-Cola, GM, Kroger, Miller Brewing Company, and Anheuser-Busch), was broadcast on the Turner Broadcasting System's superstation. The Right Honorable Perry Gladstone Christie, then prime minister of the Bahamas (who happens to belong to a Jonkonnu group), was presented a Global Achievement Award. In his thank-you speech, he reminded the largely African American audience that Bahamians and African Americans share a great many things in common and that the Bahamas nation has contributed to African American achievements, beginning, of course, with the actor Sidney Poitier. He ended with the following insightful words, which are relevant to the themes of this chapter, especially as those themes relate to the African diaspora. He said: "An expanse of water separates us, but an expanse of water should never divide us. One family insoluble under God."

Acknowledgments

This was originally a keynote address delivered at the annual meeting of the Southern Anthropological Society (SAS) in February 2003 in Baton Rouge, Louisiana. I would like to thank Helen Regis for inviting me and encouraging me to distill ideas I had been rehearsing for many years. As program chair, she was responsible for organizing the conference as well as its Key Symposium, whose theme pertained to Southern and Caribbean connections. She so generously allowed me to choose how I would participate in the meeting. I had the options of presenting a paper in the Key Symposium, serving as a discussant, or giving the keynote lecture, which would give me twice as much time to lay out my ideas. Obviously, I could not resist the temptation of the latter option. I also appreciate the conversations, e-mail correspondence, and hotel room sharing I have enjoyed with Rosalyn Howard, whose research on the Black Seminoles contributed to my excitement about the common ground in the cultural history of the South and Caribbean. I am so glad I was in my office that afternoon she telephoned me to ask my advice about graduate programs in anthropology. A mutual friend, Marvin Haire, had encouraged her to contact me. Since then, we have been in each other's amen corner. I appreciate the warm Louisiana hospitality that folklorist and ethnomusicologist Joyce Jackson and her husband, documentary photographer J. Nash Porter, extended during the SAS meeting. Their insights into the performing arts and cultural imagination of the Mardi Gras black Indian masking tradition are remarkable. I especially look forward to learning more from Dr. Jackson's ongoing research, which is shaped by her commitment as an organic intellectual working in solidarity with African American communities in southern Louisiana. I would also like to thank Brett Riggs for his conversations during his years at the University of Tennessee and more recently his reply to my e-mail request that he confirm the story he told me about Jonkonnu in eastern North Carolina. That bit of information shared several years ago reinforced my wish to remap the South's ties to the Caribbean region.

My aunt, Pearl Hamilton Harper, has been such a gem over the years. The history book she gave me quite a while ago—after she had forced herself to finish reading it—was an important turning point in my knowledge about the place our hometown occupies in the wider Atlantic world. I am so glad that her reading hobby has occasionally included local history. Another useful book, one focused on free black Norfolkians, was a gift from my uncle, the late Dr. Herbert Marshall, whose enthusiasm for my scholarship I will always appreciate.

PART III

Engaging Interlocutors in Interdisciplinary Dialogue

4. Writing against the Grain

Cultural Politics of Difference
in Alice Walker's Fiction

Introduction: Anthropology at the Crossroads

A number of sociocultural anthropologists are engaging in the process of redefining the critical anthropological project for this postcolonial, post–Cold War, postmodern era, an era in which modernist expectations of linear evolutionary and developmental change have been largely abandoned (di Leonardo 1991, 26).[1] Disciplinary canons are being critically reassessed and their mechanisms for excluding and silencing exposed. Alternative routes to knowing, understanding, critiquing, and confronting the cultural terrain of late capitalism and the cultural logic of the early twenty-first-century world are being mapped in the midst of intense theoretical and political negotiations, debates, and contestations over how to construct a more decolonized study of humankind, a more authentic study of humanity's common ground as well as its historically contingent and embedded differences.

Anthropology as we currently know it is at an important crossroads in its historical development. The directions it follows can potentially lead toward a paradigmatic shift or epistemological break from the discipline's remaining colonial legacy and the crisis that has resulted from its tensions and contradictions. The road chosen and followed can also move anthropology beyond the impasse that Robert Ulin (1991) discerns between more orthodox forms of political economy and postmodernism, particularly the trends that relativize texts and narratives and direct attention away from "the concrete conditions of [the capitalist world system] that profoundly condition the representational process" (63; e.g., Geertz 1988; Clifford 1986, 1988b).[2] A potential resolution to this impasse has already been attempted in a number of experimental studies that combine the concerns of both historicized political economy and cultural/symbolic analysis (e.g., Taussig 1980, 1987; Willis 1981; Nash 1979) and texts with greater emphasis upon the articulation of indigenous historical consciousness with wider world developments than on political economy per se (Rosaldo 1980, Price 1983). However, such attempts at reconciling the two divergent approaches have not yet produced results that are fully satisfactory. George Marcus and Michael Fischer claim that "[a]n interpretive anthropology fully accountable to historical and political-economy implications . . . remains to be written" (1986, 86). In Ulin's perspective, some postmodern anthropologists (e.g., Marcus and Fischer 1986) are "sensitive to the concerns of political-economy," but they have not adequately identified "how political-economy serves as a constraint on symbolic or communicative exchange" (Ulin 1991, 80), including that involved in writing and reading ethnographic texts. He goes on to claim that by opening ethnography to "a plurality of voices" and to relativism, which assumes an equality of voices (72),[3] even the new interpretive political economy trend complicates rather than resolves the issue of ethnographic authority: "[T]he authority of the account does not rest simply with the author's voice or those of a plurality of informants but rather through their fusion with a thoroughly mediated social world. . . . [T]he foregrounding of the informants' voices does not settle the issue of authority as these voices are not autonomous but rather stand mediated by the social conditions of their production and the potential audiences to which they are addressed. . . . The infusion of a multiplicity of voices into the ethnographic narrative, no matter how positive, is not a substitute for the critical grasp of social reality and hence leaves the authority of the ethnographic account incomplete" (80–81).[4] Ulin argues that incomplete authority—the result ultimately of postcolonial challenges to anthropology—presents both an epistemological and political problem for a discipline with the potential and practical intent of challenging exploitation and offering an uncompromising vision of human emancipation (81–81).

According to Richard Fox (1991b), to restore the credibility of, and confidence in, its knowledge claims, anthropology must *recapture* authority by reentering the real world with strategies such as writing against culture (Abu-Lughod 1991), reading social life with class-sensitive lenses (Ortner 1991), engaging historicism and new culture history (Vincent 1991; Fox 1991a), excavating an archaeology of anthropology (Trouillot 1991), and transnationalizing the discipline's conceptual terrain (Appadurai 1991). Although Fox and the other contributors to *Recapturing Anthropology* clearly underscore nontextualist and nonrhetorical means of reconstituting authority, critical anthropology need not go so far as to eliminate textual experimentation and theory from its project(s). The concern with writing innovative texts can be included without being based on relativist assumptions and without being elevated above or deflecting critical epistemological and political issues. Indeed, textual strategies should be embedded within the wider task of producing politically grounded and responsible ethnographic analysis and used as a literary medium to facilitate and enhance anthropology's ability to describe, analyze, interpret, and explain to its readership.

In revising anthropology as a critical discipline, it is important to draw upon the experimental antipositivist impetus that is so much a positive feature of "the postmodernist turn"[5] and combine this feature with the strengths of other critical discourses, particularly a historicized political economy, as Ulin advocates. Our understanding of political economy and of a larger critical anthropological project, however, should be expanded and enhanced by insights from a feminism sensitive to the racial, ethnic, class, and national differences that condition gendered experience as well as by understandings from the sociopolitically grounded critical intellectual trajectories of non-Western, Third World, and racialized ethnic peoples.[6] As I will discuss in greater detail later, much of anthropology—whether critical or conventional—remains guilty of underestimating and bracketing the power and force of gender and race dynamics within both the discipline and the world at large. Will the shift toward a reconstructed and revitalized critical anthropology make possible a more inclusive, decolonized, multicultural, and multiracial disciplinary discourse, or will it inadvertently reinscribe gendered and racialized neocolonial relations that marginalize subaltern social analysis from centers of authority and validation? To what extent is anthropology's ability to recapture authority contingent on the integration—not token inclusion nor subordination—of subaltern sociocultural analysis and on a concomitant redistribution of intellectual capital and power? In my view, these questions are absolutely crucial to the postmodern and postcolonial era's critical anthropological project—or projects. Ultimately, the answers will depend upon the outcome of sociopolitical struggles over a range of interrelated issues, among them canon re-formation, the definition and legitimation of new research priorities, and the recruitment, hiring, and retention of more diversified faculty in training and research programs. Ultimately, these struggles are over the power and authority to define, produce, and confer legitimacy on the ideas and goals that constitute anthropological knowledge and praxis. As I understand them, power and authority may be analogically present and rhetorically structured in texts, but, more germane to this particular discussion, they are forces embodied, enforced, and contested in the real-world institutionalized contexts within which anthropologists develop careers and accumulate academic and professional capital by competing for grants, doing research, writing texts, publishing in juried outlets, and participating in other aspects of academic and nonacademic work.

An important role of critical or radical anthropologies of various persuasions—none of which are mutually exclusive—is to struggle for a more democratized anthropology wherein Westerners and non-Westerners, men and women, class privileged and class oppressed can engage on more leveled terrain in an anthropological enterprise that no longer objectifies, appropriates, or nativizes ethnographic others. In other words, our role and goal is to remake and transform the discipline. In order to influence the direction and scope of anthropological inquiry toward this goal, authority to validate knowledge claims and particularly those modes of interpretation and explanation recognized as theory is required. The historical reality is that access to such authority is differentially and unequally structured, however, with race, gender, class, and national origins as salient conditions (Collins 1991, 1998).

In succinct terms, this is my view of anthropology at this juncture (see also Harrison 1991). It is from this particular vantage point that I will examine a set of issues related to the general problem of Third World and minoritized women's, specifically black American women's, relatively peripheral location in the prevailing structure of intellectual production. Here I am not focusing on the small number of celebrities, stars, who have been commodified. I am more concerned with the rank-and-file variety of intellectuals, the more typical uncelebrated intellectual *workers*. My position is basically that critical anthropologists need to appreciate and understand what black women—as well as feminist and subaltern intellectuals generally—have to say and write about the cultural terrain of the late twentieth century and the history that unfolded it—whether their writings are ethnographies or fiction. This directive applies even to Eric Wolf (1982), Robert Ulin (1984, 1991), and William Roseberry (1989), who have written invaluable assessments of anthropology, as well as to third phase feminist anthropologists (Moore 1988) concerned with deconstructing and de-essentializing gender.[7] It is instructive that some of the latter, notably Mina Davis Caulfield (1979), Karen Sacks (1989), and Micaela di Leonardo (1991), have been much less inclined to negate the contributions of women of color than have other critical analysts (e.g., Cassells 1977; for review of Cassells's book, see Harrison 1990a).

In the ensuing chapter, I make the claim that the fiction that African American women have written is embedded in a broader interdisciplinary and intertextual discourse wherein themes, issues, and concerns of definite anthropological import are prominent. Moreover, I argue that fiction, specifically Alice Walker's novel *The Temple of My Familiar*, can be read for its implications for and insights into ethnographic and ethnohistorical analysis and writing, particularly analytical writing on questions of race, gender, class, and the politics of knowledge and culture in the postcolonial and postmodern world. If, as James Clifford (1986) claims, ethnography is fiction—that is, contingent and fashioned from a partial and embodied perspective—then fiction may be viewed as a form of ethnography, especially in the case of a writer like Alice Walker, who traces her intellectual genealogy to Zora Neale Hurston, who was both an ethnographer and a novelist. My reading and analysis of Walker's fiction are intended to illuminate the anthropological significance of a particular form and genre of critical discourse and cultural resistance, not to advocate that anthropology in its conceptual and methodological breadth be refashioned largely as a literary enterprise.

The Politics of Canon Formation and Contentions over the Critical Anthropological Project

As I already have pointed out, in Ulin's assessment the critical anthropological project will emerge from bridging the impasse between the two major contenders, political economy and postmodernism, both of which have limitations. For instance, there is a tendency in some versions of political economy to treat symbolically mediated social action as a mere epiphenomenon of the logic of production. Equally problematic is the trend within postmodernist writing to "advance a notion of theory that is insufficiently connected to praxis and a grasp of the social world as a totality" (Ulin 1991, 63, 82). Both approaches, however, are not without redeeming qualities that can provide the basis for a synthesis and reconciliation.

Although I am in basic agreement with the thrust of Ulin's discussion, I find it problematic that he acknowledges the role that "the feminist trajectory" plays in the critical project with only a brief endnote that claims that including feminist concerns in the main text of the article would distract from the issues he chooses to highlight. Although it is completely within his right to select his focus, his choice not to integrate feminist perspectives results in the inadvertent reinforcement of a problematic pattern of erasing or placing feminism out of focus and into peripheral vision. With only a peripheral vision of salient feminist concerns, his critique of postmodern anthropology is not attentive to the latter's implicit gender politics, which also weakens postmodern anthropology's grasp of the social world, which is fundamentally gendered.

James Clifford and George Marcus's *Writing Culture* (1986) is revered as one of the sacred texts of anthropology's postmodernist turn in the United

States. In the introductory essay, Clifford claims to have excluded feminist ethnographic analysis from his anthology because feminists have supposedly failed to theorize much about ethnographies as texts, and when they have, they have only done so on feminist grounds. This suggests that feminism's culture-bound character makes it an inappropriate basis for cross-culturally valid theorizing and experimentation. Implied here is the arrogant presumption that postmodernists are somehow less culture bound because of their appropriation of an anticolonial rhetoric and their skepticism about "the grounds of . . . authority, assumption, and convention" (Fischer 1986, 194; see also di Leonardo 1991, 23).

In an analysis of citation patterns, Catherine Lutz (1990) has forcefully argued and documented that for the most part women's important contributions have been and are being erased from the anthropological canon. This exclusion is not only limited to conventional, established, or bourgeois anthropology; it unfortunately also exists in the space of critical anthropology, as defined by such theorists as Ulin. Although women have been and are still being put in their marginal places outside the center of anthropological authority, those anthropologists who are non-Western, from the global South, or of color have been even more invisible (cf. Pels and Nencel 1991, 18). If we believe Ulin, there are apparently no minoritized, or Southern Hemisphere intellectual trajectories that could potentially influence the direction the anthropological project will take in the twenty-first century. In earlier work (Harrison 1988a), I have demonstrated that anthropologists concerned with global dynamics and their effects on urban phenomena have neglected to take advantage of an important literature produced decades ago by African American scholars such as W. E. B. Du Bois, Oliver Cromwell Cox, Allison Davis, and St. Clair Drake "in the periphery of American academic and intellectual life" (111). That periphery, although formed in large measure by discrimination and exclusion, has historically been a significant, innovative intellectual front for antiracist and anticolonialist struggle (114). The anthropological preoccupation with cultural differences has not stimulated many (beyond subaltern anthropologists) to consider that the anthropological project might in fact benefit from non-Western and nonwhite cultural and intellectual perspectives (see Harrison 1992).

The core of anthropological discourse has been historically constituted largely as a Western, white male domain, in which the language of objectivity and value neutrality has served to mask and obscure mechanisms of silencing the voices and subjectivities of white women and the female and male descendants of the colonially conquered people denied history and access to anthropological authority. Any prospective critical anthropology should confront and counteract the subjugation of subaltern knowledges.

The Postmodernist Turn and the Recolonization of the Ethnographic Other

Notwithstanding Ulin's and Clifford's implicit gender and racial biases, post-modernism is indeed one of the most visible contenders in anthropological debates. Postmodernism can be characterized as a general epistemological orientation influenced by poststructuralism, hermeneutics, and neo/post-Marxism. Its claim to fame rests partly upon its apparent anticolonial stance—something it certainly shares with Marxist/neo-Marxist traditions; its forthright and reflexive concern with power, authority, difference, and otherness; and its recognition of and attempt to resolve the crisis of representation in realist ethnographic writing. Perhaps its most important contribution, however, lies in the role it has played in liberating anthropology from what Victor Turner (1987) described as its dysfunctional legacy of positivism. The modernist/positivist anthropological canon legitimated the authority of the outsider Western researcher in the study of non-Western societies. According to the received model of science, knowledge production must occur under conditions of unbiased objectivity outside the realm of values and politics. The observer/self/subject is disconnected from the social processes that condition the observed object of study, the ethnographic other. The ethnographer who adheres to reliability/validity prescriptions becomes omniscient and able to make truth claims based on "correct" interpretations of data (Wilson 1988, 46).

In view of the historic fact that the great masters of ethnography (e.g., Bronislaw Malinowski) have been Western men, the positivist posture—in effect even if not in design—has masked and authenticated the underlying logic and politics of a Eurocentric and patriarchal intellectual supremacy. Overwhelmingly, Western women and peoples of color—both male and female—have been distanced from the center of intellectual legitimacy in which the authority to theorize and explain the universal and the particular is conferred. The ideological underpinning of this phenomenon is that cultural, epistemological, and theoretical perspectives outside the Euro- and androcentric canon have been evaluated as less objective, less universal, and less scientific.

Relating this logic to the location black women have in the structure of Western intellectual production, Barbara Johnson (1987) notes that white men are authorized to make statements of universality; white women, statements of complementarity (indicating their ambiguous relationship to the seat of power); black men are permitted to make statements of the other—oppositional statements whose meanings are still dependent on their relationship to the canon; *and black women "must do with what's left"* (quoted in Wallace 1990, 216; emphasis mine). Consequently, black women are forced to operate as the other of the other, but in that restricted space they often manage to make something meaningful out of nothing.

Renato Rosaldo argues that the received positivist notion that objectivity depends on cultural distance between the observer and the observed is fallacious, because "social analysis can be done—differently, but quite validly—either from up close or from a distance" (1989, 188). The traditional cultural-distance criterion, however, has actually been compromised by an unspoken double standard. The cultural-gap prescription has only applied to Westerners. Delmos Jones (1970) pointed out that small numbers of natives have long been recruited to conduct fieldwork in their own or in similar societies, indicating that the native's ability to collect valuable and otherwise inaccessible data has been acknowledged. The prospect of an African or Melanesian studying Anglo-Americans or Europeans, however, would make Malinowski and maybe even Franz Boas roll over in their graves. Both Jones and Christine Obbo (1990) attest to the tendency for native ethnographers to be treated as fieldwork assistants or as glorified key informants—subordinates not expected to develop theories and generalizations, an area in which rules regarding objectivity and cultural distance have been more consistently applied.

Writing of her own experience, Obbo recounts how several Western colleagues have read her field notes with the objective of appropriating them (1990). At the Makerere Institute of Social Research in Uganda, where she was initially trained, it was once customary for foreign anthropologists—who spoke little or none of the local language—to use Africans, many with limited knowledge of English, as assistants and translators. The distortions that resulted from data collected in this manner prompted "shrewd investigators" to seek out "local colleagues who would unwittingly play the role of unpaid research assistant" by being brain picked during the Institute's tea hours or, worse, by having his or her field notes read—with or without permission (Obbo 1990, 295). In one of Obbo's own experiences, a foreign colleague who shared her research interest in economic activities in Kampala's low-income neighborhoods boldly went into her office and read her field notes without her prior knowledge. One week later at an international conference, Obbo witnessed the man present a paper that plagiarized her field notes (296).

In another incident, a foreign woman anthropologist who was a guest in Obbo's home arrogantly demanded access to her African colleague's data. One evening when her host went out for dinner, the guest remained in the house to search—without any success—for the data. Upon Obbo's return, the woman had the audacity to admit she could not find the field notes despite an intensive search. Experiences such as these—as well as a few involving some work on suburban whites in the United States—convinced Obbo that Western anthropologists are, even today, vulnerable to the barely conscious presupposition that Westerners are "better at analyzing data than their counterparts from developing countries" (297).

Although the postmodernist turn has certainly destabilized positivism, its epistemic skepticism, relativism, explanatory nihilism, theoretical agnosticism, and sense of political impotence present troubling problems (West 1991, xxii). A number of critics argue that postmodernism represents an intellectual response largely by Western white males to challenges to Western hegemony and white supremacy in a world marked by the ascendance of postcolonial nationalisms, Japanese capitalism, and feminism (West 1988, 27). There are feminists who go so far as to assert that postmodernism is "fundamentally a sexist response that attempts to preserve the legitimacy of androcentric claims in the face of contrary evidence" (Mascias-Lees, Sharpe, and Cohen 1989, 15). They point out that postmodernist literary experiments that undermine the ontological status of the subject have become popular just when women and Third World theorists are challenging the universality and hegemony of received traditions and thereby asserting their subjectivities. The correlation between postmodernism—which is not a monolith—and sexism/patriarchy, however, is not absolute nor universal. In the postmodernist postcolonial feminism of artist and analyst Trinh Minh-ha, the female subject is destabilized, but not according to a relativist assumption of an equality of positioning for all subjects. In Trinh's view, owing to women's "social, sexual and symbolic experiences," they are characteristically subjects in the making and subjects on trial (1989, 102). The destabilized female subject has important sociopolitical implications in that a "r-evolution of subjects" is required for a "social-political r-evolution . . . in order to shatter the social codes . . . reject everything . . . definite, structured, loaded with meaning, in the existing state of society" (102). It appears that for Trinh, the destabilized r-evolutionizing subject is "situated" (Haraway 1991; Collins 1991) in a field of critical locations marked by an inequality of positioning. This view is unlike a relativist approach that would assume an equality of positioning and, thus, deny the differential sociopolitical stakes and responsibilities invested in multiple knowledge-engendering locations (Haraway 1991, 191).

Although postmodernist experiments in ethnographic writing highlight difference, otherness, power, and authority, issues that were originally fore-grounded by Third World and feminist thinkers, many of these experiments inadvertently reinscribe neocolonial domination, wherein the other is ob-jectified and appropriated. Textual strategies and literary techniques tend to privilege the force of rhetoric over substantive concern with concrete institutional relations of power (di Leonardo 1989; Jordan 1991.). Authority dispersal is conceived largely in terms of dialogic and polyphonic narratives rather than as a substantive means of empowering informants by creating new forms of ethnographic relationships—for example, concrete collabora-tions involving coauthorship and coeditorship and leveling the ethnographic terrain by imparting research and writing skills to informants so that they can become cosubjects (Jordan 1991, 1992). Ethnographers as authors employ the power of poetic license to write texts that orchestrate "a cacophony of voices," but these texts tend to belie the structured inequality of social con-texts in which "all 'genres, texts, and voices' are *not* created equal" (Polier and Roseberry 1989, 251–52).

There is also a disturbing absence of attention in the poetic discourse on power to racism and class inequality.[8] Renato Rosaldo (1989) is one of the few analysts in the ethnography as narrative discourse who attempts to come to terms with the reality of racism for blacks and Latinos and with the implications of subaltern subjectivity for anthropological analysis. He boldly turns anthropology on its head when he argues that "the dominated usually understand the dominant better than the reverse. In coping with their daily lives, they simply must" (189).

The relative absence of interest in the ethnographies, creative literature, and literary criticism produced by blacks and other peoples of color is un-derscored by bell hooks, a black feminist theorist and cultural critic, who argues that the approach that Clifford articulates "in no way challenges the assumption that the image/identity of the ethnographer is white and male" (hooks 1990, 126). She states that:

As a script, [Clifford and Marcus's *Writing Culture's*] cover does not present any radical challenge to past constructions. It blatantly calls attention to two ideas that are quite fresh in the racist imagination: the notion of the white male as writer/authority . . . and the idea of the passive brown/black man who is doing nothing, merely looking on. . . . Significantly, we cannot discuss the brown female gaze because her look is veiled by the graphics of the cover, a black line drawn across her face. Why does this cover doubly annihilate the value of brown female gaze, first by the choice of picture where the dark woman is in the shadows, and secondly by a demarcating line? . . . [W]hat politics of representation are enacted by these images[?] Is it possible that an image, a cover can undermine radical writing—can reinscribe the colonizing anthropology/ethnography that is vigilantly critiqued in *Writing Culture*? (1990, 127)[9]

Postmodernism tends to privilege poetics over politics (Fabian 1983), and what politics it has is that of academia and not that of the world at large (Jordan 1991; Rabinow 1985; Polier and Roseberry 1989). A genuinely critical and radical anthropology must "challenge exploitative and hegemonic social practices and social formations" (Ulin 1991, 81), and the deployment of in-novative narrative strategies alone cannot do this. Nonetheless, provided they are appropriately politically grounded and conceptually framed, textual and rhetorical techniques can play an important part in intellectually challenging oppressive structural power.

Anthropology, Fiction, and Unequal Relations of Intellectual Production

Although Zora Neale Hurston (1935 [1978]), John Gwaltney (1980), Betty Lou Valentine (1978), and others whose ethnographic work has deconstructed the conventional wisdom of ethnographic practice are virtually absent from anthropology's postmodernist discourse, it is more surprising that contem-porary fiction writers who have attained much more visibility are also absent from a discourse that blurs genres and disciplinary boundaries, draws upon literary theory and techniques, and begins from the premise that ethnograph-ic texts are characteristically partial and therefore fictive. Michael Fischer is one of the few exceptions to this trend, in that he has directed some attention to ethnic literary genres, specifically autobiography and autobiographical fiction. For him, postmodernism "is . . . the general condition of multicul-tural life demanding new forms of inventiveness and subtlety from a fully reflexive ethnography" (Clifford 1986, 23). He looks to ethnic autobiography for insights into the way culture operates in "pluralist, post-industrial, late 20th Century society" (Fischer 1986, 195). He believes that this genre, both its form and content, can potentially revitalize and refashion ethnography as a mode of cultural criticism. He states that "the ability of [these] texts . . . to deliver cultural criticism without the stereotypic distortions that traditional cross-cultural categorizations have often produced is an important model for ethnography" (201–2).

I take Fischer's approach one step further to claim that ethnic/minority fiction—not just autobiography—is a salient genre that more ethnographic writers should explore because it represents a rich mode of *writing the cul-*

tures, cultural politics, and history of our multicultural world structured in
relations of dominance and colored by the contradictory dynamics of resistance. I am particularly interested in what black women writers such as
Alice Walker have written from the vantage point of gendered and racialized experience and their particular predicament and crisis as black female
cultural workers struggling against the grain of exploitative objectification
and alienation from the means of intellectual production. Chandra Talpade
Mohanty (1991a, x) asserts, as many others (e.g., Harrison 1991) have, that
"questions of race, class, sexuality, colonialism, and imperialism are . . . constitutive of knowledge production in a number of disciplines (not merely
ghettoized in marginal fields)." If racial, gender, and class inequalities are
indeed at the heart of the postmodern/postcolonial experience, then certainly
the subaltern should have something significant to contribute to the social
analysis of the postmodern era.

Whatever postmodernism's paradoxes and flaws, its intertextual and
blurred genres approach can be constructive, as Fischer's discussion reveals.
This framework permits us to view anthropological inquiry as an interrelated
and mutually corresponding component of a much larger and inclusive corpus of intellectual enterprises. In this context, we can examine black women's
fiction and consider how it relates to and resonates with anthropological
discourse.

Black feminist cultural critic Michelle Wallace and others have noted that
black women's most prolific, articulate, and concentrated intellectual production is found in creative endeavors, fiction being key among them. Black
women have "concealed their best articulations of self under the cloak of
fiction" (Wallace 1990, 182). Fiction, it appears, has served as a sanctuary, a
refuge, offering greater freedom for the imagination and for critical explorations of the cultural, psychological, and historical dilemmas of the black
and human experience. In some respects, the concealed, coded articulations
that fiction allows seem to be opaque interreferences and challenges to social
science's exclusive and monopolistic claims to the verification of social/cul-
tural knowledge and truth. The ideology of science as Eurocentrically and
androcentrically defined objectivity has to a considerable extent denied black
women the legitimacy to make reliable truth claims that white males can
replicate. What black women know to be their experience of social reality is
reduced to subjective belief or fantasy, overreactive emotionalism, "chip-on-
her-shoulder" propaganda, and feelings—often neurotic. As Trinh Minh-ha
(1989) points out, the canon elevates masculinist thinking and writing to
the realm of the universal, objective, rational, logical, and intelligible. The
nativization of Third World women and the construction of anthropology

as a scientific conversation of man with man lead to an oppressive situation wherein women, particularly women of color, by ideological definition and cultural construction, are at a definite disadvantage in authorized intellectual productivity (6, 7). In this context, fiction writing has freed black women from the burden of pressures to write like (white) men and from epistemological and methodological strictures that suppress, subjugate, and colonize their blackness and femalenesss, disfiguring them into raceless and desexualized distortions of self. *Fiction encodes truth claims—and alternative modes of theorizing*—in a rhetoric of imagination that accommodates and entertains the imaginable. Fiction resists, protests, and works against the grain of those constructs of validity and reliability that in practice as well as in ideological representation privilege elitist, white male representations and explanations of the world.

Lest I erroneously imply that literary production is free from racial and gender domination, let me qualify my argument by indicating that the literary milieu is also stratified and segmented to black women's disadvantage. The visibility of only a chosen few—however deserving they are—obscures the reality for the majority of black women writers. Michelle Wallace and bell hooks view the visibility of Alice Walker, Toni Morrison, Gloria Naylor, and a few others as a "symbolic substitute for substantive black female economic and political power" (Wallace 1990, 215). hooks argues that much of the current interest in black women's writing emanates from consumer capitalism's "spirit of commodity fadism," which promotes the commodification of blackness, at least its most stylish, creative aspects (hooks 1990, 5, 7, 8). hooks claims that this trend is a strategy of colonization in a postmodern society in which social identity is formed through mass-mediated image control (8).

Black women writers must struggle against forces that commodify their creative labor in order "to speak [critically and oppositionally] from the still radically unspeakable position of 'the Other'" (Wallace 1990, 227). For the most part, they are denied the power and authority to classify, interpret, and analyze as well as to critically assess the nature of classification, interpretation, and analysis.[10] This denial is most evident in black women's relative absence from the ranks of literary criticism. It is not accidental that the most prominent critic of Afro-American literature—black women's creative writing included—is a black man, Henry Louis Gates. Wallace points out that black women's muted voices in literary criticism is part of a general phenomenon in academic knowledge production that participates in a broader hegemonic scheme—"a scheme in which black women . . . are systematically denied the most visible forms of discursive and intellectual subjectivity" (215).

The extent to which black females may internalize this hegemonic violation of their subjectivity is illuminated in Jacqueline Jones Royster's analysis of students' response to a survey she administered as director of a writing program at Spelman College, a historically black women's institution (Royster 1990). She asked a sample of successful students who were writing interns two questions: first, "Do you consider yourself to be a writer?" and second, "Do you consider yourself to be a scholar or intellectual?" The results indicated that although the "interns were rather comfortable in claiming themselves as writers and as competent and capable people who expect to be successful . . . they were not so eager to claim and name themselves . . . scholars [or] intellectual beings" (1). The students accepted a false binary opposition between creativity and intellect and associated their best abilities and prospects with the former.[11] Royster questions the "sociocultural influences [that] have shaped African-American women to the extent that academically successful students would readily claim authority as learners and as creative writers, but would be more reluctant to claim a comparable authority as scholars or intellectuals" (4). She goes on to ask, "What is the genesis of authority? What are pathways to empowerment?" (4).

For black women to engage in creative writing is perhaps less threatening than for them to theorize about literature, society, and the world in more direct recognizable ways. In a hegemonic scheme that attributes to blackness and to femaleness the natural ability to create and to be aesthetically expressive, and that elevates a masculinist science to the most privileged and rewarded echelons, writing fiction is an acceptable behavior for a token few black women. According to the popular imagination, black women are more likely to be able to sing, dance, perform, entertain, and stimulate imagination and sensibilities than their white counterparts (who—if they are to be successful in the postmodernist crossover popular culture—must model their aesthetic practice after quintessential black performers). The sad reality is that if a black woman cannot sing, dance, or entertain in some fashion, she has very few outlets and critical mass bases of support for publicly expressing her humanity. In this context, for black writers and other artists to work effectively against the grain, they must convert the narrow spaces within hegemonic cracks into places where dissent and rebellion can take root and grow.

The overwhelming concentration of black women in aesthetic and commercial entertainment arenas and their underrepresentation in literary criticism and the social sciences are then consequences of a racist/sexist/classist structure of opportunity and domination. This structure permits black women to write novels but makes it difficult for them to engage in literary criticism. It celebrates the talents of a token few but renders invisible the creativity of the mass. With respect to anthropology, this hegemonic structure accommodates limited black participation in rank-and-file ethnographic production—particularly as glorified field assistants "on the cheap" (Obbo 1990, 291; Jones 1970)—but limits positive, validating sanctions for their formulating cross-culturally testable explanations of data. When radical black women write fiction or ethnography, they do so against the grain of a hegemony that peripheralizes them yet appropriates the value of their creative and critical productivity.

Alice Walker as Anthropology's Interlocutor

The experimental moment permeating anthropology can be constructive and indeed liberating, depending on how it is used and whether it is grounded in responsible worldly praxis. I suggest that we look to some of black women's fiction for insights into how writing culture can be both experimental and potentially liberating. I emphasize the word *some,* because black women's fiction is not automatically subversive or counterhegemonic. As Michelle Wallace admits, black women's literature "alternately conspires with and rebels against . . . current cultural and political arrangements" (1990, 250).

Alice Walker is readily identified with feminism/womanism, civil rights, and other social justice struggles. Moreover, she is one of the token few black women who have enjoyed the esteem of the literati. I see Alice Walker as one of anthropology's less visible interlocutors. This relationship with the discipline emerged most clearly at the point in her career when she searched for and rediscovered Zora Neale Hurston for herself and for the world of readers and thinkers. Walker, along with Robert Hemenway (1977), is probably most responsible for revitalizing interest in the enigmatic and forgotten Hurston. That revitalization, however, has affected and involved literary scholars more than it has anthropologists. Gwendolyn Mikell (1982, 1983, 1989b) is one of the few anthropologists who has thoughtfully examined Hurston as one who was just as much an anthropologist as she was a novelist, as one whose fiction was grounded in a contextual, participatory ethnographic subjectivity, which during her lifetime had no comfortable home in U.S. anthropology.[12] This professional homelessness is reflected in Hurston's relationship with Columbia, where during the graduate phase of her studies the faculty "were either ambivalent about her work, hostile to her methodology and research techniques, or scandalized by the depth of her participation in cultural practices" (Mikell 1999, 64).

For Walker, Hurston represents a cultural ancestress, who, along with Billie Holiday and Bessie Smith, "form[s] a sort of unholy trinity" (Walker 1983, 91).

Walker first "became aware of [her] need of" Hurston's work when she "was writing a story that required accurate material on [V]oodoo practices among rural Southern blacks of the thirties" (83).[13] She was sorely disappointed and insulted by the literature written by racist anthropologists and folklorists of the period, so she searched until she came upon *Mules and Men* (1935 [1978]). When she and her rural Southern relatives read and talked about the tales, Hurston reported, Walker learned from her family's reaction that the material Hurston had collected was valid. This was the beginning of her special relationship with Hurston—and obliquely with anthropology.

The interrelationship between the use of historical and anthropological literatures as sources for facts and ideas, and the writing of culture in fictive rhetoric, is salient in Walker's work, which strongly resonates with discourses in a number of scholarly disciplines, particularly anthropology. With her ancestor's blessings, Walker wrote fiction that is ethnographic and ethnohistorical, even if not as deliberately or as self-consciously as Hurston's was.[14] Whereas Clifford and others claim that ethnography is fiction, I, then, propose the idea that Alice Walker's fiction, as was that produced by Hurston, is ethnography. This is evident if one reads her work to discern interreferences to issues and concerns in anthropological discourse. An intertextual reading of Walker's short stories and novels, especially *The Temple of My Familiar* (1989), reveals how Walker's creative inscription of culture, politics, and history—and her cultural critique of the colonial/postcolonial world system—can be seen to be embedded within a larger interdisciplinary discourse to which anthropologists contribute. As in the case of the ethnic autobiographies that Fischer examines, Walker's literary production "parallels, mirrors, and exemplifies contemporary theories of textuality, of knowledge, and of culture" (Fischer 1986, 230). Her writing is consistent with postmodernist ethnographic experiments in its deployment of a number of techniques. Key among them are bifocality or reciprocity of perspectives (i.e., seeing others against a background of ourselves and ourselves against a background of others), the juxtapositioning of multiple realities, interlinguistic play (e.g., moving from standard English to dialect [code switching] to Spanish and back to English), comparison through families of resemblance, and the foregrounding of dialogue and discourse.

In brief, Walker's *The Temple of My Familiar* is an intricate story of several people's stories of past and present experiences in love and friendship relationships, in families, and in precolonial, colonial, and postcolonial contexts of gender, race, and class oppressions. The diverse stories converge in the lives of two San Francisco couples, one African American and the other mixed Latino and African American. These couples are multiply connected through work (at a college or university), an extramarital affair, a masseuse-client relationship, and their common ties to a wealthy, globe-traveling Anglo-American woman. As presented, the various personal dilemmas and conflicts that the two couples (and their relatives and friends) experience are embedded in and indeed implicate the wider status quo in both national and international contexts. The characters' many narratives and conversations open windows on a historically dynamic world marked by dramatic differences as well as basic commonalities.

The novel's main characters are Carlotta, a Latin American immigrant and women's studies professor; her mother, Zedé, a feather goods seamstress and former schoolteacher who escaped political persecution in Latin America; Carlotta's husband, Arveyda, a popular African American singer and musician with the power of spiritual healing; Suwelo, a black history professor who inherits his dead Great-Uncle Rafe's house in Baltimore and struggles over his relationships with women; Mr. Hal, Uncle Rafe's best friend and a talented painter with the gift of delivering his wife's babies; Miss Lissie, Mr. Hal's wife, who was also a common-law wife to Uncle Rafe, with whom she, Hal, and their daughter Lulu shared a home; Fanny, Suwelo's wife/ex-wife, a former literature professor and college administrator, who must come to terms with her kinship to Africa and her relationship to Suwelo—in and out of marriage; Olivia, Fanny's mother, a nurse and lecturer on African affairs who came of age in a family of black American missionaries in Africa; Ola/Dahvid, Fanny's father, former freedom fighter and political prisoner, prominent playwright, and minister of culture in a postcolonial African nation with a white-settler colonial past; Nzingha, Ola's African daughter and Fanny's half-sister, who struggles to assert her womanhood and find a new place in a male-dominated postcolonial society; and Mary Ann/Mary Jane, a committed radical from a rich Anglo-American family, Ola's wife of convenience (for the sake of her immigration status), and art school founder and director, who in her youth helped Zedé and Carlotta find refuge in the United States and in her mature years committed herself to the people of postcolonial Africa.

Through the intersecting and at times parallel experiences and memories of these characters—as well as of their more extended networks of relatives and friends—the novel moves the reader back and forth across a long-distance itinerary linking urban and suburban neighborhoods, universities, museums, and massage parlors in San Francisco, Baltimore, and London with mountain villages, export-crop plantations, and political prisons in Latin America and all of these with government ministries, art schools, grassroots theaters, and rural villages in postcolonial Africa. All of the personalities, situations, and conflicts in Walker's novel are complex and multidimensional. The predicaments related to, for example, love triangles—and rectangles (Carlotta, Arveyda, and Zedé; Carlotta, Suwelo, Fanny, and Arveyda; and Hal, Lissie, and Rafe)—and to, as another example, exile (in the cases of Zedé, Mary Ann/Mary Jane, and M'Sukta, a human museum exhibit) provide poignant points of entry into and shed light on wider fields of knowledge, power, and possibility.

Walker's novel is a world cultural history from a transnational feminist, or womanist, perspective. As feminist/womanist herstory, the novel de-essentializes gender as well as race and class. Like the work of cultural critics and theorists bell hooks and Michelle Wallace as well as the anthropological analyses of Christine Obbo (1980), Filomina Chioma Steady (1981), Ifi Amadiume (1987), Johnnetta Cole (1986), Patricia Zavella (1991a), and Sandra Morgen (1988), *The Temple of My Familiar* challenges the universalization of Western, middle-class women's experience by exploring cultural, racial, class, and national differences while pointing to possibilities for clearing a common ground. The book adumbrates, or foreshadows, directions for feminist analysts willing to cross the threshold of the third phase that Henrietta Moore discusses in her *Feminism and Anthropology* (1988). This novel should be seen as an integral part of the broader literature on the politics of representing gender, race, and culture history. The monolithic Third World victims reified "under Western feminist eyes" (Mohanty 1991b) are nowhere to be found in Walker's narrative. In this respect, her understanding of women's multidimensional experiences concurs with those advanced by Mohanty (1991a, 1991b) and Amadiume (1987), whose analyses are anchored in a critique of Western feminist constructions of the female other.

In *Temple,* Walker writes an enabling history geared toward informing present and future struggles for the full humanization of men and women around the world. The novel is a gender- and race-sensitive complement to and friendly critique of ungendered texts such as Eric Wolf's *Europe and the People without History* (1982).[15] Despite Taussig's (1989) caustic and, in my view, not completely convincing criticism of Wolf's concern with commodities rather than with commodity fetishism, Wolf's anthropological history is a watershed that expands the stage and action in world history to include the diverse peoples anthropologists have traditionally studied. Although Wolf sets new standards for the study of historicized political economy and the world system, his contribution does not give visibility to women's historical agency. His vision and approach are necessary but insufficient for a feminist project in culture history—a project that privileges the role of consciousness and experience in resistance and contestation.

The works that Walker challenges most forcefully are those blatantly racist and sexist Eurocentric histories that objectify or render invisible the majority of the world's peoples, both male and female. In Walker's fictive history of the world and of humanity, she foregrounds the agency of the colonized (especially the women) and of counterhegemonic Western women. She amplifies agency by focusing sequences of events and extended dialogues around the life stories and memories of several individuals and their kin and friendship networks. These parallel networks intersect at various points in historic time and extend across four continents—North and South America, Africa, and Europe—and eventually converge in the ethnohistorical present of contemporary northern California.

Walker explores the interrelationship among history, myth, and "the painful dream world of memory" as she weaves together myths, legends, magical realist accounts, and documentable historical reconstructions in her depiction of African, African American, (U.S.) Latino, and Latin American experiences and dilemmas. In Walker's writing, myth is not history's binary opposite. For the great masters of social anthropology (key among them Malinowski and Alfred Radcliffe-Brown), history was absent and unknowable among so-called primitive others, whose mythical minds were functions of social structures fossilized in an ahistoric present. In *Temple,* however, myth provides an idiom and narrative form for encoding queries, recollections, and constructions of the distant and not-so-distant past. Suwelo, Fanny, Carlotta, and Arveyda come to resolve their personal and marital crises collectively through the reconciliation between, on one hand, the formal knowledge that they as historians, literary scholars, and artists have attained from both within and without "academic plantations" and, on the other hand, the experiential, mythical, magical narratives their elders—Miss Lissie, Mr. Hal, and Zedé—transmit to them as counsel. The younger generation's rediscovery and reclaiming of the suppressed folk knowledge of human origins, the subjugation of female humanity and deities, and the psychological and cultural consequences of colonial and postcolonial oppression help steer them along a growth-inducing route to more decolonized and gender-egalitarian consciousness and lifeways.

Walker foregrounds and privileges black/brown intellectual discourse in her reconstruction of history; her critique of postcolonial states and their sexist, class-biased, and too often militarized strategies of national development; and her excavations of the deeply implanted distortions and discontinuities in the psychic and sociocultural experiences of both the oppressed and the oppressive in unjust social orders of both the former First and Third Worlds. Black and brown characters whose subjectivities had been thwarted and warped in hegemonic situations and contexts collectively come to voice by talking with each other, sharing painful memories of their past experiences, and revealing and coming to terms with multiple and sometimes clashing facets of self. This coming to voice, however, is not predicated upon the exclusion, erasure, or negation of critical Western discourse. The intellectual subjectivity of the minoritized and the global South is depicted as a dialogic encounter between formal knowledge producers and those articulate and expert in folk wisdom. Intellect and knowledge, then, are not elitist and exclusive; they are based on a collective, historicized consciousness in which the experience and wisdom of the folk can invoke authority in negotiating the resolutions that the younger, formally trained intellectuals make in their thinking and in their lives. Walker's depiction is compatible with Helán Page's analysis (1988), in which she demonstrates that subaltern communities can in fact exert authority and influence outcomes in dialogic negotiations of interpretations and meaning. Subaltern authority notwithstanding, Walker's novel highlights and accentuates the ongoing crisis of being a black or brown intellectual. Fanny, Nzingha, Ola, Suwelo, and Carlotta grapple with, talk extensively about, and seek to understand the dilemmas stemming from living under conditions of racist and sexist domination. As professional intellectuals, they struggle to come to terms with their formal education as a means of conquest that they must resist and overcome. This dilemma is most acute in Nzingha's painful experience. As a small child, she was taken away from her illiterate mother, who had fought in the armed struggle that won the country its liberation but subsequently had no respected place in postcolonial society. At boarding school and later at university in France, Nzingha underwent an enculturation that alienated her from her mother and people. This disjuncture that schooling created between Nzingha and her mother eventually resulted in the severance of their tie, leaving Nzingha in a painfully liminal position, for the negation of her mother and all she symbolized was not at all offset by a welcoming assimilation into the Western culture on which her education was based. After recounting the trials and tribulations of her youth, Nzingha shares this lament with her sister Fanny: "being educated by people who despise you is also conquest" (Walker 1989, 265). In resistance, however, Nzingha, like her father, invests her educational capital in cultural projects designed to raise popular consciousness and to mobilize social forces for political and economic democratization.

Fanny, Suwelo, and Carlotta all eventually decide to leave academia for more creative vocations in music, playwriting, massage, and carpentry, in which they find greater peace and freedom. This fictive solution to the crisis of the black/brown intellectual is tantamount to a strong indictment against

U.S. academia at a juncture when the conservative political backlash against multicultural and feminist subjectivities is on the rise.

Through her characters' struggles for self-knowledge, Walker illuminates the dynamic, nonessentialist, and culturally constructed nature of social identity. She, like the authors of autobiography that Fischer (1986) examines, elucidates how each generation reinvents and reinterprets race, ethnicity, gender, and class. These reconstructions are based on a process of interreference between two or more cultural traditions (cf. Fischer 1986), and they are also anchored in critiques of past and present "rhetorics [and ideologies] of domination" (Fischer 1986, 198). The sense that social identity and self-knowledge emerge from the cross-fertilization and conflicts within cultural/class borderlands is consistent with Renato Rosaldo's remark that borders have the potential of "opening new forms of human understanding" (1989, 216). He goes on to comment that "[a]ll of us [not just the subaltern] inhabit an interdependent late-twentieth century world marked by borrowing and lending across porous national and cultural boundaries that are saturated with inequality, power, and domination" (217).

The multidimensional self or the multiplicity of selves is a recurrent theme in Walker's novel. This, combined with her concern with the ambiguity of boundaries, is most powerfully symbolized through the character of Miss Lissie, an elderly black woman who shares her memory of her innumerable reincarnated lives that span both evolutionary and historic time. Miss Lissie, having been—among other things—both male and female, and both black and white in past lives, is the metaphoric embodiment of plural and collective human experiences. Furthermore, her insight into the reification of otherness is also informed by her past life as a lion at the evolutionary juncture when humans estranged their animal familiars. She recalls that in the earliest and most peaceful days of human existence, familiars were closely associated with women and children, who interacted with animals in much the same way they interacted with other people. Eventually, men forced familiars away from women's fires. This antagonistic act occurred around the time that the social foundations were laid for male domination and the carnivorous consumption patterns associated with hunting. Human society was, hence, re-created in the interests of power-hungry men, who subjugated women and killed and ate their former familiars.

The influence of multidimensional selves on racial and ethnic identity is also illuminated by Walker's techniques of bifocality and comparison through families of resemblance (cf. Fischer 1986, 201). Zedé and her daughter Carlotta, refugees from a repressive Latin American republic, see images of themselves in Arveyda, the African American singer/musician who marries

Carlotta. Arveyda's combined Indian-Chinese-African features and kinky hair remind Zedé of her mate, a Latin American Indio with traces of African ancestry. Fanny, an African American borne of a black missionary and an African freedom fighter and playwright, is described as having an Apache-like nose. Even her native African half-sister, Nzingha, has this nose, at once symbolizing political-economic parallels between Native Americans and native Africans in settler colonialism and the fallacy of notions of racial purity. Interethnic fusions and similarities are mentioned throughout the novel. They reflect Walker's human-centered multiracialist sense that "when [she] look[s] at people in Iran and Cuba, they look like kin folk" (Fischer 1986, 213). This view effects a penetrating critique of the very concept and historically constituted realities of "race," which severely constrain enactments of alternative selves (213).[16]

Walker's provocative treatment of marriage and family illuminates the tension between conjugality and blood and fictive-blood relationships (see Sudarkasa 1988). She exposes the severe limitations of forms of marriage constrained by patriarchal values and explores alternative arrangements such as polyandry (e.g., Miss Lissie, Mr. Hal, and Suwelo's Uncle Rafe) and extended marriages in which co-couples form fictive familial units. Although such arrangements are indeed controversial, especially at a time when monogamy is advanced as a defense against the spread of HIV/AIDS, Walker's treatment of marriage and kinship resonates with the extensive literature on African and African American kinship that elucidates the traditional primacy of the mother-focused consanguineal core over conjugal units, which tend not to be focal points in extended-family contexts. As Niara Sudarkasa (1988) points out, the stability of extended families is not dependent on the stability or permanence of marriage. In both *The Color Purple* and *The Temple of My Familiar,* reinvented families encompass blood kin, friends, co-lovers, and co-spouses. Fanny, for instance, had two grandmothers—Mama Celie and her partner/lover Mama Shug—both of whom had had intimate relations with Celie's husband Albert. In these communalist configurations, women take the lead in establishing ties of sisterhood as an alternative to the destructive sexual rivalry that exists in situations in which clandestine polygyny and its exploitation of women prevail.

The Temple of My Familiar articulates an opaque but penetrating critique of anthropological discourses that nativize and objectify Third World women. A poignant allegory of the reification of the African woman is found in M'Sukta's plight. M'Sukta, the last survivor of her annihilated people, was taken to England, where she lived in a replica of an African village at the Museum of Natural History. She, along with the material culture, was on exhibit to demonstrate her vanished way of life and to pass on "the history of her people's ancient way of life" (Walker 1989, 233). She no longer had a home outside the colonial museum—or outside a colonizing system of anthropological data collection, analysis, and representation.

Walker contrasts this discursive system with that adumbrated, for example, by African American missionaries, who embedded ethnographic accounts in letters and reports during the late nineteenth and early twentieth centuries. In her youth, Fanny's aunt Nettie had written letters to her sister Celie about the indigenous African societies she encountered and the oppressive impact of colonialism (see *The Color Purple*). St. Clair Drake (1990, 5), in work describing the hidden contributions of Africans and diasporic blacks to early ethnography, noted that the ethnographic descriptions that black missionaries wrote were generally more sympathetic and less susceptible to the ethnocentric and racist biases found in the standard missionary and travelogue ethnography of that time. The latter ethnographies provided evidence for armchair ethnology, however, whereas the former have virtually been forgotten. Interestingly, "by the time World War I ended," black missionaries, whose antiracist and anticolonial accounts can possibly be revisited "in the files of the national Baptist conventions and the two African Methodist Episcopal Churches" (Drake 1990, 5), "were suspected of being a subversive influence and attempts were made to reduce their numbers" (5). Drake points out that "[t]his was the same period when the first large foundation grants were made for a study of various African peoples using the techniques and theoretical frameworks of the infant field 'functional anthropology'. Needless to say, no Black graduate students were sent out by the British who administered these American donations nor did the International African Institute—also American subsidized—offer an opportunity to any Blacks from the West Indies or the U.S.A. to participate in its research. Africans were extensively used, but as 'informants'" (5).

Walker's critique of anthropology is one predicated on a keen awareness that alternative and oppositional perspectives and voices exist both within and outside the discipline's boundaries. After all, she is more than aware of Hurston's precarious place within professional anthropology and of her decision to write against the grain with the aid of instruments of creative writing.

Interestingly, compared with *The Color Purple,* to which it can be seen as a sequel, *Temple* has not stimulated considerable debate or discourse. Perhaps many people do not know exactly what to say about the book, whose content extends beyond the fictive turf black women writers have traditionally been allowed to control. Walker, I think, has defiantly gotten out of the place reserved for writers like her. She has moved beyond the internal dynamics and conflicts within Southern black life to the whole wide world and some of its most pressing contradictions—racial, sexual, class related, political economic, environmental, and intellectual.

Hers is a holistic fiction that reflects her vision of a global yet human-centered set of interlocking experiences. Her creative work boldly envisions and interprets. The responsibility for subjecting her truth claims to proof or disproof lies not in her literary project but in those discursive/intellectual realms in which testing, falsification, and explanation are characteristically expected, demanded, and undertaken. These latter realms, however, which include, of course, the social sciences, operate in relations of complementarity and cross-fertilization with the arts and humanities. Alice Walker's provocative work does not and should not be expected to prove anything. Nonetheless, empirical evidence for grounding and providing meaningful cultural contexts and interpretation for much of her creative license can be found within the wider intertextual and interdisciplinary discourse within which her writing is embedded.

Conclusion: Subaltern Voices "Talking Back"

Let me reiterate that Alice Walker is only one of the most visible participants in a wider, more inclusive domain of subaltern intellectual production. Within this domain, which is largely peripheral to established scholarly canons, writing cultural politics of difference and locating it in wider contexts of history and power are salient. Subaltern intellectual production is not and should not be confined to creative writing, and I am not advocating that anthropology reconstruct itself as (subaltern) fiction. As the most interdisciplinary of all the social sciences, however, anthropology can benefit from combining the strengths of the current "experimental moment" (Marcus and Fischer 1986) with those derived from the more conventional wisdom that has permitted anthropology, particularly its multiple critical expressions, to contribute to our understanding of societies and cultures all over the world. When anthropologists undertake imaginative literary experiments, the latter should be grounded in worldly praxis.

At this experimental moment in U.S. anthropology's trajectory, the creative and theoretical insights and the sociopolitical sensibilities of the subaltern should not be erased. The postmodernist "fetishizing of [textual and rhetorical] form" (Clifford 1986, 21) and sharply separating it from intellectual content may be responsible in part for the near failure to engage the many substantive analyses and critiques that subaltern anthropologists have produced. Nonetheless, attempting, as some may be inclined, to excuse this exclusion or erasure with the claim that "groups long excluded from positions of institutional power, like women or people of color, have less concrete freedom to indulge in textual experimentation" (Clifford 1986, 21) and, therefore, are more likely to confront issues of data content in "the anthropological archive" (21) is a smokescreen obscuring the heterogeneity of theoretical perspectives, methodological approaches, and textual strategies that people of color and white women have actually contributed to anthropological knowledge.[17] If form is to be prioritized, then how can the virtual invisibility of Hurston (1935 [1978]), Gwaltney (1980), and interlocutors like Walker be justified? Are not the current textual experiments that Clifford valorizes attempts to resolve a crisis in ethnographic writing, analysis, and theorizing that emerged at least in part from the content of debates around the culturally, racially, and sexually biased content of the anthropology born of colonialism/imperialism? The artificial separation of form and content is contestable, as even Clifford admits. He and his colleagues must be held accountable for the implications and consequences of this, however, especially when they risk reproducing reinvented and camouflaged forms of the very relations of domination that have historically exploited the majority of humanity as well as violated and endangered its earthly habitat. This is the context within which subaltern voices—those of informants and trained intellectuals—have been rendered mute or appropriated as aesthetic and academic commodities in ethnographic representation and writing. Anthropology is at an important crossroads. In the process of redefining the critical project(s) and of reconstituting anthropological authority, we must offset the persistent pattern of relegating the work of women and that of women of color in particular to the discipline's periphery.

Acknowledgments

I would like to acknowledge a number of persons whose encouragement and constructive comments were beneficial to me in the writing and rewriting of this chapter: Ruth Behar, Deborah Gordon, Catherine Lutz, Lucy Freibert, Estella Conwill Majozo, Deborah D'Amico, Anne Francis Okongwu, Yvonne Jones, Angela Gilliam, A. Lynn Bolles, Pem Buck, and the reviewers for the version published in *Critique of Anthropology* (vol. 13, no. 4, 1993). As usual, I am deeply indebted to William L. Conwill for patiently listening to my reading of the earliest draft and subsequently offering helpful suggestions.

5. Probing the Legacy of Empire

Reflexive Notes on Caribbeanist
Gordon K. Lewis

Reading Lewis Anthropologically

In "The Making of a Caribbeanist," a 1983 working paper, the late Gordon Lewis (1919–91) offered a number of guidelines and directives to Caribbeanists (Lewis 1983b). Among them was the necessity of acquiring a complete mastery of the literature, both past and present. As a sociocultural anthropologist working in Caribbean studies, I have put forth great effort to read and study across multiple disciplinary boundaries to develop a holistic understanding of Caribbean societies and cultures. Nonetheless, there never seems to be enough time to acquire that near-complete mastery that Lewis demanded of himself and of any serious student or scholar of the Caribbean. Although I may not be as intellectually and culturally literate in things Caribbean as I would like to be, I can gladly report that during the course of my graduate training in the mid- to late 1970s and my professional work since then, I have read from Lewis's impressive oeuvre, and I have found his contributions to be staple foodstuffs for nourishing my thinking, unthinking, and rethinking.[1]

Although I cannot affirm that the direction I have followed in my own research on Jamaica's urban informal economy and the political experiences of the urban poor is directly attributable to Gordon Lewis's influence on me, I can state emphatically that Lewis's approach to Caribbean dilemmas helped confirm, crystallize, and configure my sense of commitment to the issues I have chosen to pursue as an anthropologist working in an intellectual territory—namely, that of Caribbean politics and economy—in which ethnographers tend to be less visible than economists and political scientists.

Charles Carnegie (1992) has demonstrated that, on the whole, Caribbean social science discourse, particularly that of native Caribbean social science, has been dominated by economics, with anthropology occupying a fairly peripheral place. His examination of *Social and Economic Studies* (*SES*) from the 1950s when it was founded to the late 1980s indicates that "[although] anthropology . . . with its capacity for revealing local systems of thought and modes of organization, was initially seen as central to social science discourse in the 1950s . . . [i]n subsequent decades . . . the discipline's influence, and the importance attached to ethnographic research in the other social sciences, waned markedly, becoming marginalized, as attention turned to the panacea that development economics appeared to offer" (Carnegie 1992, 10). The disciplinary distribution of the articles published is quite telling: although in the 1950s 23.6 percent (twenty-nine) of all articles published in *SES* were by anthropologists, by the decade of the 1980s the percentage had declined to 3.2 percent (ten) (13).

Gordon Lewis departed from the dominant trend of privileging the "units, models, and aggregate numbers" (Lewis 1983b, 11) of macroeconomic and macropolitical structures and being blind to the human agents who people and breathe life into them. Lewis's scholarship was informed and guided by a humanistic methodology that recognized the salience and force of culture, consciousness, and lived experience in the historical unfolding of Caribbean societies (Maingot 1991). Although embedded in his work elsewhere, this methodological framework is probably most developed in his monumental *Main Currents in Caribbean Thought* (Lewis 1983a). Although there are other political scientists with comparable interests—James Scott (1985) being prominent among them—graduate programs in political science and government typically do not privilege the study of culture in the anthropological sense of the concept.

Lewis's work was enriched by his having listened carefully to the voices of Caribbean "folk peoples." He believed that one cannot understand Caribbean societies' full reality without "listening to the report of the majority—the disinherited, the poor, the unemployed, 'the sufferers' in Jamaican street parlance" (Lewis 1984, 2). Even his studies of Caribbean intellectual history firmly situate the main ideological currents in the context of Caribbean culture; that is, the total way of life of the Caribbean masses, who are the "real custodians" of a nation's, and a wider region's, cultural development (Lewis 1983a, 19–20).

He advocated that the whole of Caribbean studies adopt a more humanist spirit to counter the compartmentalization of modern disciplines and the uncritical acceptance of the natural science model of investigation (Lewis

1983b). He saw in some anthropological work (e.g., Mintz's [1960] *Worker in the Cane* and Oscar Lewis's [1965] *La Vida*) the seeds for planting "a philosophic revolution designed to bring back the fragmentalized disciplines into a new, human totality" (Lewis 1983b, 11). This insight of his is most consistent with the holism that the best of anthropology values and seeks to live up to, and, as I shall discuss here, there is an important trend within contemporary sociocultural anthropology that seeks to bridge the conventional gap separating macrostructures and microrealities. I associate my work and that of many of my colleagues with this particular trend and direction.

Lewis's humanist spirit is the methodological feature that marks his work as anthropologically relevant. But there are other aspects of his scholarship that are especially significant to me in view of my interests in the political economy of urban poverty and polarized economic development, in local-level politics, and in the lumpen proletarianization of workers and peasants. First, Lewis offered a radical, socialist, and morally indignant critique of European and U.S. imperialism. This critique brought into bold relief the invidious, multilayered structures and ideologies of domination in a world in which multiple forms of accumulated violence have been afflicted against "the poor and the powerless" (Thomas 1988). The overwhelming majority of the "wretched of the earth," as Fanon (1963) would characterize them, are of African descent and, hence, in one form or another have confronted a dehumanizing racism. Second, related to this was his demystifying analysis of decolonization, both its political and economic dimensions. He recognized the constraints that conditions of empire—such as relations of economic dependence—impose on national sovereignty and the implementation of democracy. In fact, as Clive Thomas (1988) and Trevor Monroe (1986) have insisted, genuine democracy beyond the formal trappings is fundamentally incompatible with empire and the socioeconomic disparities of power and wealth that it has spawned. Third, reflecting his humanistic orientation, Lewis's approach to the vibrant cultural life of the folk underscored the creative ways that common people have "invented their own mechanisms of survival, in part resistant, in part accommodating" (Lewis 1983a, 20). Following a directive from Edward Braithwaite (1975), Lewis probed the intricate and subtle processes of the "inner or subterranean world" of the folk (Braithwaite, 1975, 175). A fourth and the final dimension I care to note is Lewis's interest in the impact of Caribbean slavery and colonialism on England, notably on its intellectual debates and its radical social and political thought (Lewis 1978). In the ensuing discussion, I will reflect upon the relevance and the resonance of these important features in the work I have done since I underwent my coming-of-age rites as an anthropologist.

Ethnographic Visions of Black Youth in Britain: Diasporic Connections

In an autobiographical essay on his vocation as a Caribbeanist, the Welsh-born Lewis (1983b) revealed that he was prepared for his Caribbean odyssey by informal encounters with and exposure to the black or colored experience in the United Kingdom. While a university student in Cardiff, he had gained some familiarity with Tiger Bay, Cardiff's colored quarters—or, as Glenn Jordan (1991) prefers to describe Butetown, a "multiracial" neighborhood in Cardiff's docklands. Lewis's encounter with Tiger Bay—and a few years later with the South Side of Chicago—had exposed him to a new world of heterogeneity and multiethnicity that provided a transition from the "hermetic homogeneity" of the mainstream British scene to the multilayered pigmentocracy of the Caribbean world. Lewis noted the value of his U.S. sojourn by claiming that the U.S. experience was "a dress rehearsal for any European seeking to understand the Caribbean"(Lewis 1983b, 3). That important intermediate experience was facilitated by St. Clair Drake and Horace Cayton—authors of the classic *Black Metropolis* (1945)—who guided Lewis through U.S. race and ethnic relations and African American life.

Interestingly, the path I followed to the Caribbean began in the United States, with black Britain, specifically Brixton in southwest London, being the transition that eventually led me to Jamaica. Another transitional experience that at least indirectly parallels Lewis's trajectory was my connection to the late St. Clair Drake, who, I realize now, helped ease Lewis's cultural shock in the Caribbean. I am fortunate to have been one of Drake's graduate students. After publishing *Black Metropolis,* a two-volume sociological and ethnographic study of the South Side of Chicago, Drake (1954, 1955) did fieldwork in the same Tiger Bay where Gordon Lewis had initially been introduced to questions of color and the racial dimensions of empire. Whether Drake's interaction with Lewis influenced his decision to work in Wales, I do not know, but it is an uncanny coincidence that he undertook his doctoral research in Cardiff rather than in London, Liverpool, or elsewhere in the United Kingdom. Although I had originally intended to go to London for my dissertation research, somehow, with Drake's support, guidance, and blessings, I ended up working in Jamaica, with the expectation that in due time that Third World Caribbean experience would enhance my understanding of the British situation—as my earlier experience in Brixton had surely deepened my appreciation for the Caribbean, the homeland of the majority of its immigrant inhabitants.

I trace the beginnings of my interest in Caribbean studies to an early general curiosity about the sociocultural, political, and economic commonalities and variations within diasporas—the Caribbean diaspora, the broader African diaspora, various Asian diasporas, and the Jewish diaspora. I was motivated to explore the Caribbeanization of England because of this curiosity (cf. Sutton 1987 on the Caribbeanization of New York). I also had a strong interest in international relations and cross-cultural processes and their impact on ordinary people in everyday life. Studying the great waves of African American migration from the rural agrarian South to the urban industrial North while in college had stimulated my thinking about the exploitation and deployment of black labor within capitalism at both national and international levels. I remember coming across an article in *Radical America* on black labor migration in the United States that made a profound impression on my thinking (Baron 1971). All of a sudden something clicked in my mind. As a consequence, I was inspired to think in new ways about the socioeconomic role of African-descended people in the United States as well as in the world at large.

I was originally attracted to the Caribbean migration situation because of its comparative significance for probing the general patterns and principles that characterize the African diasporic component of the larger capitalist world system. I expected to find, and in fact did, many important parallels between the U.S. black and British Caribbean situations due to comparable political-economic conditions rooted in global capitalism as well as due to what Lewis referred to as the "triangular ideological trade" that circulates ideas and perspectives among black folk in England, Africa, and the Americas (Lewis 1978, 338).

My initial research experience as a fledgling ethnographer took place in London in the mid-1970s, where, between undergraduate and graduate schools, I lived and worked—as a volunteer assistant in a youth project, the Brockwell Park Project—in Brixton among immigrants from the Commonwealth Caribbean and their black British progeny (Harrison 1975, 1976). I focused my attention on the socialization and politicization of the second generation, caught—like the generation before it—between the rock of race and the hard place of class in an imperial mother country that had relegated her colonial and neocolonial subjects to the third-class citizenship of immigrants, Britain's troublesome "outside children." Defined as a social problem jeopardizing Britain's law and order, African Caribbean youth were the focus of intense ideological contestation over how to represent, interpret, and politicize the experience and predicament of black British adolescents. These young adults, in disproportionate numbers, had been labeled uneducable and rendered unemployable because of their relative lack of skills and widespread refusal to accept what they deemed to be demeaning "shitwork." In the context of an intense economic and political legitimacy crisis, what Stuart Hall and colleagues (1978) have described as a "moral panic" emerged around issues of race, immigration status, and petty crime—specifically mugging. In government and media discourses, black youth were categorically trans-figured into criminal menaces that warranted being controlled, contained, and repressed through expanded policing and judicial measures. Economically dislocated and socially alienated black youths bore the brunt of policies designed to police Britain's social crisis in part because their presence and predicament in schools, in community life, and both in and out of the labor force challenged the basis of political leadership and cultural authority in the center of the kingdom, where the "Empire [had begun to] strike back" (Centre for Contemporary Cultural Studies 1982).

According to Hall and colleagues (1978), moral panics emerge in response to crime and perceived crime waves when there are crises of hegemony in which the basis of political leadership and cultural authority is exposed and contested. At these junctures, panic reactions are related to things other than crime per se, but crime becomes an index of the social order's disintegration. The moral panic over West Indian mugging contributed to the establishment of an authoritarian consensus or a conservative backlash in support of a law-and-order regime. Assigning the mugging label to West Indian youths legitimated the exercise of police force and judicial control while resolving ambiguities in public opinion about Caribbean immigrants.

In his work on race in postwar and late-twentieth-century Britain, Lewis (1978) showed that the contradictions of the colonial peripheries had come to be internalized through the physical presence of Commonwealth immigrants and the sociopolitical conflicts that immigration helped engender. This process has given the Caribbean legacy a prominent place in contemporary English social, cultural, and political life and, as Lewis cogently argued, particularly in English radicalism. Accordingly, any effective critique of, and opposition to, British capitalism, its structures of political and economic domination, and its cultural hegemony must be grounded in a sophisticated understanding of the interplay between race and class in the dynamics of oppression, resistance, and contestation. Understanding the complex and entangled interpenetration of the historically contingent processes of racialization, class formation, and cultural production is clearly mandatory for making sense of Caribbean social orders, which Lewis designated so colorfully and accurately as "pigmentocracies." Since World War II and particularly as we move farther into the twenty-first century, however, similarly combined processes are also increasingly constitutive of postmodern European societies. Lewis's examination of both Caribbean and British situations underscored the significance of various configurations of race, class, and culture in a contemporary global system historically constituted by a dehumanizing legacy of colonialism.

Ethnographic Visions of a "Slum of Empire"

My later work in Jamaica continued to reflect my earlier concern with the problem of criminalization and the more general issue of state policies aimed at the social control of reserve and surplus labor—that is, workers rendered marginal or redundant by a political economic system whose bottom-line principles are profitability and capital accumulation rather than human well-being. Beginning in 1978, I did ethnographic fieldwork for my doctoral dissertation in a downtown slum in Kingston. My initial analysis focused on the social and political organization of participants in the urban informal economy. I attempted to complement the many analyses concerned with macrostructures, aggregate profiles, and abstractions from statistical extrapolations with an intensive study of ordinary people engaged in the practices and struggles of everyday life in an impoverished tenement locality. In that slum of empire, chronic wage unemployment was shamefully high, "tribalism" or the too often violent rivalry between clients of the two major political parties was rampant, "Babylon" (or the repressive arm of the state) unveiled the fullness of its terror-provoking face, and reinvented memories and metaphors of plantation slavery textured the poignant discursive performances of "men- [and women]-of-words" (Abrahams 1983), the "likkle people's" social critics and political philosophers who, among other things, questioned the meaning of freedom and sovereignty for the "poor and the powerless" (Thomas 1988). Lewis also raised this question in light of the fact that independence has merely represented "a redefinition of the legal status of [Caribbean] society, not bringing in its wake a profound social metamorphosis" (Lewis 1968, 387). The "paraphernalia of sovereignty" was transferred, but the society remains one shaped by its colonial heritage (387). The unfulfilled promises of decolonization have wrought in the folk experience and sociopsychology a deep structure of feelings marked by a profound sense of disappointment, alienation, and anger.

In my ethnographic analysis of the place I call Oceanview, my basic aim was to illuminate how structural contradictions within national and international economic development and within clientelist, authoritarianized democracy are manifested and played out in local-level situations, lived experience, perceptions, and vernacular interpretations. Following trends within the locality over nearly a twenty-year period, I examined shifts in national and international climate—swings in national policy orientation and foreign response—and their trickle-down effects at the local level. I have been most concerned with the ambiguous, contradictory, and fluctuating character of sociopolitical practice and consciousness in this neighborhood and among lumpenized workers and peasants generally. My intent has been to understand how Oceanview has been affected by the rise and demise of the People's National Party's (PNP's) democratic socialism, the subsequent imposition of the International Monetary Fund's (IMF's) structural adjustment policies, the expansion and internationalization of ganja or marijuana production and trafficking, and the increased involvement of transnational Jamaican gangs or posses in cocaine transshipment and trafficking.

My approach to Jamaican politics is very much influenced and informed by the political science and political sociology that examines and attempts to explain the intra–working class divisions that are produced and reproduced by the established political system that Carl Stone (1980) and others have categorized as clientelist and that Obika Gray (1991), Paget Henry (1991), Ledgister (1998), and I even earlier (Harrison 1988a, 1988b) have characterized as a synthesis of authoritarian and democratic characteristics. Lewis's analysis in *The Growth of the Modern West Indies* (1968) highlighted the bourgeois character of both of Jamaica's mass parties, pointing out that the ideological and policy differences are only those of degree rather than kind (Lewis 1968, 168). He argued that in Jamaica the classes (i.e., the privileged classes, particularly the middle-class managers of the state machinery) reduce the masses to "nothing more than the darkened theatre audience that alternatively applauds and hisses the actors on the national stage" (190). In light of this carefully circumscribed and neutralized role for the majority of the citizenry, some of the poorest segments of the electorate gain entry into national politics via what Lewis called the "semi-military political gangs directed by the leaders of both . . . political groupings" (398). Lewis underscored the view that the political violence that is so much a feature of Jamaican-style democratic contests is routinized and indeed institutionalized as an informal arm of the political party and government system. Moreover, this pervasive political violence is rooted not in the ignorance, moral deficits, and crime-prone character of the lower class but in the violence and class defenses of the privileged. Lewis argued that the "real threat to the carefully nurtured image of inter-racial fraternalism [and interclass national unity] comes, not from the masses, but from the top groups placed on the defensive [by the challenges of independence]. . . . Most of the suppressed violence simmers on the verandahs of upper St. Andrew and not in the shacks of Western [or Eastern or Central] Kingston" (192–93).

It appears that this violence finds explosive expression in government policies for policing the sufferers who bear the brunt of the crises of development and political legitimacy that have emerged from Jamaica's precarious place within an international economy increasingly marked by instability and restructuring. As I will discuss in more detail in a later chapter, during the 1980s the Jamaica Labour Party (JLP) administration put more teeth into labor and criminal laws to enable the government to act more punitively against dangerous elements disrupting the climate for foreign investment (Harrison 1987a). To this end, it established the Special Operations Squad that was colloquially dubbed the "Eradication Squad." This security apparatus was underwritten by an unprecedented level of U.S. aid. A. Vaughn Lewis, a Caribbean political scientist, warned that the modernization of security technology as a component of the U.S. Caribbean Basin Initiative aid package drew the United States into domestic politics and the social order (Barry, Wood, and Preusch 1984, 209). This militarization of the state was all too similar to the situation in Central America. It represented yet another front through which what Gordon Lewis (1984) called the "accumulated violence" of empire was deployed in Caribbean life (2).

Although Lewis, Stone, and others indeed illuminated paradoxes and contradictions within Jamaica's parliamentary democracy, in much of their work they, nonetheless, highlighted the positive aspects of the Commonwealth Caribbean's stable constitutional systems (Lewis 1985, 227–33). Unlike Latin American and African situations, in the English-speaking Caribbean on a whole democracy works, electorates accept the status quo, and politics is relatively humane with political leaders being "[men] of the people" (Lewis 1985, 227, 230). My perspective on Jamaican politics concurs with Lewis's insistence that democracy in the form of elections, uncensored press, and intellectual and discursive freedom should be a necessary condition for a genuinely decolonized, sovereign, and economically just social order. However, I underscore the point that the formal trappings and rituals of de jure democracy are grossly insufficient when, as Stone admitted, an "authoritarian value system, . . . social violence, authoritarian styles of leadership, authoritarian institutions, nonbargaining attitudes to political conflict, and tendencies toward political religiosity and fanaticism" (Stone 1985, 26) thwart the functioning of a fully developed democracy (see also Gray 1991; Henry 1991). From the vantage point of Oceanview, it is clear that Jamaica's de facto polity is characterized by markedly unequal access to constitutional rights and protections and that unorganized or informally organized labor and the unemployed have the most precarious access to those supposedly inalienable rights of citizenship. My ethnographic observations corroborate Carlene Edie's view that Jamaican democracy, seriously flawed by its external and internal dependency and clientelism, exists largely by default rather than by virtue of widespread commitment to the values and behaviors of liberal democracy (Edie 1991, 7). Democracy is stabilized by default because dual clientelism constrains "authoritarianism by dispersing resources" (7). Since the 1980s with the entrenchment of structural adjustment policies, which I will discuss in greater detail in a later chapter, the resources that political patronage once provided to the most privileged clients declined drastically, undermining the legitimacy of the political party system in the eyes of considerable segments of ghetto constituencies.

Especially during the late 1970s and throughout the 1980s, my observations suggested that Oceanview's political scene was animated by a dialectical interplay between patterns of accommodation and various forms of resistance and protest. I have been particularly interested in the latter because of my hopeful hypothesis that such oppositional practice has the potential to create some of the conditions that engender positive microcultural change. Influenced by Carlos Vélez-Ibáñez's (1983) exemplary ethnography of grassroots politics in Mexico, I assumed that microlevel forms of resistance and change, largely by heightening social solidarity, could enhance the quality of local and extralocal life and potentially help set the stage for broader-based mobilization and more far-reaching change.

Following the leads of scholars such as Anthony Giddens (1979) who emphasize structure's duality, I sought to illuminate both the constraints and the opportunities that the multifaceted structure of domination presented to grassroots sociopolitical actors over a period of more than two decades, namely from the late 1960s to the early 1990s (see "Ethnohistorical Periodization of Oceanview's Political Climate, 1967–92"). Oral history accounts as well as a variety of other primary and secondary sources enabled me to discern several phases that seemed to reflect ethnographically salient shifts in Oceanview's overall sociopolitical temperament, particularly in relations within and among such local fields of power as party-affiliated and nonaffiliated gangs, political party groups (PNP) and branches (JLP), and nonpartisan networks and voluntary associations, many of which were female-centered (Harrison 1988d, 1997).

Ethnohistorical Periodization of Oceanview's Political Climate, 1967–92

1967–72   Phase of emergent political tribalism occurring in context of the widening social disparities that accompanied the postwar economic expansion; end of two terms of conservative (authoritarian) Jamaica Labour Party (JLP) rule and beginning of People's

National Party (PNP) political liberalization and Jamaicanization; expansion and internationalization of illegal drug trafficking.

1973–77   Phase of intensified tribalism taking place in the broader context of U.S.-supported JLP destabilization campaign against the PNP's democratic-socialist program (which was more radical in rhetoric than in substance); virtual economic collapse due to reverberations from international oil crisis, bauxite companies' politically motivated retrenchment, and in 1977 International Monetary Fund (IMF) intervention.

1978–79   Short phase marked by the rise and demise of the citywide Peace Movement organized by "top-ranking generals" (gang leaders) rather than by the politicians of the PNP and JLP; at the local level, nonpartisan, nonsectarian networks and associations activated, extralocal linkages cultivated on basis of embryonic class consciousness—kinship ties mediated these interlocality relationships.

1979–80   Transitional phase of electoral campaigning and unprecedented tribal war and casualties (800 killed); Kingston likened to Beirut and hell; life in Oceanview called "worst nightmare."

1981–82   A second transition marked by the beginnings of the JLP administration and free market/IMF/Caribbean Basin Initiative program for economic "deliverance"; consolidation of JLP control in Oceanview.

1983   Phase featuring internecine factionalism within JLP ranks, austerity policies of IMF/World Bank/U.S. structural adjustment, crisis of political legitimacy with failure of IMF test, and emergence of one-party rule in wake of uncontested elections; transnationalization of local drug posses.

1984–85   Period when unfulfilled promises of economic "deliverance" triggered the mobilization of PNP and nonpartisan forces at the local level, culminating in citywide antigovernment protests.

1986–89   JLP decline, revival of PNP morale, and reelection of pro–free market PNP, increasing role of cocaine and crack in local and national drug economy; intensification of local debates and conflicts over the ethics of drug trafficking and investment of blood money; decline in partisan gang tribalism with realignments based on drug trafficking agenda.

1990–92   Unprecedented decline in the legitimacy of the two-party political system; general elections held, with PNP winning mandate; fusion of two gang hierarchies into a single network of drug posses coordinated by a powerful don; growth of crack epidemic. IMF structural adjustment program ends in 1990, but policy climate continues nonetheless.

During two of the phases, the third and seventh, some noticeable degree of microcultural change occurred. Cohorts of men and women coalesced and mobilized, projecting a sense of autonomy by defying the efficacy of the state, the power of its politics of clientelism, and the mystifying political rituals that disguise fundamental social and class cleavages. The political practices during these two phases were marked by bilateral, nonsectarian alliance building; extralocal cohort formation and various expressions of interlocal consciousness of kind; challenges to established conceptions of work and economic development; and a heightened recognition of the local consequences of structured underdevelopment and polarized economic growth. In my view, these kinds of principles and patterns of reorganization and rethinking are necessary but not sufficient conditions for engendering a mode of struggle that might lead to more far-reaching transformations, namely an alternative form of development consistent with what Guyanese political economist Clive Thomas (1988) has delineated in his *The Poor and the Powerless*. The presence, however ephemeral and unstable, of these modalities of sociopolitical practice and consciousness—including forms through which women expressed their opposition to political violence, the politicization of scarce work opportunities, and the cultural construction of militaristic, violence-glorifying definitions of ghetto manhood (Harrison 1997)—suggested to me that the common folk are able to puncture and unthink dominant ideologies of power. And perhaps the most progressive elements of the lumpen proletariat, the informal labor force, and casual workers can progress beyond desperate mercenary action and struggles over patronage to an emergent stage of class consciousness and formation (Harrison 1987b). The Oceanview case shows that however stable Jamaica's political system may be, that stability is based on a strongly ambivalent, volatile, and enforced accommodation on the part of the masses. The enforcement aspect is underestimated in many analyses that attribute political reproduction primarily to the power of hegemony or ideology (e.g., Austin 1984) while overlooking the concrete force of routinized police repression and paramilitary enforcement in the everyday life of ghetto neighborhoods. The Oceanview case suggests that domination and its reproduction are based upon multiple instruments of control and power—among them hegemony as Austin emphasizes, the institutionalization of divide-and-rule relations of patronage-clientelism as both Stone (1980) and Edie (1990) underscore, and the threat and actual deployment of both official and unofficial forms of coercion.

In my analysis, the latter two aspects are vividly foregrounded. Oceanview residents are impelled to live in a contested space of violence and terror. This lived experience provides an important basis, although not the sole one, for constituting the meanings invested in divergent local interpretations of claims to political party and government legitimacy. For example, some of the people who voted for the PNP in 1972 and 1976 had withdrawn their support by the late 1970s and 1980. This shift occurred not necessarily because the local electorate was against liberal reforms per se but because of the skepticism and distrust engendered by living in a setting in which PNP constituency dominance had been enforced through the brutal coercion of so-called socialist gangs. The PNP's socialist—or, according to Walter Rodney (1975), pseudosocialist—rhetoric and programmatic goals for the nation came to be evaluated in terms of local contradictions and conflicts and the intended and unintended consequences of those conflicts. As a result, the moral and political integrity of the entire party and its progressive strategy for change was thrown into serious doubt. The dramatic swing in favor of the JLP in 1980 may have reflected local feelings and disillusionment about the inconsistencies, paradoxes, and hypocrisy of a party that had heightened popular consciousness about salient national and international issues and about the fundamental issues of equality and justice. In other words, the PNP had successfully raised the people's expectations for progressive change in their immediate lives but then left too many of them hanging in deep disappointment.

Although my ethnographic focus was primarily Oceanview, in my effort to probe the relational character of urban poverty and disempowerment, I also attempted to "study up" (Nader 1969) as well as "study down" the social class ladder. Because the state apparatus is managed by a sector of the middle class, I examined middle-class discourses on the ghetto and its residents, class conflict, and development (e.g., Harrison 1991). This added concern with what was spoken in conversations and interviews and what was disseminated by the mass media allowed me to excavate the stratified implications of what Lewis seemed to have seen as the class and social-spatial distance between the simmering heat of the uptown veranda and the smoke and fire of the downtown ghetto yard. Among other things, many ordinary, middle-class people stereotyped the lowest sectors of the lower class as idle, immoral, and criminal impediments to national development, the form achieved via foreign aid and investment. Class conflict and polarization were often attributed to the misbehavior and pathology of ghetto people rather than to economic injustice. The very serious and escalating problem of crime was rarely placed in the context of wide social and economic disparities, labor destabilization, and the markedly uneven patterns of economic growth. The context that was discursively constructed was the narrow one of intrinsic ghetto and lower-class criminality. That bias was implicit in both PNP and JLP government policies that have prioritized the control of symptoms of economic underdevelopment but not the acquisition of the substantive economic control required for regulating the most strategic forms of private property (Calathes 1988). It appeared that middle-class discourses tended to upstage the foreign and domestic bourgeoisie while categorically criminalizing ghetto people and foregrounding them as the punishable culprits held responsible for Jamaica's deepening national crisis.

Lewis perceptively claimed that to a certain extent the Caribbean's crime problem "represents the revenge of the poor against the well-to-do" (Lewis 1985, 233). The Oceanview case illustrates that some who are being labeled criminals and outlaws view their breaches of the law as forms of rebellion and protest against "Babylon" (Harrison 1987a, 1988c). According to ethnographic observations, the lumpen proletariat is more differentiated and heterogeneous than many analysts admit. A diachronic analysis reveals the historically specific conditions under which individuals and organized social units such as the local age-graded peer networks that make up street gangs either engage or refuse to engage in social or political crime. While "choking and robbing" and politically victimizing the poor may be pervasive and preponderant tendencies, they do not exhaust the range of activities and orientations among that segment of poor people who may in fact breach or defy the law. In Oceanview, there have been considerable debate and negotiations over what constitutes ethical and moral behavior, particularly with respect to the justifiability of victimizing other poor people (Harrison 1989). There are indeed points in Oceanview's history at which the most progressive lumpen elements have struggled to articulate and adhere to ethical principles that reflect a collectivist sufferers' consciousness and conscience. Some of the most successful adherents of this position, especially during the 1970s, were identified as "True Rastas" or as those who were raised by True Rastas (Harrison 1989). Although this particular politicized social outlawry may have only been exhibited sporadically and intermittently, it was grounded to some degree in the recognition of intraclass solidarity and interclass antagonism (Harrison 1988c). These subtle nuances are often lost in macrolevel analysis that treats poor people and the criminal elements among them as an essentialized category deserving the state repression that is prevalently perpetrated through extrajudicial as well as court-approved executions. According to Amnesty International, these are Jamaica's biggest human rights violations.

Conclusions: Moved by the Spirit of Humanistic Inquiry

My research on the politics of lived experience in both Brixton and Oceanview has been anchored in the kind of humanistic, ordinary, people-centered orientation that Gordon Lewis's scholarship reflected and advocated. The work I have done, however, is only a small part of a larger corpus of anthropological research that bridges the conventional gap and disjuncture between, on one hand, macrolevel studies that may be susceptible to overgeneralization and to underestimating variation and, on the other hand, microlevel analyses that zoom in on the nuanced, intricate specificities of comparable yet variant cases. Both quantitative and qualitative, generalist and particularist, macro- and microstyles of scholarship are desirable in that they are potentially complementary and cross-fertilizing. Lewis, however, amplified the point that the uncritical dominance and overrepresentation of quantitative methodology in the social science of the Caribbean are problematic when important questions of history, culture, consciousness, and experience are relegated to an obscure periphery by virtue of methodological parameters and proscriptions. Although sociocultural anthropologists have long studied real people in natural groupings and settings, they have not always embedded their ethnographies in wider contexts of structured power. Wolf's (1982) pathbreaking anthropological history of colonial expansion and capitalist development and Sidney Mintz's (1985) cultural history of the social and cultural impact of sugar on English society are studies signaling the enlarged vision many of today's anthropologists have of what constitutes relevant and appropriate lines of inquiry. It is noteworthy that both Wolf's and, of course, Mintz's professional trajectories began in Caribbean studies, with the *People of Puerto Rico* team project (Steward et al. 1956). That watershed study claimed an expanded intellectual territory for anthropology and is in part responsible for the progress being made in Caribbean anthropology today.

Caribbean anthropology is advancing our understanding of the impact that the New World Order of capitalist globalization and restructuring is having on the everyday life experiences of Caribbean people—workers, peasants, big and small entrepreneurs, women, men, and children. In light of the accelerated mobility of capital and labor, commodities and culture, the late-modern phenomenon of transnationalism has assumed new significance for Caribbean people, whether they live, work, and die in their Caribbean or circum-Caribbean homelands or in contexts in which they have come to be twice or thrice "diaspora-ized," as Hall (1999, 10) has used the term.

These trends in scholarship have the potential "to make possible . . . the initiation of policy options that are at once more informed and more creative for having been grounded in a richer understanding of the historical and cultural processes of the people for whom [development is supposedly] designed" (Carnegie 1992, 25). Before economic and social policies can be more effectively humanized, the knowledge informing policy formulation and decision making as well as that informing the political struggles that influence those decisions must be more humanized. Gordon Lewis's directive that Caribbean studies integrate a humanistic framework into its repertoire of tools and instruments was, I believe, tied to his profound vision of and commitment to the historical possibilities for achieving genuine freedom, independence, and regional unity in the world of vibrant Caribbean folk people.

Acknowledgments

I would like to express my sincere thanks to Constance Sutton for inviting me to participate in the April 12, 1992, symposium ("Gordon K. Lewis: A Caribbean Odyssey and Legacy") that she and Lambros Comitas organized at the Institute for the Study of Man. That event prompted me to revisit several of Lewis's writings in order to reflect upon them from the vantage point of my own interests and experiences in Caribbean studies and the Afro-Atlantic. Looking back farther to formative experiences in my intellectual background, I would like to acknowledge the formative support I received from two of my undergraduate professors at Brown University: Louise Lamphere and the late George Bass. They were instrumental in my winning a Samuel T. Arnold Fellowship, whose purpose was to provide "unusually promising seniors . . . a post-graduate year of international travel and independent study . . . to promote . . . personal development and broader understanding of international aspects of human affairs" (Samuel T. Arnold Fellowship, http://www.brown.edu/Administration/Dean_of_the_College/fellowships/list/index.php?id=207). That award allowed me to spend 1974–75 in London, England, where I did exploratory research on the experiences of black, largely African Caribbean, youths. As a result of that year's experience, the notion of pursuing advanced studies in anthropology became a conviction. After completing the London project, I enrolled in the graduate program at Stanford University, where St. Clair Drake, based on his earlier work in Great Britain, deeply enriched my understanding of the history and context of Caribbean and African immigrants in Great Britain. His influence along with that of the interdisciplinary political economy seminar that economist Donald J. Harris, originally from Jamaica, coordinated—and that Bridget O'Laughlin encouraged anthropology students to attend—led me to do my dissertation research in Jamaica, where the majority of the immigrants I knew in England had originated. I was convinced that I needed to link the transnational and diasporic experiences I encountered in Britain to the uneven patterns of development and sovereignty that characterize colonial and postcolonial economies in the Caribbean, Latin America, and Africa.

PART IV

The Power of Ethnography,
the Ethnography of Power

6. Gangs, Politics, and Dilemmas of Global Restructuring in Jamaica

> Everyone is crying out for peace, yes
> None is crying out for justice . . .
> Everyone is talking 'bout crime
> Tell me who are the criminals?
> I don't want no peace
> I need equal rights and justice . . .
> And there'll be no crime
> There'll be no criminals
> —Peter Tosh, "Equal Rights" (1977)

It was no midsummer's night dream. It was a veritable nightmare, and it was real—ninety-six degrees in the shade, what little of it you could find in Kingston's concrete jungle. Newspaper headlines in both Jamaica and the United States sounded the alarm about the "terror in the city" of Kingston (*Weekly Gleaner* 2001a, 1), and the "Jamaican soldiers on guard" (*USA Today* 2001, 11A). Once things calmed down, readers were reassured that "[v]iolence [had finally] subside[d] in Jamaica, but wounds [were still festering]" (*New York Times* 2001, A3). Even today this remains true, too true for comfort—that is, for those who would be comforted by a sustained peace and all that presupposes in a society like Jamaica, where social disparities and political tensions are stark and cruel and where social suffering is chronically painful.

The July 2001 episode of violence, in which nearly thirty people were killed and forty wounded, was only one among many troubling episodes in the politics of urban Jamaica. In this instance, the violence erupted most immediately from confrontations between the national security forces and local gunmen, whom former Prime Minister P. J. Patterson described as "criminal elements [trying to] hold [the] country to ransom" (*USA Today* 2001). Although violent crime is certainly a serious problem, Jamaicans United against Police Brutality claimed that the media coverage and government account were one sided. Among the dead were innocent women, children, and elderly people caught in the police's "nonstop rounds of . . . random firing in public places like Coronation Market (Notobrutalpolice listserv communiqué, "Holding Prime Minister Patterson responsible for 27 more killings," July 12, 2001). They point out that, although the epicenter of the violence was West Kingston, people all over the metropolitan area put up roadblocks to show their "solidarity for the residents of West Kingston who were 'under police oppression'" (*Weekly Gleaner* 2001a, 2). The government legitimates that oppression by using "force as a means of solving social problems. It was Patterson who created the Crime Management Unit (CMU), which few can argue is anything but a death squad with a benign sounding name" (Notobrutalpolice listserv communiqué, July 12, 2001). Other commentators claimed that the unrest was less about uncontrollable crime than about a political tactic to incite disorder in constituencies loyal to the opposition Jamaica Labour Party (JLP) and, by so doing, "to pressure the government to call an early election" (Patterson 2001; see also Espeut 2001). Another commentator contested the notion that the unrest was primarily about party politics and, uncovering yet another dimension of Jamaica's political and economic complexity, argued instead that the source of the problem was the conflict between, on one hand, the police and security forces and, on the other, drug traffickers with big stakes in the international trade (Robotham 2001, 9).

The July 2001 flare-up happened just a few months after the controversial extrajudicial execution of seven young men—merely adolescents—in the Braeton area of the capital city. In response to the "Braeton Seven" incident along with an extensive accumulation of damning evidence on summary executions, disappearances and illegal detentions, torture and dehumanizing prison conditions (even for children), and capital punishment (Amnesty International 2001a, 2001c), Amnesty International issued a press release describing "the situation in Jamaica *as a human rights emergency*" (emphasis mine; Jamaicans United Against Police Brutality listserv message, "Jamaican Government Defies Amnesty International," April 16, 2001; Amnesty International 2001b). This human rights emergency is very real, but it must be placed in the context of "a big picture 'overstanding' of how so much of the desperation that fuels crime and repression . . . is connected to the imbalances and misery that top-down globalization, in league with local elites, is producing. Such an 'overstanding' would . . . lead to a better grasp on why young people are flinging themselves into the jaws of the police with such ferocity" (Schechter 2001, 2).

Over the years, the violence that abuses the human rights of those who live in Jamaica's urban war zones has emanated not only from the cruel excesses of policing crime but also from conflicts between rival gangs, which are usually affiliated with the two main political parties: the People's National Party (PNP) and the Jamaica Labour Party (JLP). Increasingly, these gangs have become entangled in the trafficking of drugs and guns, a sphere of the world economy that has come to be one of the few sources of income available in impoverished urban constituencies where subsistence insecurity has reached crisis proportions (Harrison 1989, 1990). The interdependence between politicians and ghetto dons, henchmen, and enforcers has a problematic history that dates back to the beginnings of independence. That garrison-constituency politics is such an integral feature of Jamaica's clientelist democracy is clearly illustrated by the fact that in May 2001 several members of the PNP, including three cabinet members, attended the funeral of a leading West Kingston don, who was memorialized in, of all places, the National Arena. This official paying of last respects to a gang leader and drug don from Arnett Gardens, a prominent PNP constituency in West Kingston, prompted the leadership of the National Democratic Movement (a third party established in the 1980s), *Gleaner* columnists and editors, and spokesmen from the Jamaica Council of Churches to question seriously whether politicians or dons were the de facto rulers of the country. One critic lamented that "[p]oliticians are prisoners, hostages of garrison politics" (*Weekly Gleaner* 2001c, 3).

Ultimately, this interdependent relationship between politicians and gangsters arises from a confluence of societal conditions. According to Jamaican sociologist and criminologist Bernard Headley, the crux of the problem is the growth of an urban wageless class, which is the "logical [outcome] of Jamaica's socioeconomic and historical processes" (Headley 1996, 22). Headley argues that three major forces are responsible for this grave situation: the decline of agricultural production leading to massive internal and external migration; the evolution of a disarticulated, underdeveloped modern economy; and an increased rate of growth among youth, without having an adequate economic base for their productive integration.

Alienated from the means of productive, legitimate work, the growing population of "urban lumpen proletarians" has come to accept illegal and often violent forms of income generation, including "political thuggery" (Headley 1996, 19), as "normal, functional enterprises" (18). As I indicated previously, since the 1970s drug-related activities have been integrated into the international narcotics and small-arms trade. The diasporic routes of drug trafficking and gunrunning bring gangsters back and forth between the island and "a foreign"—mainly North America but also Great Britain—permitting them to escape arrest in Jamaica while frustrating the police's ability to fight or contain crime. Increasingly since the 1980s, "outmigrating offenders [have been] forcibly returned to Jamaica, after being either suspected or convicted of crimes in the [United States]. [T]he restart of their criminal careers in Jamaica [has added] a new dimension to the island's crime problem" (19).

In light of these factors, Headley takes the unpopular, but I believe correct, position that "'[t]ougher' law enforcement *by itself* will never seriously reduce crime; it only displaces and perhaps delays its occurrence" (Headley 1996, xxiii; emphasis in original). As an alternative to "policing the crisis" (Hall et al. 1978) and militarizing the state and society, he recommends that the government come up with more "imaginative approaches to the law, law enforcement, and to the idea of punishment that are likely to reduce the incidence of street crime *while [Jamaicans] are trying to construct a more just society*" (Headley 1996, 63; emphasis in original). A more humane approach to law and policy would seek to rehabilitate and reintegrate "otherwise wasted and unproductive" lives into society. Although Headley's recommendations are consistent with social-justice goals, it is much easier to articulate this vision of an alternative criminal justice system than to implement it in the social and political pressure cooker that Jamaica has become since its independence from Great Britain.

Making Use of Hindsight

Intersections between politics and the criminal underground, the law and the lawless, and police and thieves have continually been a focus of heated debate in Jamaica. I was introduced to the terms of this debate in the late 1970s, when I initiated my work in the area I have called Oceanview. Since then, I have learned a great deal about the political economy of poverty, garrison constituency politics, and the consequences of both on the everyday life of poor people. In this chapter, I examine these issues as they played themselves out in Oceanview during earlier periods, including that of the still relevant period of national as well as grassroots struggle over the pros and cons of competing strategies of economic and political development, namely democratic socialism as an alternative, noncapitalist path versus the free market, privatization path of the dominant world system, the path consistent with U.S. domestic and foreign policy. I will focus my discussion on the shifts in political climate during the period between 1967 and 1992, although I will bring my narrative into the ethnographic present of 2001 by offering a few general impressions.[1]

My analysis reveals nuances and dimensions of experience that are usually absent from national and international accounts of Jamaica's problems with crime, policing, and political corruption. My intent is to offer a more three-dimensional picture of Oceanview's residents and, perhaps by implication, impoverished and disempowered people inhabiting other neighborhoods in Kingston's ghetto zone of garrison constituencies. These people tend to get lost in the homogenizing categories—ghettoes, criminals, garrison constituencies—that punctuate Jamaica's public discourse about poverty, politics, and crime. Moreover, I aim to put the persistent patterns of crime and political violence in a systemic context that will shed light on the shifting dynamics of local social organization, subsistence strategies, and political expression. I wish to present an ethnographic representation of Oceanview's sufferers and outlaws that depicts them as multidimensional, although contradictory, agents situated in a context of social crisis and change that is uneven, constrained, zigzag, and poignantly indicative of the unfulfilled promises of postcolonial sovereignty and development.

Rethinking Transformation in the Years of Postdemocratic Socialism

The 1980 demise of Jamaica's democratic-socialist PNP administration and the subsequent failure of the JLP government's alternative to generate economic growth and stability forced political analysts, including political ethnographers, interested in the possibilities of radical change in Jamaica and the Caribbean region to rethink their positions. This turn of events prompted them to identify and closely examine the varying conditions that constrain and create possibilities for sustained popular mobilization and structural transformation.

Since the 1970s, research on political processes in cities of the global South has shown that the urban poor, through their grassroots movements and other forms of political expression, play increasingly important roles in the struggle for social change (Castells 1982; Portes and Walton 1976; Singer 1982). Social scientists and political activists alike have often raised questions about the political character and potential of the growing numbers of unemployed and underemployed persons in peripheral capitalist cities (Fagen 1983, 21; Worsley 1972). This population, variably labeled lumpen—or sub—proletariat, marginals, and informal-sector labor, has possibly been more subject to stereotyping and misrepresentation than any other sector of dependent capitalist societies.

The lack of fundamental change in these parts of the world is sometimes attributed to deficiency on the part of the urban poor themselves. According to varying arguments, this group has been rendered politically conservative, apolitical, or inhibited by such factors as its peasant or rural origins (Bonilla 1962); its heavy participation in ephemeral, organizationally fragmented, small-scale economic activities; and its present-day-survival value orientation (Roberts 1978, 135). Although these factors point to the immediate conditions and sociocultural forms of the poor, other variables also stem largely from external structures and controls. These supralocal constraints include the containment of disquiet and political rebellion by police repression, government and political party patronage-clientelism (Stone 1980; Laguerre 1982; Harrison 1982), and hegemonic processes operative through mass media, schools, and churches that validate a ruling-class ideology advocating notions of the social/political inferiority of the undereducated mass (Austin 1984).

Rather than immediately asking why structures of domination persist or why the urban poor are politically disabled, as blanket questions, more scholars are approaching grassroots political practice processually, situationally, and dialectically (cf. Lessinger 1985; Susser 1982; Vélez-Ibañez 1983; Worsley 1984, 187). They have focused on the variant and multifaceted forms and phases of political expression over time, sometimes considerable spans of time. As Susser has noted, workers and the poor do not always have the opportunity to mobilize power (1982, 7). These scholars, therefore, look for the modes of struggle available under historically specific conditions, which change over time. They accept as a basic premise that *the path to empowerment and structural transformation is usually indirect and full of contradictions, ambiguities, and reversals* (Portes and Walton 1976, 110; emphasis mine).

With such an approach, it becomes possible to appreciate the significant role of "small victories" in the broader and longer-term scheme of political struggle and change. Grassroots praxis sometimes engenders meaningful microcultural change. As Vélez-Ibañez has pointed out, we must look at conditions that permit the coalescence of cohorts of men and women who project "their sense of social autonomy by defying the power of the state" and its "rituals of marginality . . . that crosscut sector and class cleavages" (1983, 241). Such occurrences, though restricted to particular localities and neighborhood movements, may have important implications for developments in political consciousness and organization.

My purpose here is to show the multidimensional and often ambiguous character of political processes in slum neighborhoods in Kingston, Jamaica. I do this by analyzing certain sociopolitical patterns in a particular locality: Oceanview. The individual and collective behaviors of Oceanview actors are viewed in the context of a specific historical period, from 1967 to 1992, during which political and economic changes at both the national and international levels engendered shifts in local-level political expressions and configurations. These shifts in grassroots politics, particularly in the field of gang relations, represent responses to the pressures, constraints, and interventions attendant upon Jamaica's status in the world system, most immediately in "Uncle Sam's backyard."[2]

The ensuing analysis suggests that the violent political rivalry, colloquially called "tribalism," generally associated with Kingston's street gangs, is not a necessary or automatic outcome of gang formation per se. It is, however, the result of gangs constituted amid rampant political clientelism, wide class disparities, and turbulent, disruptive economic change partially induced from the outside. In other words, the criminal, mercenary, and reactionary aspects of gang behavior so often underscored in public culture should be viewed as characteristics stemming from specific sets of historical circumstances rather than as intrinsic features.

The Oceanview case demonstrates that before the late 1960s gangs were largely innocuous and fairly constructive units of local organization. They provided a basis for association, cooperation, and exchange among male adolescents and adults younger than thirty to thirty-five years of age. With major changes in the downtown economy, the expansion of the marijuana or ganja trade, the introduction of guns, and the consolidation of a partisan—that is, political party mediated—economic niche, the social field that gangs constituted became increasingly vulnerable to criminalization and clientelist politicization. Over time, these processes became deeply entrenched in local political life.

Locality politics in urban Jamaica is in great measure constituted by gangs and their relationships with other local (as well as extra- and supralocal) interest networks, with government, and with political party machines, yet the complex and ambiguous dynamics of gang power are rarely seriously examined beyond a cursory acknowledgment of its mercenary opportunism, criminality, and political corruption (Stone 1973, 1980). The following discussion, therefore, represents an attempt to offset this simplistic view.

The major phases that marked Oceanview's political life during the 1967–92 period can be briefly described as follows. In the late 1960s and early 1970s, intense intergang rivalry became institutionalized and eventually assumed a partisan character. This state of affairs persisted throughout most of the 1970s and, in fact, intensified. In 1978, there was a marked shift away from the interparty and intergang rivalry, which too often characterizes patronage–clientelist politics. Instead, an extrapartisan alliance, namely the Peace Movement, emerged to challenge the conventional pattern of party and government intervention. During late 1979 and 1980, an election year, conditions promoting broad-based solidarity and consciousness among the formally unemployed and marginally employed eroded and were subverted by gang fighting, or "tribal war," of unprecedented proportions. By 1983, after nearly three years of JLP rule, the conventional polarization of political party forces had given way to intense internecine fighting between ruling party clients-henchmen. From 1984 until around 1986, the local scene was marked by the rise of a largely nonpartisan solidarity between those most alienated from the government and party system, including traditional rivals. Following this period until around 1989, support for the JLP declined and that for the PNP was revived, culminating in its reelection in early 1989. The new PNP administration, however, did not depart substantially from the JLP's neoliberal policies, which would increasingly reflect the economic strategy that prevailed internationally in the wake of the disintegration of the Soviet Union as a superpower. On Oceanview's informal economic scene, cocaine and crack played an increasing role, upstaging the traditional ganja. Partisan gang tribalism gave way to realignments based on a common drug-trafficking agenda, but these were destabilized by the electoral campaign's divisive tactics. By the early 1990s, there was an unprecedented decline in the legitimacy of the two-party system. The power and economic clout of drug posses, as units of local socioeconomic organization and as transnational formations facilitating the transshipment of illegal drugs largely, but not exclusively, to the United States, grew more entrenched. At this point in their development, gangs seriously rivaled the local presence of political parties that, due to national and international policy-exacerbated economic austerity and the growing opportunities that transnational drug trafficking made available, could no longer provide materially significant patronage to their clients. The terms of patronage were redefined from "a wok" (i.e., work contracts) to the provision of "cover from the police" (Robotham 2001, 8–9). The political plot thickened, however; politicians' control over the police and army was greatly diminished by the growing militarization of the state and, as a result, the enhancement of the military's power.

My analysis of these shifts highlights the dynamic and fluid character of local politics in urban Jamaica. Moreover, by approaching grassroots political action in situational and processual terms, I attempt to illuminate patterns of microcultural change, which may, under better conditions, clear the ground for the development of more broad-based and sustained forms of consciousness and struggle.

Oceanview: A Profile

Oceanview is a slum that in the 1980s was inhabited by approximately 6,500 people. Nearly 75 percent of the neighborhood's working-age population was—and probably still is—formally unemployed, supporting itself and its dependents largely through informal economic activities ranging from chicken raising to "selling a likkle [little]," the petty marketing of foodstuffs or manufactured goods. People also engaged in a number of illegalities, key among them the marketing of ganja, although cocaine trafficking grew in significance during the 1980s. Oceanview's economic situation, particularly in the 1960s and 1970s, was compounded by a high level of dependency because it had large numbers of children and senior citizens (Department of Statistics 1970). In the mid-1970s, the mean annual income was equivalent to U.S.$450 (Urban Upgrading n.d.). Income from the informal economy has never been sufficient for survival and has had to be combined with that from intermittent wage work, often only available in the public sector.[3] Opportunities for wage work have been, therefore, strongly politicized, accessible only through party/government connections and sponsorship and primarily available to party supporters and clients.[4]

The most strategic of the neighborhood's political fields have traditionally been those aligned with the state: constituency politics, mediated by local party associations—JLP branches and PNP groups; urban redevelopment politics, mediated by government programs concerned with housing and social welfare; and street-corner gang hierarchies, based to a considerable extent on illegally gained resources and gun power. It is this last field that will be emphasized here. The risks and dangers involved in partisan rivalry have led many people in Oceanview to retreat from "polytricks"—party politics. Consequently, much sociopolitical action has occurred in nonpartisan domains such as Parent-Teacher Associations (PTAs), churches, and kin and peer networks. These so-called nonpolitical bases of local action have represented adaptive responses to the painful and often life-threatening excesses of tribalism and patronage politics. Oceanview residents have defined for themselves a variety of nonpartisan social fields in which to pursue local goals and special interests; hence, they have found ways to behave and act politically (Swartz 1968), despite their formal political invisibility. As a general rule, local political activities tend to be pragmatic, economistic, ephemeral, and fragmented. Political positions in the various fields are usually in flux. Such flexibility and ambiguity permit the locality as a locus of power to come to terms with a contradictory and harsh socioeconomic and political environment (Leeds 1973, 23).

Tribalism and the Postwar Expansion, 1967–72

Before the late 1960s, Oceanview's political landscape was relatively unmarked by volatile partisan rivalry and gang conflicts. These became institutionalized partly in response to disruptions in the local economy produced by the country's economic boom.

Jamaica entered its postcolonial phase in 1962 during a period of rapid economic growth, which began in the 1950s and lasted through the 1960s. Although the national bourgeoisie and the middle class benefited from the expansion propelled largely by U.S. investment in the bauxite/alumina industry, the peasantry, agroproletariat, and the least skilled and secure in the urban workforce suffered a doubled rate of unemployment and received a smaller share in the national income (National Planning Agency 1978, 6; Girvan and Bernal 1982, 37).

In this context of widening disparities and class polarization, a limited form of income distribution through patronage allocation served as a means of placating sections of the impoverished majority. It also conferred some measure of legitimacy on the state, administered by a petty bourgeoisie rooted in domestic and foreign capitalist interests. In post- or neocolonial Jamaica, the political directorate has relied on clientelism to consolidate power and authority (Stone 1980) over an impoverished electorate whose interests are not being met by Jamaica's form of peripheral capitalism. The two major political parties, the PNP and JLP, are highly centralized and elitist. They restrict rank-and-file participation to electoral campaigns and voting and during terms of office to patronage allocation and enforcement, which often involves coercive tactics (Stone 1980, 97). Along with marked economic disparities, contradictions between de jure democracy and the de facto disenfranchisement of the mass of Jamaicans generate considerable disaffection, which the state cannot always contain.

Prior to the postwar decline and relocation of the port and commercial districts (Clarke 1971, 238), a great deal of Oceanview's population had found both formal and informal work opportunities in the nearby downtown. The economic disruption was offset somewhat by government-provided jobs. Labor recruitment, however, done largely through political party associations and top-ranking gangs, did not allay the widespread disaffection surrounding retrenched employment. In fact, local divisions and disparities intensified due to the differential allocation of jobs.

Another change affecting Oceanview's political relations was Jamaica's increased importance in the international ganja trade during the mid- to late 1960s (Lacey 1977, 159). With the decline in legitimate income-making opportunities, Oceanview's involvement in the illegitimate sector, especially the ganja trade, grew. Accompanying this expansion was an increased availability and use of guns, because ganja exported to the United States was exchanged for cash and arms (Lacey 1977). By the late 1960s, the means by which gangs as well as formal political brokers and bosses acquired power and access to sources of income and capitalization had changed dramatically. The entrenchment of gun use escalated local conflicts and prompted persistent tribal war.

One such long-term conflict erupted between Oceanview's two major gang hierarchies—Ethiopia and Israel—in 1967. Before this juncture, shifting alliances, realignments, and sporadic skirmishes between street gangs rarely had serious impact on the neighborhood's political and economic life. The immediate context for this war was a changing local economy, wherein traditional niches eroded and gave way to new ones in which party affiliation was increasingly a determinant.

After 1972 when the PNP won office, the war assumed unequivocally partisan dimensions. Israel became encapsulated in the PNP machine and was given control over numerous contracts for municipal-sector work, such as road maintenance. Ethiopia had ties to the JLP opposition, but these were at best sporadic and tenuous. Nonetheless, though not closely linked to JLP brokers and patrons, Ethiopia was clearly an intractable oppositional force with which the local PNP constituency had to contend.

Tribalism, the Recession, and Destabilization, 1973–77

During the middle and late 1970s, tribal divisions deepened in the midst of a national crisis that destabilized both the economy and the political and national security system. This crisis, abetted by national as well as international opposition, had its origins during the period between 1972 and 1976, during the PNP's first term of office.

Widespread political protest, set off by the social inequalities Jamaica's economic boom engendered, culminated in the PNP's 1972 succession to executive office. The Michael Manley administration instituted various reforms designed to redistribute income and secure greater national control over the dependent island economy (Girvan and Bernal 1982). Largely in response to the effects of the international recession, in 1974–75 the government initiated a series of radical moves toward Jamaicanization. It imposed a production levy on the bauxite companies; it pressed to acquire a 51 percent share in the mines; it helped form the International Bauxite Association; and it announced its commitment to democratic socialism and anti-imperialist struggle throughout the world.

The PNP's turn to the left prompted adverse reactions from foreign capital (particularly the bauxite companies), the U.S. government, and Jamaica's national bourgeoisie. The JLP, backed by the United States, designed and implemented a massive destabilization campaign to undermine PNP legitimacy and oust it from office (Keith and Girling 1978, 29). Foreign and domestic investment diminished drastically. Bauxite companies cut back production and, consequently, reduced the government's revenues and displaced workers. By highlighting anti–North American sentiments, the U.S. press discouraged tourism and thereby undermined Jamaica's second-largest foreign-exchange earner. Local entrepreneurs in large numbers closed down businesses and sought refuge in North America. By March 1976, international commercial banks ceased making loans. Jamaica's economy was brought to a near collapse.

On the political front, the JLP launched a large-scale anticommunist campaign in late 1974, two years before scheduled elections. By early 1976, political and criminal violence had reached unprecedented levels. In reaction, the government declared a state of emergency in June. In December, elections were held, and although the PNP won by a landslide, the government had to maintain acute vigilance against ongoing destabilization efforts over the next four years.

In 1977, the government's shortage of foreign exchange forced it to turn to the International Monetary Fund (IMF; Girvan and Bernal 1982, 39). The restrictive IMF policies (currency devaluation, removal of price controls, and restraints on wage increases) exacerbated the economic slump as well as the political climate and were a major catalyst for the PNP electoral loss in October 1980 (Girvan and Bernal 1982, 43; *African Mirror* 1978, 44).

Although the PNP administration made strides in democratizing an elitist polity through numerous progressive reforms, it, nonetheless, zealously continued a tradition of political patronage. The accompanying tribal violence and victimization also lived on (Ambursley 1983, 87). In localities like Oceanview, those embedded in ruling-party networks—the socialists—benefited from whatever the government had to offer the poor. Those outside of these networks—opposition-party supporters, called labourites, and the unaffiliated alike—however, were denied benefits and, in some cases, even their constitutional rights. This kind of differential access served to discredit democratic socialism in the disillusioned eyes of many at the grassroots.

Political relations in Oceanview during this period of PNP decline grew increasingly polarized and volatile. The unemployment rate rose, and jobs and job contracts were more and more frequently the object of violent local political contests. Increasingly, the only source of wage work was the government-controlled sector, which had rapidly expanded to allow the state to manage key areas of the national economy.

The economic collapse also precipitated an expansion of informal and illegal economic activities. Ganja marketing remained one of the most rampant forms of hustling, and the black market and its attendant crimes hypertrophied as goods became scarce or unobtainable on the formal market. The foreign-exchange deficit severely constrained the importation of a wide range of consumer and capital goods; consequently, these commodities became available only through illegal means.

Barred from more than occasional token jobs with a local urban redevelopment construction scheme in its immediate territory, the gang called Ethiopia specialized in illegal activities and managed to gain a competitive edge in that domain. Israel, on the other hand, monopolized local access to municipal government patronage, but as these resources waned, rivalry grew with Ethiopia over niches in the ganja trade and the black market.

Diminishing patronage, the increased politicization of contracting wagework opportunities, contentions over turf in the illegal sphere, and, as we shall see, the government's drastic repressive security measures all contributed to the volatility that made life in Oceanview a continuous nightmare and threatened to destroy Jamaica's social order.

The Peace Movement, 1978

At the very depths of the 1970s crisis, a citywide Peace Movement emerged, formed by rival gang leaders aligned with the two major political parties. One of the most significant events in Jamaican politics during the 1970s, the Peace Movement was an unprecedented manifestation of popular democracy. It permitted Kingston's so-called lumpen elements to articulate their collective interests and demands. Through it, the urban poor attempted to elevate their political consciousness and develop more coherent and sustained patterns of mobilization outside the conventional machinery of the two-party system.[5]

The Peace, as it came to be known, was catalyzed largely by the Green Bay Massacre of January 5, 1978, a tragic point in Jamaican urban politics. With the help of plainclothes military intelligence agents, the army apparently lured fourteen men from Central Kingston into an ambush at the Green Bay firing range fourteen miles outside Kingston.[6] Five senior members of one of the neighborhood's major gangs were killed. The remaining nine men managed to escape and tell of their experience. Later, the security forces claimed that the Central Kingston gang was caught while engaged in target practice and that the soldiers shot back in self-defense. However, the arms the gunmen supposedly used were never found.

Several days later, major rival gangs called a halt to their fighting. Within days, most gangs in the metropolitan area had accepted the truce and rallied their forces around a demand for equal rights and justice, which meant in this context peace, jobs, and better living conditions. The truce sought to prevent the police and national security forces from committing further atrocities against alleged criminals as well as to stabilize relations between PNP- and JLP-affiliated gangs. Realizing that the contract politics that sparked violence between rival party clients only gave security forces a pretext to attack and led ghetto youths and young men to their deaths, the peacemakers asserted their political autonomy by defying clientelist co-optation and brutal repression. The movement's discourse (as evidenced in media coverage and in local-level discussions) indicated that ghetto peace activists themselves recognized how the political patronage system benefited individual brokers while maintaining the marginalization and victimization of the popular masses (cf. Vélez-Ibañez 1983). By challenging both patronage-clientelism and repression, the Peace Movement threatened the very efficacy of the state apparatus.

The truce was operationalized by a two-tiered committee structure that formed and implemented various grassroots programs designed to create jobs and to occupy otherwise unemployed youths with constructive community projects (Stephens and Stephens 1986, 236–37). These peace programs allocated work on a nonpartisan basis, a clear departure from the conventional mode of recruitment. The two-tiered administration allowed both gang and other ghetto leaders and representatives of established institutions like the Jamaica Council of Churches, the Private Sector Organization of Jamaica, the major political parties, and the government to participate in the movement. The local-level activists belonged to a Peace Council, and the supralocal representatives constituted an Advisory Committee.

Oceanview's Peace

The 1978 truce and the movement that supported it created a climate in which Oceanview residents could again leave the refuge of their fenced-in "yards" (coresidential compounds), put down their weapons, and walk down lanes and alleys without the constant fear of death or injury. For the first time in years, it became possible for ghetto people—so-called labourites, socialists and neutralists alike—to believe they could unite to find solutions to their common "sufferation" (suffering).

The immediate effect was that local networks of kinspeople and peers extended and strengthened. Relatives and former friends, who had severed contact with those involved in gang activities, reestablished communication and interaction. Middle-aged and old people, forced by the war to stop attending evening lodge meetings and religious services, now resumed their various organizational activities. They were much less afraid of having to travel through gang territories and former war zones.

Even gang members found it possible to interact with their former enemies—albeit quite cautiously. A number of Ethiopians and Israelites, who had been schoolmates or friends before the war, managed to revive their relationships and reduce some of their ambivalence toward one another. During the height of the Peace, Ethiopians and Israelites could be seen frequenting the same bars, gambling together, and playing on the same football (soccer) field. Disputes that arose in these situations were usually resolved informally without resort to violence.

The truce also made possible the formation or renewal of extralocal networks based on kinship, church membership, and youth club activities. Although intra- and extralocal cohorts were still largely bound by common party sympathies, there were more cases of individuals who successfully managed to interact across tribal and neighborhood boundaries without contending with accusations of betrayal or physical reprisals.

Demise of the Peace

Oceanview was more fortunate than many ghettoes in that some remnant of the truce (namely, the absence of fighting) was sustained for close to two years, until the latter months of 1979. The momentum of the formally organized citywide movement was lost well within a year, however, undermined by both internal and external dynamics. Conflicts between the Peace Council and the Advisory Committee emerged over funds and illegal arms (Stephens and Stephens 1986, 236–37). Ghetto leaders, whose initiatives had provided the impetus for the movement and whose constituents were to be the direct beneficiaries, wanted control over the Community Peace Fund and the grassroots programs. Their credibility was lost when proceeds from the April One Love Peace Concert were mishandled. Their stature as responsible, legitimate leaders was even further diminished by their adamant refusal to relinquish their arms in return for government amnesty. They feared victimization by national security forces and the police, who were conspicuously absent from the peace efforts. Such fears were in fact realized when one of the key architects of the movement, Claudie Massop, was assassinated by the police in 1979.

The slow pace of local improvements meanwhile eroded the movement's popular base of support. The Community Peace Fund was too small to support the scale of enterprise and activities required to improve the lives of a chronically unemployed constituency. Hence, the peace projects turned out to be short-term palliatives, which initially raised expectations and hopes and then triggered frustrations.

Beyond these contradictions, constraints also emanated from the volatile relations between the Peace Movement and the police. Moreover, the movement had to contend with covert partisan opposition to potentially subversive political realignments, with the JLP-led, U.S.-supported government destabilization campaign, and with IMF-aggravated economic conditions.

Although the PNP and JLP were officially supportive of the movement, the two parties walked a difficult tightrope because their unofficial agenda was to maintain or to reclaim authority over their ghetto constituencies. To this end, they supported the truce while at the same time maneuvering to circumscribe the peace efforts and to keep them within the scope of the parties' and government's goals and interests. To preclude jeopardizing the party structure or either party's respective position in the contest for control of the state, the movement was curbed. It was only allowed to progress so far in its attempts to develop horizontal or class-based solidarity as an alternative to the competitive, divisive vertical alignments characteristic of the clientelist political system.

Although vulnerable to attacks from both major parties, the movement was especially susceptible to the massive force of the JLP opposition. The movement's critical focus on the state system rather than on the PNP administration per se ran against the grain of the destabilization campaign. The campaign's objective was to oust the PNP and replace it with a party sympathetic to U.S. foreign policy and economic interests. Furthermore, the movement's attempt to enforce peaceful relations between gangs and to form a broad-based alliance between lumpen elements controverted the opposition bloc's tactic of fomenting and exploiting partisan cleavages.

Wartime Campaign, Late 1979 to 1980

After late 1978 when the peace programs could not sustain adequate financial backing—because of the nation's grave economic situation and the mishandling of movement funds—one of the few remaining sources of material resources for those outside the government's pool of client workers was the JLP machine. This was generously supported by the United States. By 1980, in the context of a 35 percent national unemployment rate, rising crime, shortages of basic commodities, sharp price increases, and constant currency devaluations, large numbers of ghetto adolescents and men—desperate for "a money," "a wok" (work), or a gun for protection—had become vulnerable to the persuasion and more immediate gratification offered by labourite brokers and bosses. The general disrespect for and distrust of police and "wicked" politicians widely articulated by ghetto peace activists and followers were reinterpreted and translated into a blind hostility directed toward the PNP, whose alleged corruption, mismanagement, repression, and communist leanings had "mash up de cuntry."

Although Ethiopia, particularly its top-ranking or "vanguard" cluster, had managed to avoid becoming directly entangled in JLP brokerage networks during much of the latter 1970s, by 1980 its relations with Israel were enveloped by the hysteria of party rivalry. Ethiopia's former autonomy from the opposition party stemmed in considerable measure from its relative success in forming a resource base derived from illegal activities. At the same time, it maintained a durable relationship with the resourceful headmistress of Blessed Sacrament School, who provided intermittent welfare benefits and continuously discouraged Ethiopians from becoming involved with JLP politics and from, consequently, escalating local conflicts.

Toward the latter part of 1979, the gang's ability to resist partisan pressures waned. Several influential seniors had emigrated, and an influx of arms, channeled initially through a secondary-level gang with ties to JLP branch activists, upset the power balance within the hierarchy. The gang faction with labourite connections prevailed, and Ethiopia's fight against its traditional rival became a part of the larger contest between the JLP and the PNP, between U.S. government and corporate interests and the recalcitrant PNP.

When the PNP government announced general elections in 1980 to determine the country's economic path, the electoral campaign took political violence and terror to unprecedented proportions. A former JLP enforcer, or gunman, recounting his experiences during 1980, claimed that many youths in their teens and early twenties, himself included, were lured into the ranks of political bodyguards by the bait of the temporary good life. The prospect of accompanying "big men" politicians to posh restaurants, hotels, and other uptown settings, of having fancy foods and drink, of being able to wear stylish clothes, and of sporting guns mesmerized many ghetto youths. The young man went on to claim that henchmen commonly were drugged furtively via their food. Some of the excessively violent and inhumane behavior exhibited during the campaign can perhaps be attributed to this kind of manipulation. In the war of 1980, approximately 800 people lost their lives in either the fighting or the cross fire of an irrationally violent campaign for "deliverance."

The Unfulfilled Promise of Deliverance, 1981–89

The "deliverance" that Edward Seaga and the JLP promised Jamaicans was to have developed out of an economic recovery supported by the IMF and the

Ronald Reagan administration's Caribbean Basin Initiative (CBI). Jamaica was to become a model democracy and free-enterprise haven in a region where, during the 1970s, socialist insurrection and other alternatives to dependent capitalist development whetted the imaginations, visions, and praxis of social forces in Grenada, Nicaragua, El Salvador, and in Jamaica itself.

The CBI provided duty-free trade provisions such as softened tariffs and quotas for a period of twelve years and special tax concessions to U.S. corporations investing in the area (Girling 1983). Despite massive support from the U.S. government and international institutions, the Jamaican economy deteriorated. The prospects for the predicted boom were not at all bright. The redeployment of international capital did not favor Jamaica, which, compared to many Third World countries, had a relatively well-organized and expensive formal labor force. Moreover, "Reaganomics" militated against recovery in that high interest rates and reduced North American contributions to the IMF and World Bank served to annul the special concessions the CBI made (Ambursley 1983, 100).[7]

Although in the first year or two of the JLP administration the massive influx of loans and aid engendered optimism, by late 1983 few hints of a growth dynamic remained (*Weekly Gleaner* 1985a, 1985b). The balance-of-payments deficit grew. Whereas in 1980 the deficit was around J$200 million, in 1984 it had grown to J$600 million (*Daily Gleaner* 1984). The country's debt repayments exceeded the flow of loan funds.

Following stringent IMF directives, the government denationalized publicly-owned businesses, drastically cut back in public employment, lifted price regulations and food subsidies, imposed restraints on wages, and devalued the currency several times. These austerity measures made living conditions more severe than at the height of the crisis the former PNP administration confronted. The Jamaican people's expectations and hopes of being delivered from volatile economic recession were met by the frightening prospects of "Haitianization" (Headley 1985, 39).

The deterioration of the economy was accompanied by an erosion of democracy. Between late 1983 and early 1989, there was no official parliamentary opposition (*Weekly Gleaner* 1983a, 1983b; Headley 1985, 40). When the government failed IMF performance tests in 1983, it responded to a PNP challenge by calling early elections. The PNP boycotted the elections partly because the electoral lists were not current (*Daily Gleaner* 1984). Approximately 20 percent of the eligible voters (primarily young adults) were not included on the list, whereas 10 percent of those listed were reputed to be dead. The elections were considered bogus by nonpartisan groups like the Jamaica Council of Churches as well as by PNP proponents. As a consequence, parliament had sixty JLP representatives and eight so-called independents appointed by the governor-general on the prime minister's recommendation. They served as a pseudo-opposition (*Weekly Gleaner* 1983b). Later in 1984, the PNP lost its foothold in the Kingston metropolitan government, the Kingston-St. Andrew Corporation (KSAC) (*Weekly Gleaner* 1984b). The government subsequently disbanded the reputedly mismanaged KSAC and transferred its functions to central or national government ministries.[8]

State militarization also grew to be a problem. Evidence suggests that the government increased its capacity to repress the power of intractable gunmen, whose numbers grew since the massive influx of arms during the late 1970s and in 1980. It was also able to repress labor militancy by increasing the importation of heavy arms (*Weekly Gleaner,* 1984a). Security forces become increasingly visible, and Seaga began to speak in terms of enforcing discipline; that is, of "putting teeth" into labor and criminal laws so that the state could act more punitively against the forces of disorder—as well as those of counterhegemonic change (Headley 1985, 39, 40).

As I have argued elsewhere (Harrison 1987, 32), Seaga's Special Operations Squad, dubbed the Eradication Squad, was underwritten by the United States, which after Seaga's 1980 election victory gave Jamaica the largest per capita police aid package that the Commonwealth Caribbean had ever received (Barry et al. 1984, 207). Jamaica obviously had, and still has, strategic value as a vital cog in the U.S. security and political-economic plan for the circum-Caribbean region. The security aid was designed to improve the capability of the Jamaica Defense Force to meet threats from "externally supported subversion." A security assistance proposal noted that "the failure of the CBI would confirm the view of those who argue that cooperation with the IMF and stimulation of the private sector are fruitless. If the CBI fails to disprove its opponents and secure U.S. dominance, then military options must be available" (Harrison 1987, 32).

Caribbean political scientist A. Vaughn Lewis warned that "the . . . government emphasis on security is ultimately destructive. It draws the [United States] into local politics and establishes it and its representatives as the ultimate mediators. The modernization of the security forces has a strong ideological character beyond its technological aspects. The military gains an enhanced sense of political power as the major guardian of the social order. [This process] is all too similar to the . . . militarization politics in Central America" (Harrison 1987, 32, quoting Barry et al. 1984, 209.).

Opinion polls, the pattern of strike actions (particularly the two-day general strike against gas price increases in January 1985), and the PNP's rise in popularity demonstrated that the populace overwhelmingly lacked faith in the government's IMF/CBI policies for national development. Unlike the decade before, the upsurge in oppositional consciousness, discourse, and mobilization all across Jamaica did not produce a risk of civil war. Although in the 1970s the government confronted a massive onslaught orchestrated by North American and domestic bourgeois interests, the opposition bloc in the 1980s was largely national in scope. It relied more on labor militancy, mass rallies, and boycotts than on the use of terror. The JLP, however, with its heavy backing from the U.S. government, retained the edge in the sphere of physical coercion. The actions of government death squads did not neatly target local criminal elements. Whole communities bore the consequences of police and army deployments that too frequently were indiscriminate in applying force.

JLP Factionalism at the Local Level

After 1983, the intense rivalry between JLP and PNP supporters that marked Oceanview's political landscape after the demise of the Peace subsided. What arose instead was acute factionalism within JLP ranks: gangs vying against each other and gangs competing against JLP associations—all competitively mobilizing their forces to obtain dwindling patronage during a period of IMF-enforced austerity. The flow of heavy arms, which inundated many ghettoes during the destabilization campaign, was partly responsible for this turn of events. Illegitimate, unauthorized gun power, monopolized mainly by JLP henchmen, increasingly operated independent of party and government control (*Weekly Gleaner* 1984c). This, combined with declining patronage resources, multiplied internecine conflict, dividing and polarizing JLP supporters. The JLP's inability to discipline its gunmen effectively undermined its authority.

In May 1984, a two-day feud occurred in Rema, a major JLP stronghold. Two gang factions fought it out until seven persons were killed and many more injured. During fall 1983, there had been a similar eruption in Ocean-view. The Ethiopian gang hierarchy, once a fairly cohesive formation of allied street networks, fissioned. The corner gang with the closest, most direct ties to the JLP, in this case to the office of a member of parliament (MP), was as a consequence the most heavily armed. It attacked members of another corner network on the grounds that the latter were actually socialists. Before 1980, the latter cluster had been the highest ranked gang in Ethiopian territory, and its leadership was reputed to be fairly independent of the JLP machine.

In late 1983 and 1984, the newly emergent vanguard, or top-ranking gang, attempted to consolidate its position in the partisan niche by discrediting or eliminating its major competitor, still widely respected by most Ethiopians. Accusations and threats abounded, and gun fighting occurred in broad daylight, injuring some of the intended targets and killing an innocent person on the street. As a result of this war, many JLP sympathizers became alienated from both the vanguard gang and from the ruling party's administration.

Nonpartisan Mobilization, Antigovernment Protest, and Local Solidarity

In 1984, Blessed Sacrament School's headmistress, Sister Elizabeth, gathered support from local people to spearhead a campaign to build a job-training center and bakery adjacent to the school. Under the aegis of a major service club, J$2.1 million was raised to build the center, which opened in fall 1984. This project was deliberately designed to be a nonpartisan effort. The constituency's MP and councilors (aldermen) were not invited to become involved in any way.[9] In a locality where a large percentage of the population is disillusioned with the government as well as with both major parties, the project would have been open to question and suspicion had it been associated with partisan interests.

Throughout the 1970s, in the midst of political polarization, there had been organized attempts to build a nonpartisan basis for local action and development. The principal locus of this impetus was Blessed Sacrament School, situated on the edge of Ethiopian territory. For approximately two decades, under the administration of Sister Elizabeth, the school provided a number of social services to local people according to need rather than political identity. The school's PTA was one of the neighborhood's most active voluntary associations, tackling larger community issues as well as school problems.

Sister Elizabeth's class and institutional status permitted her access to a wide spectrum of political and economic benefits and favors. Having both relatives and friends strategically placed in the private sector and government, and able to galvanize moral and material support from Catholics both nationally and internationally (largely through U.S. connections), she managed to channel into Oceanview resources otherwise unavailable to poor slum inhabitants, especially those lacking ruling-party connections and sponsorship.

Sister Elizabeth had won the respect of most of the local population, gangs included. According to local oral tradition, she was known to have walked the streets during gun battles and successfully demanded that the fighting stop. In the mid-1970s, before the emergence of the Peace, she worked with others in the neighborhood to organize and enforce a local truce that lasted a full year—a long time by Oceanview standards. Her especially close relationship with Ethiopia was partly responsible for the former vanguard's relative autonomy from party clientelism during a considerable period before the tribal nightmare of 1979–80.

Over the years, therefore, Blessed Sacrament School's many activities—the PTA, the medical and dental clinic, the distribution center for scarce goods like rice and soap—built and sustained a base of local support across gang and party lines. The apparent success of the school's most recent and ambitious project, the training center, served to reinforce local people's hope that a peaceful, unified basis could be found to develop opportunities, which would improve living conditions and life chances.

The Blessed Sacrament project and the prevailing national mood, as evidenced by the January 1985 general strike, contributed to a promising change in Oceanview's political climate. Beyond a small number of JLP stalwarts (whose numbers were reduced by emigration), there was growing dissatisfaction with the government. Oceanview inhabitants seemed to share a common basic outlook toward the JLP administration and the painful austerity its policies imposed. During the general strike, both Ethiopians and Israelites, labourites and socialists, took to the streets, expressing solidarity in protest against unbearable local and national conditions. Although, for some, participation in mass protests such as the general strike represented support for the opposition PNP, for many others such protest actions were largely independent of party loyalty or affiliation. In fact, Oceanview's PNP groups had been dormant before the strike. Moreover, much of the population in neighborhoods like Oceanview had grown skeptical of the ability of either major party, as they were constituted then, to genuinely represent the interests of poor people (*Weekly Gleaner.* 1985c).

Hard times and "sufferation" were equally borne by Oceanview's majority under Seaga's regime. As one resident put it, without significant differences between Ethiopians and Israelites, between labourites and socialists, there was more unity in the area than there had been for a long time. The increased influence of nonpartisan sociopolitical fields, such as that occupied by Blessed Sacrament School, and the simultaneous narrowing of party and gang schisms were significant patterns. They can perhaps be viewed as adaptive processes, which enabled Oceanview to mobilize the totality of its severely limited resources for economic survival. Moreover, in the face of the increasing authoritarianization of Jamaican society, these periodic local responses created an important sense of collective defense, autonomy, and empowerment (cf. Vélez-Ibañez 1983, 246). Over the next several years, however, including those of the subsequent PNP administration, this collective sense of efficacy was harnessed into a pragmatic but, ultimately, self-defeating modus operandi—namely that of mobilizing a united front among the gangs involved in drug trafficking (Harrison 1989, 1990).

In the face of severely diminishing opportunities for legitimate employment in both the public and private sectors, the most readily available income-generation options for ghetto youths and younger adults were to be found in drug trafficking, which, paradoxically, had kept the national economy from collapsing during the crisis of the 1970s when other major commodities—bauxite and tourist leisure landscapes—had failed. Given the severe constraints of Jamaica's "capitalism gone mad," the political economy of drugs is, unfortunately, economically rational, although certainly not ideal and not without serious contradictions. Beyond the economically motivated violence related to drugs, by the early 1990s the consumption of crack cocaine had become a serious health risk.

Oceanview's being caught between a rock and a hard place—the place of "no justice, no peace" regardless of the political patrons in charge—is poignantly acknowledged in local discourse, from hushed conversations in yards to dance-hall lyrics sung at sessions, in which the ethics of drug trafficking, gang violence, and the distribution and investment of drug money in the neighborhood is ambivalently debated. Nonetheless, even a respectable, God-fearing individual sometimes admits that without "enforcers" (gunmen)—without their outlaws, their own local rebels—the community of sufferers would have nothing to protect them against political victimization and starvation and their unending vicious cycles.

The outlaws have tended to view themselves in terms of practicing redistributive and retributive justice. There are some for whom illegalities—crimes against property, the sabotage of public- or private-sector projects failing to meet local needs—are an expression of political protest. Whether political or not, crimes are not uncommonly rationalized in terms of a street code of situational ethics. An influential gang member once told me that, depending on the context, crime can be "moral and forgivable before God if one does it for a just reason, e.g., to feed one's hungry family . . . [or] burglariz[e] a store, whose proprietor lives in a big house and . . . refuses to give credit to or hire ghetto residents." He asserted that "sufferers must eat and drink the fatness of the land now" and not after death.

The code among thieves and its accompanying ethical consciousness, however, seem to have eroded over the years. Years ago, an elder suggested to me that "[g]ang members who have earned their 'manhood titles' over the past few years are more inclined to victimize ghetto people than older 'brethren' raised by '[T]rue Rastas' in the 1960s and . . . 1970s. The . . . youth coming of age since the mid-seventies are more likely to have been corrupted by the greater presence of high-powered guns and the dirty politics aided and abetted by the [United States]" (Harrison 1987). Headley (1996, 14) concurs with this assessment by pointing out that "over the course of the most recent years . . . the activities of . . . rogues and badmen have become more brutal and more depersonalized." This has occurred because of the normalization and internationalization of street crime and the subterranean drug economy since the 1970s (19).

Microcultural Change and Prospects for Structural Transformation

The Oceanview case would be nothing more than a completely sad story of violence and party clientelism in their various permutations were it not for a few hopeful phases in the locality's history: the year-long truce in the mid-1970s, the Peace in 1978–79, and the climate of embryonic unity in 1984–85. In these instances, nonpartisan relations, alliances, and social fields offset cleavages based on rival party loyalties and gang membership. In those three phases, the clientelist character of Jamaica's democratic system was challenged by the withdrawal of considerable grassroots support from the major political parties and the government and the redirection of this energy toward greater community integration. Such a radical but short-lived realignment defied the efficacy of the neocolonial state. Were those local coalitions more than ephemeral and episodic, they might have had the potentially transformative impact on local and national political life that political philosophers and organizers envision but have great difficulty achieving, especially under the volatile and insecure circumstances that characterize the social reality of impoverished and politically alienated Jamaicans.

Although a refreshing and dramatic political departure, the Peace Movement failed, and the later 1980s manifestation of nonclientelist mobilization and solidarity was subverted by the contradictions of a desperate economic pragmatism that led to the conversion of local street gangs into transnational posses hunted by the FBI while meeting the market demand, largely among the suburban middle class, for illegal drugs in the United States. Can these episodic departures from the normal state of political affairs ever lead to anything of consequence? Perhaps the very fact that the Peace Movement, as a mobilization from the very bottom, emerged at all suggests the ability of elements of the urban poor to form, with appropriate allies and support, a broader-based coalition articulating common interests and demands. The Peace Movement demonstrated that the most critically conscious sections of the lumpen were capable of more than mercenary action and skirmishes over patronage. In their mobilizations for justice and peace, they exhibited a rudimentary state of class consciousness and class formation (Stone 1980, 45). The failure of the movement to sustain its momentum and to actualize its ambitious goals was not solely because of endemic flaws in Kingston's most alienated poor. Instead, the demise of the Peace and the return to tribal warfare can be attributed, in part, to the economic and political instability wrought by the forces of North American intervention. Within this context of what many believe to have been a politically orchestrated destabilization, the police and security forces did more than their share of harm. Extrajudicial executions were on center stage in the dreadful drama that unfolded at the time. In considerable measure, the Peace Movement, along with the government's experiment with democratic socialism, was sabotaged and subverted, and, as a result, U.S. dominance in Jamaica and the Caribbean Basin was upheld. Business as usual prevailed.

Although the direction and pace of structural change in Jamaica are certainly constrained by international conditions—from U.S. dominance and IMF intervention to the international drug trade—these conditions are never omnipotent. Despite prevalent and often overpowering limitations, Jamaica's political life—its many formal institutions as well as the multiplicity of informal fields—offers possibilities, opportunities, and maneuvering spaces for agency and social change. Local-level patterns such as Oceanview's Peace and the neighborhood's later responses to austere national conditions elucidate some of the limited means those who bear the brunt of political and economic underdevelopment have for resisting "sufferation" and bringing into their collective lives some semblance of meaning and empowerment, a semblance that perhaps outlines and foreshadows what more effective struggles in the future may be able to materialize and sustain.

My tenor here may be an expression of wistful thinking in the face of dreadful prospects for the equal rights and justice of which the late Peter Tosh sang. But I am trying to envision a more optimistic and convergent destination for the labyrinthine routes that Jamaicans United against Police Brutality, Jamaicans for Justice, the Jamaican Council of Churches, the uncorrupt politicians in the established political party system (and I believe there are some), and, most important to me here, the ordinary people of Oceanview follow in their disparate but potentially intersecting pursuits of a more humane Jamaican society. The elusive dream of, and deeply felt yearning for, equality and justice are themes woven throughout the fabric of everyday life in places like Oceanview. Somehow, that precious dream has managed to survive despite the nightmare with—and against—which people in Oceanview live their everyday lives.

As I indicated in my remarks at the beginning of this chapter, I saw in a July 2001 *Weekly Gleaner* article that blockades were put up all over the Kingston-St. Andrew area, including uptown areas like Barbican, Stony Hill, and Red Hills Road. There was also mention that these popular rituals of solidarity against police oppression—Babylon—took place in neighborhoods east of the West Kingston inferno. Not surprisingly, Oceanview is listed among them. According to the newspaper article, "members of the security forces, who attempted to clear the roadblocks . . . came under heavy fire from gunmen and had to retreat. Some roads which were cleared by police were immediately blocked again by residents" (*Weekly Gleaner* 2001a, 2).

It takes an indefatigable spirit to survive as sufferers, outlaws, and rebels in a setting that many define as Babylon. This is especially true in a case in which the common-sense practices of everyday survival and resistance are incarcerated by a tragic logic of myopic pragmatism and opportunism that works against the kinds of far-ranging transformation that would free bodies and souls from many of the worldly burdens that daily assault their humanity. I cannot help but think that the freedom, justice, and equality that elude the oppressed now resonate with the emancipation for which many of our ancestors, both African Jamaican and African American, lived and died. We, the descendants of those ancestors, know now that emancipation day came but with strings attached to it. The struggle to disentangle ourselves from those sturdy strings, which at times feel like ropes and chains that bind our hands together while cutting into our flesh, persists into the present. As part of that compromised emancipation's legacy, everyday rebels in places like Oceanview continue to struggle, albeit with unreliable weapons for their trial-and-error advances. I offer these inadequate words of anthropological imagination as an expression of affinity and solidarity and as my yearning for an eventual future of peace and one love.[10]

7. The Gendered Violence
   of Structural Adjustment

An Ethnographic Window on the Crisis

"The ghetto not'ing [nothing] but a sad shanty town now." This is what one of my friends and research consultants sadly remarked to me upon my 1992 visit to Oceanview, a pseudonym for an impoverished slum neighborhood with a roughly 74 percent formal unemployment rate in the downtown district of the Kingston, Jamaica, metropolitan area. Times were so hard that the tenements had deteriorated beyond repair. The conspicuous physical decline was a marker of the deepened socioeconomic austerity that has accompanied what some critics (e.g., *Race and Class* 1992) now consider to be the "recolonization" of Jamaica by "the new conquistadors"—the policies and programs that the International Monetary Fund (IMF), the World Bank, and the successive administrations of the United States government—designed to "adjust" and "stabilize" the country's revived export-oriented economy. These strategies for delivering developing societies from collapsing economies are informed by a neoliberal development ideology that euphemizes the widening social disparities that have been the outcome of policies imposing an unbearable degree of austerity on living conditions. Hence, these policies have sacrificed ordinary people's—especially the poor's—basic needs in health care, housing, education, social services, and employment for those of free enterprise and free trade.

Since 1978, I have observed and conversed with Oceanview residents about the social, economic, and political conditions that shape their lived experiences and struggles for survival in this neighborhood (e.g., Harrison 1987a, 1987b, 1988, 1991a, 1991b). The late 1970s was a time of economic hardship and political turbulence, a time when the People's National Party's (PNP) democratic-socialist path to economic development and social transformation was vehemently contested, blocked, and destabilized by political opponents both in and outside of the country and by the concerted economic force of international recession, quadrupled oil prices, and a massive flight of both domestic and foreign capital. Life was certainly hard then, but, as one resident commented, "Cho, mahn; tings worse now." Despite the bright promises of political and economic "deliverance" made by the Jamaica Labour Party (JLP) and its major backer, the Ronald Reagan and later George Herbert Walker Bush administrations of the United States government, the 1980s and early 1990s—under the leadership of a much more conservative PNP—brought only a deepened poverty to the folk who people the streets and alleys of slum and shantytown neighborhoods like Oceanview. This deepening poverty was reflected, for example, in a serious decline in the conditions of public health. Structural adjustment policies implemented over a thirteen-year period brought about alarming reductions in government health care expenditures and promoted the privatization of more costly and less accessible medical care (Phillips 1994, 137). Those most heavily burdened by the impact of these deteriorating social conditions and capital-centered policies were women (Antrobus 1989) who served as the major "social shock absorbers" (Sparr 1992, 31; Sparr 1994) mediating the crisis at the local level of households and neighborhoods. Nearly 50 percent of all of Kingston's households are female headed, giving women the major responsibilities for making ends meet out of virtually nothing (Deere et al. 1990, 52–53). Concentrated in the informal sector of the economy, these women along with their children are most vulnerable to the consequences of malnutrition, hunger, and poor health: rising levels of morbidity and mortality (Phillips 1994, 142; Pan American Health Organization/World Health Organization 1992).

To appreciate and understand the effects, contradictions, and meanings that constitute the reality of a structurally adjusted pattern of production and trade—the effects of which persisted even after the program officially ended in 1990—we must examine the everyday experiences, practices, discourses, and common sense of real people, particularly those encouraged to wait—and wait—for social and economic benefits to trickle down. In the interest of an ethnographically grounded view of Jamaica's economic predicament during the 1980s and early 1990s, I present the case of Mrs. Beulah Brown, an admirable woman whose life story I have collected over several years, to help elucidate the impact the ongoing crisis has had on the everyday lives of ordinary Jamaicans, particularly poor urban women and those who depend most on them. A longtime household head and informal-sector worker like so many other Jamaican women, Mrs. Brown was once a community health aide with a government program that provided much-needed health services to a population to which such care would not have been available otherwise. Mrs. Brown would not have gotten or held that job for the years that she did without the right political connections, something, unfortunately, that too few poor people ever obtain. Although visible benefits from membership in the local PNP group may have set her apart from most of her neighbors, the centrality of patronage-clientelism in local and national politics makes a former political client's experience an insightful window on the constraints and vulnerabilities built into Jamaica's political and economic policies.

Highlights from Mrs. Brown's life story will, then, lead us to the more encompassing story of postcolonial Jamaica's experience with debt, export-led development, and structural adjustment and their combined impact on women workers as well as on neighborhood-level negotiations of crisis.

A Hardworking Woman's Story within a Story

In the 1970s, Beulah Brown, then a middle-aged woman responsible for a three-generation household and extended family, worked as a community health aide under the combined aegis of a government public health program and a local urban redevelopment agency, two projects that owed their existence to the social policy orientation of the reformist PNP administration. Mrs. Brown had begun her employment history as a worker in a factory manufacturing undergarments; however, she preferred household-based self-employment over the stringent regimentation of factory work. A woman with strong civic consciousness and organizing skills, she had worked her way into the leadership of the PNP group within the neighborhood and wider political division. By the late 1970s, she was no longer an officer; however, her membership in the party was still active.

Mrs. Brown was so effective at working with patients and exhibiting good citizenship that she was widely recognized and addressed as "Nurse Brown," the term *nurse* being a title of utmost respect. When Mrs. Brown made her daily rounds, she did more than what was expected of a health aide. She treated her patients as whole persons with a range of basic needs she felt obligated to help meet. To this end, she saw to it that they had nutritious food to eat, clean clothes to wear, and neat and orderly rooms in which to live. She was especially devoted to the elderly, but she also invested considerable energy in young mothers who were often merely children themselves. She shared her experiences and wisdom with them, admonishing them to eat healthful foods, read good books, and, given her religious worldview, "pray to the Lord Jesus Christ" so that their babies' characters and personalities would be positively influenced while still in the womb.

When I initially met her, Mrs. Brown was responsible for caring for her elderly father, her handicapped sister, her sister's three daughters, and her own two daughters. At earlier times, she had even minded a young niece who eventually joined her other siblings and mother, another of Mrs. Brown's sisters, in Canada. Despite many hardships, Mrs. Brown managed her household well enough to see to it that the children were fed, clothed, and schooled. Indeed, one of her nieces, Claudia, is now a nurse in New York City, and—"by the grace of God"—her eldest daughter, Cherry, is a graduate of the University of the West Indies. Unfortunately, Marie, the daughter who still remains at home, has had difficulty getting and keeping wage work, whether in the office or factory—and she has tried both. She decided to make and sell children's clothes so that she could work at home while minding her children. Despite the economic uncertainty of informal-sector work, Marie appreciates its flexibility and the freedom from the "downpressive" (oppressive) industrial surveillance about which a number of former factory workers in Oceanview complain.

Because the community health aide job did not bring in enough money to support the household, Mrs. Brown found extra ways to augment her income. The main thing she did was dressmaking, a skill and talent she had cultivated over the course of her life. Years ago, she even had a small shop in Port Antonio that catered to locals as well as some foreign tourists. That was before she gave up everything—her shop and her husband—to return home to Kingston to care for relatives who were going through some hard times. Besides her dressmaking enterprise, Mrs. Brown also baked and sold meat patties, bought and sold cheese, and sold ice from the freezer she had purchased with remittances from her twin sister in England and help from her church. Through political party connections gained through her earlier activism in the local PNP group, she also saw to it that her sister got a job cleaning streets in the government Crash Programme. Although her family managed better than most of their neighbors, survival was still an everyday struggle.

In the mid-1980s, Mrs. Brown lost her health aide job. The Community Health Aide Program suffered massive losses due to the retrenchment in public-sector employment stipulated by the structural adjustment and stabilization measures imposed by the IMF and World Bank (Le Franc 1994). Luckily, the layoff came around the time when the girls she had raised were coming of age and ready to work to support themselves and the families they were establishing. By 1988, the household was made up of only Mrs. Brown, her second daughter, Marie, and Marie's three small children. Everyone else had moved on to independent residences in Kingston or emigrated to the United States and Canada to live with relatives "a foreign" (overseas). This dispersal relieved the household of considerable financial pressure, but to make ends meet Mrs. Brown still had to intensify her informal means of generating income. She did more dressmaking as well as added baking wedding and birthday cakes to her list of money-making activities.

No matter how much work she did, she never seemed to be able to do more than barely make ends meet. With the devaluation of the Jamaican dollar and the removal of subsidies on basic consumer items like food, the costs of living had increased dramatically. What more could she do to keep pace with the inflationary trend designed to make Jamaican exports more competitive on the international market? She knew, however, that she would never resort to the desperate illicit measures some of her neighbors had taken by "tiefing" (thiefing) or dealing drugs. She simply refused to sell her very soul to the devil for some of the blood money obtainable from the activities of local gangs—now called posses—that move from Kingston to the United States and back, trafficking in substances like crack cocaine. Increasingly, especially with political patronage becoming more scarce, drug trafficking has become an important source of local subsistence and small-scale investment. However, the price paid for a life of crime is too high. She lamented that too many "youts" (youths) involved in the drug economy make the return trip home to Jamaica enclosed in deathly wooden crates.

Like most Caribbean people, Mrs. Brown has long belonged to and actively participated in an international family network extending from Jamaica to Great Britain, Canada, and the United States (Basch, Schiller, and Blanc 1994). Her sisters "a foreign" had often invited her to visit them, and they had also encouraged her to migrate so that she, too, could benefit from better opportunities. Before the mid-1980s, Mrs. Brown had been determined to remain at home caring for her family. Moreover, she loved her country, her church, and her party, and she wanted to help shape the direction of Jamaica's future. She strongly felt that someone had to remain in Jamaica to keep it going on the right course. Everyone could not migrate. "My home is here in Jamaica," she had insisted adamantly.

These were her strong feelings before structural adjustment hit the heart of her home—her refrigerator, freezer, and kitchen table. In 1990 alone, the cost of chicken—a desirable entrée to accompany rice and peas on Sunday—went up three times. The cost of even more basic staples also increased, making items such as fresh milk, cornmeal, and tomatoes (whose price increased 140 percent) increasingly unaffordable for many people (Statistical Institute of Jamaica 1991).

Between 1987 and 1992, Mrs. Brown traveled abroad twice for extended visits with relatives in England, Canada, and the United States. While away for nearly a year at a time, she "did a likkle babysitting and ting" to earn money that she was able to save for her own use and purposes. Her family treated her "like a queen," buying her gifts ("good camera, TV, radio, and ting"), not letting her spend her own money for living expenses, and paying for her air transportation from point to point along her international itinerary. The savings she managed to send and bring back home were key to her Oceanview household's survival. Her transnational family network, and the geographic mobility it offered, allowed her to increase her earnings by taking advantage of the marked wage differential between Jamaica and the countries where her relatives live (Ho 1993, 33). This particular financial advantage has led even middle-class Jamaican women to tolerate an otherwise embarrassing and humiliating decline in social status to work as nannies and domestic helpers in North American homes. International migration within the Caribbean region as well as between it and northern metropoles has been a traditional survival strategy among Jamaicans since nineteenth-century postemancipation society.

Harsh circumstances forced Mrs. Brown to join the larger wave of female emigrants from the Caribbean who, since the late 1960s, have outnumbered their male counterparts (Deere et al. 1990, 76; Ho 1993, 33). Thus far, Mrs. Brown has remained a visitor, but she acknowledges the possibility and perhaps even the probability that some day soon she will join her sisters as a permanent resident abroad. Meanwhile, she continues to take care of business at home by informally generating and allocating resources within the kinship-mediated transnational social field within which her local life is embedded.

Mrs. Brown's story and many others similar to it are symptomatic of the current age of globalization, marked by a deepening crisis that policies such as structural adjustment and its complementary export-led development strategy attempt to manage in favor of the mobility and accumulation of transnational capital. Mrs. Brown's story, however, is only *a story within a story* about the dramatic plot-thickening details of Jamaica's nonlinear struggle for substantive development and decolonization. Let us now place Beulah Brown's lived experience in broader context and, in so doing, illuminate the forces and conditions that differentially affect Jamaica's hardworking women, particularly those who work in the informal sector and free trade zone. As we shall see, their dilemmas and struggles are closely interrelated.

Once upon a Time: Dilemmas of Development

Deep into Debt

Postcolonial Jamaica, like many other Third World and Southern Hemisphere countries, is beset by a serious case of debt bondage. Jamaica is embroiled in a crisis that can be traced back to the economic turmoil of the mid-1970s. By 1980, when the conservative JLP ousted the democratic socialist PNP from power, Jamaica's debt had doubled because of the extensive borrowing undertaken to absorb the impact from the receding international economy, to offset massive capital flight (a domestic and international panic response to the PNP's move to the left), and to underwrite state-initiated development projects. To stabilize and reinvigorate the collapsed economy, the JLP administration, with the support and guidance of the Reagan administration, relied on the IMF and the World Bank for massive loans to redress its critical balance of payments and fiscal deficits. Consequently, the country's indebtedness grew by leaps and bounds. As a result, Jamaica's debt servicing exceeds what it receives in loans and grants (Ferguson 1992, 62), and it devours 40 percent of the foreign exchange it earns from its exports, which are supposed to jump-start the economy into a pattern of sustained development. The development strategy pursued since 1980—one that privileges private-sector export production—has been underwritten by these relations of indebtedness. The IMF, World Bank, and the U.S. government's Caribbean Basin Initiative (CBI) along with the United States Agency for International Development (USAID) have delimited terms for Jamaica's economic restructuring that further integrate the island into a global hierarchy of free trade relations. This global hierarchy is not only class- and racially biased (Köhler 1978); it is also fundamentally gendered (Antrobus 1989; Enloe 1989; Sparr 1944).

The Path to Economic Growth and Social Crisis

The debt-constrained, export-led, and free trade-based development path that the Jamaican economy has followed has failed to deliver the masses of Jamaican people from the dilemmas of persistent poverty and underdevelopment. Benefits from this development strategy have not trickled down the socioeconomic ladder. What have trickled down, however, are the adverse effects of drastic austerity measures, which are the strings attached to aid from the IMF and World Bank. These strings stipulate that the government denationalize or privatize public sectors of the economy, cut back social services and public employment, devalue the Jamaican dollar, impose restraints on wages, liberalize imports, and remove subsidies and price controls on food and other consumer goods (Antrobus 1989, 20). These measures along with the stipulated focus on export production have resulted in increased unemployment, a decline in real wages for those fortunate enough to have regular incomes, a dramatic rise in the costs of living, and, with these, an increase in malnutrition and hunger, a general deterioration in public health, and an escalating incidence of drug abuse and violence—including violence against women (Antrobus 1989, 23). Conditions are so severe that economist Clive Thomas (1988, 369) poignantly argues that poor people cannot afford to live as well as nineteenth-century slaves whose access to protein, carbohydrates, fuel, and work tools was more adequate. Those bearing the heaviest burden in coping with the social and economic austerity are women, a large proportion of whom have the responsibility—whether they are formally employed or not—to support households and family networks (Bolles 1991).

Although it has sacrificed ordinary people's basic needs, the debt bondage and free trade strategy has, however, been successful in restoring "the military and economic foundations of U.S. superiority . . . incorporating the Caribbean Basin countries into the U.S. military-industrial complex" (Deere et al. 1990, 157). A central aspect of the CBI has been the increased sale of U.S. exports to the Caribbean (McAfee 1991, 43). Exports from the Caribbean that receive duty-free entry into the U.S. market are produced in foreign-controlled free trade zones where items (usually apparel and electronics) are assembled from raw materials and capital goods imported often from the United States. In other words, the Caribbean has become an offshore site for branch plants that are not generating the backward linkages and horizontal integration necessary for stimulating the domestic sectors of Jamaica's economy.

Gender Inequality in Globalization

Transnational capital has appropriated the enterprising freedom to repatriate profits without any enforced obligations to invest in the host country's future; it has enjoyed the freedom to employ workers, to a great extent female, whose labor has been politically, legally, and culturally constructed to be cheap and expendable. As Cynthia Enloe (1989, 160–63) argues, economic globalization depends upon laws and cultural presumptions about femininity, sexuality, and marriage that help lower women's wages and benefits. For instance, transnational garment production has taken advantage of and reinforced the patriarchal assumptions that activities such as sewing are natural women's tasks requiring no special skill, training, or compensation; that jobs defined as skilled belong to men, who deserve to be remunerated for their special physical strength and training; that women are not the major breadwinners in their households and families and are really supported by their fathers or husbands (Safa 1995); and that women's needs should not direct the policies and practices of business management and development specialists.

The profitability, capital mobility, and structural power (Wolf 1990) constitutive of globalization are fundamentally gendered phenomena marked by a masculinist logic. Present-day strategies to adjust, stabilize, and facilitate capital accumulation implicate constructions of femininity and masculinity that, in effect, legitimate the superexploitation of the productive and reproductive labor of women, with women of color, racially subjugated women, bearing the heaviest burdens (see Enloe 1989; Deere et al. 1990; Antrobus 1989) and being the most vulnerable targets of structural violence—the symbolic, psychological, and physical assaults against human subjectivities, physical bodies, and sociocultural integrity that emanate from situations and institutions structured in social, political, and economic dominance (Köhler 1978).

The misogynistic symbolic assault against women is reflected in the language and pictorial representations of promotional materials addressed to prospective investors in trade journals and industrial magazines as well as in flyers and posters at trade shows. For instance, in a Jamaica Promotions Corporation (JAMPRO) advertisement promoting investment opportunities on the island, there is an image of a black woman's shapely lower back, protruding buttocks (in Jockey briefs), and upper thighs (National Labor Committee 1992). Inscribed across the underpants in large white print is the phrase "A brief example of our work" (44). Below this, under a sentence attesting to the high quality and productivity of Jamaican factories, is found in smaller print the statement "From jeans to jackets—from suits to shorts—smart apparel manufacturers are *making it* in Jamaica" (emphasis added). "Making it" can be construed as a double or triple entendre evoking manufacture and profit making as well as the more risqué connotations associated with female anatomy. An implicit set of meanings being manipulated is that related to the hypersexuality that historically racist/sexist ideology has attributed to women of African descent. Jamaican female labor is cheap in the dual sense of low labor costs and the myth of unrestrained sexual availability. Drawing on stereotypical notions of African Caribbean promiscuity, the advertisement informs prospective manufacturers that they can "make it" with Jamaican female workers without any legal strings attached or long-term commitment. The foreign manufacturer can take advantage of this lucrative situation for at most—and often less than—75 cents per hour or anywhere from 13 percent to 24 percent of what is paid to U.S. apparel workers (McAffee 1991, 83). According to a 1988 survey, 80 percent of Kingston's free trade zone workers earned less than U.S.$15 per week (86). Although wonderful incentive for the investor, from the vantage point of the worker, this wage purchased less than 40 percent of a family's food needs (24).

Beyond its decided class bias, Jamaica's approach to development has a definite gender bias in that women's productive and reproductive roles are expected to bear the brunt and absorb the highest risks of both the export-growth and austerity facets of present-day policies. Caribbean feminist Peggy Antrobus argues that structural adjustment policies in particular presuppose "a gender ideology [that is] fundamentally exploitative of women's time, labor, and sexuality" (1989, 19). Poor women, whether employed in free trade zone factories or informally eking out meager livelihood in their ghetto households and neighborhoods, bear the burden of policies and programs that, in effect even if not in design, contribute to what George Beckford (1972) called the "persistent poverty" characteristic of plantation and postplantation societies in the throes of recolonization (*Race and Class* 1992) in late twentieth- and early twenty-first-century capitalism.

The Trickle-Down Effects of Free Trade Zones

The free trade or export processing zones established under JAMPRO and the program organized under section 807 of the U.S. Special Tariff Provisions represent a "type of unregulated trade, investment and employment . . . that the [World] Bank believes ought to be in effect worldwide" (McAfee 1991, 84–85). The recipients of generous incentives, free trade zones do not pay "import duties and taxes on stock dividends" (84–85), and they are free to transfer their profits from host countries. A state within a state, the free trade zone is unfriendly to unions (84), and it has been given the license to exploit its host country's laborers, who are often forced to work overtime without any notice and are denied sufficient time and facilities for rest and lunch breaks. In some cases, workers are frisked before they are allowed to use the restroom and, in the worst situations, are permitted access to the restroom only once per day (Ferguson 1992, 68–69; McAffee 1991, 85).

When export processing zone workers contest the free trade zone's cheap labor policy and, consequently, organize for better wages and work conditions, they risk being fired and blacklisted, which precludes their finding work in any other free trade zone factory. Despite the severe risks, Jamaican women have not accepted dehumanizing conditions without responding organizationally. For instance, in March 1988, 2,000 women from Kingston's free trade zone went on a three-day strike (*Weekly Gleaner* 1988a, 1988b, 1988c, 1988d). The women complained of verbal and physical abuse, unreasonably low pay, and the lack of union representation. Initially, then Prime Minister Edward Seaga appointed a joint union–management council to investigate the workers' complaints; however, he eventually gave in to pressure from factory owners, who threatened that they would close their plants if the government failed to live up to promises it made and if workers continued to exhibit "poor work attitudes" (*Weekly Gleaner* 1988a).

Economic Desperation in the Informal Sector

Seaga's attitude that, no matter how bad the situation, free trade zone jobs are better than no free trade zone jobs is shared by many workers, who prefer these jobs over the insecure, unstable, and aggressively competitive work found in the informal economic sector (Deere et al. 1990). Free trade zone workers, nonetheless, are extremely vulnerable to losing their jobs. If they exhibit behavior that management construes as nonproductive and reflective of poor work attitudes, they face abuse or summary termination. Moreover, they are apt to be made expendable if factory owners decide to move on to more lucrative grounds in a country better able to enforce a cheaper wage labor force.

Although wage workers frequently augment their income with informal means of generating additional income, close to 40 percent of Jamaican women—as compared with 12 percent of the male labor force—work primarily in the informal economy, in which they predominate in household service and petty commerce (Deere et al. 1990, 67; Bolles 1992; Harrison 1991b). To maximize survival, informal-sector workers have to balance the competitive spirit of "aggressive hustling" with the cooperative spirit that sustains the extended kin and friendship networks through which goods, services, and cash are circulated for the sake of basic survival. In light of the increasing scarcity of cash, these extended exchange networks allow their impoverished participants to meet basic needs outside of formal market transactions (Deere et al. 1990, 71).

Although many women prefer having factory jobs over informal means of subsistence, the reality is that there are few such job opportunities available. Moreover, the built-in expendability of free trade zone labor means that the export processing proletariat cannot enjoy any real distance from the day-to-day reality of the informal sector and the persons—like Beulah and Marie Brown—who operate within its sphere. Although the full-time informal workforce includes those with no recourse but the underground economy, there are, nonetheless, petty entrepreneurs for whom small-scale self-employment represents a meaningful source of livelihood preferable to work conditions in the free trade zone. Local residents' social criticism of the factory regime may be unemployed workers' rationalization of the resentment they feel for being excluded from a wage-work opportunity. On the other hand, their criticism may also be an expression of a local knowledge cognizant of the contradictions and iniquities of the prevailing model of development and its structure of employment/unemployment.

Many analysts claim that the individuated and present-day oriented aggressive hustling characteristic of informal-sector activities "hinders the development of a sense of collective struggle" and contributes to "the fragmentation of the working class and a deterioration of its institutions" (Deere et al. 1990, 11, 12). This predicament, they argue, "further deepens the social crisis" (11, 12). Under what circumstances can a sense of collective struggle emerge among those without any recourse but hustling to survive? What role does gender politics play in the development of collective consciousness of kind in the sociopolitical space of structural unemployment and informal-sector work? These are questions that inform the ensuing analysis of the structural violence of poverty in the slum where Beulah Brown's story began.

Negotiating Crisis in a Downtown Constituency

Everyday life is literally a struggle against "sufferation" in a place like Oceanview where chronic wage unemployment is extremely high; the violent rivalry between gang-organized clients of the country's two major political parties, the PNP and JLP, runs rampant; "Babylon," what the Rastafari call the oppressive society and its repressive state apparatus, reveals the fullness of its terror-provoking face; and (paraphrasing Roger Abraham's [1983] book title) men-and-*women*-of-words engage in verbal performances punctuated by questions concerning the meaning of freedom and sovereignty for sufferers and "likkle people" who struggle to survive in a national context in which independence has represented a redefined legal status unaccompanied by a fundamental social and economic metamorphosis (Lewis 1968). The rising expectations and unfulfilled promises of independence and decolonization have wrought in the folk experience and sociopsychology a deep sense of disappointment, alienation, and anger, which inform agency among Oceanview's sufferers.

No-Man's-Land and Centerwomen's Space

According to most Kingstonians' cognitive maps, the uptown-downtown division is a central dimension in local social class and political geography. Also, within the space of the expansive downtown ghetto zone, partisan boundaries demarcate loci of safety, danger, and neutrality, all of which are contingent and subject to recodification. The neighborhoods that are viewed as anathema to most middle-class people who are afraid to be "caught dead" most places downtown, are highly contested sites that are often reduced to virtual war zones, especially at the height of the political violence attendant upon election campaigns.

These ghetto zones are also gendered. Territories within and between neighborhoods have been masculinized and paramilitarized according to a cluster of sociocultural criteria grounded in a popular imagination shaped and promoted by the violence-glorifying B-rated movies imported from the United States during the 1960s and early 1970s. More importantly, local constructions of masculinity are grounded in what Lacey (1977, 159) calls the guns/ganja/organized crime nexus that has internationalized Jamaican marijuana production and distribution since the late 1960s (Harrison 1990). Aided and abetted by the routinized gang-centered political violence through which many politicians expropriate power, the gunman syndrome that has swept across Jamaica's urban ghettoes draws upon and reconfigures traditional notions of lower-class African Jamaican masculinity that privileged such "reputational" attributes as virility, physical prowess, toughness, and defiance of authority (Wilson 1978; Whitehead 1986). Accordingly, masculinity is constructed in terms of the ability to be tough and defiant enough to use violence to conquer and control women and weaker men. In light of the salience of achieving a sense of "social balance" (Whitehead 1986), this militarized manhood is most valued when it is balanced by the "respectability" of being able to satisfy at least some of the material needs of one's offspring and "babymother" by "living by the gun." If a relative balance between reputation and respectability is not achieved, then the gunman is judged to be "wicked"—a form of moral weakness (Whitehead 1986).

Gunman values and power do not, however, stand uncontested. The paramilitarized masculinity of political gangs, drug posses, and their turfs and war zones is challenged both by peaceful men of street-corner networks who manage to negotiate political neutrality and by those women who claim local spaces and convert them into the sanctuaries, safety zones, and neutral interfaces (cf. Feldman 1991) of such nonpartisan fields of power as open markets, schools, churches, mutual aid associations, and some yards, or coresidential compounds. Peacemaking women, similar in many respects to the center-women that Sacks (1984) analyzes in the context of workplace struggles in North Carolina, mobilize social power rooted in the familistic values and skills that enable and empower them to engage in effective communication, goal and priority setting, decision making, and conflict mediation and resolution.

In Oceanview, the primary and most visible loci of power are government- and political party–based domains along with the rival street-corner gangs that have traditionally been aligned with the two major political parties. (Since the 1980s, gangsters—who rival the national security forces in their gun power—have increasingly operated outside of party and government control.) At certain junctures in local history, violent conflicts arising from partisanship and other significant divisions have been contained by truces negotiated and sustained for varying (but usually limited) periods of time. During peaceful phases, women-centered networks and associations (particularly the nonpartisan and multipurpose Blessed Sacrament School Parent Teacher Association, or PTA, to which Beulah Brown belonged) have been visible agents of the microcultural change that has heightened social solidarity and consciousness of kind (cf. Vélez-Ibañez 1983). These periods of calm and collective identity, however, are vulnerable to being subverted by the victimization and violence that accompany electoral campaigns.

The Structure and Meanings of Violence

The worst case of political violence was in 1980 when the heated rivalry between the PNP's democratic socialism and the JLP's free-market strategy set the stage for an unprecedented level of violence. Kingston came to be described as the "Beirut of the Caribbean," and life in Oceanview was "the worst nightmare," as one local resident described to me. More recently, in early 1993, the Weekly Gleaner (1993a, 1993b, 1993c) published numerous articles, some with front-page headlines, on violence amid the general election that took place in March of that year. Whether the expected level of violence could be contained was a major concern expressed by journalists, politicians, the police commissioner, and a respected priest who runs a mission in a downtown ghetto.

Violence—whether perpetrated by politicized gangs, criminals, the police, or men against women—is an integral feature of life in Oceanview. It is a phenomenon that conditions the climate affecting not only local and national politics but also economic activities and patterns of association and social interaction. Oceanview residents are forced to live with and against violence that provides a basis, though not the sole one, for the meanings invested in local evaluations of the legitimacy of government, its policies of development, and political participation. As an instrument and process in power contests, violence is constitutive of the sociocultural forms and meanings that inform and negotiate the terms of interaction, conflict, and political culture. Throughout Jamaica's history, violence has generated politically and culturally salient meanings since the initial colonization of the island and the subsequent formation of an exploitative plantation slavery society. Violence has not only served as an instrument of domination, it has also been deployed in protest and resistance, as exemplified in the case of slave rebellions and *marronage* (the escapes and struggles of runaway slaves) in which the moral economy and cultural politics of slavery were forcefully contested (Campbell 1977).

In its duality, violence is salient in Jamaicans' historical memory and present-day experience, and in places like Oceanview its salience is reproduced in a local Realpolitik that has been buttressed by the growing pattern of militarization affecting the state as well as criminal forces like drug posses. State militarization has been underwritten by CBI aid from the United States, which has determined that regional security and U.S. dominance be achieved in the Caribbean Basin by any means necessary (see Harrison 1987a, 32; Barry et al. 1984). The broader context within which physical violence in its various forms can be situated is that of structural violence. According to Köhler's (1978) and other peace researchers' conceptualization, structural violence encompasses such assaults and violations against human rights and dignity as food shortages and hunger, pollution and environmental degradation, and police brutality—conditions engendered by the "situations, institutions, and social, political, and economic structures" (Haviland 1990, 458) that characterize the polarized economic growth associated with the concerted IMF/World Bank/CBI strategy for development.

As suggested previously, the structural violence of free-market development relies upon constructions of masculinity and femininity that help produce and reproduce the mobility and accumulation of transnational capital. Violence-legitimating constructions of masculinity are implicit in U.S.-supported military-industrial policies implemented in Jamaica. In either direct or indirect ways, the managers and protectors of the postcolonial—or neo-colonial—social order (namely, politicians, policemen, and army officers) are expected to take high, "manly" risks and negotiate danger to ensure such desired outcomes as profitability, law and order, and counterinsurrection. Even tourism advertisements appropriate images of legitimately militarized males in police or army uniforms (and welcoming, available, and compliant females in colorful peasant attire) in order to sell the comfort and safety of Jamaica's beach resorts to prospective foreign tourists (Enloe 1989, 32).

In Jamaica's clientelist political system, a form of "democracy by default" (Edie 1990), the managers of the postcolonial social order commonly expropriate and enforce their power through paramilitary means: deploying ghetto forces or partisan street gangs. The success of this tactic depends, of course, on a social construction of ghetto masculinity that privileges the dauntless toughness of living by the gun. Such a value is rooted in the forms of complicity and co-optation embodied in the current hegemonic structure of masculinized power.

Gendered Fields of Regenerative Power

Oceanview's struggle over war and peace, over repressive militarism and people-centered democracy, is also a struggle over the reconstruction of both gender and development. On the sociopolitical terrain of peace mobilization, local agents contest and renegotiate the terms and meanings of gender identity, power, work, and development, especially as they apply to local community life.

Sociopolitical agency is constituted in gendered fields of power. Gendered politics, through which dominant gender ideologies are sometimes challenged and refashioned, plays an integral part in the microcultural processes that periodically give rise to emergent forms of class-cognizant solidarity. Such episodes enable wider networks of men and women to coalesce and defy the legitimacy of the state, whose seductively divisive rituals of marginality (Vélez-Ibañez 1983) trap clients into vicious cycles of disenfranchisement.

During the 1970s and 1980s, Oceanview's political trajectory encompassed three phases (circa 1975, 1978–79, 1984–85) in which local social relations were marked by peaceful, bilateral, nonsectarian alliances; extralocal cohort formation; and increased interlocal consciousness of kind (Harrison 1987b). At these junctures, there was a heightened recognition of the local consequences of underdevelopment and polarized economic growth and a more explicitly articulated awareness of a connection between, on one hand, local poverty and political victimization and, on the other, national (and international) development strategies. At these moments of truce and reconciliation, the values and social power characteristic of women-centered sanctuaries and safety zones became more widespread.

Through the microtransformative practices of these phases of reconciliation and solidarity, networks of local women in conjunction with peace-seeking men expressed their opposition to political violence, the politicization of scarce wage-work opportunities (generally public sector controlled), and the cultural construction of violence-glorifying definitions of ghetto manhood. In the process of contesting the paramilitarization of local masculinity as well as the masculinization of power in clientelist and partisan political spheres, these women redefined the meaning and purview of their womanhood. They reinterpreted and extended the meanings of the cultural principles of regeneration and reproduction invested in many African Caribbean notions of womanhood and mothering. According to folk sensibilities, mothering is a shared, cooperative kin network–based configuration and set of practices that involves nurturing, counseling, and healing dependents as well as fulfilling the obligations of meeting family needs through participation in the public arenas of work and sociopolitical engagement.

Oceanview's centerwomen applied these traditional principles to the extended, suprakin public domain of neighborhood redevelopment—the term *redevelopment* signifying the renewal and reconstruction of the locality as a community and fictive kindred. Through their praxis in nonpartisan, multipurpose arenas like the Blessed Sacrament School PTA, these ghetto women asserted their collective familial responsibility and motherlike authority to challenge routinized political and criminal violence and to contest the hegemony of masculinist notions of power in the space of their everyday lives and lived experience. The polluted and violated space of the partisan political constituency was, hence, reclaimed and purified as an extended yard. At once a space and a cluster of social relationships, a yard—especially as a metaphor for a protected site of greater inclusiveness and cooperation—is reminiscent of the symbolically charged notion of "family land" that is believed to be the source of cosmopolitical and physical regeneration for both biological reproduction and folk-centered economic development (Carnegie 1987). Through truce-making efforts, centerwomen and their male allies reconstituted their base of survival by reclaiming contested urban space and converting it into a shared place of community.

Local articulations of social criticism and community solidarity confront nationwide and even global forces that reduce ghetto sufferers to dispensable clients and pawns sacrificed to the secular deities of what Vélez-Ibañez (1983) calls "rituals of marginality." The challenge to the gender and class ideologies embedded in the syndrome of political violence and in current poverty-perpetuating policies is a key element in the grassroots politics of survival and rehumanization found in places like Oceanview. Underpinning this woman-centered praxis is a deep, potentially subversive knowledge of a long-standing tradition of resisting and contesting the status quo and of celebrating the power of the relatively powerless to imagine—and struggle for—a community that privileges freedom. The freedom imagined is not that of capital mobility and accumulation but that which is wedded to social justice and equality. Oceanview's centerwomen, like their counterparts throughout Jamaica and the Caribbean, are catalysts in grassroots responses to a crisis that reverberates transnationally, affecting both Southern and Northern Hemispheres. Grassroots mobilizations—in the form of action groups, cooperatives, nongovernmental organizations, and social movements—are expressing the urgent concerns and grievances of households, communities, and the informal sector in ways that the established political parties and trade unions have not (Deere et al. 1990, 101). It is not at all surprising that in light of "the specific ways in which the crisis impinges upon women," they "have been among the first to protest and organize in new ways" (106).

End of the Story within a Story—For Now

Tired from feeling the weight of her sixty-three years, especially the past ten of them, Mrs. Brown complained to me about the prohibitive costs of living and the unjust formula being used to devalue the Jamaican dollar so as to make the economy more penetrable for foreign investment. "And all at the people's expense!" As we waited at the airport for my departure time, she remarked that she did not know how she could have made it through all her trials and tribulations if it were not for the grace of God who gave her industry, creativity, and a loving family as gifts; her church, upon which she had always been able to depend for both spiritual guidance and material aid; and Blessed Sacrament School, its PTA, and the various other activities and community services based on the grounds of that strategic local sanctuary from political warfare and economic desperation. When she was abroad, she raised a respectable sum of money from her relatives and friends for the church and school that have helped sustain her family through plenty of hard times. She insisted that no amount of "gunshot or war" could ever dissuade her from giving back to and continuing to be a part of the vital organs of support and solidarity that have been integral to her sense of moral and sociopolitical agency. Although committed to her Oceanview network of support and praxis, Mrs. Brown appreciated the freedom to go as she pleased, or needed, to and from the various sites of her transnational family.

It was time for me to go to my exit, so we kissed and hugged each other good-bye as we had done several times before. We promised to write and phone until we were able to meet again—whether in Jamaica or in the United States. After all, she smiled, she had many other stories to tell me about her life as a hardworking Jamaican woman making her way in a difficult world.

I am back home now, but I cannot help but think—and worry—about Beulah Brown and Oceanview in light of the global restructuring that affects life in the Caribbean as well as in the United States, where the implementation of Northern Hemisphere versions of structural adjustment are being felt and confronted. The economic restructuring occurring in the United States is only a variation on a wider structural adjustment, neoliberal theme reverberating across the globe. Policies implemented in the United States resemble the austerity measures the IMF and World Bank have imposed on developing nations: cutbacks in social spending and public investments in housing, education, and health care; deregulation of airline, trucking, banking, finance, and broadcasting industries; corporate union busting; currency devaluation; divestment of public enterprises and the increasing privatization of public services; and dramatic alterations of the tax system, shifting the tax burden away from wealthy individuals and large corporations (Sparr 1992, 30–31).

Probing the political and moral economy of poverty in "the field" (cf. D'Amico-Samuels 1991) has led me to reconceptualize analytical units and boundaries in ways that discern and utilize points of articulation and conjuncture between, for instance, Beulah Brown and myself and Jamaica and the United States for a deeper, more broadly situated, and more personally grounded understanding of structural adjustment's gendered assaults: its invidious structural violence.

PART V

Structural Violence Here and There in the Global Era

8. Everyday Neoliberalism in Cuba

A Glimpse from Jamaica

In summer 1996, I returned to Jamaica to follow up on themes from earlier research I had done on the effects of neoliberal policies at the household and neighborhood levels. In my work on the gender politics of structural adjustment (see chapter 7), I had attempted to demonstrate that the political economy of Oceanview's deepening poverty is more adequately analyzed if we discern the major loci of empirical mediation (my adaptation of Trouillot's concept) or micro-macro articulation through which structural adjustment programs penetrate and constrain the everyday life of consumption, waged and unwaged work, and collective social and political action (cf. Trouillot 1988, 199). The loci that interested me most were households, schools, and social networks of mutual aid and cooperative labor, including the male-specific, age-graded units of local organization called gangs or, in their trans-national guise, posses. The economic austerity that structural adjustment policies exacerbated and the neoliberal policy climate that persisted even after the International Monetary Fund (IMF) mandate had formally ended had measurable effects on all of these sites. I was particularly interested in how people in Oceanview made sense of and sought to negotiate those effects, whose aftershocks had both negative and positive dimensions.

In 1996, my fieldwork plan was to update my data on gang politics (Harrison 1987) as well as continue my investigation of the relationships and resource redistribution of one particular extended family, the "Browns," whom I introduced in chapter 7. In field research, one always has to be flexible enough to adapt to changing circumstances and to go with the flow. It turned out that an escalation of gang and police conflict prevented me from collecting primary data to follow up on my gang interest, so I concentrated my efforts on an "ethnography of the particular" (Lughod 1991), a detailed ethnography of a particular household and its linkages with other households tied together by matrifocal consanguineal relationships. This interhousehold network linked the Oceanview family with relatives in three different countries: England, the United States, and Canada. Earlier observations had indicated that during the 1980s my acquaintances' transnational connections had grown in importance. As the local opportunity structure was assaulted by structural adjustment, transnational sources of resources and even employment opportunities made up the difference, more or less.

As I indicated before, the head of the kin network's main household, Mrs. Beulah Brown, lost her job as a community health aide when the government was directed to contract its spending in the social and health services as well as in political patronage. In the wake of this major change in her life, Mrs. Brown accepted invitations from her sisters to visit them and her extended kin in England, Canada, and the United States. During her extended visits, she took advantage of informal work opportunities (babysitting and being a live-in nursemaid) to earn some hard currency, most of which was used to purchase goods that were taken back to Jamaica for household use and informal retail. Through her transnational kin network, Mrs. Brown was able to participate in a small-scale version of informal commercial importing, an economic niche that expanded because of the conditions created by structural adjustment policies (Anderson and Witter 1994, 52–53; Ulysse, 2007).

My aim was to examine Mrs. Brown's household economy more closely to learn more about her experiences in Manchester, Toronto, and New York City, specifically her living and work conditions in these three cities, and her relatives' socioeconomic location in terms more detailed than what I already knew. I also wanted to know more about the extent to which other Ocean-view residents had access to and were dependent on transnational flows of resources. Was Mrs. Brown's situation fairly typical, or was it an exception? Which residents were more likely to be firmly positioned in transnational social fields and which were not?

A Serendipitous Redirection of Inquiry

Informal opportunity structures, transnational kin networks, and differential access to remittances were the key themes in my fieldwork that summer. Besides focusing on Mrs. Brown's family, I realize now that I embarked on a new direction of inquiry that presented itself rather serendipitously. That new direction has led me to begin a conceptual exploration of these themes, and others related to them, in a second western Caribbean context.

In the guest house where I usually stay when I work in Kingston, I happened to become acquainted with a number of fellow residents. A Venezuelan energy company doing contract work with Jamaica Public Services was housing a contingent of workers from Portugal, the Dominican Republic, and Cuba at the guest house. These men, several of whom were live-wire linemen, had been recruited to help maintain and expand Jamaica's electrical utilities and related infrastructure. This Venezuelan company was among the growing number of firms from Latin America, Spain, Italy, and other countries that have been operating in Cuba—and defying the U.S. embargo—during the post-Soviet aftermath, called the Special Period, *el período especial.*

For a month, I spent most of my evenings having meals, watching TV, and conversing with some of the guest workers. Because I could speak some broken Spanish, I befriended a number of the Cubans who were eager to learn English and who enjoyed the company of someone who had visited their country and was interested in learning more about it. Interestingly, most of the Jamaicans they encountered spoke absolutely no Spanish and had no idea that Cuba, which is one of their closest Caribbean neighbors, had any people who "looked like them," meaning black and brown. Of the fifteen or so Cubans who lived at the guest house, most were men of color, and five or six were definitely of African descent, with phenotypes that Cubans would identify as black or dark mulatto. These men ranged in age from their late twenties to early fifties. Some were in Jamaica for their second or third several-month term. These technical workers had accepted work contracts with the Venezuelans because of the opportunity to make better wages and to travel outside of Cuba. A few of them had been dislocated at home by the so-called rationalization, or the downsizing, that the Cuban economy underwent because of the demands of the Special Period. Consequently, an opportunity to work in Jamaica for a limited period represented a chance to better support their families as well as their national economy, which had rapidly declined due to shifts in the global economy in the post–Cold War period.

My several Cuban acquaintances, only one of whom was fluent in Jamaican English, were eager to talk to me and satisfy my curiosity about their lives in Cuba and the families and communities they had left behind. Our daily conversations led me to think more seriously about the impact of the Special Period on the everyday lives of ordinary Cubans, particularly those of African descent, who perhaps had benefited the most from the revolution and had the most to lose if Cuba were to return to the peripheral capitalist orbit and it racializing tendencies.

In the aftermath of the Soviet Union's and Eastern Europe's disintegration, Cuba had been left without its biggest source of political and economic support. Soviet aid, trade, and economic collaboration had buttressed Cuba's economic development, which—not unlike other Caribbean economies—depended on the mass production of exports like sugar, the traditional monocrop around which much of the region's colonial and postcolonial history is written. Although Cuba has perhaps been a bit more successful at agricultural and sectoral diversification than most of her neighbors, her dependence on the export of sugar has remained a structural feature—and flaw. After the revolution took its communist turn, the Soviet Union simply replaced the United States as the single most important market for Cuban sugar as well as for bananas, plantain, citrus, and cigars. In the context of this new dependency, 70 percent of Cuba's overseas trade was with the Soviet Union, which had given its Caribbean ally extremely generous terms of exchange. A corollary of Cuba's export orientation has been the country's heavy dependence on imported food. Forty percent of the country's food supply was imported before the collapse of the Eastern bloc. Not surprisingly, the disintegration of the Soviet Union and Eastern Europe combined with climatic catastrophes and "the loss of most of its oil imports and 30 [percent] of its agrochemical, machinery, and parts imports" (*Encyclopedia of World Cultures* 1995, 8: 88) precipitated massive food shortages, especially in 1993 and 1994, but since then as well.

One of the Cuban workers I befriended, whom I will call by the pseudonym "Jorge Negro," returned home a couple of months after my departure. After Jorge and his *compañeros* returned home, we maintained communication through a mutual acquaintance, a Jamaican friend who taught Hispanic Caribbean literature and culture and who knew people who traveled to and from Cuba from Jamaica for family and professional reasons. Moreover, during summer 2000, I was able to contact Jorge myself while in Cuba for a conference and cultural exchange program on the African diaspora. It was my second visit to Cuba in twenty years, and I had the good fortune to travel across the island nation to three different cities and provinces: those of Havana, Matanzas, and Santiago de Cuba. The exposure I gained gave me a concrete social context within which to situate Jorge's experiences as he had related them to me through his letters and conversations.

Three years before my trip to Cuba in 2000, my Jamaican friend visited Cuba and saw Jorge, who with a couple of friends who were of Jamaican descent traveled all the way from the eastern part of the island to see her and her partner in Havana. After returning home to Jamaica, my friend wrote me that when she first saw Jorge she did not recognize him. He had lost so much weight—his "Jamaican fat" she called it—that he looked seriously ill. It turned out that he was actually in good health but on an extremely lean diet prescribed not by a physician but by Jesse Helms and Dan Burton, the authors of the Helms-Burton bill that had tightened the terms of the U.S. embargo. While in Jamaica over a six- to seven-month period, Jorge had enjoyed the luxury of having two or three meals a day, featuring his choice of poultry and red meats. Back home in Cuba, however, the quantities of food and other basic necessities (e.g., soap, fuel, etc.) accessible to ordinary households like his in Cuba were very slim. Staple goods like peas, sugar, flour, and rice were more regularly available, but rarely were dairy products (i.e., milk and eggs) or meats. Even sugar, derived from Cuba's principal crop, was scarce. Unless Cubans had access to U.S. dollars from the tourist industry or from remittances from relatives living abroad, their food consumption was subject to the vagaries of food rationing.

Before the recent application of policies curtailing the free circulation of U.S. dollars, Cubans with dollars, which preempted the dramatically devalued peso, could shop at special stores or on the black market, where virtually anything could be had for a price. Often that price was dear—expensive. Recent reports suggest that of all Cubans, black Cubans are the least likely to have diasporic relatives who can send regular resources home (e.g., Sawyer 2006, 110–12, 177). Cuban enclaves of wealth and power in Dade County, Florida, and elsewhere are disproportionately white or socially white. Black Cubans, whether in the diaspora or at home, are overrepresented in dollar-poor sectors. This racially differentiated and, as I shall soon argue, gendered experience in social and economic austerity, which in some ways is even more severe than Jamaica's austerity, implicates the U.S. embargo against Cuba.

The embargo obstructs humanitarian aid as well as trade and investment and is a policy that only makes sense from the imperial context of U.S. geopolitical hegemony. Along with the international realignments resulting from the Soviet collapse, the intensification of the embargo is to Cuba what the IMF, World Bank, and Caribbean Basin Initiative (CBI) have been to Jamaica. The 1990s climate impelled the Cuban state to undergo a period of readjustment or what are called rationalizations. These amount to "a restoration of market relations in key areas of the economy, a partial process of privatization, especially in the service sector, and an attempt to find a niche in the world economy that will enable the country to retain and improve some of the central features of the socialist system, such as health and educational programs and public ownership of decisive industries such as sugar production" (Smaldone 1996, 21).

Pan-Caribbean Parallels and Ties

In all these years of working in Jamaica, I have made a point to embed my analysis of Oceanview in a global context; however, only implicit in that micro-macro bridging has been the intermediate presence of the Caribbean region. I see very clearly now that I, probably like many other Caribbeanists who specialize in particular cases, have merely paid lip service to the region in my work. Issues of regional commonalities and integration, however, have been recognized as an important key to Caribbean development and a potential counterpoint to bilateral dependencies.

Frequently, comparative research on Caribbean issues tends to draw boundaries that include or exclude on the basis of shared language and common colonial master rather than on the basis of factors that may actually be more significant for understanding the workings of cultural, economic, and political development. For instance, studies on Caribbean Women in Development (WID) tend to be overwhelmingly focused on the English-speaking Caribbean, putting Jamaica into the analytic mix with Grenada, St. Kitts, and Antigua while passing over Haiti, Cuba, or Curaçao. Haitian anthropologist Michel-Rolph Trouillot (1992) has criticized anthropologists working in the Caribbean because of our tendency to remain within a single speech community—and typically English-speaking communities—rather than work across linguistic boundaries to discern the contours of common pan-Caribbean experience.

In two excellent anthologies on Caribbean women and sociocultural change (Springfield 1997; Momsen 1993), a more pan-Caribbean trend has been outlined. In this newer trend, the Hispanic islands are being reintegrated into Caribbean studies, and the concept of Caribbean is no longer a code word signaling the more conspicuously Africanized West Indies. The Caribbean character and experience of the Hispanic islands are now being asserted by scholars who identify themselves primarily as Caribbeanists rather than Latin Americanists. Of course, these two categories overlap, but there has been a tendency to position Cuba, the Dominican Republic, and to some extent the colonial commonwealth of Puerto Rico within Latin America, neglecting the strong commonalities these territories have historically and still today share with their immediate neighbors.

From my teaching as well as from my educational background, I know very well that the Greater Antillean islands of Jamaica and Cuba share similar colonial histories. In fact, both were colonies of Spain, which lost the smaller island to the English in 1655. Both islands were sites for the development of plantation production, although in Cuba's case, the plantation sector was not the most central until the nineteenth century. Both societies incorporated massive influxes of enslaved Africans; however, Cuba was as much a European settler colony as it was a colony of exploitation based on racial slavery. Both societies share cultural histories in which the creolization, transculturation, and syncretization of indigenous and Asian but especially European and African cultural material have enriched the sociocultural legacy that shapes present-day lifeways, identities, and forms of resistance. The common cultural ground between Jamaican and Cuban culture was also cultivated by late nineteenth- and early twentieth-century migrations channeling agricultural workers from Jamaica, Haiti, and elsewhere to sugarcane fields in Cuba. Many of those cane harvesters never returned to their original homes; hence, there are kinship ties that bind some Cubans and Jamaicans. The direction of migration, however, has not only been toward Cuba. Gayle McGarrity (1996) has documented the history of Cuban migrants in Jamaica. Jamaica offered refuge to Antonio Maceo and Jose Martí, the leading heroes of Cuba's late-nineteenth-century struggle for independence, as well as to a stream of Cubans who fled the Communist revolution and, more recently, the austere conditions associated with the Special Period.

Another axis of convergence, as well as divergence, between the two islands is related to racial formation. In both Jamaican and Cuban societies, constructs of race have been fashioned to make sense of the population's phenotypic and sociocultural heterogeneity, which has evolved from the history of intergroup contact. Caribbean notions of social race, however, depart from North American ideas of mutually exclusive and bipolar races, based on an opposition and unbridgeable distance between blackness and whiteness. In Jamaica, the racial pyramid is complicated by the presence of intermediate social categories and formations, primarily those associated with the social class locations construed in terms of brownness. Although blackness and whiteness also have significance in the Hispanic Caribbean, they represent not mutually exclusive categories that order the majority of the population into either/or camps but poles representing the limits for a wide-ranging socioracial or color continuum. The classificatory focus is on the multifarious gradations between the black and white poles. No clear-cut boundaries are drawn between these gradations, and when boundaries are established they tend to be situation specific. Cuba's socioracial continuum, however, as compared with that of Puerto Rico, for instance, has been marked by the presence of sizable, visible, and largely endogamous black and white poles (see Hoetink 1985). Before the revolution, this color configuration was correlated with class. The national bourgeoisie was overwhelmingly white, whereas Afro-Cubans were overrepresented in the lowest sectors of the socioeconomic structure. Although this pyramidal pattern of race has been, to a considerable extent, dismantled since the revolution, vestiges of it certainly remain. For example, the national leadership is still conspicuously white or very light skinned. This has been the persistent pattern in a country where only about 37 percent of the population is classified as white; the remaining population is approximately 51 percent mulatto, 11 percent black, and 1 percent Chinese (*Encyclopedia of World Cultures* 1995). According to U.S. criteria, based on principles of hypodescent (or the fancy anthropological term for the "one drop" rule), more than 60 percent of the Cuban population is black, meaning of some known African descent.

Both Jamaica and Cuba along with the rest of the region also share a general pan-Caribbean culture of gender. According to Cynthia Mesh, "[w]ithin the Caribbean regional diversity of ethnicity, class, language, and religion, there is an ideological unity of patriarchy, of female subordination and dependence. Yet there is also a vibrant living tradition of female economic autonomy, of female-headed households and of a family structure in which men are often marginal. So Caribbean gender relations are a double paradox: of patriarchy within a system of matrifocal and matrilocal families; and of a domestic ideology coexisting with the economic independence of women" (Mesh 1997, 28). Also related to this, both Cuba and Jamaica have gender cultures in which femininity and masculinity have been ranked by race and class. As I will make clear later, stratified, color-coded notions of womanhood and sexuality have not been erased from present-day Cuban narratives of national identity.

Despite the differences between peripheral capitalist and socialist formations, Jamaica and Cuba share a number of commonalities in economic structure and orientation. Both economies have remained extroverted, export dependent, and focused on a very few primary commodities. Both are heavily dependent on imports of food, capital goods, and intermediate products (e.g., oil). Both economies are heavily indebted and vulnerable to chronic balance-of-payments deficits. In Cuba's case, however, up until the demise of the communist bloc, the Soviet Union subsidized and absorbed Cuba's deficit. Both Jamaica and Cuba have extensive informal or underground economies with thriving black or grey markets. In both countries, these economic spheres have made goods and services available when they were otherwise unavailable through official shops. In Cuba, those official shops sell according to a quota or ration system that limits what any household can purchase. A Cuban woman explained: "We all resort to the underground market because the authorized quotas in the state stores are sufficient for perhaps 12 of the 30 days of the month" (Calderón 1995, 19; NACLA 1995).

Finally, both Jamaica and Cuba are now experiencing conditions under which social and economic disparities are widening. The stark juxtaposition of austerity and abundance that is so characteristic of Jamaica and other parts of the Caribbean region appears to be reemerging in Cuba, where unemployment and a declining safety net became social facts of the Special

Period. These conditions have led some Cubans to flee as refugees to the United States, to the U.S. base in Guantánamo, and to potential sanctuaries in neighboring Caribbean islands, such as Jamaica (McGarrity 1996).

Expanding the Discourse on Structural Adjustment

Since my 1996 summer experiences, I have been stimulated to think more seriously about the parallels in Jamaican and Cuban experience with economic austerity, and, as a result, I have expanded my thinking on structural adjustment and related neoliberal policies to include the Cuban experience. Although in my Jamaican research I have focused on the specific interventions that the IMF, the World Bank, and the U.S. CBI have made in Jamaican daily life (Harrison 1997), I am now inclined to go beyond the specificity of those institutions and their programs in order to conceptualize structural adjustment in broader terms. As I indicated in my earlier chapters on Jamaica, even after the IMF's mandates for structural adjustment had officially ended in 1990, the national policy climate and everyday socioeconomic conditions did not undergo a drastic change. Thirteen years under structural adjustment had set in motion an entrenched, neoliberal dynamic. In the context of this discussion, beyond the direct intervention of the IMF, structural adjustment also signals a general development orientation and policy climate driven by neoliberal assumptions concerning economic growth and change. I will use structural adjustment as a metonym for the restructuring and realignments constitutive of present-day globalization. In this sense, the concept is applicable to the economic restructuring and political realignments that have occurred in the United States over the past twenty years since the President Ronald Reagan era as well as to the readjustments and rationalizations that Cuba has implemented to keep its economy afloat.

At this historic post–Cold War juncture when capitalism appears to have triumphed over its socialist and communist alternatives, a neoliberal worldview or regime of truth has been intensified, projecting its historically contingent model of development as an inevitable course of history and a naturalized state of being *homo economicus*. Based on assumptions of competitive individualism and rational choice, neoliberalism enshrines the notions that free- and private-market forces will automatically lead to efficient and productive economies and that the less government regulation and intervention, the better. The neoliberal package of structural adjustments, privatizations, and free trade that the global North has been imposing on the global South, especially over the past twenty years, represents "a sort of primitive accumulation against [what had become conventional capitalist economic forms even in the Third World] . . . industrial production for the domestic market, . . . small-scale capitalist or cooperative agriculture . . . and . . . the tenuous but crucial social safety net" (Wilson 1997, 30). Just as happened with classic primitive accumulation, the result has been massive economic dislocation and the creation of a vast pool of people desperate for jobs, even at wages below subsistence levels. The era of the second primitive accumulation is a flagrant instance of capitalist expansion and the unequal consolidation of wealth at the expense of basic human needs, subsistence security, and economic justice. Under this process, Caribbean countries such as Haiti, Jamaica, and the Dominican Republic have been converted into cheap industrial labor reserves where women factory workers are paid slave wages. In 1996, Haitian women workers at the Disney factory earned only 28 cents per hour, whereas Haitians consider 58 cents per hour a living wage (National Labor Committee 1996).

It is important to watch Cuba more closely and include its struggle within the discourse on the structural assaults being unleashed by neoliberal hegemony. Cuba represents the last stronghold for an egalitarian alternative to the vagaries of the capitalist order. Will neoliberal worldview and practice win out there as well? Will Cuba be able to maintain its achievements in health care, education, and the social services while adopting some market principles of economic organization? Can Cuban socialism be sustained as a sanctuary under siege?

Everyday Life under the Intensified Embargo

During the Special Period (which officially ended in the 1990s) and the continued hardships of the aftermath, Cuba has had to find ways to promote more food self-sufficiency and diversify its links to the international community. Over the past several years, it has undertaken internal adjustments, or rationalizations, that it hopes will enable it to negotiate its most challenging economic crisis since its 1959 revolution. In a period of only a few years, an extreme crisis of insufficient rations, energy shortages, transportation cuts, and shutdowns of entire industries made daily life for everyone, but especially women, a traumatic struggle for basic survival.

Although the Cuban state has legitimated the nuclear family as the principal unit of family and community organization, in reality, only extended families, often three-generational, provide the social base that allows ordinary Cubans to pool their limited resources to resolve the growing problems of food shortages, housing shortages, and unemployment (Bengelsdorf 1997, 232). Those who live outside of this supportive structure are at a decided disadvantage.

Even before the Special Period, *machista* elements were still extant in Cuban culture making women's double day a customary reality (Bengelsdorf 1997; Safa 1995). Despite the existence of the laudable but unenforceable Family Code, which legally codified the "joint responsibilities of husbands and wives for household maintenance and childcare," women's double day of working in the factory, field, or office and then returning home to do the housework continued to be the general rule rather than the exception. The double burden was made more bearable, however, because of extensive supports in child care, medical care, social services, and education from the state. As political scientist Carollee Bengelsdorf (1997, 232) points out, however, "as the state structures which formerly guaranteed material existence crumble, it is the family unit which has inherited the task of guaranteeing survival. . . . The time-consuming jobs of standing in lines to get all that is available as it becomes available on rations and of hunting down necessary supplementary food, whether in the newly opened agricultural markets . . . or on the black market, are . . . accomplished by" the cooperative labor of female-centered kin networks.

Drawing on surveys and ethnographic interviewing, anthropologist Helen Safa (1995) reports that race has important implications for household organization and resources. Black women are much more likely to be household heads and participants in interhousehold networks in which men are relatively marginal contributors to the resource pool. This suggests that, on the average, black households and family networks operate with more limited resources. As noted earlier, contributing to the problem of household subsistence is the differential flow of foreign remittances. Black Cubans, unlike their white compatriots (*compadres y comadres*) or some of their black Jamaican neighbors, have less access to resources from overseas kin. This suggests that even more pressure is on Afro-Cuban women to make ends meet. Like their counterparts in the Anglophone Caribbean, they, too, are expected to "work miracles" (Senior 1991).

The public sphere of work and political participation has also been adversely affected by the current crisis. Unemployment has become a problem as administrative structures are downsized and workplaces are closed when they "can no longer be supplied with raw materials or the energy to make them into finished products" (Bengelsdorf 1997, 236). The criteria for rationalizing the labor force have not been gender neutral. Seniority and standards of efficiency tend to favor men over women. Women's household responsibilities, which have increased over the past several years with massive cuts in state support services, have affected their abilities to commit themselves 100 percent to their jobs outside the home. Because of women's higher levels of absenteeism, they are not perceived by their male colleagues as equally efficient and committed workers. Male workers and management also view women as physically weaker and constrained by "nature's workshops" (i.e., their reproductive organs). Accordingly, the perception of women's liabilities emerges as salient when criteria for layoffs or occupational advancement are judged (Safa 1995, 145; Bengelsdorf 1997, 239).

As more women and men are rationalized out of the formal labor force, they are forced to look to informal means of generating income, which have become such an important sphere of economic activity that the state has begun to accept and license some forms of it. Self-employment, or *trabajo por cuenta propria*, however, is largely a male domain. Of the nearly 150,000 self-employed workers that the government licensed by March 1994, 77 percent of them were men (Bengelsdorf 1997, 237). This suggests a gender bias in the types of private occupations and private workers or entrepreneurs that the state is authorizing. The privatized enterprises that women seem to be pursuing are those in which domestic products and services are offered for sale. This is similar to the situation found in Jamaica. Generally, these domestic-based enterprises are the least lucrative forms of self-employment. If these trends continue, the current shift toward a rationalized and privatized economy may well produce the Cuban variant of the feminization of poverty (Bengelsdorf 1997, 240).

One form of women's unlicensed *trabajo por cuenta propria* that has grown in significance since the hard times of the Special Period is *jineterismo* (see Harrison 2002). This idiom connotes prostitution as well as other forms of hustling, or "riding" tourists as jockeys do horses. This line of sex-trade work is not only gendered (not only with feminine meanings, because men— *pingueros*—also pursue this line of work), it is also raced. Prostitution is linked to the resurgence of tourism. The revitalization of tourism has been one of Cuba's main strategies for generating hard currency and promoting economic growth. To this end, a Caribbean paradise, with all the necessary amenities and luxuries, has been fashioned to attract tourists. This vacation world of foreign luxury has been visibly erected alongside the everyday Cuban struggle for basic survival. Tourist hotels, restaurants, and stores flaunt material affluence before people who have been abruptly reduced to abject poverty and hunger. Those Cubans who have access to Yankee dollars through employment in the tourist industry or through foreign remittances are much better off than everyone else. The average Cuban only makes the equivalent of US$10 (or 300–400 pesos) per month; however, a bottle of beer in a club costs about $7.00.

Sex tourism and romance tourism have blossomed into significant sources of income for women. Research suggests that Afrocubanas are disproportionately among the most economically needy, with the least access to a kin-mediated inflow of dollars from the United States. It appears, then, that *jineterismo* is one of the few dollar-generating activities available to them. Of these women, those who fit the stereotype of *la mulata* find that there is a special niche for them. The magnetic image of the *mulata*, or mixed-heritage woman, is being used to attract male tourists from Spain, Italy, and Canada, among other places. One Cuban researcher laments that "to lure foreigners, the government [itself has been manipulating racial clichés by] showcasing 'traditional' Afro-Cuban religious rituals and art, 'traditional' Afro-Cuban music, and . . . Afro-Cuban women [who are foregrounded as performers in these contexts]" (Fusco 1996, 67).

The *mulata's* sexual exoticism has long been celebrated in racial narratives of Cuban womanhood, manhood, and nation. Cuban national identity, with the bonding it entails across race, ethnicity, and class, has been built over the bodies of women. The successful construction of the independence and revolutionary movements—which sought to dismiss race as a thing of the colonial or prerevolutionary past—was written on the body of the archetypical *mulata*, who has been ideologically positioned at the center and in the dangerous borderland between the races in Cuban sexual ideology (Bengelsdorf 1997, 245). Bengelsdorf argues that in the context of the current economic crisis, traditional racial narratives of gender and sexuality appear to be reasserting themselves, or they are being rewritten according to the specificities of recent restructuring.

For many women, and not just those of African descent, foreign *pepes* (the colloquial term for johns) have replaced the government as a source of the necessities of life (Fusco 1996, 64). The lyrics to one of the top salsa hits in January 1996 advised women to find a *papiriqui con mucho juaniquiqui*, in other words a sugar daddy. It is reported that young girls as young as fourteen and fifteen are leaving their provincial homes for tourist centers where they are likely to come in contact with tourist *pepes*. *Jineteras* exchange escort and sexual services for food, clothing, and hard currency. In some cases, they open up their homes as guest houses for tourists interested in a grassroots experience. Sometimes romantic relationships develop in which contact is extended beyond the tourist companion's vacation. In these cases, sexuality appears less as a commodity and more as a socially appropriate or morally acceptable expression of love and affection.

According to the testimonies of young *jineteras* themselves, to cater to client tastes "white girls are perming their hair [making it curlier] so they look more like *mulatas*" (Fusco 1996, 65). "The Spaniards really like black girls with braids, so all the *negritas* are wearing their hair like that now. The Italians like *mulatas* with wild hair" (65). Although clearly the discursive focus is on the erotic and economic edge that Afrocubanas are believed to have, Diaz, Fernandez, and Caram's (1996) research suggests that white women may actually predominate in the *jinetera* ranks. Their presence, however, seems to be rendered virtually invisible or unmarked by a racialized gaze—at once national and international—that projects differential meanings onto Cuban women's interactions with white tourist men (Fernandez 1999).

I cannot help but wonder if, according to this distorted gaze, Afrocubanas cater to the desires of sex tourists while their lighter counterparts are positioned to engage tourists in romance, an experience presumed to be outside of the market. Given what is called tourist apartheid, which entails keeping black Cubans out of the hotels, restaurants, and clubs that tourists frequent (unless they have reason to be there as security guards or as other workers), their interactions with foreign tourists are more likely to take place on the streets, for all to see and interpret as hustling rather than as socializing. On the other hand, white Cubans, who are more likely to have dollars, are allowed to enter restaurants and clubs as guests. Moreover, they are hired to work behind the desks and cash registers, as hostesses and waitresses, and in other capacities in which they come into daily contact with tourists. Hence, they can meet and socialize with foreigners in ways that disguise and camouflage sex work as well as in ways that may engender more sustainable relationships as friends and lovers. Some observers have noted that some *jineteras* are after more than money and consumer objects. Some are looking for love and a better life outside of Cuba (Stout 1995). Some tourists make return trips to maintain and renew relationships, and in some of these cases, marriages have resulted. For example, one of Jorge's neighbors had an international courtship with a Canadian whom she had met in Veradero, Cuba's most developed tourist resort about a two-and-a-half-hour drive from Havana. Eventually, they married and had two children, with the husband visiting Cuba as often as he could. In time, after many trials and errors with immigration on the Cuban side, he was able to complete the legal work to have his family join him in Canada. He admitted that initially the relationship with his wife was largely entertainment, but in time he committed himself to a serious relationship.[1] Jorge's former neighbor, a lighter skinned woman probably categorized as *blanca*, fits the description found in the literature of the Cuban women who are more likely to experience romance rather than simply a trick of the trade. Further interrogation of the relations and blurred boundaries between romance and sex tourism, however, is necessary to discern whether a sound empirical basis exists for a racialized division of labor among women who, by a variety of informal means, jockey for dollars.

According to the advertisement and discussions on the Internet, over the past fifteen years Cuba has gained a reputation as "pussy paradise." A male tourist even admitted to a Cuban American researcher and cultural critic that "[n]o one comes to Cuba for ecotourism. What sells this place is right on the dance floor—rum, cigars, and *la mulata*" (Fusco 1996, 63). Tourist packages are advertised to attract males (and females) interested in acting out their sexual fantasies in an affordable setting free from police intervention. Whether intentional or situational, sex tourists have tastes and fantasies that are shaped by particular racialized ideologies that can be acted out in Cuba without any accountability. According to one Canadian tourist who spoke quite candidly with a sociologist, "You can call a Nigger a Nigger here, and no one takes it the wrong way" (Davidson 1996, 46). The left-of-center version of this finds expression in the racial liberalism that is supposedly demonstrated by having sex with friendly black and mixed women.

In many cases, Cubans themselves buy into the same racial and racialized gender stereotypes that drive sexual tourist behavior. They often subscribe to the belief that blacks are naturally hypersexual, athletic, and rhythmic; the belief that black and *mulata* women are *caliente* (hot) and that black sexuality is more untamed, primitive, uninhibited, and exciting than white sexuality; and the notion that black people "have a natural love of music and dance so well" (Davidson 1996, 46). When I was in Cuba in 2000, I remember coming across a vendor selling wood carvings at a beach resort outside of Santiago de Cuba. The vendor was a black man, perhaps categorized as mulatto, who claimed to be the artist of the carvings on display. As I was passing by on my way to the dining room, one piece in particular caught my attention: a carving in dark wood, perhaps mahogany, of a masculine figure with an erect penis, one that was extremely long and curved. Some artistic license had obviously been taken for the erect penis to extend from the groin all the way to the vicinity of the head. I asked the artist what his art work symbolized, and he replied with an unelaborated statement about male potency and fertility. In my view, the carving seemed to epitomize the narrative of black male hypersexuality that some black Cubans themselves reiterate with considerable pride.

Are these emergent trends in tourism and related jockeying undermining the progress Cuba has made in creating conditions for racial equality? For the past decades, black Cuban imagery and aesthetic expressions have served as a compelling symbol for revolutionary Cuban nationalism. Ethnographer Yvonne Daniel's (1995) study of rumba, a powerful folkloric dance complex, documents how in the past decades rumba has become an important emblem of Cuba's egalitarian ethos. Those who were previously the most stigmatized, the most disfranchised, and the most economically exploited symbolize the transformations that have eased if not completely eliminated the burdens of racism and class oppression. Of course, racial equality as symbol and as concrete reality are not the same thing. The varying intersections of color, gender, and class that have serious implications for Cubans' life chances and quality of life warrant closer scrutiny and interrogation.

Although I have focused on negative patterns that suggest the reemergence of the gender, racial, and class hierarchies that the revolution sought to destroy, it is important to emphasize that Cuba still has a critical mass of patriotic nationalists who support Fidel Castro's dream and admire his charismatic defiance. I recall the simple but deeply felt words of my friend Jorge, who told me, "I love my family and my country. That is why I am here in Jamaica, to help them both." This commitment to help one's country and compatriots finds expression in the open displays of mutual aid and solidarity that characterize everyday life in many communities. Mirta Calderón, a Cuban journalist, writes optimistically of the Cuban people's fervent commitment to preserve the best of Cuba's achievements. Reflecting on the ethical dilemma of "good revolutionaries" participating in the black market, or in hustling tourists for a hearty meal, she states the following: "We have few conflicts of conscience over the [implicit] double standard . . . because we face the choice of surrendering or surviving, of maintaining pride in our nation or . . . formally or informally [entering] into a state of . . . annexation to the United States" (Calderón 1995, 19). She goes on to write that despite the contradictions in today's Cuban society, "our children are also growing up in the shadow of a great many expressions of solidarity and open displays of human generosity. If the old lady on the corner needs some medications, the necessary amount of tablets or antibiotics will invariably appear from many houses on the block. . . . Usable clothing and shoes change owners, and voices of encouragement and friendship abound in the neighborhoods. Absolute hunger afflicts no one. Solidarity redistributes what little there is. . . . As life becomes more difficult here, people think about [what it means to be Cuban]. With all the good and the bad, this Cuba is ours. It belongs to no one else as long as we can preserve it" (19).

Somewhat consistent with this line of thought, poet Georgina Herrera (a member of the former women's nongovernmental organization MAGIN —from iMAGINation—which the government closed down because of its controversial views) expresses the view that Afro-Cuban women who feed their families by "giving their bodies" should not be seen as "vulgar prostitutes" and criminals. She claims that their families rarely evaluate their actions in these terms of "bourgeois" concepts of morality (Herrera 2000,

123–24). She feels strongly that "everyone has a right to seek a living any way they can, especially when there's inequality . . . no food . . . the price is very high. . . . You see how wretched it is. So a girl who knows she's attractive takes advantage of it. . . . I have friends who tell me that if they were twenty years younger they wouldn't think twice about going out on the streets" (124). Contrary to the official position of the FMC, the government-controlled Cuban Women's Federation, she and her comrades in the former MAGIN insist that the young women who take to the streets are fortified with high self-esteem and a clear understanding of what their values and commitment to their families, communities, and nation are.

Conclusions

Ordinary Cubans, like the ordinary Jamaicans I have come to know over nearly thirty years, are struggling to survive and retain their dignity in the face of difficult changes occurring in the multiple contexts of nation, region, and global system. Now that I have met Jorge and his *compañeros* and caught a glimpse of their lives in Cuba, I cannot help but wonder how they are adapting to the vagaries of their country's struggle to negotiate and, when possible, resist the formidable obstacles that the U.S. embargo and the Special Period's rationalizations have presented. Like many other Cuba watchers and sympathizers, I question whether neoliberalism will capture Cuba and tame its defiant quest for autonomy. Although Cuba *libre* remains the national goal, Cuba's internal adjustments reflect the extent to which the country has been pressured to buy into hegemonic notions of efficiency and productivity, which favor whiter Cubans over blacker Cubans and privilege men over women, who are more vulnerable to being relegated to economically precarious positions that increase their dependence on husbands, boyfriends, extended families, and *pepes*. In at least some respects, Cuba's ongoing crisis is being negotiated over the bodies of Cuban women, with *negras y mulatas* expected to bear the deepest assaults on what remains of one of the last socialist sanctuaries.

As I reflect on the racial and gender implications of neoliberalism and structural adjustment in the Caribbean region, I must extend my ruminations to the role that the U.S embargo plays in directing or circumscribing change. Although the embargo is the most flagrant form of foreign intervention in the region, the mandates of U.S.-led multilateral institutions such as the IMF and World Bank are also interventions that thwart Caribbean sovereignty and impose a model of economic organization and geopolitical hierarchy that is not necessarily the most culturally, structurally, or ecologically appropriate.

The U.S. embargo, like structural adjustment policies, is premised on an ideology of power, recolonization, and ranked capitals that assumes that Cubans deserve to be forced out of their defiant opposition and resistance to U.S. dominance. In order to accomplish that, other foreign interests in trade relations with Cuba must be subordinated to the U.S. agenda. The same general ideology that rationalizes the unregulated spread of commodification into all spheres of social life implies that Cuban bodies can be bought and sold on the auction block of imposed economic austerity without any accountability on the part of the biggest *papiriquis*—the sugar daddies of global capital. According to this line of thinking, Cubans deserve to suffer the hardships the embargo engenders if their dysfunctional national values mislead them from the U.S. version of rational choice. If they as a deviant nation or rogue state refuse to adhere to principles of democracy and free enterprise, then they themselves are responsible for their predicament and decline. Those who are unfit to belong to the global capitalist community have no enforceable rights to subsistence security.

The virtually Spencerian blame-the-victim line of thinking described here has problematic implications for basic human rights. The subtext I have outlined, however, is basically the same as that undergirding the conservative discourse on poor people and outlaws in Jamaica. It is also strikingly similar to the ideological underpinnings of current domestic policies in the United States. Recall the arguments mobilized to justify punitive policy reforms in the areas of welfare, crime, and affirmative action. In all of these cases, ideologically constructed others are being targeted, demonized, and, in the worst-case scenario, sacrificed. This purging—or ethnic cleansing—of dangerous and troublesome elements depends on ordinary folk like us buying into mystifying moral panics that scapegoat others for the fears and anxieties that systemic flaws generate within us. Despite our differences, the islands of the Greater Antilles—Cuba, Jamaica, and Haiti as well—are not really that far away from the United States in either geographic or ideological space. It is within our purview as stewards of democratic principles to hold our government accountable for domestic and foreign policies that fail to do justice to our sense of humanity.

Since my serendipitous encounters at that Kingston guest house, I have found it hard to resist the temptation of following my inductive insights down a path of further reflections, tentative inferences, and new questions. My journey through a maze of Greater Antillean common ground will hopefully permit me to find my way out onto a wide-open field where I can continue to rethink the Caribbean and the kinds of research directions I would like to follow in the years to come.

Acknowledgments

I might not have explored the meaning and impact of the U.S. embargo against Cuba without inspiration from my fellow residents of the guest house mentioned in this chapter. I thank them for sharing their stories with me and, in Jorge Negro's case, corresponding with me after I returned to the United States. I am grateful to the colleague and friend who mediated my communication with Jorge once he left Jamaica for his home in Cuba. I appreciate the informative letters she wrote me on her observations during her visit to Cuba. I want to thank Janis Hutchinson, past president of the Association of Black Anthropologists (ABA), for organizing the ABA conference and cultural exchange that were held in Cuba during summer 2000. The conference and subsequent educational tour of Havana, Matanzas, and Santiago de Cuba enabled me to visit Cuba a second time, renew contact with Cuban friends, and make new acquaintances. All the members of the ABA conference group, especially Gina Ulysse, Cheryl Rodriguez, Maria Vesperi, Jay Sokolosky, and Dawn-Elissa Fischer helped make our sojourn in Cuba a special experience.

9. Global Apartheid at Home and Abroad

Situating Urban Apartheid

In a provocative essay on urban apartheid, Philippe Bourgois (1996) called our attention to the persistent savage inequalities and racialization within U.S. social stratification and political economy. This was an important intervention at a moment when much public discourse and litigation assumed—and today still assumes—either the declining significance of race or a radically different definition of racism in the post–civil rights United States. California's Proposition 209 and the Texas-based Fifth Circuit Court Hopwood decision both assumed that currently the major targets of racism—or so-called reverse racism—are whites, principally white males. The notion that white males are *racially* oppressed and *more* racially oppressed than blacks and other people of color dangerously undermines the credibility and legitimacy of genuinely antiracist struggle, and it naturalizes the iniquities of the social system.

Apartheid is a policy of enforced separation between races, but the term is also used to characterize any invidious structure and practice of racial inequality—intended or unintended. According to Gernot Köhler (1978 [1993]), a peace researcher, the notion of apartheid is most apt for denoting the current world situation in which a minority race (of whites and honorary whites) dominates the majority of humanity, which is composed of a variety of "peoples of color." In its global, de facto form, apartheid is even more severe than its South African exemplar. The disparities in wealth, power, military control, health, and life expectancy that characterize the world system or global macrosociety are extremely wide and growing.

The system that Köhler designates as *global apartheid* with its built-in

forms of structural violence is consistent with what sociologist Howard Winant (1994) describes as the global racial entity we know as capitalism, whose
genealogy implicates the compounding and interdependence of race and
class. Winant reminds us that in virtually every corner of the earth, dark
skin still correlates with inequality. Although race is clearly internationalized,
Winant points out that "we cannot assume an overarching uniformity. . . .
[E]ach nation-state, each political system, each cultural complex necessarily constructs a unique racialized social structure, a particular complex of
racial meanings and identities. Thus the global similarities, the increasing
internationalization of race, can only be understood in terms of prevalent
patterns, general tendencies; in no sense can such generalizations substitute
for detailed analyses of local racial formations" (Winant 1994, 123).

When Bourgois employs the term *apartheid,* he clearly calls attention to
race as a pervasive, persistent, and intensified reality. Notwithstanding the
centrality of race in constituting U.S. social structure, inequality in the United
States and the world at large is structured around more than a single axis of
difference and separation. In other words, any useful analysis of apartheid—
be it local, national, or global—should take interlocking and intersecting
stratifications into serious account, not as additive features but as mutually
and simultaneously constitutive dimensions of social reality, lived and experienced in multiplicative relationality (cf. Mullings 1997, 6).

In view of the importance of matters of social geography and geopolitics in
contextualizing the inner city's racial economy, a dimension of difference that
is often neglected is that of space and locality; that is, the differences related
to inner-city and suburban sites, to urbanness and ruralness, and to regional
disparities. Anthropologist and urban theorist Anthony Leeds (1994) conceptualized *urban* as a type of society in which the hierarchy of central places or
nodal localities is dominated by demographic and specialized institutional
nucleations called cities. If we apply this understanding to urban apartheid,
we cannot focus our attention on the inner city without at least acknowledging the everyday violence of poverty, unequal economic development, and
environmental degradation in the lives of the rural poor, who in parts of the
world constitute the most "wretched of the earth" (Fanon 2004 [1961]).

In Southern Appalachia where I lived for thirteen years, the majority of
those bearing the burdens of difference and separation from the centers of
white wealth, power, and cultural capital are not members of any targeted
racial minority. The complex and contradictory dynamics of class, race, and
regional political economy and ecology have a lot to do with white Appalachians' social locations in a "South within the North"—that is, the Northern
Hemisphere. Is their plight not a symptom or by-product of urban apartheid,

in the broader Leedsian sense? Is it not a by-product of global apartheid whose ideologies of race perpetuate social disparities in part by blinding poor people to their commonalities with other poor people across the railroad track, interstate highway, or national border? The virtually automatic association of wretched poverty with supposedly undeserving and stigmatized racial minorities erases from public conscience and consciousness the social fact that the impoverished majority in the United States is European American in a land where European descent and whiteness symbolize the power and privilege of social, political, and economic domination. In my view, it is important to contextualize inner-city problems in terms that preclude the misrecognition of the inequalities affecting those whose white-skin privilege is positioned in ironic status incongruity and is largely psychodiscursive rather than material. The relative invisibility of the poor white majority from the public gaze makes sense only in the socially constructed logic of urban and global apartheid—a logic that marginalizes the poor whites, so-called hillbillies and white trash, whose greater visibility threatens to destabilize hegemonic constructions of whiteness as a normative site of privilege and power (cf. Hartigan 1999; Buck 2001).

Another axis of difference, class, though decentered and obliquely marked on the ideological and political stage in the United States, is central to the workings of apartheid. The myth of classlessness and that most Americans are middle class is belied by data showing that—thanks to Reaganomics—by the early 1990s the top 1 percent of Americans owned 53.2 percent of all assets, and the top 10 percent owned 83.2 percent of all assets (Robinson 1996, 23). This means that the bottom 90 percent owned only 16.8 percent of the nation's assets. What does middle class mean in the context of such a skewed distribution of wealth?

In multiracial societies like the United States, class can never be fully understood outside of its interaction—and dialectical tension—with race, which always has class consequences (Winant 1994, 128) and often embodies "surplus antagonisms" from the displacement and denial of class (Ortner 1991, 185). Apartheid's construction and manipulation of race is responsible for the disproportionate concentration of workers of color in class locations within secondary labor markets, reserve armies, and underground economies. Barbara Ransby (1996) claims that mechanization and automation advances have transformed the most vulnerable segments of the black working class from an exploited labor force to economically expendable outcasts socially controlled and contained by punitive and authoritarian mechanisms for "policing the crisis" (Hall et al. 1978). A symptom of this predicament is the fact that more black young-adult males are in prison or on probation than in the postsecondary educational pipeline. Furthermore, of the 3,000 inmates on death row, 40 percent of them are African American, "a figure far exceeding Black representation in the population" (Ransby 1996, 8). Of course, one can propose an explanation of these disturbing trends by fore-grounding dysfunctional family values, matrifocality, or even unintelligent and violent genes, or one can take into account the structural violence of urban apartheid and situate urban agency, no matter how contradictory and problematic, in a context of systemic socioeconomic dislocations and the growing undervaluation of the minds and bodies of poor blacks and other people of color. Poor blacks are viewed as such menaces to society that the violation of their human rights is being rationalized and legitimated as a necessary evil. Their human rights are being violated through the structured deprivation of livelihood and the denial of citizenship rights through repres-sive policing and incarceration. Once "on the inside" of prison, a lifetime of disenfranchisement often ensues. According to Ransby, "nearly all states deny prisoners the right to vote, over half deny voting rights to individuals on probation, and nearly a third of states deny even ex-offenders the ballot. . . . The conviction of a single crime can mean lifelong exclusion from the body politic. Once you have 'a record,' the authorities have a right to moni-tor and restrict you in ways that they do not vis à vis other fully fledged citizens" (Ransby 1996. 8). In the past decade, struggles for reform and/or abolition of the prison system have prompted a few states to reconsider bans on postprison voting, but overall the disenfranchisement of prisoners and ex-convicts is a serious problem that is part and parcel of the human rights problem that the prison industrial complex represents to the United States and to the world (Davis 2003).

Gender is another important dimension of difference and hierarchy that must be recognized before we can understand the ways of the unjust world and how to change them. Gender, of course, is as relevant to men as to women, a point that is too often missed. The criminalization of inner-city males is influenced, in part, by social and cultural constructions of mas-culinity, both dominant and oppositional constructions that may compete or converge. The race- and class-specific, mass-mediated construction of black manhood—particularly young black manhood—inclines many whites to presuppose criminal and physically threatening intent upon seeing or encountering African American youths. The Simi Valley, California, jury's decision on Rodney King's litigation against the Los Angeles Police Depart-ment was premised on this ideological view (Gooding-Williams 1993). The predominantly white suburban jurors saw in the videotaped scene of King being beat to the ground by a contingent of policemen the hyperphysicality of a "dangerous black predator." The bestialization and demonization of black masculinity blinded the jurors to the objective social fact that the police outnumbered and overpowered King, who had been forced into a prone or supine position.

Oppositional constructions of black masculinity that emphasize hypersexuality, physical prowess, and defiance to authority paradoxically converge with the dominant gaze, though positive values are assigned in place of the negatives. The injured masculinity or emasculation of subjugated men who can never live up to mainstream standards of manhood may sometimes lead to overcompensations in more accessible attributes such as sexual prowess and virility, athleticism, control over or conquest of women, and the ability to deploy violence. Because real power and control are virtually unattainable in these cases, sexual conquest is symbolized through the use of misogynistic language (denigrating women as "hos" and "bitches"), noncommittal relationships, and, not uncommonly, physical abuse. Whether vulgar (as in gangsta rap) or respectable (as in the black patriarchal yearnings for masculine redemption [Pierce and Williams 1996] expressed in the Million Man March), compensatory masculinity is a double-edged sword. It may defy mainstream morality and notions of order, but at the same time by perpetuating gender asymmetries, it undermines the transformative potential within subaltern communities. As Tony L. Whitehead's (1997) research has shown, gender constructs have serious consequences for risk-taking behaviors related to illegal economic activities (e.g., drug entrepreneurship) and sexually transmitted diseases, namely HIV/AIDS (see also Harrison 1997a).

Although there is a tendency for many African American analysts, especially males, to take the position that black men are an endangered species, implying that black women are somehow more protected and privileged, it is important to point out that women are also adversely affected by the law-and-order regimes established in many inner-city localities. Women and children often find themselves caught between a rock and a hard place. They are often caught between, on the one hand, indiscriminate police raids and lockdowns and, on the other hand, the drive-by shootings that gangs perpetrate against rivals and innocent bystanders. Ransby (1996, 7) amplifies this point by arguing that "Black women and children are the primary residents of public housing in most major cities and these housing projects increasingly resemble minimum security prisons—at best." It is also important to note that Black women "are not exempt from . . . the punishment industry. Incarceration rates for Black women have risen [78 percent nationally and in some states well over 1,000 percent] in the last [two] decade[s]" (Ransby 1996, 6; Davis 2003, 19; Sentencing Project 2006).

The experience of urban apartheid is clearly gender differentiated, with men and women being affected and responding in different ways. It is important to recognize that women, however, bear the multiple burdens of rising rates of incarceration, being held captives in local police states targeting primarily male offenders, having the sole responsibility for supporting households based on inadequate wages and/or punitive welfare, and being assaulted by a racialized, gendered public discourse that implicates their morality, problematizes their sexuality, and jeopardizes their reproductive rights.

At this historical moment on the U.S. political front, race and gender are particularly salient. Backlash movements have assaulted antiracist and antisexist social policies, which are claimed to undermine individual merit, family values, and a color- and gender-blind interpretation of constitutionally based democratic rights. In this climate of drastically reduced safety nets and a rapidly withering welfare state, poor women of color, particularly African Americans and Latinas, have become the targets of a racialized gender and gendered racial ideology that pathologizes poor women of color, blaming them for the disproportionate female-headed households, structural unemployment, problems of law and order, dysfunctional schools, and community blight that deindustrialization and transnational capital-friendly economic restructuring have exacerbated. Although these macrostructural processes actually affect whites as well as nonwhites, and poor people as well as the increasingly vulnerable middle class, public discourse is decidedly color and class biased. Its focus has clearly been on racially marked inner cities and not on the affluent suburbs where more illegal drugs are bought and consumed than in crime-infested inner cities and where the threatening forces of downward social mobility are threatening to dislocate people from once taken-for-granted social positions based on the unfair privileges and power of whiteness.

From Urban to Global Apartheid

Recent trends in anthropology point to the usefulness of conducting research across multiple sites. This especially makes sense in light of the fact that anthropologists are increasingly thinking with deterritorialized concepts of culture and nation and are more apt to organize research around analytical units such as diasporic and transnational social fields (Appadurai 1991; Basch, Schiller, and Blanc 1994; Gupta and Ferguson 1992). As the beneficiary of multisited analyses, anthropological inquiry and applications must reject "the false dichotomy between First and Third Worlds" (Nash 1994, 9). As June Nash (1994, 9) writes, we must recognize "the commonalities in the welfare problems faced by women trying to feed their families and keep their children alive, whether they live in drug-war-devastated inner cities of industrialized [or deindustrialized] countries or in militarized countries where conflicts are exacerbated by U.S. arms shipments." On a similar note, Owen Lynch (1994, 37) argues that in light of the current globalized context, "what [anthropologists learn] about those living in one city often has implications or linkages of space-time distanciation with those living in another." He goes on to state that "it behooves . . . anthropologists to take time-space [distanciation] into account and not remain with the localized fragmentations of place and identity to which postmodernism has so forcefully, but narrowly, redirected our attention" (49).

Social analysts who are taking the implications of globalization seriously are able to see that the Contract with America (advocated by controversial Speaker of the House Newt Gingrich during the Bill Clinton administration), and, before it, Reaganomics, the "Daddy Bush ditto," and continuities through Clinton and George W. Bush, are the U.S. variants of a broader process of structural adjustment, which, as I suggested earlier, is more than just the institution-specific programs and conditionalities that the International Monetary Fund (IMF) mandates debt-ridden economies in the Third World to follow (Sparr 1992). Beyond these, structural adjustment is an international and transnational policy climate and development strategy informed by a neoliberal macroeconomic paradigm and worldview, which valorize laissez-faire capitalism. This worldview assumes that free-market forces will automatically lead to efficient and productive economies in the long run. According to this logic, the less government regulation and the more privatization, the better. Structural adjustments, then, are put into place to redefine and redirect the role of the state and to expand the rule of the market, which supposedly has the capacity to meet all needs. Consequently, government subsidies of goods and services are eliminated or drastically reduced. Neoliberalism underpins export-led industrialization in free trade zones around the world, IMF agreements and conditions, World Bank programs, the North America Free Trade Agreement (NAFTA), as well as former president Clinton's so-called welfare reform, the Hopwood decision delegitimating affirmative action, and the fact that more money is being channeled into the military and prisons than into public schools.

Although the effects of structural adjustment have not been uniform, overall they have exacerbated global apartheid and the structural violence it unleashes against the well-being and sustainability of people and ecosystems alike. Global integration has resulted in the growing erosion of subsistence security in both the North and South (Nash 1994). As sociologist William

Robinson (1996, 22) has written, "[u]nder globalization there has been a dramatic growth of socioeconomic inequalities and of human misery. . . . The gap between rich and poor is widening with each country, in both the North and South. Moreover, inequalities between North and South have increased sharply." While the divide between North and South is growing, increasingly the human species has come to be stratified along transnational class lines, and, nationally as well as internationally, class is segmented and stratified by race and gender. As a consequence, racially subordinated peoples all over the world are disproportionately represented in labor's most vulnerable lowest strata, both in the United States and abroad.

The current global regime of export-led development, structural adjustment policies, and debt servicing—which could perhaps be characterized as a second primitive accumulation and an era of recolonization—are resulting in massive economic dislocations and the creation of a vast pool of men and women desperate for jobs, even at wages below subsistence levels. Under these conditions, many developing—or underdeveloping—countries have been converted into cheap industrial labor reserves, the most recent versions of imperialism's colonial frontiers (Mies, Bennholdt-Thomsen, and von Werlhof 1988), where women are often especially earmarked for factory work paid at nearly slave wages. For example, according to information from several years ago, Haitian women workers at the Disney factory earned only 28 cents per hour, nowhere near a living wage by either Haitian or U.S. standards (National Labor Committee 1996).

It should not be surprising that women bear the brunt of global apartheid. Seventy percent of the world's absolute poor are women, and these women disproportionately subsidize the production and accumulation of wealth and development with their unwaged and waged labor—labor that is socially constructed and ideologically defined as cheap or, in unwaged contexts, free. Women are especially vulnerable to the ideological and physical assaults of nationalist militarization, economically induced environmental degradation, and the economic restructuring and political realignments mediated by neoliberal policies. Increasingly, women's as well as their families' and communities' subsistence security and human rights are being eroded in a post–Cold War climate in which capitalism appears to have triumphed over its alternatives and is projecting its model of development as an inevitable course of history and regime of truth. That regime of truth legitimates an international division of flexible labor that depends on the naturalization of gender and racial hierarchies, as manifested in so-called women's work and men's work (Alexander and Mohanty 1997, 5). These categories are undergirded by the patriarchal assumptions that tasks such as sewing, assembling electronic components, or pursuing home- and community-based informal activities are extensions of women's natural activities requiring no special skills, training, or compensation and that skilled jobs belong to men who, as natural breadwinners, deserve greater remuneration for their special strength and training. With their labor socially constructed in these terms, poor women of the world—whether as participants in export industrialization, informal-sector activities, or other spheres of work—subsidize the production and accumulation of the world's wealth, which, more than ever, is being concentrated at the top of a transnational ladder. This upward redistribution of wealth is made possible at least in part by cultural production, a process of producing discourses and images through which presuppositions about subordinate womanhood, sexuality, domesticity, and marriage are mobilized. This discursive practice naturalizes women's subordination and helps lower their wages and benefits. According to Aihwa Ong (1991, 289), "reinventing principles of male and racial superiority, this process of cultural production rests upon the articulation that transnational labor relations have with local norms, including the norms expressed in the policies and practices of the postcolonial state."

Following feminist political scientist Cynthia Enloe, we know that gendered meanings, relations, and practices are thoroughly infused in international politics and political economy. Established forms of power depend on assumptions and expectations of masculinity and femininity (Enloe 1989, 4). For instance, the international order, as evidenced in its current structural adjustment strategy of development, depends on "ideas about masculinized dignity and feminized sacrifice" (4). As a consequence, the politics of international debt, for instance, does not impact only women. It works in the first place because of widespread expectations and gender-role hierarchies that ensure that women will be shock absorbers taking up the slack when jobs and social safety nets are slashed or eliminated (Enloe 1989; Sparr 1992, 1994). According to economist Pamela Sparr, "women [around the world, North and South] have mortgaged their lives helping nations weather the painful adjustments" (Sparr 1992, 33). A UNICEF report for the Americas pointed out "that if it were not for poor women working harder and longer hours, the poorest third of the population in that region [women, men, and children] would not be alive today" (Sparr 1992, 33–34; UNICEF 1989).

Feminist research on women in development demonstrates that globalization in its neoliberal form is fundamentally a gendered phenomenon marked by a patriarchal logic. From the interventions that multiracial and postcolonial feminisms have made, we know that this masculinist logic is informed by racialized assumptions and meanings. Present-day strategies to facilitate capital accumulation implicate a racialized gender ideology and politics that legitimate the superexploitation of the productive and reproductive labor of women, with women of color bearing the heaviest burdens and being the most vulnerable targets of structural violence. These women are concentrated in the Southern Hemisphere. Disproportionately but not exclusively, they occupy subordinate racial, ethnic, and class statuses grounded in diverse histories of inequality that are context specific but, at the same time, cross-culturally comparable and connected by continuities related to "the logic and operation of capital in the contemporary global arena" (Mohanty 1997, 28).

Gender, as only one axis in a more complex matrix of domination (Collins 1991, 1998), is inextricably tangled up with other hierarchies and processes of difference making. In view of the intersection of multiple axes of inequality and power, and the injustices accompanying them, it is not a coincidence that the superexploited Haitian workers to whom I referred earlier are black and second-class citizens of the poorest nation in the Western Hemisphere. Consequently, their bottom-level position in the international hierarchy is conditioned by their race, gender, class, and national status. Although all these dimensions of difference and inequality are flagrantly marked in Haiti's case, the international racial ranking of human subjects extends well beyond Haiti and is not always as visibly marked; "the [neoracist] order of . . . power relations . . . [does not necessarily] proceed through readily apparent notions of superiority and inferiority" (Gilroy 1991, 40; Balibar 1991) nor through explicitly articulated notions of race.

Implicit or coded articulations of race, and of race's intersection with gender, may appear in the language of "heightened nationalism" (Williams 1996, 7), which can have the effect of racialization. In the former Yugoslavia, the ethnonational conflicts that have erupted are expressed in a language emphasizing irreconcilable, immutable cultural/political differences that can be resolved only through ethnic cleansing. In the context of this violent conflict, full-scale military strategies have been inflicted on tens of thousands of women whose racially marked bodies have become battlefields (Kesiæ 1996, 51). The heinous campaign of ethnocide and its equivalents elsewhere (e.g., Rwanda) are being deployed by violating women's bodies and, through their bodies, destabilizing the assaulted nation's moral integrity and reproduction. To this horrendous end, the "wombs of nationalist respectability" and the prospects for preserving "racial patrimony" have been violated (Williams 1996, vii). In this case and in many others, rape is being deployed as a masculinist weapon not only against individual women but against their families, communities, and supralocal solidarities that dare to assert their right to self-determination and to imagine a future of national sovereignty.

In this context, rape is deployed as a means of racialization, "a means of imposing a permanent partition between territories as well as two previously co-existing and symbiotically related peoples" (Harrison 2000, 51).

Confronting Apartheid:
Local and Transnational Strategies

Local Responses with Global Implications

Whether encoding personal or social criticism in their songs or oral poetry (Price 1993 [1984]; Abu-Lughod 1986), being possessed and attacked by spirits on the factory floor (Ong 1987), or organizing a needed rural cooperative or a human rights organization to fill important gaps (Harrison 2004), racially situated women's agency is not precluded by the weight of the multiple oppressions with which they live. Interlocking oppressions are often discussed in the additive terms of double or triple burdens, evoking either an image of a poor black or indigenous woman overwhelmed by the weight of oppressions or a romanticized image of a superwoman exhibiting remarkable strength. Ethnographic analysis of ordinary women corroborates the practice theory notion that within structures of domination, no matter how severe, there exist constraints on as well as spaces and opportunities for resistance and contestation. Agency assumes a variety of forms that are influenced by historically specific circumstances shaped by the interplay of such factors as local culture and community power dynamics, state policies, and the local workings of transnational capital as played out in varying economic sectors, including the informal or underground sector (cf. Ong 1991, 296).

As Ong suggests, women's responses to the impacts of recolonization can frequently be seen as diverse, localized instances of cultural struggles for claiming moral personhood and human dignity rather than as clear-cut expressions of gender, class, or racial consciousness. Ong claims that a "cryptic language of protest" is embedded in the isolated individualized and covert tactics of resistance that she observed in Malay factories. She found that although those rituals of rebellion rarely coalesced into more organized collective actions with explicit demands, they "silently negotiated the contours of daily work relations" and exposed the injustices of a postcolonial industrial logic (Ong 1991, 301), which institutionalizes hierarchies and inequalities of race and gender (289).

In other cultural and national contexts, such as Korea (Ong 1991) and Jamaica (Harrison 1997b), women workers have contested the dehumanizing conditions of their economic subordination in more direct and militant ways. Like their North Carolinian counterparts whose struggle as hospital workers Karen Brodkin Sacks (1988) documents, they have drawn on familial and community-based cultural values and principles of social organization for mobilizing collective protests (e.g., strikes). In my own research, I have found that the segment of Jamaican women who, for the most part, eke out a living by doing informal rather than industrial work engage in cultural struggles centered in their communities. Activating social networks connected to neighborhood-based, nonpartisan, voluntary associations, their struggle has focused on such problems as rampant political violence and political victimization in the distribution of public-sector wage work. In this color- and gender-stratified social context, these political assaults tend to target downtown blacks rather than uptown browns and whites. In efforts to restore a greater measure of peace to their troubled downtown neighborhood, women-centered networks and voluntary associations have challenged ghetto-specific constructions of black masculinity that glorify the defiant employment of (gun) violence as well as interrogated, at least implicitly, the domestic and international policy climate responsible for exacerbating economic austerity.

Also in Jamaica, a quite explicitly articulated form of gender, race, and class-conscious critical cultural production has been undertaken by Sistren, a predominantly working-class drama troupe engaged in collaborative research for working-class conscientization and empowerment. This innovative project emerged in the late 1970s out of the relationship that developed between twelve women government service workers and the Jamaica School of Drama, which had been commissioned to provide resource persons to support the development of a workers' cultural festival (Ford-Smith 1997). Over the years, the goals of the organization have been somewhat thwarted by race/color and class dynamics that recreated conventional power disparities between the black working-class rank-and-file members and their middle-class allies with the professional skills and social capital to administer and serve as credible brokers and spokespersons for an organization dependent on the largesse of bourgeois donors.

This brief overview of an array of gendered and raced agencies would be terribly incomplete without acknowledgment of the emergence of transnational praxis; that is, forms of social and political action consistent with what Alexander and Mohanty (1997) refer to as projects of "cross-border feminist democracy." As you will see in the ensuing discussion, despite the intensification of local identities and political fragmentation that many scholars consider symptomatic of postmodernity, there are labor and grassroots activists who are learning to organize transnationally against corporate exploitation, subsistence insecurity, and other manifestations of intersecting inequalities.

Seeking Transnational Strategies of Activism

Making meaningful change in this global era entails acting locally and thinking globally, as the popular slogan goes, but simply following this directive is
no longer sufficient. We need to see more connections made between local
actions and organizing efforts involving higher levels of integration and coordination. As I have shown, permanent unemployment, subsistence insecurity,
homelessness, drug-related violence, and savage inequalities in public education and health all implicate processes, conditions, and power dynamics at
the international and transnational level. To reform current welfare reform
in light of the empirical reality of urban apartheid in the United States, we
must understand how national-level political decisions are embedded within
wider contexts of organizational and structural power. As we confront policy
deformities in the various states and in Washington, DC, some of us need to
direct our energies to the major loci of policy making at the transnational
and global level. This necessarily involves our deconstructing and then reconstructing—and hopefully transforming—the very meaning and practice
of development, democracy, global order, and human responsibility.

As demonstrations in Seattle, Washington, Washington, DC, and Genoa,
Italy, against the World Trade Organization (WTO), the IMF, and the free
trade deliberations of the Group of Eight (G8; United States, Canada, Great
Britain, France, Germany, Italy, Japan, and Russia) have shown, there are
labor and grassroots activists who are learning to organize globally against
transnational capital and subsistence insecurity. Returning close to my own
former backyard, in Southern Appalachia, one of the Southern zones within
the North, the Tennessee Industrial Renewal Network (TIRN), which was
renamed the Tennessee Economic Renewal Network (TERN), like other
labor organizations around the country, responded to plant closings and the
accompanying union-bashing climate by organizing across national borders
(Ansley 1992). TERN has followed the movement of capital from Tennessee
to the Texas-Mexico border towns where it has created forums in which unemployed and potentially unemployed women factory workers from eastern
Tennessee and their *maquila* counterparts can share their respective experiences and gain a broader perspective on labor organizing that parochialism
would preclude. As political scientist Sheila Collins points out:

> Many in the labor movement now see organizing globally as a way to prevent
> companies from playing one country against another. Ideally, workers in dif-
> ferent countries employed by the same multinational company could organize
> internationally to support each others' demands for better wages and working
> conditions. Meetings between groups of U.S. workers with their counterparts in
> Mexico, El Salvador, Guatemala, the Dominican Republic, and Haiti are mov-

ing in that direction. . . . UN conferences on development related issues have seen increased activity by grassroots NGOs [nongovernmental organizations]. Taking the issues of the poor into the deliberations of official (government-sponsored) conferences, NGOs have developed vast networking apparatuses through alternative summits and by means of the Internet. A global organization of indigenous peoples whose cultures and economies face extinction due to Western development schemes is one result. (Collins 1995, 135–36)

The fact that more Northern women now have a greater understanding of gender's intersection with underdevelopment, international debt, militarism, and human rights violations—racism and xenophobia included—has a great deal to do with the profound effects of "falling from grace" (Newman 1988) or the growing downward mobility that economic restructuring has engendered in the United States. Northern women's increased political and economic literacy, however, can also be attributed to the impact that Southern women's articulations and organizational efforts have had on feminist consciousness and praxis worldwide, especially since the watershed 1985 United Nations Women's Conference and Non-Governmental Organization (NGO) Forum in Nairobi, Kenya. Whereas North-South tensions were particularly pronounced in Nairobi, ten years later in Huairou and Beijing, China, there were noticeable efforts to bridge some of the gaps and resolve some of the tensions by clearing enough common ground for confronting the global forces that cross-cut the boundary between North and South.

The post-Nairobi and now post-Beijing spirit of cooperative work and struggle is reflected in Alternative Women in Development (Alt-WID), a working group of feminist researchers and activists (Sparr 1992). In the late 1980s and early 1990s, Alt-WID produced an important case study of Reaganomics as a form of structural adjustment so that women—and their male allies—in the North and South could see their commonalities more clearly and, consequently, become better prepared to build transnational coalitions linking action at local, national, and global levels. Alt-WID is a Northern sister organization of DAWN, the acronym for Development Alternatives with Women for a New Era, which is a network of largely southern hemisphere activists, researchers, and policy makers (see Sen and Grown 1987). I see these two organizations as models for integrating applied social research into activist agendas and projects.

Can Anthropologists Make a Difference?

To what extent are anthropologists involved in these kinds of coordinated efforts? Whatever our response to this question, we need to be even more involved wherever we find ourselves on the terrain of struggle. If we can transcend the limitations of the professional or entrepreneurial individualism that informs much of anthropologists' involvement with change-inducing agencies (from the local to global levels), we may be in the collective position to mobilize the potentially powerful knowledge, cross-cultural networks, and institutional pipelines we have achieved as a discipline toward the end of creating conditions for an alternative, sustainable future that is more ordinary people centered and earth friendly. It is absolutely urgent that we find more effective ways to confront apartheid both at home and abroad.

Perhaps we can put our mobilizing capacities to the test by taking advantage of the opportunities for national and transnational networking and coalition building that are opened up by United Nations conferences, such as the World Conference against Racism, Racial Discrimination, Xenophobia, and Related Intolerance (WCAR) that was held in Durban, South Africa, in 2001. That important human rights conference, along with its parallel forum for nongovernmental organizations, was devoted to examining and combating the heightening problems that racism, as a human rights violation, presents to the world (Harrison 2001, 2005).

Within the UN-based human rights system, racism's intersection with gender oppression has received a great deal of attention. The Special Rapporteur on Racial Discrimination has noted the importance of understanding that racially subjugated women suffer a gender-specific form of racism that obstructs their ability to exercise their basic rights (Harrison 2000, 60; Harrison 2001, 115). Consequently, the fight against global apartheid must deploy ideas, models of change, and plans of action that take multiaxial realities into consideration. This means that tools and weapons of antiracism need to be integrated into advocacy campaigns and projects focused on women's rights, migrants and refugee's rights, indigenous people's rights, children's rights, social and cultural rights, economic and work-related rights, and the rights to development and environmental sustainability. In turn, it also means that antiracism mobilizations need to integrate gender, sexuality, class, and other relevant concerns into their strategies for change. To achieve this more holistic, integrative approach to human rights struggle, coalitions and united fronts need to be organized in ways that offset some of the unwitting political fragmentation that the proliferation of rights (e.g., women's rights, children's right, refugee's rights, indigenous rights, etc.) and the growing numbers of conventions and covenants associated with them have helped create.

Under the aegis of the International Union of Anthropological and Ethnological Sciences (IUAES), specifically that of the IUAES Commission on the Anthropology of Women, an international group of anthropologists with a few other social scientists and human rights activists participated in the

WCAR NGO Forum (Harrison 2001, 2005). We went to Durban because of our convictions about the importance of social researchers having sustained cross-pollinating dialogues and connections with activists committed to dismantling the negative effects of racial oppression, especially as it is experienced and struggled against by women and the people whom they love and care about. Dialogue is a prerequisite for, and integral to, cooperative and coordinated action. Anthropologists have so much to learn as well as to teach about human rights. Witnessing and being a small part of that megaforum with its countless plenary speeches, workshops, sessions, and extraprogram activities that went on everywhere we turned, were important learning experiences that exposed us to some of the ways that antiracists—and antiracist feminists—across the globe are attempting to make a difference in this world of heatedly politicized and too frequently militarized differences. With those lessons in hand, our renewed and expanded repertoire of tools should enable us to become better anthropologists, committed to finding more effective ways to practice what we preach by situating our projects in a coalition of knowledges and mobilizations (Harrison 2000, 62). Toward that end, more of us can find the means to face up to global apartheid and act upon the ethical and moral responsibilities that our growing knowledge of human rights abuse carries with it.

Beyond Seeking Sanctuary in White Public Space

In his provocative 1996 essay, Philippe Bourgois challenged anthropologists to struggle against the grain of ideologically murky social analysis that more often than not relies on "elite projections of class- and race-biased fantasies" (249) for interrogating and theorizing the complex and contradictory phenomena of inner-city poverty and street agency. He asserted that anthropologists frequently seek refuge in "safe settings where white public space is dominant" (cf. Page and Thomas 1994) and avoid the harsh reality of inner-city life and violence succumbing to the cultural and class logic of U.S. apartheid. The class and racial segregation of U.S.-style apartheid make the everyday lives of the urban poor largely inaccessible to privileged intellectuals who—if they are interested in poor people—are more inclined to "crave the protective cocoon of schools" than to "venture into . . . the surrounding streets, tenements, and housing projects" (Bourgois 1996, 251). To confront urban apartheid more effectively and honestly in both analytical and applied terms, more of us need to overcome the fears and insecurities that obstruct the more widespread pursuit of ethnographic inquiries, such as Bourgois's research project (1995) on the underground economy in Spanish Harlem.

Bourgois should be applauded for bringing the issue of the structured oppression and violence of urban apartheid to our attention, challenging us as anthropologists committed to various forms of praxis to do more than pay lip service, project liberal or conservative fantasies, or engage in inquiry primarily from the perspective of metaphoric as well as physically real windows on the everyday violence of poverty. Although I think his critique of many school ethnographies, for instance, is sound, at the same time I suspect that he may have overstated his criticism and the uniqueness of his contribution. After all, it is not new for anthropologists to take life-threatening risks to conduct fieldwork in troubled places in the world. Very often, we have confronted these risks by default rather than by choice and unusual self-sacrificing courage. Anthropologists often cultivate such courage and conviction through negotiating the vicissitudes of difficult and dangerous fieldwork experiences. Although there are those of us who make a point to avoid troubled spots, nowadays it is hard to find places immune to the everyday violence of apartheid in some form or another. The apartheid to which Bourgois refers is widespread, indeed global. Those of us studying populations ostensibly disadvantaged by interlocking stratifications of race, class, and gender have few places to hide, especially as the forces of globalization accelerate and penetrate lifeways in North and South, East and West. There is virtually nowhere to hide as the cultural logic of transnational capital accumulation and free trade diffuses to every corner of the planet, jeopardizing the sustainability of subsistence systems and ecosystems as well as the most valorized pattern of capitalist development.

Bourgois's ethnographic analysis and cultural critique are important food for thought for applied and activist anthropologists, but they should be situated in a wider intertextual and discursive context within which we may find a growing body of anthropological work that confronts urban and global apartheid, both from the streets and from various strategically located windows. Much of this work has not gained the visibility and canonized status that it deserves; however, it can be retrieved by anyone willing to do his or her homework and confront the hierarchical ordering of knowledges within anthropology. Do not forget that the Valentines—parents and children—lived in a New York ghetto for several years studying "hustling and other forms of work" and survival (Valentine 1978). Do not forget that a number of anthropologists—myself included—have investigated informal economies, gangs, insurgents, and social movements and that even more have worked in parts of the world where indigenous peoples, peasants, and urbanites are struggling for their very survival, often at great personal and political risk. Although there may not be any theoretical or political consensus within this work, and though there may indeed be too much ideological murk, I believe that embedded in the record anthropologists have helped produce are many of the necessary—if not completely sufficient—elements for constructing frameworks and models for interpreting, analyzing, explicating, and acting against the invidious reality of global apartheid. The challenge is for us to build with and upon these elements, learning from their strengths and limitations, developing new syntheses and strategies for more effective and, I hope, transformative praxis in the twenty-first century.

10. Justice for All

The Challenges of Advocacy Research in the Global Age

In late spring 2002, I received an e-mail message from an anthropology student at the City University of New York's (CUNY's) Graduate Center. I was pleasantly surprised that Angela Queeley had the idea of nominating me for the Delmos Jones Visiting Scholars Program, a year-old program named in memory of the late African American anthropologist who had worked at the Graduate Center for nearly twenty-seven years. Like the W. E. B. Du Bois Visiting Scholars Program before it, the program was designed to bring three or four minority scholars to the Graduate Center every year to spend a few days interacting with students and faculty. Visiting scholars are asked to deliver a formal public lecture, give a more informal colloquium on some aspect of their current research, and meet with interested students and colleagues, in groups or as individuals. They also meet with administrators, all the way up to the university president. I was honored by the idea of the nomination but felt somewhat uncomfortable about it. Perhaps a more senior person would be more appropriate for such a prestigious nomination. The deadline for submitting the materials was only two or three days away, so I did not have much time to decide.

How could I say no to such a wonderful gift? The nomination itself was enough of an honor. The fact that the idea had come from the Africana Studies Group, which was organized by graduate students, meant a great deal to me. When I was a grad student at Stanford, I had coordinated a similar interdisciplinary group of students interested in the African world, including, of course, the diaspora. That cohort experience contributed to my higher education in ways to which I am forever indebted. With the support of the African and African-American Studies (AAAS) Program and through the framework offered by an undergraduate course in which a few of us found ourselves serving as voluntary teaching assistants, we organized a lecture series in which a handful of nationally recognized scholars from around the country were invited to present on different aspects of race, class, and power.

The lecture series was an ad hoc plan that emerged from ongoing conversations between students and the coordinator and director of the AAAS Program. It was an empowering experience to see an idea translated into action in the context of an undergraduate lecture course whose substantive focus was reshaped to explore the questions that engaged our minds and hearts at that time. Fortunately, Stanford's Multicultural Student Affairs had the resources to support us in our endeavor.

I decided to accept the CUNY nomination, not expecting to get an invitation to visit. The PhD program in anthropology had to submit the official nomination, and the executive officer, Louise Lennihan, did so with great enthusiasm. If the nomination were accepted by the vice provost's office, I would be the first anthropologist and the first woman to be appointed a Delmos Jones Visiting Scholar. The nomination was approved, and along with economist Glenn Loury and historian and medieval scholar William Chester Jordan, I was invited to visit the Graduate Center the following academic year.

I was at the Grad Center in April 2003. That was the time when the U.S. Supreme Court heard the Michigan affirmative action case and when the country's war against terrorism had led to a declaration of war against Iraq. I met with the newly established Women of Color Group in the anthropology program and had a luncheon and roundtable discussion with an interdisciplinary group of students involved in the Magnet Fellowship Program. Both of these groups were interested in survival issues, strategies for getting through graduate school, and what to expect afterward. I interacted with a wider group of students and faculty during a colloquium, and then the whole two-day marathon culminated with the public lecture and, following that, a reception and dinner party. I returned home two days later with a strong dose of stimulation and inspiration to carry on.

Because I feel that the Delmos Jones Visiting Scholar Lecture was probably the most significant address I had given up to that point in my career, I present it here without deleting its lecturelike features. I was given the platform to speak truth to power in memory of a supportive senior colleague whose writings were—and, as you shall see, still are—an important source of insight and inspiration to me. In fact, the words in one of his essays had helped plant the seeds of "decolonizing anthropology" in my head.

I dedicate this chapter to my intellectual ancestor, Delmos Jones, and to students preparing to emerge as a new generation of scholars working in the social justice–centered tradition that Delmos Jones represented.

Introductory Remarks

It is truly an honor for me to be here as one of this year's Delmos Jones Visiting Scholars and to bring closure to this year's lecture series. I thank the Africana Studies Group for initiating the nomination and the PhD program in anthropology for its supportive partnership in bringing me here. I am at once honored and humbled because of the respect and admiration I have for the important work that Dr. Jones did throughout his career as an anthropologist and throughout his life as a person of principles with a strong sense of social responsibility and political commitment.

The academic and political dimensions of his life came together in scholarship that advanced the goals of social equality and social justice. He was committed to doing a critical native anthropology that honestly and unapologetically confronted "issues of domination and oppression" from the vantage of one who had experienced domination and oppression (Jones 1995, 58) as a member of a racially subjugated people, one of the many peoples who were historically relegated to the ranks of "the natives" by colonial overlords. His broader goal, however, was to contribute to a transformative—and not merely oppositional—social science. In his view, a transformative social science can potentially be practiced by those who experience racial, class, and gender subordination *or privilege*. Ultimately, political vision and commitment are more influential than membership in any particular social category for shaping the kind of social science any researcher pursues—whether it is part of a received tradition or whether it is paradigm shifting. Delmos Jones was an advocate for developing a transformative social science, one that offers a critique of the destructive, exploitative, and alienating conditions of capitalism as well as a social analysis of "the multiple realities, dilemmas, [and] constraints" (Jones 1995, 69) that ordinary people negotiate while making choices in their efforts, their struggles, to "bring about [meaningful] change" (63). To envision a transformative agenda for the social sciences means that one has a commitment to academic freedom, which depends on the implementation of profoundly democratic values in places where knowledge is produced, learned, and translated for wide-ranging application.

I would like to thank this institution, this place of higher learning, for recognizing Delmos Jones's contributions and the powerful significance of his presence here for nearly thirty years. I would also like to thank his many colleagues, especially those of you in the anthropology program who provided an immediate intellectual community receptive to the ideas that informed his research, teaching, and public service. I want you to know that the work you do here makes a difference that is contributing to the kind of anthropological and broader social scientific inquiry that your late colleague envisioned and worked so hard to put into practice. Whether you call what you do critical anthropology, feminist anthropology, urban anthropology, Marxist anthropology, post-Marxist anthropology, postcolonial anthropology, indigenous anthropology, or just plain ole anthropology, you represent different facets and strategies of what is ultimately a shared project to recapture and remake the discipline so that it can more effectively meet its goal of studying the diversity and commonality among human societies as they have developed over time and space and as they are changing in the current age with its many challenges and dilemmas.

As I stand before you on this day in early April, I cannot help but sense the significance and the broader social context of this lecture, whose title underscores the key words *justice* and *advocacy*. I am very much aware of and grateful for being a beneficiary and part of the legacy of the civil rights, women's liberation, and antiwar movements that created the social and political conditions for policies and programs that, among other things, opened the gates wide enough for people like me—and many of you—to enter the great halls of academia, particularly academia's historically white institutions. Regardless of the decision to which Clarence Thomas and his colleagues come, I am not ashamed of being a member of the generation of affirmative action babies. Nor am I ashamed of having come of age and social consciousness during a time when many had the courage to stand and be counted for believing that the imperial role the United States played in Southeast Asia was wrong and inconsistent with the American Dream that many had for a nation claiming to exemplify the best of democratic principles and a commitment to promoting justice for all. The varied voices of dissent insisted then that justice should mean more than "just us"—wealth, power, and privilege for some of us but not for most of them. Do we want "just us" or "justice"? That is a question whose relevance continues to resonate today as the nation and the world community struggle over the meanings of this important concept and set of principles.

The platform and the charge you have so generously given me this afternoon have inspired me to revisit some of Delmos Jones's writings and to reflect upon them as I consider my own thinking about justice, advocacy, and the role of organization in directing social change in this age of globalization and at this moment of fear and panic in which our civil rights and civil liberties are the focus of debate, struggle, and legislative change. The meanings of patriotism, democracy, constitutionality, and national identity are being redefined in more restrictive terms, informed by nativist anxieties and a narrowed nationalism, while sweeping new powers have been given to the state. In this troubling context and during these troubling times, we may well have to become stronger advocates for the public space to express diverse ideological views and for the academic freedom and authority to do critical work that may result in analytical accounts of the world that will not accord with those being promulgated by the White House and the Pentagon.

Promoting a Critical "Native" Anthropology and the Decolonization of Knowledge

In his widely read, cited, and critiqued "Towards a Native Anthropology," originally published in 1970, Jones addressed issues related to the ethics and politics of fieldwork methodology as well as the epistemology of the discipline. To my knowledge, he was one of the earliest anthropologists to raise direct questions about standpoint, perspectivism, and positionality, issues that have since been widely debated and theorized, to a great extent by feminist scholars. Years later in a 1995 essay entitled "Anthropology and the Oppressed: A Reflection on 'Native' Anthropology," Jones refined his position on these matters, clarifying and underscoring the basic thrust of his earlier argument for a critical native anthropology that would contribute to the decolonization of anthropology and, by implication, the decolonization of the social sciences generally. He reinforced his view that social science but particularly anthropology (with its focus on human diversity and cross-cultural analysis) can benefit and be enriched by diversifying its ranks and subjecting both mainstream and native anthropologies, neither of which are monolithic, to critical scrutiny. He posited that the critical decolonization of knowledge is "now needed more than ever" (Jones 1995, 69). He understood that diversifying anthropology involved not only opening the gates to more people of color and non-Westerners but, beyond that, democratizing academic space to include multiple political persuasions and ideological commitments.

Although he strongly advocated the inclusion of their perspectives and experiences, he did not at all romanticize or essentialize native anthropologists, anthropologists who come from or belong to oppressed peoples. He knew that just because an anthropologist or a lawyer is from Pinpoint, Georgia, or a sharecropping farm in Alabama does not mean that she or he will automatically become a transformative thinker and actor on the stage of social change. But he also knew, based on his own life, that experience can be an excellent teacher that enables one to see through bifocal or multifocal lenses and to develop a critical double or even a multiaxial consciousness. This epistemological vantage never develops simply because of one's blackness or womanhood or poverty. When it does develop, it emerges from a struggle that is part of a wider political commitment. As Delmos Jones pointed out, that kind of commitment can free an individual from "the destructive tendency to be loyal to one's own group, 'right or wrong'" (1995, 60).

Delmos Jones also understood that decolonization was not an unproblematic concept or process; however, he used it as a point of entry into a conversation about the possibilities of transformation, both in academia and in the world at large. He dared to imagine a transformative decolonization that transcends the limitations of much of what we have seen in the existing postcolonial world in which the transition from formal colonial domination led, in most instances, to patterns of leadership succession that reproduced the very problems that many fought against during the anticolonial phase. Opposition without transformation is not what Delmos Jones had in mind when he wrote about decolonization.

The Responsibility of Social Researchers in the Age of Recolonization

Over the years, I have found Delmos Jones's writings to be a source of inspiration and insight in my own work as an anthropologist, and that work has ranged widely from the political ethnography of urban poverty in Jamaica to the comparative study of race and racism and their intersections with other inequalities, notably those along lines of gender and class, to the critical anthropology of anthropology's history, particularly those neglected chapters about ancestral skeletons that have been hidden in the closet. I have characterized my work in its multiple facets and phases as *a critical project in decolonizing anthropology*. Like Delmos Jones, I am well aware of the limitations of actually existing decolonization. However, I would argue that decolonization, in my sense of what it should be, has yet to take place in much of the world, which has been restructured along lines of neocolonialism under the guise of independence and postcolonial pseudosovereignty. Sovereignty for much of the Southern Hemisphere has been sovereignty without emancipatory substance, particularly in the political-economic realm. Indeed, the conditions engendered by the most recent phase of global restructuring and geopolitical realignment suggest that the world is undergoing a veritable *recolonization* under the dictates of a regimen of neoliberal, free-market economics. This regimen has shifted major regulatory functions from the nation-state to transnational/global entities such as the International Monetary Fund, World Bank, and the World Trade Organization, units of decision making that are technically multinational but overwhelmingly influenced by the priorities of particular core states, whose interests and purview are transnational in scope. Among these core states with disproportionate influence over these global institutions is the United States, whose domestic and foreign policies constitute two sides of the same coin.

Under conditions of recolonization, which is increasingly being crusaded by the ideological mystique and military might of American Empire expansion, the aggressive political economy and culture of commodities encroaches upon virtually everything. June Nash's work has illuminated how the human security that was once sustained by zones of traditional subsistence and biodiversity is now being severely assaulted by the forces of global integration that recognize no limits to their expansion and control (Nash 1994). The resultant socioeconomic dislocations that are being accelerated are creating "a vast pool of people desperate for jobs, even at wages below subsistence levels" (Harrison 2002a, 49). In a world in which everything is being subjected to commodification, everything can be placed on the auction block to be bought, sold, owned, and eventually consumed as private property—cultural heritage, intellectual property, body parts (as Nancy Scheper-Hughes's research demonstrates), and entire bodies, such as the exoticized, eroticized bodies of women and men, even children, whose means of livelihood are, more and more, being severely restricted to options or impositions like sex work and sex trafficking (Scheper-Hughes 2002). The planet's final frontiers, human as well as ecological, are being captured, colonized, and exploited without any serious concern for our sustainable future. As Sweet Honey in the Rock's poignant song lyrics warn us, "if the Earth could run away, so far away, then she'd be running for her life . . . running for her blessed life . . . struggling to be free from cruel humanity" ("Battered Earth").

Understanding the Intensified Abuse of Human Rights

In this recolonized world, a transformative decolonization is needed now more than ever. The production of knowledge about the existing world and its peoples needs to be decolonized and transformed now more than ever. *Now* when many states' ability to protect rights to education, health care, and humane work conditions has been drastically compromised by internationally mandated policies and programs (e.g., structural adjustment) that give higher priority to corporate rights and the rights of transnational capital than to the basic needs and dignity of ordinary human beings. *Now* when the social contract that once existed between states and citizens in the more democratic countries is eroding and quickly disappearing. *Now* when disparities in wealth, military power, health, and life expectancy are extreme and still growing. *Now* when human rights are increasingly jeopardized and being denied to peoples whose bodies, cultural practices, and social locations across national and transnational space are being racialized—whether with idioms and symbolic meanings drawing on notions of biological determinism, or cultural fundamentalism, or moral essences.

The intensification of discrimination and violence against racial others is one of the gravest human rights problems the world is facing. Although it does not really exist in nature, race is a very real social distinction, material relation, and dimension of social stratification that is mutually constituted by class, gender, ethnicity, and increasingly national and transnational identification. Understanding the intricate workings of these interlocking axes of inequality, power, and human rights conflict is a necessary part of the research agenda for critical social scientists of the order that Delmos Jones envisioned when he called for a transformative praxis that explicates the mechanisms of oppression and the matrices of domination that constrain and repress human potential.

Understanding the Political Culture of Achievement

His concern with the dynamics of local organizations, however, demonstrated his awareness that matrices of domination that constrain, co-opt, and neutralize local actions also, despite themselves, provide opportunities and spaces for critical, creative agency. Actually, I should say that critical, creative human agency makes space for itself in the crevices and interstices of structures of power. An important part of a critical social science agenda is to illuminate how, often against all odds, oppressed peoples manage to go against the grain of domination and create maneuvering spaces for seeking rehumanization, freedom, and justice. It is important to understand, as Delmos Jones's research illuminated, how they sustain not a culture of poverty or a culture of oppression but a culture of achievement and, thereby, continue to imagine alternative communities even when they fail time and time again to realize their dreams (Jones 1993). Jones found evidence of a culture of achievement even when local organizations fail to survive beyond the incipient stage or, when they do survive, they are co-opted, depoliticized, and converted into service-provisioning bureaucracies that are de facto extensions of the state. Social research needs to document how, despite dynamics like these, local actors resiliently rebound and continue their struggles under new guises and with renewed energy. Marc Edelman's (1999) observations of peasant movements in Costa Rica are quite relevant here. He found that activists who were involved in struggles that petered out reemerged in later struggles with the knowledge, skills, and experience gained from earlier periods of movement building.

Delmos Jones never romanticized local organizations that claim a commitment to social change and loyalty to the people. His work attests to the importance of an honest and critical examination of the zigzag trajectories of the actual experiences oppressed people have with organizing for change. His work underscores the importance of revealing the conflicting agendas that organizations frequently embody and the contradictory interfaces they tend to occupy between local populations and supralocal institutions "concerned with coordination, administration, and the maintenance of order" (Jones 1987, 100, quoting Leeds 1973). His observations illuminated how the call for unity within organizations and networks of organizations can sometimes mask contradictions that need to be confronted and sorted out before the important work of organizational efficacy and change can be achieved.

Studying Human Rights Struggles from the Local to the Global via a Regional Coalition

Recently, the work I have done over the past decade on the political and cultural economy of racism and antiracism has taken an explicit turn to human rights advocacy. This shift coincided with and was inspired by the momentum that many antiracist activists around the world were building up for the United Nations (UN) World Conference against Racism (WCAR), which was held in Durban, South Africa, in 2001. My writings on race and racism (e.g., Harrison 1995, 1998) led to my being invited to participate in an international human rights conference in spring 2000 that the Danish Centre for Human Rights organized in preparation for Durban. That rich learning experience, in which I exchanged ideas with human rights researchers and advocates from all over the world, made something click in my head. Since then, I have looked more closely at the UN human rights system and the arenas and instruments it provides worldwide struggles against racism and related forms of intolerance—related in the sense that they are similar to racism (e.g., caste oppression) and in the sense that they intersect or are entangled with racism (e.g., gender, class, ethnonational status; Harrison 2000, 2002b). The instruments the UN provides include the International Conventional for the Elimination of All Forms of Racial Discrimination (ICERD) and the Convention for the Elimination of All Forms of Discrimination against

Women (CEDAW). These are treaties, which many countries, notably the United States, fail to ratify or, even if ratified, fail to implement or enforce. The arenas the UN provides human rights organizations, or nongovernmental organizations (NGOs), include megaregional preparatory conferences (called "prep coms" in UN lingo) and world conferences with parallel NGO forums at which delegates of states and of NGOs exchange and debate ideas, network, and collaboratively craft blueprints for policy change that are called declarations and programs/plans of action.

My interest in the human rights system within the UN is not restricted to the political dynamics of world conferences. I am especially interested in what this system, with its conferences, treaties, declarations and plans of action, means for antiracist organizing on the ground in specific local and regional settings around the world. Although eventually I would like to undertake a multisited, cross-cultural political ethnography, in the meanwhile I am beginning this project in my own backyard.

Seven months after my amazing experience at the human rights conference in Denmark, I attended a southeastern regional human rights conference at Clark-Atlanta University, the historically black university where W. E. B. Du Bois worked when he worked within academia. That regional conference, like the international conference in Copenhagen, was organized to educate activists about, and to prepare some of them for, the WCAR in Durban. The conference brought activists from all over the U.S. South to Atlanta. There were also people from other parts of the United States and abroad, so there were national and international dimensions to what was largely a regional event organized by a network of activists (which I shall call by the pseudonym Southern Human Rights Coalition) working in local and supralocal organizations devoted to combating the problems faced by racially oppressed people, women, workers, immigrants and refugees, and communities, usually impoverished communities, affected by environmental racism. Right after the conference ended, a few of the coalition's central activists, mainly African American women, rushed to the airport to catch a flight to Santiago, Chile, where they participated in the megaregional prep com for the Americas. Less than a year later, representatives from the Southern Human Rights Coalition also made their way to Durban and then back home to their respective everyday lives at the local and regional level, where their struggles continued.

Although Delmos Jones focused his ethnographic lens on the developmental cycles and the internal as well as the external dynamics of local organizations, I am interested in examining the complex dynamics of local-regional-global articulations; that is, the ways that activists and advocates for the human rights of racially marked people are taking the issues of local politics into higher-level fields and arenas of lobbying and coalition building, translating a variety of struggles for change into the language and practice of international human rights advocacy. The local-regional-global articulation that the Southern regional coalition represents is, in many ways, still an incipient organization after only eleven years of beginning to build bridges across diverse organizations, a wide range of issues, and racial differences, working within an intersectional framework for understanding and combating multiple yet interrelated social injustices.

Possibilities, Challenges, and Vulnerabilities of Regional and Global Coalitions

If, as Jones illuminated so poignantly, there are problems with the cohesiveness, effectiveness, and viability of local voluntary associations, then when you add regional, national, and global agendas to the complexity of local organizations, the problems can be confounding. Yet, during this post-Fordist, postmodern age (i.e., post–Henry Ford's or the Ford Motor Company's model of assembly-line industrialism) when the demography and political economy of the southeastern region are being reconfigured by the effects of national and global restructuring, can advocates for change and human rights act effectively locally without thinking globally, as the maxim goes? Can local activists act effectively without understanding local manifestations of, and responses to, globalization and transnationalism? Does strategically embedding local organizations in regional and global networks and coalitions make a difference in local organizing? What difference does it make for the capacity and development of organizations? What about for the organizers themselves, whose political longevity or ability to recycle may extend beyond the life span of specific organizations? How do they interpret and use human rights language and the networks cultivated from preparatory conferences and world conferences on women, racism, social development, and the environment? In other words, what do these activists, particularly those with organic connections to the grassroots, bring to the interactions and deliberations that happen in places like Durban 2001, and what do they take back home?

These are some of the questions that I am beginning to ask in the hopes that I will be able to answer them as my research progresses. I am asking these questions because I believe that at this juncture of neoliberal globalization, agents of change need to learn how to negotiate and, if possible, overcome the obstacles and complications that accompany political organizing within various kinds of transborder fields of cultural diversity, power, and political economy. Whether we like it or not, local and regional struggles are structurally embedded within transnational and global spaces, and, as a consequence, there are implications that can be drawn for how to go about envisioning and strategizing for transformative change.

Given its particular history and its changing state of current affairs, the U.S. South is an interesting and significant setting for doing human rights research. According to the National Center for Human Rights Education, which is based in Atlanta and very much committed to improving conditions in the South, "[t]he South leads the country in the unfair application of the death penalty and in environmental racism. Underdeveloped educational systems, a massive prison-industrial complex and the lack of unions . . . for low-wage workers perpetuates a caste system, the remnant of a slave-based economy. The exploitation of migrant farm workers and sharecroppers and the brutality of police repression characterize living conditions for many Southerners" (National Center for Human Rights Education 2002).

I would like to remind you that Delmos Jones was originally from rural Alabama, the son of sharecroppers who migrated, like so many others in their predicament, to other regions of the country (Susser 2000). In one way or another, his background in racialized rural poverty informed his work on social inequality in the Southwest, Thailand, Australia, and right here in New York City. In one of his essays (Jones 1997), he recounted that while being socialized in anthropology his teachers warned against his tendency to compare his earlier experiences as a poor black country boy in Alabama with what he observed on American Indian reservations. He was being trained to zoom in on and read "real authentic Indianness" with all its continuities with the cultural past into the data he collected. In other words, during those days, problems of social change, social inequality, and the common ground that poor reservation Indians and poor rural African Americans shared were not what mainstream anthropology was largely about. It would take many, many years before he would write authoritatively about the *family resemblance* American Indians shared with poor blacks and *poor whites* in Alabama and elsewhere in the country, and I am pleased that he wrote about this in the epilogue he contributed to the second edition of *Decolonizing Anthropology* (Harrison 1997).

Organizing in the Postmodern South

Of course, Alabama and the rest of the South have changed a great deal since Delmos Jones's youth and since his days in grad school. The South today is known as the New South. In some ways, however, even the New South remains a lot like the old. For instance, just last month (March 2003), in fact, only a couple weeks ago, there was a Ku Klux Klan rally in Greeneville, Tennessee, not all that far from where I live (*Knoxville News-Sentinel* 2003). About thirty members demonstrated for White Power. After beginning the rally with a prayer, Klansmen and women shouted slogans and messages, among them "We can't allow Negroes to teach our children" and "You allow those Mexicans to take your jobs." Several hundred counterprotesters were also present along with one hundred law enforcement officers to keep the peace. It was quite an event, dramatizing a demonstration and counterdemonstration over the meanings and consequences of diversity, the increasing diversity that is reshaping human relations in the South.

Several months before, I myself participated in a different kind of demonstration, in fact, in three interrelated demonstrations in Miami, Florida, where the South has historically met and merged with Latin America and the Caribbean. Although on first thought, Miami and South Florida might appear to be different from most of the South or not really part of it, in a recent paper I have documented how the South's coastal plain or low country, extending all the way from the Chesapeake Bay tidewater area to the Gulf Coast, has historically been a zone that has been influenced by and linked to the Caribbean within a transcolonial and transnational social field of culture and political economy (Harrison 2003). The movement of capital, commodities, culture, knowledge, and people, both enslaved and free, back and forth between Jamaica, Antigua, and Barbados, on the one hand, and port towns like Norfolk, Virginia, and Charleston, South Carolina, on the other, was a key element in the development of subregional localities and cultural identities within what became the U.S. South. Farther south, the Gulf Coast and Florida were integrated into circuits of commerce and cultural production that tied the South to the Hispanic and French Antilles. Although South Florida certainly has its own unique flavor and intensity, the articulation between the South and the Caribbean is not at all a new phenomenon.

In December 2002, Miami was the venue for the Southern Human Rights Coalition's fourth biannual conference. After all the plenaries, workshops, banquets, and powerful musical and spoken-word performances had fired us up, the conference sponsored a Tour of Shame that took four busloads of people, a multiracial and even multinational group of activists, to three different sites that symbolized the injustices that local and statewide organizations were protesting and organizing against. Before this tour, few of the local organizations had ever worked together to connect their respective campaigns in a unified front.

The first stop on that historic direct-action tour took us to the ghetto, a housing project in Liberty City, where a local organization of low-income African American women (Low Income Families Fighting Together, or LIFT) are organizing to resist Hope VI's urban removal vision for their future. The second stop was at a strategically located Taco Bell. Before reaching an agreement in 2005, the Coalition of Immokalee Workers were boycotting Taco Bell because of the inhumane wage and working conditions for the workers, largely immigrants from Mexico and Guatemala, who pick the tomatoes that the Bell buys from its Florida suppliers, including Mount Olive. The final stop on the tour was just across the street from Taco Bell, which just happened to be located in the vicinity of Miami's Immigration and Naturalization Service (INS) Building. The third rally, which was even more dynamic than the earlier ones, was situated right across the street from the INS, where a long line of vigilant policemen guarded the entrance to the building. The purpose of that demonstration was to protest the indefinite detention of Haitian refugees, including small children, and the overall immigration policy that discriminates against Haitian refugees yet welcomes refugees from Cuba. We stood in solidarity with the Haitian American Grassroots Coalition and Haitian Women of Miami. We stood and we chanted in the rain, which did not dampen our spirits.

On that historic Tour of Shame, people from all over the South and well beyond it, people who represented quite an impressive spectrum of the human rainbow, Mayans from Guatemala, Mexicans, Dominicans, Puerto Ricans, Haitians, Jamaicans, Native Americans, African Americans, Africans, Asians, and Euro-Americans, marched, carried signs, chanted, and sang songs in English, Spanish, and occasionally Kreyòl. One of the chants was "*What* does democracy look like? *This* is what democracy looks like! I said *what* does democracy look like? *We're* what democracy looks like!" After consecutive call-and-response renditions of that cheer, another favorite was shouted: "¡*El pueblo unido jamás será vencido!* The people united will never be defeated!" Quite a contrast to the imagined community expressed at the Klan rally, where the ideas of a common ground and an interracial or potentially nonracialized "family resemblance" were antithetical to the old-fashioned white supremacy that is being reworked in the context of a rapidly changing South.

The Changing Regional Political Economy

Today's South is more culturally and racially diverse than it has ever been. The traditional bipolar system, which of course always understated the presence of indigenous peoples and interstitial populations, "is being displaced [by i]ncreased immigration from Mexico . . . Central [America], [the Caribbean,] and Southeast Asia" (Smith 1998, 165). This displacement "does not mean that white privilege and black oppression have diminished; rather, other racial-ized relationships and new forms of racialized exploitation are altering what has long been perceived as a bipolar dynamic, a two-part invention" (165). The changing demographics of the region stem from its location within "the increasingly global labor market." The South has become "a destination for new foreign capital and people; a point of departure for traditional, low-wage industries, seeking lower costs in other countries" a generation after having moved to the South from the deindustrialized North; and "a place of historic racial division and economic impoverishment, where the postmodern and global meet the 'pre-modern' and rural" (165).

The New South has become a Postmodern South, a region whose political economy has become flexible and post-Fordist, changing within the context of the new international economic order. Capital is moving in and out "at rates exceeding that of all other regions in the [United States]" (Smith 1998, 171). While capital flows in and out of the region, so do people, although their mobility, particularly that of immigrants, is subjected to more regula-tion. Carol Stack (1996) has written about the return migration of African Americans from the northern Rust Belt. Other scholars have written about the socioeconomic dislocation in Mexico and the Caribbean that is driving foreign nationals into the South in search of economic opportunities. The regulatory obstacles in a global city like New York are pushing some of its new immigrants out of the city and into the South. Paul Stoller (2002) points out that West Africans, mainly men, who have extended their dispersed, long-distance trade communities in West Africa to Paris, London, and New York are now migrating to the U.S. South to find work in factories and McDonalds. In the spirit of occupational multiplicity, they are also establishing informal trade networks to take advantage of local and regional markets in the New South (Stoller 2002, 142). One of the Southern cities that has attracted mobile merchants from Niger is Greensboro, North Carolina, where along with other parts of the Carolinas, the rate of increase for Latinos is even higher.

Sociologist Barbara Smith summarizes the things that are attracting capital and labor to the South:

> Corporate managers of capital-intensive industries such as petrochemicals and automobiles are attracted to the South for the same reasons that manufacturers began opening plants there over a century ago: relatively low wages, a weak labor movement, and low taxes related to meager levels of social provision. Compared to the economic requirements of employing a European or Japanese work force, the U.S. South appears extremely attractive: First World amenities without First World costs. The engineers, scientists, and other highly educated employees that they require may be relocated to the South or recruited from

anywhere in the [United States]. . . . Interstate 85 from Atlanta to Richmond is becoming an international corridor of economic activity, attracting migrants from all over the South, the nation, and the world. (Smith 1998, 171)

By the way, there is a Greensboro exit off I-85.

Transborder Political Projects

Throughout the New South, there are "powerful crosscurrents of opportunity and dispossession" (Smith 1998, 170), and those crosscurrents are creating the conditions for new, or if not really new then revitalized and intensified, strategies for organizing across differences of race, class, gender, sexuality, ethnonational identity, and issue-specific politics. One instance of this is the turn toward human rights language and advocacy by the veteran civil rights, labor, and environmental justice activists who came together to form the Southern Human Rights Coalition as an umbrella under which a wide range of injustices can be articulated and combated. This shift has taken place within the past decade, during which time human rights NGOs like Amnesty International-USA (AI-USA) have become more open to addressing human rights violations within the United States rather than externalizing the problem by treating human rights violations primarily as an issue for the rest of the world, particularly the East and the global South.

The Southern Human Rights Coalition is not alone in its efforts. Other significant developments include the participatory action research being done by organizations like the Highlander Research and Education Center in East Tennessee and Project South, which has its main office in Atlanta and another in Washington, DC. These organizations "conduct popular political and economic education and action research for organizing and liberation" (Project South n.d.). Project South is addressing the problems of globalization by participating in "the hemispheric COMPA," which stands for Convergence of Movements of the Peoples of the Americas, a three-year-old network of more than 1,000 organizations and networks, including sixteen from the United States. It represents a move toward "border movement building," and its understanding of movement building involves creating the space for "grassroots/lower-income organizations" and for leadership that reflects the gender, class, and racial diversity of the movement's base. Project South and COMPA recognize that they have a long way to go. In their view, movement building involves three stages: consciousness, vision, and strategy. They acknowledge that they are only at the consciousness stage, but they believe that through popular education they can develop the new leadership needed to advance the movement to the stage of vision and strategy.

Another organization I have watched over the years, even before my turn to human rights, is TERN, Tennessee Economic Renewal Network, an organization that promotes strategies of sustainable development, fair trade, and transborder organizing in East Tennessee. TERN has responded to the deindustrialization and capital mobility reshaping Southern Appalachia by making it possible for East Tennessee workers and displaced workers to visit the Texas and Mexico border zone where corporations that used to employ them in East Tennessee have relocated. In other words, the organization is following the path of transnational capital, which commonly targets a female workforce and subjects it to objectionable working conditions, conditions that violate workers' rights to job safety and a living wage.

Because of language barriers, TERN has developed a popular theater pedagogy for facilitating communication between East Tennessee women and their Mexican counterparts. Both groups communicate about their respective work and labor-organizing experiences by performing in skits and, of course, through interpreters. Although this is a creative way to circumvent language differences, language competence is a serious issue that needs to be confronted if transborder organizational capacity is to be enhanced. The problem of language differences is also relevant in the Southern Human Rights Coalition's case. For example, at the fourth conference of the Southern Human Rights Coalition, it was obvious that very few of the African American activists, including those who were in the Coalition's leadership, were competent in Spanish. They had to rely on the interpretive abilities of bilingual Latinos and the college-age whites who worked with Latino farmworkers. This meant that very few of the African Americans present were able to have substantive exchanges with the African descendants from Colombia and the Dominican Republic without the intermediation of interpreters, most of whom were white. Some substantive diversity training is obviously needed to effectively work—and negotiate trust—across language and cultural divides. I am pleased to say that one of the leading activists in the Coalition was preparing to leave for Cuba where she was to spend five weeks studying Spanish.

Problems in Coalition Politics

There is a long history of failed coalition building, or the petering out of coalitions. Will the coalitions being built in the South today be more sustainable? Will transborder alignments with grassroots and international NGOs be productive and sustainable? By definition, coalitions and alliances, both horizontal and vertical, are vulnerable to fissioning and disintegration. Based on research in Guatemala, Richard A. Wilson has shed interesting light on the relationship between local organizations and international human rights agencies—an alliance that may sometimes border on patronage-clientage and all the baggage it can carry. He discusses several cases in which, for instance, foreign human rights advocates have imposed legalistic and decontextualizing accounts and, by implication, organizational strategies upon complex local conflicts over human rights violations (Wilson 1997). Not uncommonly, these codifying accounts do not mesh with the locality's "heterogeneous field of interpretations . . . memories" (138), and biographical narratives, which reveal that abuse, social suffering, and structural violence involve more than the violation of abstract, natural rights (146) that belong to "universal individuals" (148).

Wilson argues that the decontextualizing practices of some international human rights organizations have inadvertently "depoliticize[d] human rights violations by drawing attention away from structural processes of class or ethnic power, and reduce[d] violations to a set of technical problems concerning the functioning of the legal system" (Wilson 1997, 148). This problem is likely to emerge in situations in which the connections that NGOs have to ordinary people's lives are mediated through thick layers of class, spatial, and political difference and distance. These kinds of political problems may exist within well-intentioned networks, especially when there are major disparities in resource base and differences in political ideology and consciousness. Delmos Jones himself wrote about organizing strategies that "appear to be liberating [but] do not adequately address . . . and [actually] obscure issues of inequality and subordination" (Jones 1997, 196). In other words, "some of the positions that seem to favor the oppressed are actually reinforcing the status quo" (198). To what extent do these kinds of problems apply to the Southern Human Rights Coalition, which includes activists who belong to diverse organizations, from small local organizations to the southern branch of an international NGO, AI-USA, and attempts to represent the interests of an increasingly diverse population in a region whose many sociocultural and political-economic landscapes are changing in significant ways?

Conclusions

Although I cannot answer my question in any detailed, definitive way at this time, I can venture the suggestion that, yes, the kinds of problems I have only sketched here are likely to apply to the Southeast as well as to other regions of the country and the world, where networks and coalitions of activists are situating their local struggles in larger contexts, particularly the context of international human rights advocacy. I have shown that Delmos Jones's painstaking studies of local organizations among the oppressed are rich with insights that continue to be relevant and useful in many of the current contexts within which we do our fieldwork This is certainly true for me, and it may also be the case for many of you. Although our deceased colleague is no longer walking with us, his ideas continue to live in our warm memories of him and in the reproduction of his contributions that is accomplished by our continuing to read, teach, cite, and think with his work. His gifts to anthropology and the social sciences remain alive when we take the many implications of his work to heart and action.

As I indicated earlier, one implication of Delmos Jones's oeuvre is the importance of building and advocating a democratized space in which academic freedom can be enjoyed by all, particularly by those of us who "come to voice" against the grain of conventional wisdom and with that voice "talk back," as bell hooks (1989) urges, in the spirit of critique and with the goal of remaking social analysis within our respective disciplines and interdisciplines. Delmos Jones hoped that a critical mass of "native anthropologists" would be an integral part of that project, linking its intellectual objectives with practical political action for promoting social justice. Promoting justice does not warrant supporting one's people or any political project, right or wrong. Rather, it requires intellectual and political honesty about problems, contradictions, and unintended consequences that if left unattended will reproduce the status quo rather than change it into a more justice-promoting alternative.

In the epilogue to *Decolonizing Anthropology,* Delmos Jones wrote that "the just society is never achieved . . . it is a continual process of becoming, and this always involves struggles" (1997, 198). He went on to say that the anthropologist should "remain involved and committed but distant enough to appreciate and identify the dialectics involved in all social processes" (199). This is exactly what he did in his relationship with the Community Action Group about which he extensively wrote, and this is what I will strive to accomplish in my observations and political ethnography of the Southern Human Rights Coalition as it negotiates the challenges and contradictions of transborder advocacy, as it expands the space for democratic participation at home and abroad, all the while envisioning a hopeful answer to the question "What *can* democracy look like?"

Acknowledgments

I want to express my thanks to Andrea Queeley and the Africana Studies Group for their supportive response to my writings and for coming up with the idea of nominating me for the CUNY Graduate Center's Delmos Jones Visiting Scholar Program. I am truly indebted to the PhD program in anthropology for supporting the Africana Group and helping make it possible for me to deliver this lecture in memory of Delmos Jones, an anthropologist and a person whom I deeply admired and respected. I also want to thank Louise Lennihan for coordinating my visit and Joan Mencher for opening her home to me then and on many other occasions. The University of Tennessee's Lindsay Young Professorship made it possible for me to participate in the regional human rights conference that is discussed in the lecture. I gladly acknowledge the ways that the College of Arts and Sciences and the university supported my research and professional activities while I worked there. I also appreciate all the support, inspiration, and feedback that I have received from colleagues, friends, and family many too numerous to list here. Without research assistance from Nancy Anderson, long-distance telephone conversations with Marilyn Thomas-Houston and Gina Ulysse, the e-mail pep rallies that feature Ann Kingsolver and Cathy Winkler as cheerleaders, and unconditional love from William L. Conwill and our sons, I would not have made it to CUNY with script in hand, mind, and heart. Thanks to everyone in my amen corner!

PART VI

Blurring Boundaries between Academia and the World Beyond

11. Teaching Philosophy

"We come from a family of teachers," my cousin Kenneth said to me, as though to compliment me for having carried on the tradition and "keeping it in the family." We chatted as we walked across the campus of the prominent northeastern university where we both had been undergraduate students during a time when, as African Americans and especially African Americans from the South, we were still novelties and, from some people's narrow point of view, trespassers on the exclusive property rights of the nation's elite. After his graduation in 1969, he had settled down there, but I had moved away to go to graduate school out West and later to assume university teaching positions in the Southeast. Many years after my 1974 graduation, I had returned to my alma mater to deliver a scholarly lecture. I had been invited by a former history professor, who just so happened to be my cousin's next-door neighbor. Our mutual acquaintance was interested in, and generously supportive of, the boundary-blurring work I was attempting to accomplish that explored some of the potentially exciting and mutually productive ways that pedagogy, theater, and the social sciences can intersect.

It was 1990, and I had recently published an essay that my former professor had come across on my experiments with dramatic performance as a medium and technique for educating and cultivating critical consciousness among wider audiences and constituencies of learners—both within the university and in communities beyond it. In the late 1980s, while still a junior faculty member struggling to learn how to teach the broad spectrum of students who took my classes, I was prompted to "act out." I acted out in front of students first, and then a while later I acted out before community audiences, such as that assembled one March 8 for an International Women's Day celebration.

I was interested in finding new and more exciting ways to challenge learners to think outside the box about themselves and their relationship to the world of cultural diversity as it undergoes rapid change. Teaching cultural anthropology at the University of Louisville and later at the University of Tennessee–Knoxville put me in an excellent position for preparing students and other learners to think more critically and creatively about what it means to be citizens of the world—especially in light of the cultural and political-economic dimensions of global restructuring or globalization, which affects the world's peoples differentially and unequally. Over the years, I have attempted to teach by creating participatory, cooperative learning environments in which I encourage students to rethink the parameters and possibilities of cultural citizenship in a world in which distances across time and space are being increasingly compressed, bringing us into new kinds of contact with neighbors we never expected to have.

Based on my own original research in the United States, United Kingdom, and the Caribbean as well as the research done by other scholars whose writings I assign in my courses, I was inspired to improvise skits and role playing as well as to write and perform soliloquies of composite characters I fashioned from my investigative encounters in the field and in the library. Through my on-the-ground investigations and through texts, I had been exposed to the experiences of ordinary women facing daunting conditions of socioeconomic austerity and political realignment in diverse settings, including inner-city communities in the United States, shanty towns and villages in the Caribbean, and townships and rural reserves in South Africa. In a performance piece called "Three Women, One Struggle," I brought the voices of three geographically distant women into close proximity in order to stimulate critical thinking about their historical and political-economic commonalities despite their cultural and national differences (Harrison 1990). The performance was meant to encourage critical thinking and reflection on how interlocking inequalities of race, class, and gender are being interpreted and negotiated in different settings around the world. I had given dramatic readings of the piece in classes, at public events, and at academic conferences as well as performed it once as a full-fledged one-woman show at a summer arts festival in Ohio. On a stage in a Dayton park, I mustered my courage to perform without reading the script but with the help of a set of simple props that I rearranged whenever I shifted into a new character, with culturally appropriate selections of audiotaped popular music setting the tone for each of the women and marking the transitions between them.

My experimental performance as a form of critical public pedagogy drew upon my earlier learning experiences in college theater and as an undergraduate student who had fortunately taken several courses from an innovative African American studies program in which the performing arts were an integral component around which cross-pollinating dialogues among social scientists, playwrights, and actors were encouraged. In that setting, making one's research results public meant not only publishing articles or books or going about teaching in ordinary, conventional ways. It also meant the freedom and support to translate scholarly understandings into more accessible, engaging, and, indeed, dramatic terms.

That boundary-blurring standard of excellence had a profound impact on my thinking as a social scientist and on my pedagogical practice in classroom and continuing-education settings. Of course, performing an educationally enriching one-woman show is not something I do every Tuesday morning as part of my class lectures. I do on occasion, though, incorporate into my presentations some of my more creative material, including videos of past dramatic readings. More regularly, however, I integrate the music, fiction, and dramatic and dance performances of more professionally accomplished artists into my social science teaching to make the material exciting and fun. My commitment as an educator is to introduce my students, especially the undergraduates unlikely to become anthropologists, to holistic, interdisciplinary perspectives and to show them how anthropology can be useful as a window through which to view the far-reaching cross-cultural landscapes that social researchers, writers, artists, and other world citizens map, interpret, and theorize with what are, ultimately, complementary sets of conceptual and methodological tools and complementary expressions of social imagination.

Besides my emphasis on holism and an analytical tool kit built by the blurring of boundaries among the social sciences, humanities, and fine arts, I also practice a teaching philosophy informed by a critical pedagogical model of participatory learning. This is the approach that I use in smaller upper-division undergraduate classes and the intensive graduate seminars that I enjoy teaching. According to my understanding of this model, which in many respects is consistent with the overlapping values and objectives of feminist pedagogy and Paulo Freire's (1970) "pedagogy of the oppressed," students are encouraged to assume more active responsibility for their learning. Toward that end, they create, through cooperative interactions among themselves and with their professor, a more democratized learning environment in which the latter plays the role of a facilitator rather than that of a pedantic expert making deposits of consumer-friendly packages of information into the banking-oriented minds of passive recipients. In the critical-learning community that I attempt to build with my student collaborators, we develop a dynamic

in which we engage course contents in intellectually honest and critical dialogues that permit us to question the authority, adequacy, and normativeness
of received traditions of knowledge and power. We help one another cultivate
the necessary skills for crafting and applying a more inclusive repertoire of
concepts, theoretical strategies, and methods. To the extent possible, we
ground our collective studies in both personal experiences and the wider
social world beyond the ivory tower.

A few years ago, several students from my "Forms of Social Inequality"
seminar accompanied me to a regional conference on human rights held
at Clark-Atlanta University, W. E. B. Du Bois' academic home for part of
his exemplary career as a social scientist, antiracist social critic, and advocate for human rights. The conference exposed the students to the practical
problem-solving-oriented discourse of human rights organizers, who are
beginning to link their local and regional struggles to the debates, lobbying,
and coalition building emerging in transnational and global arenas such as
those the United Nations system offers to nongovernmental organizations.
We could not have organized a more enriching field trip to supplement the
reading assignments for the course.

The very next semester, I offered another seminar in which we addressed
hard-hitting issues such as racism in various contexts around the world,
parallel public policy shifts in the United States and New Zealand (Aotearoa),
and the McDonaldization of work in the deindustrialized spaces of the urban
U.S. information–service economy. I assigned a particularly provocative
book, *Worked to the Bone* (Buck 2001), on the history, culture, and political
economy of whiteness in rural central Kentucky, not at all far from eastern
Tennessee in more ways than one. Our poignant discussion on that book
had a profound impact—both intellectual and personal—on each and every
student, all of whom were white except one. Teaching that specific text was a
particularly meaningful experience for me, because its author, Pem Davidson
Buck, was one of my earliest graduate students from my years of "learning
how to teach" in Kentucky. I was surprised and deeply honored when I read
the very first sentence in the acknowledgments in which she kindly claimed
that it was I who had planted the seed for her book when I urged her, a
concerned, well-meaning white woman, to "deconstruct whiteness." I had
no idea of the powerful influence those words would have on her trajectory
as a scholar who, consistent with black feminist theorist and cultural critic
bell hooks's (1994) vision, "teaches to transgress."

Pem Buck's success in bringing her book project to fruition, in part, attests
to the positively constructive impact that a critical pedagogical approach to
teaching and mentoring can have on students. Her success as an author of

a boldly courageous cultural critique demonstrates how a critical learning experience can help one accept the risks—and manage the pain—that may be involved in learning how to think difficult thoughts with insights from different and sometimes contradictory standpoints (e.g., insights from the racially subordinate). I would like to think that the critical learning experience that Buck had under my guidance at the University of Louisville enabled her to cultivate the critical consciousness she needed to assume a traitorous identity as a critic of white privilege. As her generous words of acknowledgment suggest, the commitment to studying normative and, hence, otherwise unmarked and unnamed sites of privilege and power as well as to *unlearning* white supremacy grows from seeds sown in the fertile fields on which critical learning relationships and communities are built.

My cousin Kenneth was right. We have come from an extended family with more than its share of teachers, whose goal has been to educate and to prepare students for a changing world of new possibilities. Long before I was born, my maternal grandmother, Tola Brinkley Harper, was initiated into womanhood by assuming the responsibilities of teaching in a resource-impoverished one-room country school. For the most part, her students were the children of tenant farmers and sharecroppers, most of whom were unable to enjoy the privilege of more advanced studies. The dream of that privilege eventually motivated my grandmother to migrate from the countryside to an urban setting where the children she would bear, and eventually her children's children, would be able to enjoy the benefits of improved educational opportunities and social mobility. I remember so clearly my grandmother's many stories about teaching in that small rustic school and all the creatively resourceful ways she managed to expose her students to the basics of grammar, geography, history, literature, and math—without the assistance of textbooks. Despite the severe constraints she faced, she worked long and hard to get her message across and to inspire her students to think beyond the limits of the box that Jim Crow racism built to contain and undermine their potential. With her wonderful stories, she taught me lasting lessons about both the value of being educated and the value of serving one's community by teaching, which she considered to be a nearly sacred vocation comparable to being called to preach the Word of God. Of course, pursuing a career path as an educator took on heightened significance for her generation, for she had lived through the hard times in which our people faced gross disadvantages and repressive exclusions, making their formal pursuit of knowledge a courageous challenge of considerable social and political import.

I can see very clearly now that the values and vision that my grandmother imparted influenced my philosophy of education, initially, as a student eagerly seeking to learn and, many years later, as a full professor still seeking to learn and to improve my repertoire of best teaching practices. With those invaluable pedagogical principles and strategies, I strive to become more effective and creative in the role I play facilitating students' efforts to make personally and socially meaningful sense of the world's changing cultural, political, and economic landscapes.

12. Academia, the Free Market, and Diversity

Toward an Anthropology of Minoritized Anthropologists at Work

Situation I: In Search of Black Anthropologists

Several years ago, Yvonne Jones, a former contributing editor for the Association of Black Anthropologists (ABA) unit news in *Anthropology Newsletter* (*AN*), now *Anthropology News,* told me that a *Los Angeles Times* reporter contacted her for information on what black anthropologists do. He had already been informed by sources he would not divulge that black anthropologists have not really produced anything—only critiques and derivative work. He had been given Jones's phone number by the American Anthropological Association (AAA) office, which he had contacted for information. He told her that the AAA did not have any information, nor did the person with whom he spoke know of any publications to recommend. Erased from memory were the special issues of *Transforming Anthropology* (the ABA's journal that for many years had the status of only a "review" among AAA publications) and the ABA/AAA publication *Decolonizing Anthropology* (Harrison 1991b), which had two editions (and a "third revision") sell out. Fortunately, Jones's phone number was published in her *AN* column. The reporter contacted her, and she in turn contacted me to ask if she could refer him to me as well as to a few other black anthropologists who could set the record straight about the character of black intellectual production within anthropology.

Situation II: Advising the Social Science Research Council

Apparently, the AAA had included my name on a list of potential reviewers or panelists. I was invited to serve on an advisory committee charged with the responsibility of helping the Social Science Research Council (SSRC) formulate its policy for a new program in international research. I spent a full day in New York City participating in deliberations that involved a group of several social scientists from mostly top-ranking research universities. Only two of us were women, and I was the only person of any color other than white. The other woman was reticent for most of the meeting; three of the men were quite outspoken and even arrogant, giving me the impression that they were competing for center stage. Determined not to allow the situation to intimidate me, I made a point to participate in the discussion, interjecting comments and queries whenever I felt an anthropological or qualitative research orientation was particularly warranted. A month later, the program coordinator sent out copies of the meeting summary. When I read my copy, I was shocked, disappointed, and hurt to see that only one remark was attributed to me. A statement I had made concerning the tradition of international research at historically black universities such as Howard and Clark-Atlanta was included in the record without any identification of its source. I had said other things as well, but they had not made it into the record. It appears that they had not been regarded as significant enough to warrant inclusion, or perhaps they had not even been heard. Issues I had raised about how qualitative research methods would be evaluated vis-à-vis the quantitative methods of the so-called harder social sciences were attributed to one of my white male colleagues who had reacted to my input. His voice and not mine had been heard and credited. My ideas had provided the data that allowed an authorized voice to speak conclusively. Does this not represent a relation of appropriation? I tendered my resignation that very afternoon. I refused to be used as a vacuous symbol of diversity and equal opportunity. Regretfully, I did not have the confidence then—more than twelve years ago—to openly contest the document's accuracy for fear of having my reaction construed as unfounded whining and hostility.

Situation III: Paranoia or Crisis of Native/Subaltern Intellectuals?

An invited session, which was to be given "Presidential Session" status, organized by the AAA's Commission of Minority Affairs members Robert Alvarez and George Bond was cancelled two months before the 1995 annual meeting. A letter explaining the reason for the cancellation of a session organized to show the AAA's "commitment . . . to the epistemological contribution of native anthropologists and those of us concerned with and part of the subaltern class" was published in the November issue of *Anthropology Newsletter* (*Anthropology Newsletter* 1995, 2, 6). Written by Robert Alvarez, the letter was sent on behalf of ten of the individuals, myself included, who were to present papers on the timely theme of "Race, Cultural Pluralism, and the Anthropological Promise." From the letter's contents and my personal communication with Alvarez, it seems that an unintended conflict in scheduling was not handled in the most diplomatic and sensitive way, and this complication came to be seen as the proverbial straw that broke the camel's back.

As the staff at the AAA headquarters reminded us, schedule conflicts are color-blind in that they affect and complicate the conference participation of whites as well as minorities. In fact, some highly visible and quite famous white male anthropologists have had to deal with being scheduled for two sessions at once. Why did the late Beatrice (Bea) Medicine (1924–2005), a prominent senior American Indian anthropologist, become so upset about the scheduling error? After all, she had experienced such errors before. Why did she not just choose one session over the other to bring the matter to a quick resolution? Why do "those people" suspect racism and expect special treatment whenever things like this go wrong? After Medicine altogether withdrew from the program rather than choose between two equally important sessions, why did the ten remaining people not go on with the session? On what basis was the unanimous consensus the letter articulated reached?

The ordeal that Dr. Medicine experienced, and that her colleagues understood, unfolded in a multilayered context bigger and more complex than the coordination and complications of the annual meeting's program. Although a single straw may be barely recognizable or felt, when it contributes to the weight of a cumulative load, it becomes a burden too heavy for a camel to bear. Being the only one, or one of very few, not only having to negotiate a climate of hostility or ambivalence but also having to struggle to break out of the limits imposed by alterity and nativization, all these and more constitute the burden that Bea Medicine and other anthropologists of color have had to carry over the course of their careers. And the seniors are witnesses to the past as well as the present. They have witnessed how things have changed and how we have come a long way over the years; however, they also witness how some things have yet to change even though the packaging has been modernized and postmodernized.

Implications

Today's is an especially turbulent climate, especially in view of the restructuring, retrenchment, and conservative backlash that contribute to the crisis of the subaltern intellectual. Students and scholars of color are being targeted by the symbolic assaults of a revival of biological determinism and a co-optation of multiculturalism that put every minority in its place. These may be the best of times and the worst of times, however. Good times may have been evident, for instance, in Yolanda T. Moses' past presidency of the AAA (1995–97) and in the growing visibility of dark and female faces in the leadership of various professional associations, committees, review panels, and editorial boards. Hard times still confront us, though. Erasure, peripheralization, and a racialized, gendered politics of reception and reproduction (Vincent 1991, 47–49) assume more subtle forms than before; nonetheless, they persist insidiously. This raises the question of whether the new voices of diversity within the academy are really being listened to and understood for what they can teach about negotiating differences democratically. Are today's new voices any more audible than the old voices virtually erased from disciplinary or institutional memory? Even if the answer is yes, it must be qualified in view of hierarchy-producing assumptions, discourses, and practices that tend to position certain—even if not all—categories of subalterns outside the centers of authorization.

Interventions from the Global Free Market

Jagna Sharff and Hanna Lessinger (1994) and Hans Baer (1995) are among those within anthropology who called for more concerted and sustained interrogations of the growing power of corporate capital in academic life. In a poignantly insightful analysis of the casualization of academic work that is occurring as an outcome of the global restructuring of capital accumulation and labor control, Sharff and Lessinger made the point that the new global orientation "requires corporations to eschew all local, nation-based obligations and loyalties" (1994, 13). To the extent that local interests exist, they "are focused on the provision of high-tech services for corporations' management headquarters, on the low wage service sector, and on innovative, potentially profit-making research. . . . [They underscore that] U.S. universities are increasingly drawn into the provision of such services for corporations" (13).

In his call for studying—that is, studying up—academia's linkages with big business and government, Baer warned of the dangers that "the fiscal crisis in higher education and the anti-intellectual assault . . . fueled by conservative elements" present to critical thinking and the ability to create/re-create conditions and opportunities for academic freedom in the most democratized sense of the term (1995, 5–6). The redefinition and reordering of academic priorities in favor of conservative and corporate interests is leading to the reallocation of material and moral support away from the so-called softer fields of study such as the humanities and social sciences. The destabilizing assaults of retrenchment are compromising work conditions, displacing entire programs and departments, and undermining the legitimacy of interdisciplinary programs. For the past thirty-five years, programs in ethnic and women's studies have offered sanctuaries for the production of oppositional and transformative knowledges that counteract and compensate for the many gaps, silences, and subjugations that have made conventional disciplinary practice and departmental life inhospitable and unreceptive to critical thinkers relegated to discursive minor streams and peripheries (i.e., streams of thought outside the mainstream). The extent to which these programs have been successful in democratizing intellectual practice, and producing and applying new knowledges within and beyond the academy, is now a measure of their vulnerability and expendability during a period when feminism, multiculturalism, and even liberalism are being contested. The neoconservative backlash claims to be color and gender blind, but its position in the culture wars is to defend the purity and supremacy of a masculinist Western canon—lest U.S. standards of excellence diminish. In a commentary in *The Chronicle of Higher Education*, Evelyn Hu-DeHart (1995, B1–B2) describes some of the common practices being undertaken to undermine the legitimacy of even successful ethnic studies programs and research centers: installing weak directors and heads even against the wishes of faculty, hiring few full-time faculty and swelling the ranks with part-timers, dividing teaching and research functions into separately administered units, and delaying approval of degree programs. She argues that such administrative slights have precluded ethnic studies from gaining the secure foothold and programmatic advances that many women's studies programs now enjoy.

Academic values are being increasingly penetrated and redefined by a postcolonial yet recolonizing corporate hegemony. It is important to note that this reconfiguration is emerging at a historical conjuncture when biodeterminist scholarship such as that represented by *The Bell Curve* (Herrnstein and Murray 1994) is being revived and legitimated and when gender and race cognizance is being repudiated by political assaults on the social contract (namely, affirmative action and welfare). Also within this historically specific context, issues of economic need are being manipulated rhetorically in a divisive politics marked by mean-spirited policies that facilitate both the dislocation of labor and the upward redistribution of wealth. During these unstable times, anthropology is as vulnerable as it is necessary for what it can contribute to public intellectual debates over issues of growing consequence for both academia and the world.

Anthropology is strategically positioned on the intellectual landscape by virtue of its broad scope, which extends from the natural sciences to the humanities, and by virtue of its commitment to questions concerning diversity and common ground—absolutely important concerns at a time when the problems of negotiating diversity appear to be growing and intensifying around the world. Anthropology, however, compromises its ability and promise to account for and resolve struggles over diversity when it neglects to hear and understand its new voices speaking from a variety of perspectives and positions. Anthropologists should be receptive to these new perspectives because of our chosen field's extensive ethnographic record on otherness and its orientation toward participatory inquiry. As a potent investigative strategy and style, participant observation demands the kind of sensibilities, communication, and interpersonal relationships that give us access to both public and hidden transcripts of peoples too often denied both historical and intellectual agency.

Universities are faced with the challenge of negotiating diversity: confronting old and new problems and embracing new opportunities. Currently, these negotiations—which span the conservative–progressive political continuum—are being undertaken in the face of a growing ambivalence and, very often, visible hostility toward the politically salient and emotionally charged differences designated by conservatives as special interests, which supposedly contradict and undermine the interest of the larger national body. In the conservative view, the nation is envisioned in terms of either putatively homogeneous values or a naive, facile pluralism that denies the structured inequalities that order relations among ethnicities, races, and other interest groups.

An instance of flagrant hostility is evidenced by the experience of former law professor Jennifer Russell, who was subjected to racial harassment in the form of receiving an anonymous copy of *National Geographic* with a cover photograph of a gorilla. This incident occurred in the aftermath of two events: white students' objections to her teaching about the subtle workings of racism and a racially charged hiring of a minority over a white male candidate (*Women's Review of Books* 1996). In an informative and very useful report written for the Association of American Colleges' Project on the Status and Education of Women, Yolanda T. Moses (1989) documented black women's perceptions and experiences of hostile academic environments, whose double standards and racist and sexist biases impose barriers to their success. Another work that illuminates black women's struggles for space within academia is the edited collection by Joy James and Ruth Farmer (1993), *Spirit, Space, and Survival: African American Women in (White) Academe,* which contains a number of essays—including that of anthropologist Helán Page (1993)—concerning matters of philosophy, theory, autobiography, and pedagogy. The essays express a shared sense of opposition and confrontation to the forces and obstacles that would alienate and demoralize weaker spirits.

Even well-intentioned attempts to come to terms with diversity are being infused with assumptions and values from the prevailing corporate ideology. During the 1990s, a former chancellor of the University of Tennessee–Knoxville (UTK), William Snyder, produced and circulated a document, *Toward a Climate for Enhancing Diversity on the UTK Campus,* that articulated his vision and position on diversity for a university that has a long history of exclusionary policies and practices (Snyder n.d.). The university was under the obligation and watch of a state court order to desegregate, and the results from a survey indicated that the climate for women was hostile. Snyder's *Toward a Climate for Enhancing Diversity* was written in the wake of growing agitation from both women and African Americans. A past dean of the school of engineering, Snyder had been involved in a successful long-standing engineering program designed to recruit and retain minority students, so he has a track record that lends credibility and intellectual honesty to the document, which asserts that "diversity [must] be embraced as a moral imperative as well as an opportunity for personal growth and development . . . [and that] a philosophy of collective ownership of all institutional problems should exist" (Snyder n.d., 5).

Recognizing that diversity is "no longer an option but a necessity," Snyder wrote of the striking technological, organizational, and demographic shifts that have "drawn all of us into their vortex" (Snyder n.d., 5). Diversity, he wrote, is an admired principle in both the natural and business worlds. To "continue to play a strategic role in the future of our nation and the world . . . the land grant university of the 21st century will continue to be an essential partner with business and industry in enhancing the global competitiveness of the United States" (10). The chancellor's famous motto was that UTK must be "value driven, customer oriented, and learning focused" (5) to be a university of choice.

Although Snyder should be commended for articulating a vision in which diversity is seen as an opportunity that should be embraced, his attempt to accommodate diversity within a model of university development oriented toward corporate constituencies and the market values of customer orientation was problematic, to say the least. The market analogy presented a false image of fair and free exchange when in the real world of free-market development—with its rampant indebtedness and structural adjustment programs—buyers and sellers are differentially and hierarchically positioned. That inequality of positioning by race, gender, class, and their intersections with national or transnational status places concrete limits on how diversity can be managed and integrated into the university's core culture. The commodification of information and the uncritical alignment of higher education with the agenda of an increasingly transnationalized corporate capital reproduce or—if the upward redistribution of wealth is any indication—even intensify the very inequalities that Snyder claimed to want to overcome.

Instructively, Snyder pointed to a number of models of and for diversity enhancement within the university: an influential Fund for the Improvement of Secondary Education (FIPSE) program that used video to help faculty and staff work through their own prejudices and racism, the minority engineering program already mentioned, the Office of Minority Student Affairs, the Women's Center, and the Office of Diversity Resources and Educational Services, established to replace the more controversial Affirmative Action Program. I think it is rather paradoxical that the chancellor, the top-ranking officer of an institution of higher learning and research, neglected to mention the good works and successes of academic units such as the African and African-American Studies and Women's Studies Programs. Those accomplishments were erased from the map he charted of routes to progress and diversity promotion. In a university in which the main order of business is supposed to be pedagogy and knowledge production, academic programs were not included as important and deserving sites for investing moral and material support. Can we interpret this omission as an indication of the status of women and people of color at UTK? In my view, this unfortunate erasure is reflective of a deep-seated ambivalence regarding what new voices of diversity have to offer.

Mixed Messages

The once growing and now contracting numbers of people of color and women who have come to people academic institutions have had to make sense of mixed messages being sent from trustees, administration, faculty, and students. I speak of mixed messages rather than outright hostility. Although the latter certainly shows its face often enough and may even dominate the climate in particular places at particular times, I think that we are living through a period marked by considerable duality. For instance, in professional anthropology, women are well represented in graduate schools and in faculty ranks, though mainly in the lower ranks. They are professionally active, productive, and their extensive scholarship—whether feminist or not—has contributed important new data, perspectives, and modes of theorizing to the field. Nonetheless, despite having come a long way since, for instance, 1954, women's scholarship does not seem to be read, appreciated, and cited according to the "principles of equal opportunity employment" that prompt departments and universities to hire us and admit us into training programs

(Lutz 1990). The politics of reception and reproduction (Vincent 1991) within the discipline, and academia at large, intervenes in the formation of the disciplinary canon, whose gender equality or inequality can be discerned through citation patterns and required reading lists for core graduate seminars (Lutz 1990, 1995). The canon and the core body of ideas represented within it seem to have a gender, and that gender is masculine.

The politics of reception and canon formation is not only gendered. The value and power disparities within which intellectual validation and authorization are conferred also have a raced or racialized dimension. This dimension is operative even within intellectual arenas in which feminists and other critical anthropologists are active (Bolles 1995; duCille 1994; Harrison 1991a, 1993; Lutz 1995). The racial economy of anthropology is constituted by hierarchy-producing assumptions, discourses, and practices that result in the peripheralization of anthropologists of color (Harrison 1995b). This outcome is particularly evident among those whose people symbolize the bottom rungs of U.S. society and, hence, are less likely to be conferred the status of honorary whites (Harrison 1995a). Paradoxically, in a discipline that claims human diversity and commonality as its central concern, anthropology is less racially and culturally diverse than some of its sibling fields in the humanities and social sciences. Alvarez (1994) shed some light on this contradiction in his contribution to *Race,* based on data that are now dated (Gregory and Sanjek 1994). According to the AAA's 1995 survey, not quite two out of every ten new PhDs in anthropology were minorities (American Anthropological Association 1995–96, 308). Slightly updated data from two years later indicate that minority PhDs made up 15 percent of all new PhDs (Givens, Evans, and Jablonski 2000). The composite minority PhD was mostly of Asian origins with a hint of a Hispanic accent, three drops of African blood, and a barely discernable trace of American Indian quantum (American Anthropological Association 1995–96, 308). Whether the demographics of the profession have improved any in the past decade is a question that concerned anthropologists are still asking. Alan Goodman, the AAA's president for 2005–7, has established an ad hoc commission to collect more complete data and to monitor the profession's diversity along lines of race, ethnicity, and class.

Bifurcated Positioning

It is heartening to see that dark faces have become more visible and that a number of the celebrities among the nation's public intellectuals are African American; however, the commodification or commodity faddism of a handful of African American cultural critics—bell hooks, Cornel West, Henry Louis (Skip) Gates, and the like—is no reliable indicator that racial divisions of intellectual labor are unproblematic. Indeed, in the age of *The Bell Curve* and structural adjustment here at home and abroad, racialized/gendered relations of intellectual production are all the more significant as a front of intense ideological and intellectual struggle. The hyperprivileging (Dominguez 1994) of a few colored people as stars occurs in a context of academic market segmentation within which a wider pool of intellectual workers bears the brunt of less disguised forms of racialization. Unlike the stars, ordinary rank-and-file subalterns infrequently experience any privilege of otherness apart from the benefits they may enjoy from belonging to a community of kindred spirits often formed in opposition to the intense hostility, alienation, and depreciation built into many academic environments (cf. Moses 1989). The widely felt vulnerability of minority intellectuals, particularly women, to invisibility, isolation, misrepresentation, and attack was underscored at the 1994 megaconference held at the Massachusetts Institute of Technology entitled "Black Women in the Academy: Defending Our Name, 1894–1994." A number of black women anthropologists participated in that historic meeting at which black women shared their frustrations, yearnings, critiques, and visions for a prospective agenda and more supportive spaces within U.S. academia.

If we take seriously the voices of those women as well as of all women of color who have expressed themselves in other forums, organizational activities, and published works, we can learn from their stories and experiences important things about, at worst, hostile and, at best, ambivalent work conditions within departments and programs. These women's experiences can teach us about the politics of intellectual discourse and professional practice. They can also teach us about the constructive potential of interfaces and collaborations between departments and interdisciplinary programs. Last, but certainly not least, these stories and struggles teach important lessons about new data, theoretical perspectives, and methodological strategies and repertories, which—if engaged and embraced—diversify the intellectual work that can propel disciplines and interdisciplines further into the twenty-first century. In the case of anthropology, both new voices and older voices that have never really been carefully heard or understood shed important light on the dangers of treating anthropologists of color, and those of feminine gender, as glorified key informants or "mammyfied" providers of professional service, rather than as colleagues in the fullest sense of the term for the formal and informal organization of our profession and the intellectual development of our disciplinary modes of thought (Harrison 1991, 1993, 1995a; Obbo 1990). Francis Hsu's (1973) warnings about the counterproductive effects of prejudice on the field should be revisited today in light of more current arguments concerning the discipline's still powerful Eurocentric and androcentric biases.

Paradoxically, certain changes in the world are taking us back thirty years or more. Are we progressing with one foot only to regress with the other? Although there is certainly a critical mass of black intellectuals on the national scene, we cannot claim to have transcended the "crisis of the Negro intellectual" that Harold Cruse (1967) problematized three decades ago. A disturbing trend has emerged in which black women are being targeted for public depreciation and discredit. Lani Guinier's legal scholarship (e.g., Guinier 1994), which won her tenured positions at the University of Pennsylvania and Howard University, was erased from media coverage on the debate over her merits for an appointment in the leadership of the Department of Justice during the Bill Clinton administration. Her voice as an innovative legal scholar was muted by her portrayal as a so-called quota queen, a putative spokeswoman for inner-city welfare queens who supposedly make up the undeserving and dangerous poor (see Guinier 1998). A few years ago, Angela Davis was appointed to a prestigious chair of excellence at the University of California at Santa Cruz. The Board of Regents, however, initially opposed the appointment because of her politics and the supposed questionable quality of her scholarship as a philosopher who has dared to work outside of a more narrowly and conventionally defined field of competence. Highly acclaimed bell hooks, who has been catapulted into intellectual stardom by the media, was misrepresented in a front-page article published in *The Chronicle of Higher Education* (Leatherman 1995). This high-profile article trivialized the substance and underpinnings of her scholarship by paying more attention to her rich and famous lifestyle in New York City. In an essay published in leftist *Z Magazine*, hooks (1995) claims that although the actual interview seemed to focus on the ideas that she brings to feminist discourse and cultural criticism, those spoken ideas were not included in the published article. This pattern of erasure and selective, stereotyped misrepresentation illustrates that even the most visible and famous are not immune from being "put into their places," regardless of whether they are seen as exceptions to the presupposed rule of black intellectual inferiority. This troublesome pattern is also recounted in ordinary black women's stories about their experiences in academia.

Erasures, Silencing, and Peripheralization as Limits on Academic Freedom

Peripheralization or erasure can result from the way an academic audience receives an intellectual product such as a publication. As Catherine Lutz's (1990) work demonstrates, this can be measured by citation and content analyses. Erasure and silencing also take place in the everyday and not-so-publicly displayed behaviors constitutive of the conditions under which ideas are developed—or underdeveloped. Among these behaviors are the communications and interactions that influence—by facilitating or obstructing—the production of work deemed to be publishable. The editing and revisions required before scholarly work is considered publishable can become entangled in a struggle over the values and meanings of scholarly significance and merit. Of course, peer review and the consequent revisions are a necessary component of intellectual production that should and can serve the purpose of quality control and enhancement. This I do not dispute; however, sometimes the line between fair, constructive criticism and censorship can be crossed in a patterned way that implicates problematic, divisive, and hierarchizing biases. For instance, several African American anthropologists of earlier generations have told war stories about having had research papers rejected by mainstream anthropology publications on grounds that many of us would question and disapprove of today. Ironically, most of these rejects were eventually published in ethnic and other social science journals. We should be vigilant concerning the values that operate in evaluation now, because if we are not, their unintended consequences may implicate a racial/gendered economy of knowledge. It is not uncommon for black women in anthropology and other disciplines to report informally how their writing, published primarily as descriptive accounts, has been denuded of much of the theoretical and metatheoretical content of earlier drafts. In other words, at least some of their experience with peer review suggests an enforcement of an intellectual division of labor by gender and race, which assigns them the housekeeping role of collecting and describing data (Lutz 1995). Because publishing is the key to career development, denuded articles are better than more theoretically elaborate manuscripts buried among unpublished papers. Nonetheless, the ubiquitous publish-or-perish phrase might be rephrased as "publish while perishing" for minority and feminist scholars whose productivity fails to lead to scholarly authorization and canonization. Another common experience that one can surmise from the stories black women anthropologists tell to each other is that even when theory survives revision and editing, their work tends to be read and cited largely for its description. In other words, the theoretical elements embedded in the texts are subjected to a process of "whiting-out" (Jackson 1993). Whiting-out is a form of the partial erasure or tracking that I have described elsewhere (Harrison 1991a, 7).

Lutz (1995) argues cogently that theory (or the authority/power to explain and set the terms of authoritative discourse) has a gender as well as a race and class. If we take her insight seriously, then it is important to understand the intellectual and sociopolitical processes through which much of black women's scholarship comes to be written and/or read as particularistic description—storytelling in the narrowest sense of the term—rather than as data-grounded explanation with relevance for cross-cultural inquiry. Also needed is a critical examination of the processes whereby abstract, jargon-laden discourse is likely to be labeled theory, whereas concrete ideas accessible to women and men on the street are, too often, presumed to be atheoretical. As literary theorist Barbara Christian (1987, 52) pointed out, much of the theorizing that people of color do assumes "forms quite different from . . . Western . . . abstract logic. . . . [Their] theorizing . . . is often [embedded in narratives]." An ethnocentric and class-biased reading of such storytelling, however, would interpret it as theoryless. Christian's analysis alerts us to the importance of situating black women's writing, analysis, and theorizing—in its multiple forms—in relation to both the politics of reception and the politics of resistance to the ethnocentric and sexist elitism many authorized discourses represent. In the specific context of feminist scholarship's ambivalent reception to difference, literary theorist Ann duCille (1994) interrogates the racial politics of white feminists' reading of black women's texts. She argues that black women are commonly excluded from the category of feminist theorists and are read through lenses clouded by essentializing fantasies that lead white readers to expect "to leave high theory behind when [they] go slumming in low culture" (duCille 1994, 610). This bias may lead them to read low culture into the texts and fail to appreciate or acknowledge anything else. It may predispose them to read the texts as unconvincing and threatening, aggravating the common fear and anxiety that some whites have of black feminists. Critical black women thinkers are frequently cast "somewhere between monster and mammy: demanding, demeaning, impossible to please" (duCille 1994, 609). At the same time, black feminists may be imagined to possess "irresistible custodial power and erotic allure as the larger than life (racialized) Other" (609).

This sort of blatant racial division of labor that duCille describes may be breaking down now, but until literary criticism, anthropology, and any other disciplinary field are no longer racially biased, issues of theory and other forms of academic capital will continue to be salient. As long as both racism and sexism persist, black women's intellectual production—whether written as narrative, abstraction, or a synthesis of the two—will be a site of struggle over the authority and power to produce knowledge.

Toward a More Proactive Anthropology

Decolonizing and democratizing anthropology are imperative to the field if it genuinely prioritizes diversity, minority affairs, gender equality, and tolerance and respect for the forms of alterity constitutive of anthropological practice today. Representation and voice are issues relevant to all spheres and sites of anthropological practice: organizations, committees and boards, review panels, editorial committees, advisory and policy-making bodies, and the cohorts of students and faculty that make up departments. We must be aware of the gatekeeping and gate-opening roles of these organized bodies. We must also recognize the importance of having the most strategic units of organized anthropology outreach to the public, bringing anthropology into the intellectual debates that inform political decision making on the part of citizens and leaders.

Within the academy, anthropologists ideally need strong, supportive departments; however, sometimes individual anthropologists and departments do not have legitimacy until their significance is realized on the outside, particularly by programs and departments with some measure of institutional clout and credibility. Cross-fertilization with outsiders can be fruitful to disciplinary development, but whether cross-fertilization is an explicit goal, organizational connections and bridge building are absolutely integral to the alliance building and constituency expansion that is politically expedient and necessary for anthropology's institutional well-being. This kind of political organizing is particularly imperative for departments and programs (e.g., ethnic studies) that are being jeopardized in the current climate of fiscal instability and exigency. Effective political mobilization can create conditions more conducive to the academic freedom and institutional democratization that anthropology's postcolonial intellectual advances presuppose. Ultimately—and I believe we have already reached this point—anthropology's well-being and the material and ideological contexts within which its well-being can be achieved demand that anthropologists intervene in the public sphere and not restrict themselves to academic circles. The discursive circle around the ivory tower can become a vicious cycle if little input or direction is offered to those worldly debates that have practical consequences for real people's everyday lives. This means that we have to overcome the biases academic purists and elitists have about advocacy, political engagement, and popularization. Moreover, we need to embrace and seek effective means of articulating and bridging the plurality of anthropological knowledges and the diversity of existential situations—and predicaments—that make them possible. Outside of this web of connections (Haraway 1991) and the shared conversations and debates emerging from them, anthropology could very well reach a point of diminishing returns and face its displacement. The repositioning of anthropology within a more democratically restructured academia and society should, among other things, be linked to a repositioning of the subaltern, whose voice should not be heard as noise to be drowned out or silenced.

13. A Labor of Love

An Emancipated Woman's Legacy

Rethinking the Role of Rescue Projects and Love

Virginia Dominguez (2000) has offered a perceptive reflection on the politics of love that informs some anthropological analysis. Her point of entry into this discussion is a 1997 conference, a rescue project, "Having Our Say (*a como de lugar*): Women and the Legacy of *The People of Puerto Rico* into the 21st Century" that a committed group of Puerto Rican women organized at the University of Illinois at Urbana-Champaign. The conference was organized to "feature, recognize, and galvanize scholarly work on Puerto Rico and Puerto Ricans done by women over the past half century" (Dominguez 2000, 361). Dominguez, who is Cuban and not Puerto Rican and very little of whose work has addressed questions concerning Puerto Rico, was invited to be the keynote speaker. Puerto Ricanness and identity politics were not the criteria used for determining which women were included in the program and as honorees in the special awards ceremony. The organizers based their planning on "a politics of correction—an affirmative action based . . . on love and caring for particular individuals who in their assessment had not been sufficiently recognized in public for their professional accomplishments" (Dominguez 2000, 362).

Against both James Clifford's (1988) critique of the "salvage paradigm" and the unintended essentialism that results from some rescue efforts, she recognizes the intellectual integrity of inquiry, critique, and representation grounded in love, tough love, an emotion that has been hard—no, nearly impossible—to express openly in conventional social scientific writing, with its emphasis on "objectivity and formality" (Dominguez 2000, 378). In her

insightful examination of a number of publications on Puerto Rico, Dominguez makes the interesting observation that "feelings of love and genuine
affection often do enter the body of an anthropological work, albeit usually
unremarked on and often not even consciously" (378). Anthropologists are
often able to express the respect, admiration, and love they feel for the people
they work with through the photographs they select for their books. Dominguez points out that photographs occupy "a space seen, felt, and thought to be
less regulated by the conventions of scholarly writing" and, hence, represent
a "space in which to say something nonverbally that may communicate messages the author does also care about" (378).

Over the past fifteen years, the taboo against revealing feelings and emotions in social science inquiry and writing has subsided, as reflexivity and
positionality have moved onto the center stage in some important streams
of ethnographic writing. As a consequence, an ethnographer's sentiments
are more likely to be expressed in open, and not merely occluded, spaces.
Sentiments can still be found in the space of graphic selections, but they are
also found in explicit declarations integrated into the expository substance
of texts. We've come a long way, baby—that is, some of us have.

During fall 2001, I attended a workshop organized by qualitative researchers in the College of Education at the University of Tennessee, my previous
place of employment. The workshop was designed to extend and enrich the
education of graduate students in a college in which good research is typically assumed to be quantitative, objective, impersonal, and as value-free as
possible, despite—and perhaps because of—the impact that postpositivist and
even antipositivist methodologies and epistemologies have had on educational research over the past two decades. I attended the workshop because I
find that researchers outside of anthropology who employ ethnography and
other qualitative methods tend to conceptualize and defend their choices
in methodological design in thoroughly thought-through terms that many
anthropologists take for granted or have taken for granted before our own
polarized debates over science and nonscience in anthropology.

The presenter who was responsible for covering ethnographic methods
had her PowerPoint slides so beautifully organized that, at first, I wish I had
required my undergraduate and graduate students in anthropology to attend
that intensive course in thinking about research methods. Everything was
going so smoothly, and I was nodding my head after all of her important
points, totally in agreement with my colleague from the College of Education,
when all of a sudden I realized that I heard her say, and I saw her PowerPoint
slide spell out, something about how ethnographers, unlike the people within
the culture or cultural situation being studied, should *restrict their feelings*

toward their research subjects. Ethnographers, she said, should not go so far as letting themselves love their informants or consultants. That would be getting too involved and jeopardizing their objective distance, which is so necessary for reliable research, blah, blah, blah. I did not nod my head. The self-other, researcher-researched distinction was being adamantly upheld. This sort of adamant stance would force a researcher who feels love to disguise, deny those feelings in her write-up and maybe even overcompensate for having gotten much too involved, risking the contamination of data and interpretive validity. Oh dear!

This fairly recent experience, Dominguez's thought-provoking *Cultural Anthropology* article (2000), and the objectives of the "Challenging Disciplinary Acts through and within a Politics of Love and Rescue" session I participated in at the 2001 American Anthropological Association meeting have stimulated my thinking about the politics of emotions in ethnographic inquiry and representation. They have stimulated me to reflect upon my own work as an anthropologist and how my critical project of reworking and remaking anthropology and the sentiments integral to it have been sustained over the years through my relationships with other anthropologists, whose passion for anthropology as a repertoire of critical and creative tools has intensified the passion I have long felt for anthropology as a locus of critique, debate, experimentation, and critical reconstruction.

Expanding the Scope of Anthropological Praxis

The politics of emotions that informs and undergirds anthropological praxis can best be discerned by examining bodies of work or projects and reading across them for patterns and connections that may convey important messages about how scholars think and feel about both their work and the people whom they have studied. As we expand our ideas about the role of emotions in inquiry and textual production, we must also expand our understanding of what constitutes an anthropological project and anthropological praxis. I want to posit the idea that projects are not necessarily evidenced mainly in academic books or what academics typically consider to be major publications. Of course, when they are, scholars are likely to be highly rewarded, but when we examine some wider projects, some of the works that make them up may not even be published or written down. Although there are definite limitations to this sphere of nonpublished works, it is important, I think, to make the point that anthropological praxis, broadly conceived in the most inclusive terms, is not limited to publications in mainstream journals and academic presses. Nor, in some cases, is it limited to written scholarship.

Expanding the notion of project allows us to acknowledge and accommodate difference and differential location within the profession and broader intellectual life. It allows us to acknowledge and consider the implications of the idea that ethnographic analysis and representation—with all the emotions invested in them—can also be found, felt, experienced, and employed in diverse spaces, including those created, for instance, by everyday (work) life, social/political action, and poetic/dramatic performance.

Widening the scope and contours of our reflection beyond Dominguez's wonderful intervention is especially important in light of the life histories and lived experiences of several minoritized and critical anthropologists whose contributions have inspired me and the particular anthropological project to which I am committed, one that I have characterized in earlier work as a decolonizing project (Harrison 1997a [1991]).

A space for expressing respect, admiration, and love for the people with whom anthropologists work can be found in social action and political practice outside of the ivory tower. In the late 1970s, politically committed scholar-activist Bridget O'Laughlin, a former teacher of mine, left U.S. academia to be closer to the front lines of struggle in southern Africa. An Africanist and Marxist political economist, she wanted more than to liberalize the children of the bourgeoisie at Stanford University. The rewards and benefits of liberal education and academic career development conflicted with the passionate commitment she felt toward Africans struggling against colonial and neo-colonial oppression. She chose to use her academic skills as an economic anthropologist to work in an applied and activist research setting in Maputo, Mozambique, a research center at the University of Eduardo Mondlane that trained and assisted government-policy implementers involved in agrarian reform. Her research there was closer to, in fact integral to, the pulse of change. Her anthropology—that is, some of the discipline's conceptual and methodological principles—became a concrete tool in Mozambique's early postcolonial transformation. Her anthropology, the way she practiced it, was a labor of love for the liberation of Mozambique's people.

Of course, working in that role was risky, much more risky than teaching graduate seminars at Stanford. Indeed, Bridget was seriously injured by the very letter bomb that assassinated her colleague Ruth First, a South African exile and member of the African National Congress (ANC) and South African Communist Party (SACP). The passion Bridget felt for her work and the contribution it made to Mozambique's postarmed struggle reconstruction was clearly expressed in her everyday life in Mozambique during the late 1970s and early 1980s, the early postcolonial phase, which gave way to subsequent phases of a desperate struggle for sovereignty and basic survival in a regional context of encroaching military and political-economic violence. South African–backed RENAMO (Mozambican National Resistance) terrorists sabotaged agricultural production and maimed and murdered peasants in the countryside. The vision for which the liberation movement and later ruling party FRELIMO (Front for the Liberation of Mozambique) had dared to put its comrades' lives on the line lost its sharp focus as Mozambique became trapped in a vicious cycle of economic austerity, famine, and neoliberal economic policy strings.

I remember the wonderful letters Bridget wrote from Maputo around the same time I was in Jamaica doing my dissertation research, struggling to make sense of what I saw and what I would be able to do. Her letters were a source of deep inspiration that helped sustain my commitment to my work and, more generally, to a critical project in anthropological praxis as I had come to understand its possibilities under the guidance of professors like Bridget O'Laughlin and another influential professor also at Stanford, the late St. Clair Drake, an Africanist and scholar of the African diaspora on whom I will reflect a bit later.

A close look at minoritized experiences in anthropology reveals that it is not uncommon for intellectuals of color to maximize the opportunities that nonacademic spaces present. Ella Deloria's (1988) ethnographic understanding of the Dakota Sioux made her posthumously published novel, *Waterlily,* possible. This creative work, written but not published in the 1940s, reflected her historical anthropology and interest in going beyond the limits of realist ethnographic reportage in representing her people in caring, three-dimensional terms. Another Franz Boas–influenced anthropological researcher, Zora Neale Hurston (1935), excelled in ethnographically rich fiction and in folkloric narrative that read like fiction. She also experimented in the dramaturgical arts as a writer, director, and performer (Harrison 1990). Katherine Dunham (1969), trained under Robert Redfield at Chicago, took her anthropological knowledge to the concert stage after translating it into the choreography and dance performance informed by what came to be the internationally renowned Dunham method (Aschenbrenner 1999). A much lesser known pioneer with whom I have had the privilege to become familiar is Manet Fowler (Harrison 1993). As I explained in chapter 2, I worked on an intellectual biography of this fascinating applied anthropologist, who was probably the first black woman to earn a PhD in anthropology in the United States. In order to reconstruct her trajectory as an anthropologist, I had to rely on sources other than a conventional publication record. Most of her writing was in the form of newspaper articles in black newspapers like the *Pittsburg Courier* (which is no longer in print) and the many contract research reports that she was not free to make public. She had, however, published prizewinning short stories rich in social criticism and autoethnographic insights into the lives of people whom she wanted more people to respect and admire for their tenacity and courage in the face of racism's physical and symbolic assaults.

For a variety of reasons, several of the anthropologists (Hurston and Dunham included) whose biographies are published in *African-American Pioneers in Anthropology* (Harrison and Harrison 1999) were unable to build standard academic careers as anthropologists. Of course, racism and sexism did more than their share of harm, but sometimes personal choices based on sociopolitical principles and convictions led some of them not to follow academic conventions. St. Clair Drake, for instance, decided against publishing his PhD dissertation because he felt that the data and analysis he presented in that tome were too politically charged and sensitive for making public at that time. To protect the confidentiality of his acquaintances and research consultants in Cardiff, Wales—many of whom were politically active colonial subjects from different parts of the British Empire—he sacrificed the academic capital he might have accumulated had he published his ethnography on racial politics in Tiger Bay, a multiracial port community in Cardiff (Drake 1954).

That decision, along with many others like it, led him away from the centers of anthropological discourse and right smack into the anticolonialist and antiracist praxis in which many Pan-Africanist intellectuals were engaged. If we read between the lines, his publications in African studies and African American studies tell us a great deal about his politics and the emotions he invested in his interdisciplinary and activist anthropological praxis. Even more telling of the passion that informed his commitment as a neo-Marxist Pan-Africanist, however, are his extensive unpublished works, thousands of pages of uncompleted manuscripts, such as his encyclopedic study of the black diaspora that he had hoped to finish. This manuscript, along with countless others, is archived in Harlem at the Schomburg Center of the New York Public Library. Beyond the invaluable archives housed in the Schomburg, it was his storytelling that most convinced me that love motivated his activist intellectualism.

Anthropology Articulated through Storytelling and Other Performances

That storytelling often rambled on and on beyond the normal limits of class time, office hours, and the time spent talking while walking down bicycle paths on our way to our respective homes. Drake told countless stories about the struggle in Mississippi in the 1930s, the West Side of Chicago in the 1940s, Tiger Bay in the late 1940s and early 1950s, Liberia and Ghana in the late 1950s and early 1960s, and then back to Chicago and other hot spots across the United States during the 1960s and 1970s. Whew! I marvel at the phenomenal, encyclopedic knowledge that was stored in that man's head and at his ability to convey that knowledge in the most accessible way to undergraduates as well as graduate students. Drake's stories, most of which were related not in print but in colorful active voice, were a remarkable space where he expressed love, a love that deeply touched his students, inspiring us to carry on the struggle that activist intellectuals must undertake across a number of fronts both within and outside of the academy. This story I tell of my late teacher, Drake, punctuates the important point that sometimes we have to read between the lines and beyond the lines of written text before we can discern the emotional frame and dimensions of intellectual representation and praxis. In Drake's case, the space of his everyday life as a teacher and mentor conveyed important messages, emotional as well as intensely intellectual, about the kind of anthropological project he embraced and indeed embodied.[1]

Of course, I do not have to limit my reflections to ancestors and elders in our field to illuminate the significance of the poetic voice and political commitment in an expanded notion of what constitutes anthropological praxis, especially one grounded in a terrain made fertile by love. In September 2001, I had the good fortune to attend a provocative conference at Bates College in Lewiston, Maine: "Haiti: Exploding the Myths." Faculty and staff associated with the Africana Studies Department and the Multicultural Center organized it collaboratively, but a young anthropologist, Gina Ulysse, certainly played a leading role in framing the extended dialogue and taking it well beyond where most academic conferences dare to go. Gina's conference was part of a project to rescue Haiti and Haitians from the myths that denigrate them. Gina moderated the three-day affair, punctuating the breaks and transitions between sessions with her unique poetic voice, expressing an acute consciousness of her ancestors' and elders' sacrifices and struggles. Her ethnoperformance style of recasting ethnographic and autoethnographic representation in poetry is a most poignant and powerful way to relate the depths of her feelings and thinking. Her poignant recitation of her own poetic creations made the conference an extraordinary performative event, but even her ordinary articulation was performed with such artful spontaneity that it, too, came out as yet another expression of poetics, a poetics that is politically charged and provocative and that has the ability to rock the boat of comfortable complacency.

Gina's creative consciousness of things poetic and performative—and of matters inexplicable with only the tools of normal science—adds powerful dimensions to her conceptual, interpretive, and methodological repertoire. It adds powerful dimensions to her project as a feminist ethnographer whose elucidation of transnational fields of political economy, power, and agency comes alive with experiential dimensions of race, color, gender, and class that are so often lacking in even some of the best ethnographic representation of Jamaican and broader Caribbean life. Her ethnoperformance perspective on matters about which she cares deeply is refreshing and emotionally stirring, capable of conjuring up feelings typically buried deep beneath the surface of normal anthropological science. She has also thought a great deal about the ancestral legacy, diasporic identity, and the formidable neo-oppressions that colonize our minds and bodies just as much as the cold and hard chains that oppressed our foreparents many generations ago in Haiti, Puerto Rico, Cuba, Virginia, and South Carolina—all over the New World diaspora. She has thought a lot, imagined a lot, about how to break free, liberate ourselves from present-day matrices of domination, violence, and pain that assault us physically as well as symbolically and structurally. Although she writes as well as performs her poetics and politics (e.g., Ulysse 2001, 2005), the textual representation can never do justice to the power of live performance. The next best thing is videographic dissemination, something she as an experimental videographer and filmmaker may well consider to expand the audience for her ethnoperforming arts.

Gina's critical analytical insights and poetic mode of interpretation helped debrief me from a trip we made to Cuba during summer 2000. At a conference on the African diaspora that the Association of Black Anthropologists (ABA) organized in collaboration with the Canada-based Eleggua Project, I presented a paper on responses to global apartheid within the African diaspora. Well beyond my conference session, the theme was woven into our conversations in Cuba, in Toronto right afterward, and then later once we had returned home. We talked about what we had seen, in fact, only caught in an impressionistic glimpse. We had gone on a fantastic three-city and province tour having a cultural exchange with Cubans in a variety of settings, mainly cultural in the sense of the performance of folklore, which includes Afro-Cuban religions that are much more than relics from the cultural past. Everywhere we went, we saw evidence of the extant correlation among blackness, economic marginality, and formal powerlessness. The most economically challenged Cubans tended to be of obvious African descent. The most run-down neighborhoods in Old Havana, Santiago de Cuba, and rural communities tended to be predominantly black. In those settings, Afro-

Cubans danced, drummed, sang, and, for donations of U.S.$5.00, posed for photographs. Gina was seriously working with the idea of global apartheid, the global scope of apartheid's structural violence, and how even countries like Cuba are not immune from its injuries—which seem to include what is colloquially referred to as tourist apartheid, or the exclusion of darker Cubans from tourist establishments, especially hotels and clubs.[2]

One day Gina called me up on the phone to share a poem she had just written. I had to sit down and stop everything. It was impossible to listen to the lyrics and to the cadence of her voice without tears welling in my eyes and without my becoming conscious of the big lump in my throat. Her poem, "My Rules of Engagement," stirred a number of emotions—anger, sadness, disappointment, pride, joy, love—yes, the tough love that is needed to have the courage to tell it like it is, to tell the hard and ugly truth that contradicts and contests the romanticized positive images that many racial identity advocates insist upon to offset the ubiquitous bombardment of negative images, negating images that confuse us and sap our esteem and knowledge of ourselves. Her ethnopoetic gaze zoomed in on subtleties some of us would prefer not to see at all. But once we acknowledge awareness of them, we actually feel relieved, refreshed, and empowered to take the next step in developing our critical consciousness and our courage to refuse to be complicit in the forces of our subjection.

Gina has been an inspiration to me. She has helped me come to better terms with aspects of my own anthropological project that have meant a great deal to me but that have not been major foci in my work. Like her, I, too, have been concerned with the challenge of expanding the audience for anthropological knowledge and understanding. I, too, have an interest in developing ethnographically informed performance for academic and nonacademic audiences. In the inaugural issue of *Transforming Anthropology*, I published an article on my experimentation with what I call anthro-performance, which I cast in terms of a broadly conceived public pedagogical technique for critical conscientization (Harrison 1990). Beyond that publication, which may give some readers the idea that the author has found an interesting way to channel and mobilize her emotions, I have dabbled with performance—dance but especially dramatic readings of scripts I have written to translate my ideas about African and African diasporic women's political agency into a more accessible and engaging form. Performance also allowed me the space to fashion three-dimensional characters that ordinary people can relate to, identify with, and, I hope, care about.

"Oh, I just loved that woman from the 'isle-lands' you brought to life on that stage!" A figure of speech, perhaps, but maybe the possibility is there for audiences to interact with characters that are represented lovingly as believable and engageable persons whose three-dimensionality would be flattened in objectivist social-scientific writing. That was and is my wishful thinking about the need to experiment with genre and medium, to combine and go beyond ethnographic writing and theoretical exposition to reach folks out there beyond the halls of academic life.

I may not be as effective as I would like in convincing you of the communicative and representational power of performance, but I believe I know what I am talking about! The first time I gave a full-fledged dramatic reading of an anthropologically inspired work was when I did "Three Women, One Struggle" in the late 1980s (Harrison 1990). This was a performance piece that was organized around the voices of three black women: a working-class woman in "Chocolate City," Washington, DC; an unemployed Jamaican woman with a powerful critique of Jamaican politics and the political economy of tourism as a major source of economic development; and a South African township schoolteacher, fired for her political activism and faced with the difficult challenge of speaking at a mass funeral for some of her former students. I rehearsed what became my one-woman show at a cultural program I had helped organize for Louisville, Kentucky's, International Women's Day.[3] We, my sisters and I in the Alliance against Women's Oppression and Somos Hermanas, the international solidarity wing of the Alliance, wanted to do more than preach to the choir and the already converted. So we decided against organizing yet another political rally or program with speeches that the same people listen to every year. We wanted a more heterogeneous audience representative of a wide cross-section of the community: black and white, straight and queer, civil rights and environmentalists, gospel music lovers and aficionados of world beat. We organized quite a show, and yours truly mustered up the courage to be in the program with her anthro-performance, food for thought for rethinking international connections and solidarity across national boundaries, oceans, and linguistic differences.

I assert that among the works that constitute my critical anthropological project are my anthro-performances that even when published are much more than what can be read from a printed page. Although performances can be recorded through video or film and, hence, viewed by bigger audiences, the dynamics of the wider social event(s) of which a performance is a part may be hard to capture. The responses to my performance, what members of the audience saw in it and took away with them, were integral to the experience. "Miz Conwill, hello, Miz Conwill, I'm Aphelia Jones.[4] I'm in your huzbin's group, Dr. Conwill's group, down at the Center. He had all of us keep journals 'bout our lives and how we feel 'bout things. Did he let you read my journal? He wasn't 'sposed to! Oh, he didn't? Humph, I thought you'd read 'bout my life when you did that black woman thang up on that stage. It was like you was telling my story. Lord, I can identify wi' dat woman. I know her. She real to me. You did a real good job. And you say you teach at the university? What you teach? I need to take a class from you!"

Reaching Multiple Audiences and Bringing Anthropology Home

Part of my project in decolonizing and democratizing anthropology and in rescuing the people I care about has been to find ways to expand or multiply the audience(s) for anthropological analysis. I mean audience in at least two ways. First, there is the abstract sense of readers out there not especially interested in anthropology per se but open to what anthropologists have to say, provided, of course, that we say it in accessible, engaging terms. Audience expansion also has another significant meaning for me. It is my dream to be able to write, even if not everything I write, in a format and language that would whet the intellectual appetites of my own family and extended kin. Of course, they are impressed with my credentials and proud of the fact that I earned a doctorate and have become an intellectual and all that jazz, but most of them do not really understand what anthropology has to do with anything that means something to them. "Hmm, now tell me again what anthropology is." "But what do anthropologists *do* besides teach?!" I remember my maternal grandmother, a former schoolteacher, who enjoyed reading and watching documentaries and soap operas on TV, asking me questions like these almost every year I visited home during my years in graduate school. Something was really wrong, I thought, if nothing I say seeps in. It was nice that I could get to see some of the world beyond Norfolk, Virginia, because of anthropology, and the stories I told about the Caribbean and the other far off places I had visited for my work were welcomed, more or less. Every year, however, the same questions would pop up again: "Explain again what anthropology is and what you do and why? Why you interested in that?" I remember being so annoyed at having to explain why I was interested, even passionate, about the research I did in the field "over there." Even though I worked among skinfolks (Williams 1996), those intriguing Jamaican black folks were "those islanders over there" to my relatives. There was no concrete sense of urgency about their lives being extensions of ours "over here." There was no sense that the discipline I had adopted into my life, with its blurred boundaries between personal and professional, personal and political, meant anything to anyone other than me. "Faye's an anthropologist. That's something like a sociologist, I think, but I'm not really sure."

But then things changed a bit in the early 1990s when I was inspired to bring my anthropological gaze into my own backyard and onto the old home place that one of my maternal ancestors established in the years of post-Reconstruction in an eastern North Carolina county. Being inspired by a family reunion I had attended, I decided to examine my own family's tradition of ancestor-focused reunions, modeled after the tradition of emancipation celebrations that exists in many parts of the United States, using the tools of anthropological scrutiny and analysis. In the mid-1990s, I published a paper on this autoethnographic research that examined the sacred and secular rituals that confer meaning and identity on geographically dispersed kindred and the place(s) it defines as home (Harrison 1995b). I wrote the essay in the language of social science and in the third person without any reference to "I," "me," or "my"—except in the one note at the end in which I acknowledged all the kinfolk who had assisted and inspired me. The language of that note was unambiguously one of affection for family and respect for the sacrifices family had made to make my professional achievements possible in the first place, well before the achievement of that piece of writing and the research it represented. Interestingly, even though I had already published reflexive, autoethnographic essays elsewhere (e.g., Harrison 1997b [1991], 1995a), that interpretation of my own kindred's rituals of identity formation and genealogical connections was written in a language of social science possibly to offset the perception of my analysis being compromised because of personal attachments to those studied. Indeed, although most of the family being reunited were strangers, I was related to them and was among those being studied; hence, there was none of the objective distance that the University of Tennessee College of Education colleague whom I mentioned earlier insisted is necessary for reliable and valid ethnographic analysis. Despite this, the loving message written between the lines of the social-scientific text was comprehended by my extended kinspeople. The organizers of the family reunions expressed their heartfelt appreciation for my gesture of kinship solidarity by giving me an award at the next reunion. In their view, I had given our family's history an official status and dignified our ancestors' struggles by placing them in a rich context of local and national politics. My efforts reinforced and elaborated intergenerational stories that made long-dead ancestors amenable to being respected, admired, and, perhaps, even loved by living members of the kindred that the ancestress Susan Brown and her sons and daughters, my great-grandfather included, made possible.

The publication my family reunion paper was in did not include any photographs. If it had, I would have selected the family portrait of Susan Brown surrounded by most of her sons and daughters along with three grandchildren and one great-grandson. It was taken around 1930 when Grandma Susie was well over one hundred years old. My maternal grandfather's father, the Reverend Burgess Harper, a freedman, a family man, and a religious and civic leader, is standing beside two of his brothers and two of his sisters, most of whom were born in freedom. That distinction was an important one to them, and it still is when older family members identify who is who in the old photographs that are brought to family reunions for all there to see. Right now, the Brown-Harper family portrait decorates the wall in my home between the great room and my sons' rooms. When I visit other relatives, the same picture can sometimes be found, if not on walls, then in family photo albums. It is one of my favorite old family pictures, and if I could have published a picture with my family reunion chapter, it would have been that one with my ancestress Susan Brown seated in the center, showing a century of hard work and faith in the meaning of freedom on her old, seasoned face.

When I was a child, I was told stories about "the old folks at home" as my maternal grandparents remembered them in the days before they migrated from their Carolina farm to the southeastern coast of Virginia. Since those storytelling days of my formative years, Grandma Susie has been a potent symbol for me of a black woman who survived and rebounded against all the odds and then lived to claim and enjoy the fruits of her labor with her family and community. I think of it as poetic justice that she lived much longer as a free woman than she did as one enslaved. She outlived her former master and most of his family—that is, his *white* family. At least two of her children, the eldest Burgess Harper definitely, were said to be among the former master's more inclusive network of kin. R. T. Smith (1987) has explained that a distinction is made between family and kinship in the dual marriage systems of the Caribbean. Kinship, whether we like it or not, often connects people divided by lines of race, class, and gender. Family, however, tends to be more exclusive and endogamous. This kind of cultural system has also existed in the U.S. South, and several of my ancestors, Burgess as well as Grandma Susie herself, were products of it.

Honoring the Ancestors' Legacy

Susan Brown's rich legacy is the self-conscious kindred that assembles periodically to engage in symbolically charged activities that, among other things, reiterate and redefine collectively shared values that include the importance of family, faith, hard work, education, and civic participation. Her legacy is also reflected in me and what I do, both personally and professionally. My anthropology, as I practice it in the academy and beyond, is part of her legacy. With that in mind, I realize that if my project is to be a genuine labor

of love, whether that labor results in standard publications, anthro-performances, or other expressions of civic consciousness and participation, then
my work must rescue tools from anthropology with which to plant seeds
for the elaboration of an alternative and decolonized anthropology (Buck
2001, 7; Harrison 1997a [1991]). As Buck points out, an alternative anthropology privileges perspectives and analyses that "take account of the view
from under the sink" (2001, 7) and from other positions in which ordinary
folk work themselves to the bone, both in gainful employment and in other
forms of struggle. According to my vision, an alternative and reconfigured
anthropology must be grounded in praxis and, as a consequence, effectively
bridge the gap, both conceptually and institutionally, between theory and
practice. It must also have a historical consciousness and, hence, show love
and respect to the ancestors—those who, like my emancipated ancestress
Susan Brown, could not read as well as those who, like Ella Deloria, Zora
Neale Hurston, Allison Davis, St. Clair Drake, Vera Green, Eleanor Leacock,
John Gwaltney, William Roseberry, Delmos Jones, Jagna Scharff, and Beatrice
Medicine, could read *and write* anthropology quite well.

The Political and Intellectual Significance of Maintaining Balance

The legacy of my Great-Great-Grandma Susie's local consciousness and folk
praxis along with the legacy of W. E. B. Du Bois's internationalized brand of
activist scholarship have both had deep influences on the way I have gone
about making anthropology and its possibilities for being reworked and
remade an integral part of my life. I like to think that my critical project is a
lifelong labor of love that will continue to be informed by a holistic philosophy that values the ability to create meaning, balance, and synthesis from
the plural elements of personal and family life, professional development,
and political engagement, the latter of which has been key to my sense of
identity as an intellectual worker belonging to a subjugated people whose
oppression is deepening rather than disappearing.

Over the years, my civic participation has included abolitionist work
against the death penalty, international solidarity politics (allied with liberation movements in southern Africa, Central America, and the Caribbean),
Rainbow Coalition involvement, antiracist organizing, activities addressing
women's issues, and lots of political education of various sorts—including
the performative. It has always been important for me to have some concrete
grounding in a social-justice community and to bring principles of social
justice into my academic work, whether by teaching and researching the hu-

man rights implications of racial and xenophobic discrimination (Harrison 2005) or by working for greater justice in the "racial [and gender] economy of [anthropological] science" (Harding 1993).

During the 1980s, during the years of Reaganism and Reaganomics, which marked the shift toward a Northern variant of neoliberal structural adjustment, I felt very strongly that my work in political anthropology and anthropological political economy needed to be informed by my own political participation in struggles at home against problems—be they the increasingly repressive law-and-order regime, attacks on affirmative action and welfare, environmental injustice, or savage inequalities in public education—whose ramifications are global, reaching into other parts of the world, including into the underdeveloped world of which Jamaica's Oceanview is a part.

Conceptualizing a holistic philosophy of life is one thing, but applying it consistently in the real world of late twentieth-century and now early twenty-first-century academia, is quite a challenge. This is especially so because academic incentive and reward systems tend to privilege more alienated and commodified forms of work and career development. In many research universities, productivity is defined in a way that devalues the kinds of organic or vernacular intellectualism that would seriously address the problems and priorities of working-class and minoritized communities in substantively meaningful ways. Public service is typically defined in relatively innocuous, depoliticized terms that assign it to the bottom ranks in the institutionalized hierarchy of activities that, once the distribution of effort is evaluated, determines the merits of the professorate. Heavy penalties are applied if the balance between research, teaching, and service does not contribute to institutional goals, and if those goals are to remain in, or to move up to, the highest tiers of academia, then the quality and quantity of research and publication, often assessed according to elitist criteria, outweigh everything else. The epitome of productivity in many universities, especially within the humanities and social sciences, is the book, the single-authored, solo book, published preferably by a prestigious academic press. Ideally, candidates for tenure and promotion demonstrate their productivity and worthiness of job security with evidence of having produced books and juried articles published in high-ranking journals. All other publications and professional activities, too often teaching included, are less significant, if considered significant at all.

In 1987–88 when I was an untenured assistant professor, I was awarded a Ford fellowship to write a book on the politics and political economy of urban Jamaican "outlaws and sufferers," which would have refined and extended the analysis found in my dissertation (Harrison 1982). The juggling act that compelled me to balance being a wife and a mother of, then, two small children against the demands of an academic career was complicated by the commitment I felt to being politically grounded, especially during a time when black and other minority communities were being assaulted by the mean-spirited policies—comparable in many ways to structural adjustment—of a neoconservative and neoliberal regime. The need for a political alternative, and for progressive coalitions that would work toward it, was imperative. In Louisville, Kentucky, where I was living at the time, the Rainbow Coalition offered a logical organizational context for building bridges across differences of race, class, gender, and the issue specificity that fragments the political landscape inhabited by organizations and movements devoted to civil rights, women's rights, gay and lesbian rights, worker's rights, environmental justice, international solidarity, and peace. Well beyond the ostensible objective of the 1984 and 1988 U.S. presidential elections to get Jesse Jackson elected, the Rainbow Coalition offered a broad vision, a progressive platform, and a common-ground model for building a multiracial social movement that could unify Americans across their potentially bridgeable differences.[5] In the midst of all the debate and the mobilization for change that was being galvanized, I simply could not write an armchair book about "sufferation," resistance, and the struggle for change. I wanted to write my book as a social-justice activist who was raising her children to live in a better world.

I had strong feelings about wanting my sons to grow up in a world in which they would be able to realize their full potential, something that is denied to many African Americans and other oppressed peoples. My oldest son, Giles, was born on November 5, 1980. That date is deeply significant for another reason as well: Ronald Reagan was elected to the U.S. presidency during my thirty-hour labor. I will never forget it, because I was in the hospital in the throes of an unexpectedly difficult and prolonged delivery. I was determined to have a natural childbirth, but I had reached a stage in my labor when I did not know if I could bear any more pain. In the middle of yet another intense contraction, a nurse walked into the delivery room where I was being monitored because of complications. She announced that Ronald Reagan was the new president of the United States. Her excitement about the Republican victory was matched by my deep disappointment, genuine concern, and heartfelt *fear* for my baby's future. In ways that are difficult to express in words, I sensed that my son's future would be marked by a vulnerability to racial profiling by the police, hate crimes, and other forms of discrimination probably much more subtle than what his parents and grandparents had experienced. As these thoughts raced through my mind, I visualized the lynching of black men, a stark metaphor for the state of jeopardy and disempowerment that I was afraid a right-wing regime would engender. I remember wanting to cry and desperately wanting to erase that ugly image from my mind. Needing to convince myself that I was up to the challenge of motherhood, I told myself that I had the responsibility to protect my child from danger, including the danger unleashed by the problematic political climate that was likely to develop. Would I be able to live up to that expectation? Would I be a good mother to this child I was struggling to bring into such a contradictory world?

During my Ford fellowship year several years later, I found a way to juggle several balls while commuting every month to the University of Illinois at Urbana-Champaign (UIUC) for a week of using the library and consulting with my Ford mentor, Norman Whitten Jr. Because of my family responsibilities and the insufficient funds from the fellowship program (which was obviously designed without scholars with growing families and civic involvement in mind), I could not move to Illinois for the year. Instead, I worked at home and traveled to UIUC every month for a week. Perhaps not surprisingly, although I did not realize it then, the interstate commute, my family responsibilities, and my Rainbow Coalition commitment made it difficult for me to make the progress I had expected on the book that year. With another baby born a year later, a move to the University of Tennessee–Knoxville, where I had the chance to teach in a graduate program, and involvement in the exciting decolonizing activities of the ABA, my uncompleted political ethnography on urban poverty in Jamaica remained on the back burner for so long that its momentum was eventually lost.

Some academics would probably say that I made the mistake of getting much too involved in professional and public service and that I failed to put enough of my time and energy into being productive as a scholar. Had I been more productive in the conventional sense, I would have finished the Jamaica book and had a different career trajectory, perhaps even one that moved me up the academic ladder to one of the nation's leading research universities earlier in my career. "You can buy your own ticket once that book is out." That is what a senior colleague told me back then when I was a young assistant professor. Did I spread myself too thin, losing sight of what should have been my top priority? According to the standard values and priorities of many research universities, the answer is definitely an affirmative one. At this stage of my life, however, I prefer to think differently. Of course, I would have liked to have finished *Outlaws and Sufferers*. My work in Jamaica meant a great deal to me, so I am disappointed that I did not finish the book I had in mind then. Nonetheless, I cannot imagine reliving those years of my life without the political involvement or a family. One of the highlights of my several years of living in Louisville was the rich experience

I gained from being a part of its diverse social-justice community. Perhaps as a blessing in disguise, working at the University of Louisville and later at the University of Tennessee rather than at the kinds of research universities where I was educated and trained allowed me the flexibility and support—although, admittedly, never enough—to lead a more holistic and meaningful life, one in which I have been better able to balance and weave together the commitments to family, career, and social justice that have been so key to my sense of who I am. Without these experiences—these intense struggles and edifying opportunities—and the lessons I have learned from them, the ideas expressed in this chapter and in this book, which reflect all the major facets of my oeuvre, simply would not be.

Notes and References

Introduction

NOTE

1. This list includes scholars of color whom I discuss in subsequent chapters. Hurston is typically better known for her fiction. Davis and Drake, mentor and protégé, made important contributions to the study of racial and class dynamics in U.S. society. Drake was also an Africanist and African diaspora scholar. Robeson is known more for being the wife of the performer and leftist activist Paul Robeson. Maureen Mahon (2006) is working on an intellectual biography of E. Robeson, and earlier I did some preliminary research on Robeson's anthropological career that is summarized in Harrison and Harrison (1999, 23–24). Carneiro was an Afro-Brazilian ethnographer whose support and friendship with U.S. anthropologist Ruth Landes made her research on Afro-Brazilian religion possible. Lachatañeré was an Afro-Cuban ethnographer who insisted that Santería or Lucumí not be misrepresented as and reduced to criminal, antisocial activity. Deloria was a Yankton Dakota anthropologist who worked closely with Franz Boas. Paredes was an esteemed Mexican American folklorist who presented a critique and alternative to racist representations of Chicanos. See chapter 1 for further discussion and relevant citations.

REFERENCES

Angela, Frances. 1990. Confinement. In *Identity: Community, Culture, Difference,* ed. John Rutherford, 72–87. London: Lawrence and Wishart.

Buck, Pem Davidson. 2001. *Worked to the Bone: Race, Class, Power, and Privilege in Kentucky.* New York: Monthly Review Press.

Collins, Patricia Hill. 1990. *Black Feminist Thought: Knowledge, Consciousness, and the Politics of Empowerment.* New York: Routledge.

Di Leonardo, Micaela, ed. 1991. *Gender at the Crossroads of Knowledge: Feminist Anthropology in the Postmodern Era.* Berkeley and Los Angeles: University of California Press.

Eisenstein, Zillah. 2004. *Against Empire: Feminisms, Racism, and the West.* London: Zed Books.

Harrison, Faye V. 1991 [1997]. Anthropology as an Agent of Transformation: Introductory Comments and Queries. In *Decolonizing Anthropology: Moving Further toward an Anthropology for Liberation,* ed. Faye V. Harrison, 1–14. Arlington, VA: American Anthropological Association.

Harrison, Faye V., and Ira E. Harrison. 1999. Introduction: Anthropology, African Americans, and the Emancipation of a Subjugated Knowledge. In *African American Pioneers in Anthropology,* ed. Ira E. Harrison and Faye V. Harrison, 1–36. Urbana: University of Illinois Press.

Llobera, Josep R. 1976. The History of Anthropology as a Problem. *Critique of Anthropology* 7 (Autumn): 17–42.

Mahon, Maureen. 2006. Eslanda Goode Robeson's *African Journey:* The Politics of Identification and Representation in the African Diaspora. *Souls* 8(3): 101–18.

Chapter 1: Reworking Anthropology from the "Outside Within"

REFERENCES

Abu-Lughod, Lila. 1991. Writing against Culture. In *Recapturing Anthropology: Working in the Present,* ed. Richard G. Fox, 137–62. Santa Fe, NM: School of American Research Press.

Alvarez, Robert R. 1994. Un Chilero en la Academia: Sifting, Shifting, and the Recruitment of Minorities in Anthropology. In *Race,* ed. Steven Gregory and Roger Sanjek, 257–69. New Brunswick, NJ: Rutgers University Press.

American Anthropological Association. 1973. *The Minority Experience in Anthropology: Report of the Committee on Minorities and Anthropology.* Washington, DC: American Anthropological Association.

Angela, Frances. 1990. Confinement. In *Identity: Community, Culture, Difference,* ed. John Rutherford, 72–87. London: Lawrence and Wishart.

Anthropology Newsletter. 1994. Stamp of Approval. 35 (4): 1, 6.

Appadurai, Arjun. 1986. Theory in Anthropology: Center and Periphery. *Comparative Studies in Society and History* 28 (1): 356–61.

Asad, Talal. 1975. *Anthropology and the Colonial Encounter.* London: Ithaca Press.

Baker, Lee D. 1998. *From Savage to Negro: Anthropology and the Construction of Race, 1896–1954.* Berkeley and Los Angeles: University of California Press.

Behar, Ruth, ed. 1993. Women Writing Culture. Special issue, *Critique of Anthropology* 13 (4).

Behar, Ruth, and Deborah Gordon, eds. 1995. *Women Writing Culture.* Berkeley and Los Angeles: University of California Press.

Biolsi, Thomas, and Larry J. Zimmerman, eds. 1997. *Indians and Anthropologists: Vine Deloria, Jr. and the Critique of Anthropology.* Tucson: University of Arizona Press.

Bolles, A. Lynn. 1995. Decolonizing Feminist Anthropology. Paper presented at the 94th annual meeting of the American Anthropological Association. Washington, DC.

Borofsky, Robert. 2002. The Four Subfields: Anthropologists as Mythmakers. *American Anthropologist* 104 (2): 463–80.

Bourgois, Philippe. 1996. Confronting Anthropology, Education, and Inner-City Apartheid. *American Anthropologist* 98 (2): 249–58.

Bourgois, Philippe, and Nancy Scheper-Hughes. 2004. Commentary on Paul Farmer's

"Sidney W. Mintz Lecture for 2001: An Anthropology of Structural Violence." *Current Anthropology* 45 (3): 305–25.

Brodkin, Karen. 2001. Diversity in Anthropological Theory. In *Cultural Diversity in the United States,* ed. Ida Susser and Thomas C. Patterson, 365–88. Malden, MA: Blackwell.

Brodkin Sacks, Karen. 1989. Toward a Unified Theory of Class, Race, and Gender. *American Ethnologist* 16 (3): 534–50.

Buck, Pem Davidson. 2001. *Worked to the Bone: Race, Class, Power, and Privilege in Kentucky.* New York: Monthly Review Press.

Carneiro, Édison. 1936. *Black Religions: Notes on Religious Ethnography.* Rio de Janeiro: Civilizaçao Brasileira.

———. 1937. *Bantu Blacks: Notes on Religious Ethnography and Folklore.* Rio de Janeiro: Civilizaçao Brasileira.

Chronicle of Higher Education. 1997. Nota Bene: Indians and Anthropologists. May 9, A17.

———. 2002. Hot Type: Citation Traffic. July 26, A18.

Clifford, James, and George Marcus, eds. 1986. *Writing Culture: The Poetics and Politics of Ethnography.* Santa Fe, NM: School of American Research Press.

Cole, Sally. 2003. *Ruth Landes: A Life in Anthropology.* Lincoln: University of Nebraska Press.

Collins, Patricia Hill. 1990. *Black Feminist Thought: Knowledge, Consciousness, and the Politics of Empowerment.* New York: Routledge.

———. 1998. *Fighting Words: Black Women and the Search for Justice.* Minneapolis: University of Minnesota Press.

Cruz Takash, Paule, and Faye V. Harrison. 1999. Anthropology at the Millennium: Retrospectives from the Disciplines' Critical Center(s). In *Abstracts: American Anthropological Association 98th Annual Meeting.*

Dash, J. Michael. 1978. Introduction to *Masters of the Dew,* by Jacques Roumain. Trans. Langston Hughes and Mercer Cook. Oxford: Heinemann Educational.

Davis, Allison, Burleigh B. Gardner, and Mary R. Gardner. 1941 [1988]. *Deep South: A Social Anthropological Study of Caste and Class.* Los Angeles: The Center for Afro-American Studies, University of California, Los Angeles.

Deloria, Ella Cara. 1941. *Speaking of Indians.* New York: Friendship Press.

———. 1988. *Waterlily.* Lincoln: University of Nebraska Press.

Diggs, E. Irene. n.d. Du Bois' Contribution to Anthropology and Scholarship. Unpublished manuscript.

Dominguez, Virginia. 1994. A Taste for "the Other": Intellectual Complicity in Racializing Practices. *Current Anthropology* 35 (4): 333–48.

———. 2000. For a Politics of Love and Rescue. *Cultural Anthropology* 15 (3): 361–93.

Drake, St. Clair. 1954. Value Systems, Social Structure, and Race Relations in the British Isles. Unpublished PhD diss., University of Chicago.

———. 1959. Destroy the Hamitic Myth. In "The Unity of Negro African Cultures," special issue, *Presence Africaine* 24–25: 215–30.

———. 1960. Traditional Authority and Social Action in Former British West Africa. *Human Organization* 19 (3): 150–58.

————. 1966. *Race Relations in a Time of Rapid Social Change: Report of a Survey.* New York: National Federation of Settlements and Neighborhood Centers.

————. 1974. In the Mirror of Black Scholarship: W. Allison Davis and *Deep South.* In *Education and Black Struggle: Notes from the Colonized World.* Institute of the Black World. Harvard Education Review Monograph No. 2, 42–54. Cambridge, MA: Harvard Educational Review.

————. 1980. Anthropology and the Black Experience. *Black Scholar* 11 (7): 2–31.

————. 1987/1990. *Black Folk Here and There: An Essay in History and Anthropology.* Vols. 1 and 2. Los Angeles: Center for African American Studies (CAAS), University of California, Los Angeles.

————. n.d. *The Black Diaspora.* Unpublished manuscript. New York: Schomburg Research Center, New York Public Library.

Drake, St. Clair, and Horace Cayton. 1945. *Black Metropolis: A Study of Negro Life in a Northern City.* New York: Harcourt, Brace.

Du Bois, W. E. B. 1903. The Talented Tenth. In *The Negro Problem: A Series of Articles by Representative Negroes of Today,* 33–75. New York: James Pott.

Erickson, Paul. A. 1999. *A History of Anthropological Theory.* With Liam D. Murphy. Peterborough, ON: Broadview Press.

Farmer, Paul. 2003. *Pathologies of Power: Health, Human Rights, and the New War on the Poor.* Berkeley and Los Angeles: University of California Press.

————. 2004. Sidney W. Mintz Lecture for 2001: An Anthropology of Structural Violence. *Current Anthropology* 45 (3): 305–25.

Farred, Grant. 2003. *What's My Name? Black Vernacular Intellectuals.* Minneapolis: University of Minnesota Press.

Firmin, Anténor. 1885 [2002]. *The Equality of the Human Races.* Trans. Asselin Charles. Urbana: University of Illinois Press.

Fluehr-Lobban, Carolyn. 2002. Introduction to *The Equality of the Human Races,* by Anténor Firmin. Urbana: University of Illinois Press.

Fogel, Robert William, and Stanley L. Engerman. 1974. *Time on the Cross: The Economics of American Negro Slavery.* Boston: Little, Brown.

Gacs, Ute, Aisha Khan, Jerrie McIntyre, and Ruth Weinberg, eds. 1988. *Women Anthropologists: A Biographical Dictionary.* New York: Greenwood Press.

Gershenhorn, Jerry. 2004. *Melville J. Herskovits and the Racial Politics of Knowledge.* Lincoln: University of Nebraska Press.

Goodman, Alan H., and Thomas L. Leatherman. 1988. *Building a New Biocultural Synthesis: Political-Economic Perspectives on Human Biology.* Ann Arbor: University of Michigan Press.

Green, Dan S., and Edwin D. Driver. 1976. W. E. B. Du Bois: A Case in the Sociology of Sociological Negation. *Phylon* 37 (4): 308–42.

————. eds. 1978. *W. E. B. Du Bois: On Sociology and the Black Community.* Chicago: University of Chicago Press.

Gupta, Akhil, and James Ferguson. 1999. Beyond "Culture": Space, Identity, and the Politics of Difference. In *Culture, Power, Place: Explorations in Critical Anthropology,* ed. Akhil Gupta and James Ferguson, 33–51. Durham, NC: Duke University Press.

Hall, Stuart, Charles Critcher, Tony Jefferson, and John Clarke. 1978. *Policing the Crisis: Mugging, the State, and Law and Order.* New York: Holmes and Meier.

Haraway, Donna. 1988. Situated Knowledge: The Science Question in Feminism and the Privilege of Partial Perspective. *Feminist Studies* 14 (3): 575–99.

Harrison, Faye V. 1975a. British Race Relations and Community Organization: A London Case Study. Unpublished paper written for graduate core course in applied anthropology, Department of Anthropology, Stanford University.

———. 1975b. West Indian Adolescent Stereotypes: Implications for Class Conflict. Unpublished paper written for graduate course "Modernization, Development, and Population." Department of Anthropology, Stanford University.

———. 1976a. Down Mean Brixton Streets: Youth, Community, and Conflict. Spring paper in lieu of a master's thesis, Department of Anthropology, Stanford University.

———. 1976b. Social Mobility and a Caribbean Migration. Unpublished paper written for course "Race and Culture Contact in the Caribbean," Department of Anthropology, Stanford University.

———. 1982. Semiproletarianization and the Structure of Socioeconomic and Political Relations in a Jamaican Slum. PhD diss., Stanford University.

———, guest ed. 1988a. Black Folks in Cities Here and There: Changing Patterns of Domination and Response. Festschrift in honor of St. Clair Drake, *Urban Anthropology and Studies of Cultural Systems and World Development* 17 (2–3): 111–277.

———. 1988b. Introduction: An African Diaspora Perspective for Urban Anthropology. In "Black Folks in Cities Here and There," special issue, *Urban Anthropology* 17 (2–3): 111–41.

———. 1991a [1997]. Anthropology as an Agent of Transformation: Introductory Comments and Queries. In *Decolonizing Anthropology: Moving Further toward an Anthropology for Liberation,* ed. Faye V. Harrison, 1–14. Arlington, VA: American Anthropological Association (in cooperation with the Association of Black Anthropologists).

———, ed. 1991b [1997]. *Decolonizing Anthropology: Moving Further toward an Anthropology for Liberation.* Arlington, VA: American Anthropological Association.

———. 1991c [1997]. Ethnography as Politics. In *Decolonizing Anthropology,* 88–109. Arlington, VA: American Anthropological Association.

———. 1992. The Du Boisian Legacy in Anthropology. In "W. E. B. Du Bois and Anthropology," special issue, *Critique of Anthropology* 12 (3): 239–60.

———. 1993a. Foreword to Comparative Perspectives on Slavery in New World Plantation Societies. Theme issue, *Annals of the New York Academy of Sciences* 292: ix–xv.

———. 1993b. Writing against the Grain: Cultural Politics of Difference in Alice Walker's Work. *Critique of Anthropology* 13 (4): 401–27. Condensed version reprinted in *Women Writing Culture,* ed. Ruth Behar and Deborah Gordon, 233–45. Berkeley and Los Angeles: University of California Press, 1995.

———. 1994a. The Academic Maroon. *Brown Alumni Monthly.* Special insert, "Why I Teach/What I Learn," May, 7. Reprinted in *Why I Teach/What I Learn: Brown Faculty on the Joys and Challenges of Teaching,* 31. Providence, RI: Brown Alumni Monthly and the Continuing College, Brown University.

———. 1994b. Beyond Postal Recognition. Correspondence on Allison Davis' "Stamp of Approval." *Anthropology Newsletter* 35 (6): 2, 58.

———. 1995a. "Give Me that Old Time Religion": The Genealogy and Cultural Politics of an Afro-Christian Celebration in Halifax County, North Carolina. In *Religion in the*

South: Diversity, Community, and Identity, ed. O. Kendall White Jr. and Daryl White, 34–45. Athens: University of Georgia Press.

———. 1995b. The Persistent Power of "Race" in the Cultural and Political Economy of Racism. *Annual Review of Anthropology* 24: 47–74.

———. 1997a. Allison Davis. In *The Dictionary of Anthropology,* ed. Thomas Barfield, 107–8. Oxford: Blackwell.

———. 1997b. The Gender Politics and Violence of Structural Adjustment: A View from Jamaica. In *Situated Lives: Gender and Culture in Everyday Life,* ed. Louise Lamphere, Helena Ragoné, and Patricia Zavella, 451–68. New York: Routledge.

———. 1997c. St. Clair Drake. In *The Dictionary of Anthropology,* ed. Thomas Barfield, 130–31. Oxford: Blackwell.

———. 1998. Introduction: Expanding the Discourse on "Race." In "Contemporary Forum: Race and Racism," guest ed. Faye V. Harrison, special issue, *American Anthropologist* 100 (3): 609–31.

———. 1999. New Voices of Diversity, Academic Relations of Production, and the Free Market. In *Transforming Academia: Challenges and Opportunities for an Engaged Anthropology.* AES Monograph No. 8, ed. Linda Basch, Lucie Wood Saunders, Jagna Sharff, and James Peacock, 72–85. Arlington, VA: American Anthropological Association.

———. 2000. Facing Racism and the Moral Responsibility of Human Rights Knowledge. In "Ethics and Anthropology," special issue, *Annals of the New York Academy of Sciences* 925: 45–69.

———. 2001. Foreword: Medicine Woman. In *Learning to Be an Anthropologist and Remaining "Native": Selected Writings,* by Beatrice Medicine, ed. Sue-Ellen Jacobs, xiii–xvii. Urbana: University of Illinois Press.

———. 2002a. Global Apartheid, Foreign Policy, and Human Rights. *Souls: A Critical Journal of Black Politics, Culture, and Society* 4 (3): 48–68.

———. 2002b. Unraveling Race for the 21st Century. In *Exotic No More: Anthropology on the Front Lines,* ed. Jeremy MacClancy, 145–66. Chicago: University of Chicago Press.

———. 2004. Global Apartheid, Environmental Degradation, and Women's Activism for Sustainable Well-Being: A Conceptual and Theoretical Overview. *Urban Anthropology* 33 (1):1–35.

———. 2006a. Anthropology and Anthropologists. In *Encyclopedia of African-American Culture and History: The Black Experience in the Americas,* 1: 95–103. Detroit: Macmillan Reference Books.

———. 2006b. Commentary: Building on a Rehistoricized Afro-Atlantic Anthropology. In *Afro-Atlantic Dialogues: Anthropology in the Diaspora,* ed. Kevin A. Yelvington, 381–98. Santa Fe, NM: School of American Research Press.

Harrison, Faye V., and Ira E. Harrison. 1999. Introduction: Anthropology, African Americans, and the Emancipation of a Subjugated Knowledge. In *African-American Pioneers in Anthropology,* ed. I. Harrison and F. Harrison, 1–36. Urbana: University of Illinois Press.

Harrison, Faye V., and Donald Nonini. 1992. Introduction to W. E. B. Du Bois and Anthropology. Special issue, *Critique of Anthropology* 12 (3): 220–37.

Harrison, Ira E., and Faye V. Harrison, eds. 1999. *African-American Pioneers in Anthropology.* Urbana: University of Illinois Press.

hooks, bell. 1984. *Feminist Theory: From Margin to Center.* Boston: South End Press.

Hymes, Del. 1969 [1974]. *Reinventing Anthropology.* New York: Vintage Books.

James, Joy. 1997. *Transcending the Talented Tenth: Black Leaders and American Intellectuals.* New York: Routledge.

Jones, Delmos. 1970. Toward a Native Anthropology. *Human Organization* 29 (4): 251–59.

———. 1971. Social Responsibility and the Belief in Basic Research. *Current Anthropology* 12 (3): 251–59.

———. 1997. Epilogue to *Decolonizing Anthropology: Moving toward an Anthropology for Liberation,* ed. Faye V. Harrison. 2nd ed., 192–200. Arlington, VA: American Anthropological Association.

Jordan, Glenn. 1991 [1997]. On Ethnography in an Intertextual Situation: Reading Narratives or Deconstructing Discourse? In *Decolonizing Anthropology,* ed. Faye V. Harrison, 42–67. Arlington, VA: American Anthropological Association.

Keesing, Roger. 1994. Theories of Culture Revisited. In *Assessing Cultural Anthropological Anthropology,* ed. Robert Borofsky, 301–12. New York: McGraw-Hill.

Lachatañeré, Rómulo, 1938 [2005]. *Afro-Cuban Myths: Yemayá and Other Orishas.* Princeton, NJ: Markus Wiener.

Lamphere, Louise. 2004. Unofficial Histories: A Vision of Anthropology from the Margins. *American Anthropologist* 106 (1): 126–39.

Landes, Ruth. 1947. *The City of Women.* New York: Macmillan. 2nd ed. Albuquerque: University of New Mexico, 1994.

Leatherman, Thomas, and Alan Goodman, eds. 1998. *Building a New Biocultural Synthesis: Political-Economic Perspectives on Human Biology.* Ann Arbor: University of Michigan Press.

Lewis, Gordon. 1968. *The Growth of the Modern West Indies.* New York: Monthly Review Press.

Lewis, Herbert S. 1999. The Misrepresentation of Anthropology and Its Consequences. *American Anthropologist* 100 (3): 716–31.

Llobera, Josep. 1976. The History of Anthropology as a Problem. *Critique of Anthropology* 7 (Autumn): 17–42.

Lutz, Catherine. 1990. The Erasure of Women's Writing in Sociocultural Anthropology. *American Ethnologist* 17 (4): 611–27.

———. 1995. The Gender of Theory. In *Women Writing Culture,* ed. Ruth Behar and Deborah Gordan, 249–66. Berkeley and Los Angeles: University of California Press.

MacClancy, Jeremy, ed. 2002. *Exotic No More: Anthropology on the Front Lines.* Chicago: University of Chicago Press.

Mafeje, Archie. 1997. Who Are the Makers and Objects of Anthropology? A Critical Comment on Sally Falk Moore's *Anthropology and Africa. African Sociological Review* 1 (1): 1–12.

Magubane, Bernard Makhosezwe. 2000. *African Sociology: Towards a Critical Perspective.* Trenton, NJ: Africa World Press.

Magubane, Bernard M., and James C. Faris. 1985 [2000]. On the Political Relevance of Anthropology. In *African Sociology: Towards a Critical Perspective,* by B. Magubane, 499–516. Trenton, NJ: Africa World Press.

Marcus, George E. 1999. *Critical Anthropology Now: Unexpected Contexts, Shifting Constituencies, Changes Agenda.* Santa Fe, NM: School of American Research.

Marcus, George E., and Michael M. J. Fischer. 1986. *Anthropology as Cultural Critique: An Experimental Moment in the Human Sciences.* Chicago: University of Chicago Press.

McClaurin, Irma, ed. 2001. *Black Feminist Anthropology: Theory, Politics, Praxis, and Poetics.* New Brunswick, NJ: Rutgers University Press.

Medicine, Beatrice. 1988. Ella Cara Deloria. In *Women Anthropologists: A Biographical Dictionary,* 45–50. New York: Greenwood Press.

Medicine, Beatrice. 2001. *Learning to Be an Anthropologist and Remaining "Native": Selected Writings.* With Sue-Ellen Jacobs. Urbana: University of Illinois Press.

Merton, Robert K. 1972. Insiders and Outsiders: A Chapter in the Sociology of Knowledge. *American Journal of Sociology* 78 (1): 9–47.

Michaelsen, Scott. 1999. *The Limits of Multiculturalism: Interrogating the Origins of American Anthropology.* Minneapolis: University of Minnesota.

Moore, Henrietta, ed. 1999. *Anthropology Theory Today.* Cambridge: Polity Press.

Moore, Sally Falk. 1994. *Anthropology and Africa: Changing Perspectives on a Changing Scene.* Charlottesville: University Press of Virginia.

———. 1998. Archie Mafeje's Prescription for the Academic Future. *African Sociological Review* 2 (1): 50–55.

Mukhopadhyay, Carol, and Yolanda T. Moses. 1997. Reestablishing "Race" in Anthropological Discourse. *American Anthropologist* 99 (3): 517–33.

Mwangi, Wambui, and Elisa Forgey. 1996. Of Prepositions and Propositions: Perspectives on Feminism and the Epistemology of Africanist Collaboration. *Penn African Studies Newsletter,* November/December, 2–6. http://www.africa.upenn.edu/Newsletters/afstd_1296.html.

Ong, Aihwa. 1999. *Flexible Citizenship: The Cultural Logics of Transnationality.* Durham, NC: Duke University Press.

Ortiz, Fernando. 1906. *Hampa Afro-Cubana. Los Negros Brujos (Apuntes para un studio de etnología criminal).* Madrid: Libería de Fernando Fe.

———. 1940 [1995]. *Cuban Counterpoint: Tobacco and Sugar.* Durham, NC: Duke University Press.

Pandian, Jacob. 1985. *Anthropology and the Western Tradition: Toward an Authentic Anthropology.* Prospective Heights, IL: Waveland Press.

Paredes, Américo. 1958. *"With His Pistol in His Hand": A Border Ballad and Its Hero.* Austin: University of Texas Press.

———. 1978. On Ethnographic Work among Minority Groups: A Folklorist's Perspective. In *New Directions in Chicano Scholarship,* ed. Ricardo Romo and Raymund Paredes, 1–32. La Jolla, CA: Chicano Studies Monograph Series.

Patterson, Thomas. 2003. *A Social History of Anthropology in the United States.* New York: Berg.

Prah, Kwesi Kwaa. 1997. North/South Parallels and Intersections: Anthropological Convergences and Divergences in the Study of Africa. *Critique of Anthropology* 17 (4): 439–45.

Price-Mars, Jean. 1928 [1983]. *So Spoke the Uncle (Ainsi Parla l'Oncle).* Trans. Magdaline W. Shannon. Washington, DC: Three Continents Press.

———. 1978. Anténor Firmin. Port-au-Prince. Haiti: Imprimerie Seminaire Adventiste.

Ramos, Arthur. 1935. Black Folklore of Brazil (O Folk-Lore Negro do Brazil). Rio de Janeiro: Civilizaçao Brasileira.

Ramphele, Mamphela. 1995 [1999]. *Across Boundaries: The Journey of a South African Woman Leader.* New York: Feminist Press at the City University of New York.

Robotham, Don. 1997. Postcolonialities: The Challenge of New Modernities. *International Social Science Journal* 49 (3): 358–71.

Rosaldo, Renato. 1989. *Culture and Truth: The Remaking of Social Analysis.* Boston: Beacon Press.

Roseberry, William. 1996. The Unbearable Lightness of Anthropology. *Radical History Review* 65: 5–25.

Roumain, Jacques. 1944 [1978]. Masters of the Dew. Trans. Langston Hughes and Mercer Cook. Oxford: Heinemann Educational.

Rubin, Vera, and Arthur Tuden, eds. 1993 [1977]. *Comparative Perspectives on Slavery in New World Plantation Societies.* Special issue, *Annals of the New York Academy of Sciences* 292: vii–703.

Scheurich, J. J., and M. D. Young. 1997. Coloring Epistemologies: Are Our Research Epistemologies Racially Biased? *Educational Researcher* 26 (4): 4–16.

Segal, Daniel A., and Sylvia J. Yanagisako, eds. 2005. *Unwrapping the Sacred Bundle: Reflections on the Disciplining of Anthropology.* Durham, NC: Duke University Press.

Shaw, Carolyn Martin. 1995. *Colonial Inscriptions: Race, Sex, and Class in Kenya.* Minneapolis: University of Minnesota Press.

Sims, Lowery Stokes. 2002. The One-Man Crisis in Modernism. *Chronicle of Higher Education.* July 19, B15.

Smedley, Audrey. 1993 [1999]. *Race in North America: Origin and Evolution of a Worldview.* Boulder, CO: Westview.

Srinivas, M. N. 1997. Practicing Social Anthropology in India. *Annual Review of Anthropology* 26: 1–24.

Taylor, Council. 1971. Clues for the Future: Black Urban Anthropology Reconsidered. In *Race, Change, and Urban Society,* ed. Peter Orleans and William R. Ellis Jr., 219–27. Beverly Hills, CA: Sage.

Thomas-Houston, Marilyn. 2005. Personal communication, May 17.

Tuden, Arthur. 1993. Preface to Comparative Perspectives on Slavery in New World Plantation Societies, ed. Vera Rubin and Arthur Tuden. *Annals of the New York Academy of Sciences* 292: vii.

Ulin, Robert. 1991. Critical Anthropology Twenty Years Later: Modernism and Postmodernism in Anthropology. *Critique of Anthropology* 11 (1): 63–89.

Warner, W. Lloyd, and P. S. Hunt. 1941. *The Social Life of a Modern Community.* Yankee City Series, vol. 1. New Haven, CT: Yale University Press.

———. 1942. *The Status System of a Modern Community.* Yankee City Series, vol. 2. New Haven, CT: Yale University Press.

Warner, W. Lloyd, and L. Srole. 1945. *The Social Systems of American Ethnic Groups.* Yankee City Series, vol. 3. New Haven, CT: Yale University Press.

Weismantel, Mary. 1995. Making Kin: Kinship Theory and Zumbagua Adoptions. *American Ethnologist* 22 (4): 685–709.

Whitehead, Tony L. 2005. E-mail message, February 26.

Whitten, Norman E. Jr., and John Szwed, eds. 1970. *Afro-American Anthropology: Contemporary Perspectives*. New York: Free Press.

Williams, Brackette F. 1989. A Class Act: Anthropology and the Race to Nation across Ethnic Terrain. *Annual Review of Anthropology* 18: 401–44.

———. 1991. *Stains on My Name, War in My Veins: Guyana and the Politics of Cultural Struggle*. Durham, NC: Duke University Press.

Wolf, Eric. 1982. *Europe and the People without History*. Berkeley and Los Angeles: University of California Press.

———. 1990. Facing Power—Old Insights, New Questions. *American Anthropologist* 92 (September): 586–96.

Yelvington, Kevin A. 2003. An Interview with Johnnetta Betsch Cole. *Current Anthropology* 44 (2): 275–88.

———. ed. 2006a. *Afro-Atlantic Dialogues: Anthropology in the Diaspora*. Santa Fe, NM: School of American Research Press.

———. 2006b. The Invention of Africa in Latin America and the Caribbean: Political Discourse and Anthropological Praxis, 1920–1940. In *Afro-Atlantic Dialogues: Anthropology in the Diaspora*, ed. Kevin Yelvington, 35–82. Santa Fe, NM: School of American Research Press.

Chapter 2: Unburying Theory, Repositioning Practice

NOTE

1. I would venture to add that her work was also embedded, or perhaps buried, within collaborative authorship. For example, she contributed to the book *Strangers Next Door: Ethnic Relations in American Communities* (Williams et al. 1964), in which the senior author acknowledged that Fowler synthesized and drafted a manuscript from the extensive material the several-year team research yielded. "Her draft [was] heavily utilized in the writing of [the] book" (Williams et al. 1964, xii). On the cover page, Fowler's name is listed along with several others who participated in the research project. These names are several spaces beneath and in much smaller print than Williams' name and those of two collaborators recognized as coauthors. Although she wrote the first draft of the book, she was not a full-fledged coauthor.

REFERENCES

Anthropology Newsletter. 1994. Stamp of Approval. 35 (4): 1, 6.

Behar, Ruth, and Deborah Gordon, eds. 1995. *Women Writing Culture*. Berkeley and Los Angeles: University of California Press.

Christian, Barbara. 1987. The Race for Theory. *Cultural Critique* 6 (11–19): 51–63.

Clifford, James, and George Marcus, eds. 1986. *Writing Culture: The Poetics and Politics of Ethnography*. Berkeley and Los Angeles: University of California Press.

Daily Reflector. 2001. Friday's Go! Guide Events. Jonkonnu Celebration. http://www.reflector.com (accessed February 24, 2003).

Davis, Allison. 1945. Caste, Economy, and Violence. *American Journal of Sociology* 51: 7–15.

———. 1983. *Leadership, Love, and Aggression*. San Diego: Harcourt Brace Jovanovich.

Davis, Allison, and John Dollard. 1940. *Children of Bondage: The Personality of Negro Youth in the Urban South*. Washington, DC: American Council on Education.

Davis, Allison, Burleigh Gardner, and Mary Gardner. 1941. *Deep South: A Social Anthropological Study of Caste and Class*. Chicago: University of Chicago Press.

Di Leonardo, Micaela, ed. 1991. *Gender at the Crossroads of Knowledge*. Berkeley and Los Angeles: University of California Press.

Douglass, Lisa. 1992. *The Power of Sentiment: Love, Hierarchy and the Jamaica Family Elite*. Boulder, CO: Westview.

Drake, St. Clair. 1974. In the Mirror of Black Scholarship: W. Allison Davis and *Deep South*. In *Education and Black Struggle: Notes from the Colonized World*, 42–54. Institute of the Black World. Harvard Education Review Monograph No. 2. Cambridge, MA: Harvard Educational Review.

Drake, St. Clair, and Horace Cayton. 1945. *Black Metropolis: A Study of Negro Life in a Northern City*. New York: Harcourt, Brace.

———. 1993. *Black Metropolis: A Study of Negro Life in a Northern City*. Rev. and enl. ed. Chicago: University of Chicago Press.

Foucault, Michel. 1980. *Power/Knowledge: Selected Interviews and Other Writings, 1972–1977*. New York: Pantheon Books.

Fowler, Manet. 1942. Review of *Color, Class, and Personality*, by Robert L. Sutherland. *American Anthropologist* 44 (4): 706–8.

———. 1952. The Case of Chef A: An Inquiry into and Analysis of a Human Relations Situation. Unpublished PhD diss., Cornell University.

———. 1953. Review of *Jamaican Personality and Cultural Dynamics: Personality and Conflict in Jamaica*, by Madeline Kerr. *Phylon* 13 (2): 217–19.

Fox, Richard, ed. 1991. *Recapturing Anthropology: Working in the Present*. Santa Fe, NM: School of American Research.

Fraser, Gertrude. 1991. Race, Class, and Difference in Hortense Powdermaker's *After Freedom: A Cultural Study in the Deep South*. *Journal of Anthropological Research* 47 (4): 403–16.

Free Press. 2001. Tryon Palace Celebrates Two Centuries of Christmas Tradition. http://www.kinston.com/entertainment/palace_33421_article.html/tryon_christmas.html (accessed February 24, 2003).

Haraway, Donna. 1991. Situated Knowledges: The Science Question in Feminism and the Privilege of Partial Perspective. In *Simians, Cyborgs, and Women: The Reinvention of Nature*, 183–201. New York: Routledge.

Harding, Sandra, ed. 1993. *The "Racial" Economy of Science: Toward a Democratic Future*. Bloomington: Indiana University Press.

Harrison, Faye V., ed. 1991. *Decolonizing Anthropology: Moving Further toward an Anthropology for Liberation*. Washington, DC: American Anthropological Association.

———. 1993. Writing against the Grain: Cultural Politics of Difference in the World of Alice Walker. *Critique of Anthropology* 13 (4): 401–27.

———. 1995. The Persistent Power of "Race" in the Cultural and Political Economy of Racism. *Annual Review of Anthropology* 24: 47–74.

———. 1993. Manet Fowler: Living, Surviving, and Celebrating Professional Commitment to Anthropological Practice. Unpublished manuscript.

Harrison, Ira E., and Fay V. Harrison. 1999. *African-American Pioneers in Anthropology.* Urbana: University of Illinois Press.

hooks, bell. 1989. *Talking Back: Thinking Black, Thinking Feminist.* Boston: South End Press.

James, Joy. 1993. African Philosophy, Theory, and "Living Thinkers." In *Spirit, Space and Survival: African American Women in (White) Academe,* ed. Joy James and Ruth Farmer, 31–46. New York: Routledge.

Jordan, Glenn. 1991. On Ethnography in an Intertextual Situation: Reading Narratives or Deconstructing Discourse? In *Decolonizing Anthropology,* ed. Faye V. Harrison, 42–67. Washington, DC: American Anthropological Association.

The Journal of Blacks in Higher Education. 1994. Black Heritage Award for an African-American Educator. No. 3 (Spring): 23.

Kluger, Richard. 1976. *Simple Justice.* New York: Knopf.

Leacock, Eleanor. 1987. Theory and Ethics in Applied Urban Anthropology. In *Cities of the United States,* ed. Leith Mullings, 317–36. New York: Columbia University Press.

Lutz, Catherine. 1995. The Gender of Theory. In *Women Writing Culture,* ed. Ruth Behar and Deborah Gordon, 249–66. Berkeley and Los Angeles: University of California Press.

Marcus, George, and Michael Fischer. 1986. *Anthropology as Cultural Critique.* Chicago: University of Chicago Press.

Mascia-Lees, Francis E., Patricia Sharpe, and Colleen B. Cohen. 1989. The Postmodernist Turn in Anthropology: Cautions from a Feminist Perspective. *Signs* 15 (1): 7–33.

Moore, Roger. 2001. *Stupid White Men . . . and Other Sorry Excuses for the State of the Nation!* New York: ReganBooks.

Powdermaker, Hortense. 1939. *After Freedom: A Cultural Study of the Deep South.* New York: Viking.

Practicing Anthropology. 1995. Commentary on Elitism and Discrimination in Anthropology. 17 (1–2): 42–56.

Rosaldo, Renato. 1993 [1989]. *Culture and Truth: The Remaking of Social Analysis.* Boston: Beacon Press.

Shaw, Carolyn Martin. 1995. *Colonial Inscriptions: Race, Class, and Gender in Kenya.* Minneapolis: University of Minnesota Press.

Singer, Merrill. 1994. Community-Centered Praxis: Toward an Alternative Non-dominative Applied Anthropology. *Human Organization* 53 (4): 336–44.

———. 1995. Reflections on Elitism in American Anthropology. *Practicing Anthropology* 17 (1–2): 44–46.

Smith, R. T. 1987. Hierarchy and the Dual Marriage System in West Indian Society. In *Gender and Kinship: Essays toward a Unified Analysis,* ed. Jane Collier and Sylvia Yanagisako, 163–96. Palo Alto, CA: Stanford University Press.

Stocking, George W. Jr. 1992. *The Ethnographer's Magic and Other Essays in the History of Anthropology.* Madison: University of Wisconsin Press.

Transforming Anthropology. 1990–present. A publication of the Association of Black Anthropologists. Arlington, VA: American Anthropological Association.

Trinh Minh-ha. 1989. *Woman, Native, Other.* Bloomington: Indiana University Press.

Ulin, Robert. 1991. Critical Anthropology Twenty Years Later: Modernism and Postmodernism in Anthropology. *Critique of Anthropology* 11 (1): 63–89.

Vincent, Joan. 1991. Engaging Historicism. In *Recapturing Anthropology,* ed. Richard Fox, 44–58. Santa Fe, NM: School of American Research Press.

Wallerstein, Immanuel. 1991. *Unthinking Social Science: The Limits of Nineteenth-Century Paradigms.* Cambridge: Polity Press.

Warry, Wayne. 1992. The Eleventh Thesis: Applied Anthropology as Praxis. *Human Organization* 51 (2): 155–63.

West, Cornel. 1991. *The Ethical Dimensions of Marxist Thought.* New York: Monthly Review Press.

Williams, Robin, John P. Dean, and Edward A. Suchman. 1964. *Strangers Next Door: Ethnic Relations in American Communities.* Englewood Cliffs, NJ: Prentice-Hall.

Willis, William Jr. 1974. Skeletons in the Anthropological Closet. In *Reinventing Anthropology,* ed. Dell Humes, 121–52. New York: Vintage Books.

———. 1975. Franz Boas and the Study of Black Folklore. In *The New Ethnicity: Perspectives from Ethnology,* ed. John W. Bennett, 307–34. St. Paul, NM: West.

Wolf, Eric. 1990. Distinguished Lecture: Facing Power—Old Insights, New Questions. *American Anthropologist* 92 (3): 586–96.

Chapter 3: Remapping Routes, Unearthing Roots

NOTE

1. The term *Creole* is used in a number of ways, including as a generic designation for culture, language, and people that are products of New World processes of change and exchange. It has also been invoked as a social or ethnic identity by some segments of certain Caribbean and circum-Caribbean societies.

REFERENCES

Abu-Lughod, Lila. 1991. Writing against Culture. In *Recapturing Anthropology: Working in the Present,* ed. Richard Fox, 137–62. Santa Fe, NM: School of American Research Press.

Baber, Willie L. 1988. *The Economizing Strategy: An Application and Critique.* New York: Peter Lang.

———. 1999. St. Clair Drake: Scholar and Activist. In *African American Pioneers in Anthropology,* ed. Ira E. Harrison and Faye V. Harrison, 191–212. Urbana: University of Illinois Press.

Basch, Linda, Nina Glick Schiller, Christina Szanton Blanc. 1994. *Nations Unbound: Transnational Projects, Postcolonial Predicaments and Deterritorialized Nation-States.* Langhorne, PA: Gordon and Breach Science.

Bettelheim, Judith. 1988. Jonkonnu and Other Christmas Masquerades. In *Caribbean Festival Arts: Each and Every Bit of Difference,* ed. John W. Nunley and Judith Bettelheim, 39–83. Seattle: University of Washington Press in association with the Saint Louis Art Museum.

Bogger, Tommy L. 1997. *Free Blacks in Norfolk, Virginia: The Darker Side of Freedom.* Charlottesville: University Press of Virginia.

Chevannes, Barry. 1994. *Rastafari: Roots and Ideology.* Syracuse, NY: Syracuse University Press.

Clarke, Kamari Maxine. 2004. *Mapping Yoruba Networks: Power and Agency in the Making of Transnational Communities.* Durham, NC: Duke University Press.

Cooper, Matthew. 1999. Spatial Discourses and Social Boundaries: Re-imagining the Toronto Waterfront. In *Theorizing the City: The New Urban Anthropology,* ed. Setha M. Low, 377–99. New Brunswick, NJ: Rutgers University Press.

Davis, Allison, Burleigh B. Gardner, and Mary R. Gardner. 1941 [1988]. *Deep South: A Social Anthropological Study of Class and Caste.* Los Angeles: Center for African American Studies.

Deagan, Kathleen A., and Darcie MacMahon. 1995. *Fort Mosé: Colonial America's Black Fortress of Freedom.* Gainesville: University Press of Florida.

Dominguez, Virginia. 1986. *White by Definition: Social Classification in Creole Louisiana.* New Brunswick, NJ: Rutgers University Press.

———. 2000. For a Politics of Love and Rescue. *Cultural Anthropology* 15 (3): 361–93.

Douglass, Lisa. 1992. *The Power of Sentiment: Love, Hierarchy, and the Jamaican Family Elite.* Boulder, CO: Westview.

Drake, St. Clair. 1987. *Black Folks Here and There: An Essay in History and Anthropology.* Vol. 1. Los Angeles: Center for Afro-American Studies, University of California, Los Angeles.

———. 1990. *Black Folks Here and There: An Essay in History and Anthropology.* Vol. 2. Los Angeles: Center for Afro-American Studies, University of California, Los Angeles.

Foster, Laurence. 1931. Negro-Indian Relations in the Southeast. PhD diss., Columbia University.

Frucht, Richard. 1971 [1967]. A Caribbean Social Type: Neither "Peasant" nor "Proletarian." In *Black Society in the New World,* ed. Richard Frucht, 98–104. New York: Random House.

Funk and Wagnalls New Encyclopedia. 1986. Norfolk. 19: 135–36. Chicago: Rand McNally.

Goody, Jack. 2003. Globalization and the Domestic Group. *Urban Anthropology and Studies of Cultural Systems and World Economic Development* 32 (1): 41–56.

Gupta, Akhil, and James Ferguson. 1992. Beyond "Culture": Space, Identity and the Politics of Difference. *Cultural Anthropology* 7 (1): 6–23.

Hall, Stuart. 1995. Negotiating Caribbean Identities. *New Left Review* (209): 3–14.

———. 1999. Thinking the Diaspora: Home-Thoughts from Abroad. *Small Axe* 6: 1–18.

Harding, Sandra, ed. 1993. *The "Racial" Economy of Science: Toward a Democratic Future.* Bloomington: Indiana University Press.

Hargrove, Melissa. 2000. Marketing Gullah: Identity, Cultural Politics, and Tourism. Master's thesis, Department of Anthropology, University of Tennessee, Knoxville.

———. 2005. Reinventing the Plantation on Gullah-Contested Landscape: Gated Communities and Spatial Segregation in the Sea Islands. PhD diss., Department of Anthropology, University of Tennessee, Knoxville.

Harrison, Faye V. 1997. The Gendered Politics and Violence of Structural Adjustment. In *Situated Lives: Gender and Culture in Everyday Life,* ed. Louise Lamphere, Helena Ragoné, and Patricia Zavella, 451–68. New York: Routledge.

Howard, Rosalyn. 2002. *Black Seminoles in the Bahamas.* Gainesville: University Press of Florida.

————. 2004. Yoruba in the British Caribbean: A Comparative Perspective on Trinidad and the Bahamas. In *Yoruba in the Atlantic World,* ed. Toyin Falola and Matt Childs, 157–76. Bloomington: Indiana University Press.

Kirsch, Max, 2003. The Politics of Exclusion: Place and the Legislation of the Environment in the Florida Everglades. *Urban Anthropology and Studies of Cultural Systems in World Economic Development* 32 (1): 99–131.

Knight, Franklin W., and Peggy K. Liss, eds. 1991. *Atlantic Port Cities: Economy, Culture, and Society in the Atlantic World, 1650–1850.* Knoxville: University of Tennessee Press.

Landers, Jane. 1990. Gracia Real de Santa Teresa de Mosé: A Free Black Town in Spanish Colonial Florida. *American Historical Review* 95 (1): 9–30.

————. 1999. *Black Society in Spanish Florida.* Urbana: University of Illinois Press.

Morales, Beatriz. 1995. Returning to the Source: Yoruba Religion in the South. In *Religion in the Contemporary South: Diversity, Community, and Identity.* Southern Anthropological Society Proceedings No. 28, ed. O. Kendall White Jr. and Daryl White, 124–30. Athens: University of Georgia Press.

Price, Jacob M. 1974. Economic Function and the Growth of American Port Towns in the Eighteenth Century. *Perspectives in American History* 8: 123–86.

————. 1991. Summation: The American Panorama of Atlantic Port Cities. In *Atlantic Port Cities: Economy, Culture, and Society in the Atlantic World, 1650–1850,* ed. Franklin W. Knight and Peggy K. Liss, 262–76. Knoxville: University of Tennessee Press.

Pulis, John W.. 1999a. "Citing [Sighting]-Up": Words, Sounds, and Reading Scripture in Jamaica. In *Religion, Diaspora, and Cultural Identity: A Reader in the Anglophone Caribbean,* ed. John W. Pulis, 337–401. Amsterdam: Gordan and Breach.

————. 1999b. The Jamaican Diaspora: Moses Baker, George Liele, and the African American Migration to Jamaica. Paper presented at the School of American Research Advanced Seminar, "From Africa to the Americas: New Directions in Afro-American Anthropology," Santa Fe, New Mexico.

————. ed. 1999c. *Moving On: Black Loyalists in the Afro-Atlantic World.* New York: Garland.

————. 2006. "Important Truths" and "Pernicious Follies": Texts, Covenants, and the Anabaptist Church of Jamaica. In *Afro-Atlantic Dialogues: Anthropology in the Diaspora,* ed. Kevin A. Yelvington. Santa Fe, NM: School of American Research Press.

Reid, Ira de A. 1942. The John Canoe Festival: A New World Africanism. *Phylon,* 4th Quarter, 349–70.

Regis, Helen. 1999. Second Lines, Minstrelsy, and the Contested Landscapes of New Orleans Afro-Creole Festivals. *Cultural Anthropology* 14 (4): 472–504.

————. 2001. Blackness and the Politics of Memory in the New Orleans Second Line. *American Ethnologist* 28 (9): 752–77.

Schuler, Monica. 1979. Myalism and the African Religious Tradition in Jamaica. In *Africa and The Caribbean: Legacies of a Link,* ed. Margaret E. Crahan and Franklin W. Knight, 65–79. Baltimore: Johns Hopkins University Press.

Smith, R. T. 1987. Hierarchy and the Dual Marriage System in West Indian Society. In *Gender and Kinship: Essays toward a Unified Analysis,* ed. Jane F. Collier and Sylvia Junko Yanagisako, 163–96. Stanford, CA: Stanford University Press.

Stack, Carol. 1996. *Call to Home: African Americans Reclaim the Rural South.* New York: Basic Books.

Sudarkasa, Niara. 1996. Interpreting the African in African American Family Structure. In *The Strength of Our Mothers: African and African American Women and Families; Essays and Speeches,* 123–41. Trenton, NJ: Africa World Press.

Walser, Richard. 1971. His Worship the John Kuner. *North Carolina Folklore* 19 (4): 160–72.

Wertenbaker, Thomas J. 1962 [1931]. *Norfolk: Historic Southern Port.* 2nd ed. Durham, NC: Duke University Press.

Whitehead, Tony L. 1986. Breakdown, Resolution, and Coherence: The Fieldwork Experiences of a Big, Brown, Pretty-Talking Man in a West Indian Community. In *Self, Sex, and Gender in Cross-Cultural Fieldwork,* ed. Tony L. Whitehead and Mary Ellen Conaway, 213–39. Urbana: University of Illinois Press.

———. 1997. Urban Low-Income African-American Men, HIV/AIDS, and Gender Identity. *Medical Anthropology Quarterly* 11 (4): 411–47.

Willis, William Jr. 1971. Divide and Role: Red, White, and Black in the Southeast. In *Red, White, and Black: Symposium on Indians in the Old South* ed. Charles M. Hudson, 99–115. Athens: University of Georgia Press.

Wilson, Peter. 1973 [1995]. *Crab Antics: The Social Anthropology of English-Speaking Societies of the Caribbean.* Repr. Prospect Heights, IL: Waveland Press.

Chapter 4: Writing against the Grain

NOTES

1. The unity of critical anthropology cannot be treated as a given. Robert Ulin, however, probes the conceptual terrain on which there are "competing claims . . . to define the critical project of anthropology" (1991, 63–64). He writes of a single yet multifaceted project because of his view that the present impasse between political-economy and postmodern anthropology can be bridged. For a thoughtful discussion of the intellectual underpinnings of the postmodern era, see di Leonardo (1991).

2. The intellectual parameters, meaning, and boundaries of anthropology's postmodernism, which is a fairly recent invention, are intensely contested; consequently, one cannot safely write of a unified domain of postmodernist anthropology. Various trends and tendencies are categorized together for the sake of Ulin's argument, upon which I base my point of departure. A particularly insightful treatment of the multiplicity of perspectives associated with postmodernism is found in Lutz (1993).

3. According to Donna Haraway, as an unsatisfactory alternative to totalizing claims to scientific authority, "relativism is a way of being nowhere while claiming to be everywhere equally. The 'equality' of positioning is a denial of responsibility and critical enquiry" (1991, 191).

4. In much of the discourse associated with the postmodernist turn, the concern with authority is focused primarily on the various modes or paradigms of authority structured into texts (e.g., Clifford 1988a). Marcus and Cushman (1982, 38) define textual authority as "the combined structure of a covering legitimation and the styles of evidence derived

from it for the page-by-page descriptions and claims of a text," which establishes credibility for and readers' confidence in what an author or authors present. My emphasis in this chapter is on the broader intellectual and institutional parameters that engender differential authority in sociopolitical contexts of knowledge production and legitimation. Authority in this broader disciplinary and institutionally structured sense has been at worse ignored or at best underemphasized in postmodern anthropology's conceptual toolkit.

Since the end of political colonialism in the 1960s, anthropology, more than any other social science, has experienced an epistemological and political crisis around the discipline's "capacity to define authoritatively the non-Western other" (Pels and Nencel 1991, 3). In light of the discipline's sexist, racist, and imperialist genealogy, the authority, legitimacy, and purpose of anthropological knowledge have been seriously thrown into question. With "the complex of classical anthropological [knowledge]—[based on] university education, value-free theory, the brokerage of cultural difference, the legitimation of fieldwork as a politically innocent method—[becoming] suspect," postmodern anthropologists have responded with textual and rhetorical strategies for decentering and relativizing the ethnographer's authority vis-à-vis the "voices" of their native informants (Pels and Nencel 1991, 7). Shared or dispersed narrative authority, however, belies the structured inequalities of the social contexts within which ethnographers do fieldwork, write up, and publish texts. In these contexts all voices and narratives are not equal (Polier and Roseberry 1989, 252).

5. Antipositivism acknowledges that values and politics help shape research and knowledge. Alan Banks, Dwight Billings, and Karen Tice discern a democratic temper in postmodernism's avoidance of universalism and essentialism through its "fluid, plural, uncentered, and ineradicably untidy approach" (1992, 291).

6. Although the concept of the Third World is problematic and contestable, I use it in the qualified sense that Mohanty, Russo, and Torres indicate in their edited volume on Third World women and feminist politics (1991, ix–x). They use the term to refer to "the colonized, neocolonized, or decolonized countries (of Asia, Africa, and Latin America) whose economic and political structures have been deformed within the colonial process, and to black, Asian, Latino, and indigenous peoples in North America, Europe, and Australia" (ix).

7. Henrietta Moore describes the development of feminist anthropology in terms of three phases. The first phase was concerned mostly with the anthropology of women to correct male bias in ethnographic description and analysis. The second phase was marked by a focus on gender. The third phase brings us to the present with the concern with deconstructing sameness and understanding class, ethnic, and racial differences among women.

8. Michael Taussig and Richard Price are exceptions to this trend. They both have published experimental ethnographies that illuminate racial and class exploitation and oppression in Colombia and Suriname, respectively. These works, however, do not have as their primary purpose the interrogation or probing of the racism that affects the experiences of Afro-Americans in the two South American contexts. Also, Clifford's aesthetic and cultural criticism (e.g., 1988b) includes essays that perceptively touch on the artistic and ideological dimensions of blackness and Africanism in Aimé Césaire's poetry and

in art museum exhibitions of so-called primitivism and an essay on the negotiation of cultural (and so-called racial) identity and tribal status of a coastal Massachusetts community of heavily acculturated and miscegenational Mashpee Indians.

9. Deborah Gordon (1988) offered one of the earliest critiques of *Writing Culture* and its cover's photo images. She argued that the foregrounding of white male ethnographic authority reflects a central tension in the book related to gender, feminism, and theories of writing (8); so-called experimental ethnography, as reflected in Clifford and Marcus's collection (1986), is grounded in a masculinist subjectivity that seeks to "manage feminism." Peter Pels and Lorraine Nencel (1991, 16) also criticize the cover photograph, pointing out that Stephen Tyler is shown working "ass backwards" with his back toward the native "co-producer[s] of his text."

10. Although black women creative writers and literary critics may in fact produce theoretically rich works, these discourses and texts are rarely recognized and valorized as such. Indeed, in elitist academic language, theory, criticism, and fiction are generally presumed to be disparate, virtually mutually exclusive productions. Consequently, those literary works that bridge the conventionally imposed gap between theory and creativity are underappreciated and misunderstood by critics who adhere to the established canon.

11. The Spelman students' response may also suggest their resistance to the narrow elitist, exclusionist constitution of scholarship as something distinct from and perhaps elevated above the more open-ended and heterogeneous category and domain of creative writing. The very language of Western academia poses serious problems for black women writers (personal communication with Estella Conwill Majozo, professor of English and creative writing, University of Louisville, December 25, 1992).

12. Other analysts who have been concerned with Hurston as an ethnographer are Dorst (1987) and Gordon (1990).

13. The short story to which Walker was referring is "The Revenge of Hannah Kemhuff" (1973).

14. According to literary artist Estella Conwill Majozo, black women writers have historically expanded literary genres, blurring boundaries between them, history, and the social sciences. In this respect, both Walker and Hurston are part of a broader and older tradition (personal communication, December 25, 1992).

15. Walker's concern with rewriting not just black but global history is paralleled in anthropologist Gwendolyn Mikell's more narrowly delimited political economy of the Akan of Ghana (1989a). Mikell situates the rise and fall of Ghana's cocoa economy in the wider historical and worldly context of colonial and postcolonial capitalism. A global framework, however, does not preclude her from underscoring the lived experiences and struggles of subsistence producers and cash-cropping farmers, matrilineal kinspeople, and traditional and modern bearers of power/authority at the local as well as regional and national levels. Moreover, the history, political economy, and culture that Mikell analyzes are both gender and class focused.

16. See anthropologist Patricia Zavella (1991b, 75) for a discussion on the oppressive constraints of "crossing borders" and constructing identities. Zavella's conception of Chicano/Chicana ethnicity is grounded in her understanding of the "compounded diversity" of a set of historical experiences that has drawn upon Indian, African, and European "racial" and cultural sources (1991b, 78).

17. Clifford admits that this proposition is untenable (1986, 21). For just a small sample of the range of writing strategies and approaches among black women anthropologists, see Bolles (1983), Harrison (1988b), Mikell (1989a), and Mullings (1984) for historicized political economy and class analyses of households, informal economic activities, changes in kinship and stratification, and indigenous psychotherapy; and Bolles (1986, 1996) and Harrison (1990b) for more humanistic, reflexive, interpretive approaches to intellectual history, life stories, and the performance of ethnographic scripts.

REFERENCES

Abu-Lughod, Lila. 1991. Writing against Culture. In *Recapturing Anthropology: Working in the Present,* ed. Richard G. Fox, 137–62. Santa Fe, NM: School of American Research Press.

Amadiume, Ifi. 1987. *Male Daughters, Female Husbands: Gender and Sex in an African Society.* London: Zed Books.

Appadurai, Arjun. 1991. Global Ethnoscapes: Notes and Queries for a Transnational Anthropology. In *Recapturing Anthropology,* ed. Richard G. Fox, 191–210. Santa Fe, NM: School of American Research Press.

Banks, Allen, Dwight Billings, and Karen Tice. 1992. Appalachian Studies, Resistance, and Postmodernism. In *Fighting Back in Appalachia: Traditions of Resistance and Change,* ed. Stephen L. Fisher, 283–301. Philadelphia: Temple University Press.

Bolles, A. Lynn. 1983. Kitchens Hit by Priorities: Employed Working-Class Jamaican Women Confront the International Monetary Fund. In *Women, Men, and the International Division of Labor,* ed. June Nash and María Patricia Fernández-Kelly, 139–60. Albany: State University of New York Press.

———. 1986. African-American Soul Force: Dance, Music and Vera Mae Green. *Sage* 3 (2): 32–34.

———. 1996. *We Paid Our Dues: Women Trade Union Leaders of the Caribbean.* Washington, DC: Howard University Press.

Cassells, Joan. 1977. *A Group Called Women: Sisterhood and Symbolism in the Feminist Movement.* Prospect Heights, IL: Waveland Press.

Caulfield, Mina Davis. 1979. Participant Observation or Partisan Participation? In *The Politics of Anthropology: From Colonialism, and Sexism toward a View from Below,* ed. Gerrit Huizer and Bruce Mannheim, 309–18. The Hague, Netherlands: Mouton.

Clifford, James. 1986. Introduction: Partial Truths. In *Writing Culture: The Poetics and Politics of Ethnography,* ed. James Clifford and George E. Marcus, 1–26. Berkeley and Los Angeles: University of California Press.

———. 1988a. On Ethnographic Authority. In *The Predicament of Culture: Twentieth-Century Ethnography, Literature, and Art,* 21–54. Cambridge, MA: Harvard University Press.

———. 1988b. *The Predicament of Culture: Twentieth-Century Ethnography, Literature, and Art.* Cambridge, MA: Harvard University Press.

Clifford, James, and George E. Marcus, eds. 1986. *Writing Culture: The Poetics and Politics of Writing Culture.* Berkeley and Los Angeles: University of California Press.

Cole, Johnnetta B., ed. 1986. *All American Women: Lines that Divide, Ties that Bind.* New York: Free Press.

Collins, Patricia Hill. 1991. *Black Feminist Thought: Knowledge, Consciousness, and the Politics of Empowerment.* New York: Routledge.

———. 1998. *Fighting Words: Black Women and the Search for Justice.* Minneapolis: University of Minnesota Press.

di Leonardo, Micaela. 1989. Malinowski's Nephews. *The Nation.* March 13, 350–52.

———. 1991. Introduction: Gender, Culture, and Political Economy. In *Gender at the Crossroads of Knowledge: Feminist Anthropology in the Postmodern Era,* ed. Micaela di Leonardo, 1–48. Berkeley and Los Angeles: University of California Press.

Dorst, John. 1987. Rereading *Mules and Men:* Toward the Death of the Ethnographer. *Cultural Anthropology* 2: 305–18.

Drake, St. Clair. 1990. Further Reflections on Anthropology and the Black Experience. *Transforming Anthropology* 1 (2): 1–24.

Fabian, Johannes. 1983. *Time and the Other: How Anthropology Makes Its Object.* New York: Columbia University Press.

Fischer, Michael M. J. 1986. Ethnicity and the Post-Modern Arts of Memory. In *Writing Culture: The Poetics and Politics of Writing Culture.,* ed. James Clifford and George E. Marcus, 194–233. Berkeley and Los Angeles: University of California Press.

Fox, Richard G. 1991a. For a Nearly New Culture History. In *Recapturing Anthropology,* ed. Richard Fox, 93–114. Santa Fe, NM: School of American Research Press.

———. 1991b. Introduction: Working in the Present. In *Recapturing Anthropology,* ed. Richard Fox, 1–16. Santa Fe, NM: School of American Research Press.

Geertz, Clifford. 1988. *Works and Lives: The Anthropologist as Author.* Stanford, CA: Stanford University Press.

Gordon, Deborah. 1988. Writing Culture, Writing Feminism: The Poetics and Politics of Experimental Ethnography. *Inscriptions* 3/4: 7–24.

———. 1990. The Politics of Ethnographic Authority: Race and Writing in the Ethnography of Margaret Mead and Zora Neale Hurston. In *Modernist Anthropology,* ed. Marc Manganaro, 146–62. Princeton, NJ: Princeton University Press.

Gwaltney, John L. 1980. *Drylongso: A Self-Portrait of Black America.* New York: Vintage Books.

Haraway, Donna J. 1991. Situated Knowledges: The Science Question in Feminism and the Privilege of Partial Perspective. In *Simians, Cyborgs, and Women: The Reinvention of Nature.* New York: Routledge. Originally published in *Feminist Studies* 14, no. 3 (1988): 575–99.

Harrison, Faye V. 1988a. Introduction: An African Diaspora Perspective for Urban Anthropology. In "Black Folks in Cities Here and There: Changing Patterns of Domination and Response." Special Issue, *Urban Anthropology and Studies of Cultural Systems and World Economic Development* 17 (2–3): 111–41.

———. 1988b. Women in Jamaica's Urban Informal Economy: Insights from a Kingston Slum. *Nieuwe West-Indische Gids/New West Indian Guide* 62 (3/4): 103–28.

———. 1990a. Feminism in Anthropological Perspective. Review of *A Group Called Women,* by Joan Cassell. *Transforming Anthropology* 1 (2): 25–27.

———. 1990b. "Three Women, One Struggle": Anthropology, Performance, and Pedagogy. *Transforming Anthropology* 1 (1): 1–9.

———. 1991. Anthropology as an Agent of Transformation: Introductory Comments and

Queries. In *Decolonizing Anthropology: Moving Further toward an Anthropology for Liberation,* ed. Faye V. Harrison, 1–14. Washington, DC: American Anthropological Association.

———. 1992. The Du Boisian Legacy in Anthropology. Special issue, *Critique of Anthropology* 12 (3): 239–60.

Hemenway, Robert E. 1977. *Zora Neale Hurston: A Literary Biography.* Urbana: University of Illinois Press.

hooks, bell. 1990. *Yearning: Race, Gender, and Cultural Politics.* Boston: South End Press.

Hurston, Zora Neale. 1935 [1978]. *Mules and Men.* Bloomington: Indiana University Press.

Johnson, Barbara. 1987. *A World of Difference.* Baltimore: Johns Hopkins University Press.

Jones, Delmos. 1970. Towards a Native Anthropology. *Human Organization* 29 (4): 251–59. Reprinted in *Anthropology for the Nineties: Introductory Readings,* ed. Johnnetta B. Cole, 30–41. New York: Free Press, 1988.

Jordan, Glenn H. 1991. On Ethnography in an Intertextual Situation: Reading Narratives or Deconstructing Discourse? In *Decolonizing Anthropology,* ed. Faye V. Harrison, 42–67. Washington, DC: American Anthropological Association.

———. 1992. Beyond the New Cultural Anthropology: Subjects, Objects, and the Politics of Representation. Unpublished manuscript.

Lutz, Catherine. 1990. The Erasure of Women's Writing in Sociocultural Anthropology. *American Ethnologist* 17 (4): 611–27.

———. 1993. Social Contexts of Postmodern Cultural Analysis. In *Postmodern Contentions: Epochs, Politics, Space.* New York: Guilford Press.

Marcus, George E., and Dick Cushman. 1982. Ethnographies as Texts. *Annual Review of Anthropology* 11: 25–69.

Marcus, George E., and Michael M. J. Fischer. 1986. *Anthropology as Cultural Critique: An Experimental Moment in the Human Sciences.* Chicago: University of Chicago Press.

Mascias-Lees, Frances E., Patricia Sharpe, and Colleen Ballerino Cohen. 1989. The Postmodernist Turn in Anthropology: Cautions from a Feminist Perspective. *Signs* 15 (1): 7–33.

Mikell, Gwendolyn. 1982. When Horses Talk: Reflections on Zora Neale Hurston's Haitian Anthropology. *Phylon* 43 (3): 218–30.

———. 1983. The Anthropological Imagination of Zora Neale Hurston. *Western Journal of Black Studies* 7 (1): 27–35.

———. 1989a. *Cocoa and Chaos in Ghana.* New York: Paragon Press.

———. 1989b. Zora Neale Hurston. In *Women Anthropologists: A Biographical Dictionary,* ed. Ute Gacs, Aisha Khan, Jerrie McIntyre, and Ruth Weinberg, 160–66. Urbana: University of Illinois Press.

———. 1999. Feminism and Black Culture in the Ethnography of Zora Neale Hurston. In *African-American Pioneers in Anthropology,* eds. Ira E. Harrison and Faye V. Harrison, 51–69. Urbana: University of Illinois Press.

Mohanty, Chandra Talpade. 1991a. Introduction: Cartographies of Struggle, Third World Women and the Politics of Feminism. In *Third World Women and the Politics of Feminism,* ed. Chandra Talpade Mohanty, Ann Russo, and Lourdes Torres, 1–47. Bloomington: Indiana University Press.

———. 1991b. Under Western Eyes: Feminist Scholarship and Colonial Discourses. In *Third World Women and the Politics of Feminism,* ed. Chandra Talpade Mohanty, Ann Russo, and Lourdes Torres, 51–80. Bloomington: Indiana University Press.

Mohanty, Chandra Talpade, Ann Russo, and Lourdes Torres, eds. 1991. *Third World Women and the Politics of Feminism.* Bloomington: Indiana University Press.

Moore, Henrietta. 1988. *Feminism and Anthropology.* Minneapolis: University of Minnesota Press.

Morgen, Sandra. 1988. The Dream of Diversity, the Dilemma of Differences: Race and Class Contradictions in a Feminist Health Clinic. In *Anthropology for the Nineties: Introductory Readings,* ed. Johnnetta B. Cole, 370–80. New York: Free Press.

Mullings, Leith. 1984. *Therapy, Ideology, and Social Change: Mental Healing in Urban Ghana.* Berkeley and Los Angeles: University of California Press.

Nash, June. 1979. *We Eat the Mines and the Mines Eat Us: Dependency and Exploitation in Bolivian Tin Mines.* New York: Columbia University Press.

Obbo, Christine. 1980. *African Women: Their Struggle for Economic Independence.* London: Zed Press.

———. 1990. Adventures with Fieldnotes. In *Fieldnotes: The Makings of Anthropology,* ed. Roger Sanjek, 290–302. Ithaca, NY: Cornell University Press.

Ortner, Sherry. 1991. Reading America: Preliminary Notes on Class and Culture. In *Recapturing Anthropology,* ed. Richard Fox, 163–90. Santa Fe, NM: School of American Research Press.

Page, Helán E. 1988. Dialogic Principles of Interactive Learning in the Ethnographic Relationship. *Journal of Anthropological Research* 44 (2): 163–81.

Pels, Peter, and Lorraine Nencel. 1991. Introduction: Critique and the Deconstruction of Anthropological Authority. In *Constructing Knowledge: Authority and Critique in Social Science,* ed. Lorraine Nencel and Peter Pels, 1–21. London: Sage.

Polier, Nicole, and William Roseberry. 1989. Tristes Tropes: Postmodern Anthropologists Encounter the Other and Discover Themselves. *Economy and Society* 18 (2): 245–64.

Price, Richard. 1983. *First Time: The Historical Vision of an Afro-American People.* Baltimore: Johns Hopkins University Press.

Rabinow, Paul. 1986. Representations Are Social Facts: Modernity and Post-Modernity in Anthropology. In *Writing Culture: The Poetics and Politics of Ethnography,* ed. James Clifford and George E. Marcus, 234–61. Santa Fe, NM: School of American Research Press.

Rosaldo, Renato. 1980. *Ilongot Headhunting, 1883–1974: A Study in Society and History.* Stanford, CA: Stanford University Press.

———. 1989. *Culture and Truth: The Remaking of Social Analysis.* Boston: Beacon Press.

Roseberry, William. 1989. *Anthropologies and Histories: Essays in Culture, History, and Political Economy.* New Brunswick, NJ: Rutgers University Press.

Royster, Jacqueline Jones. 1990. The Genesis of Authority: Black Women's Pathways to Intellectual Empowerment. Unpublished manuscript.

Sacks, Karen B. 1989. Towards a Unified Theory of Class, Race, and Gender. *American Ethnologist* 16 (3): 534–50.

Steady, Filomina Chioma. 1981. Introduction to *The Black Woman Cross-Culturally,* ed. Filomina C. Steady, 1–5. Cambridge, MA: Schenkman.

Sudarkasa, Niara. 1988. African and Afro-American Family Structure. In *Anthropology for the Nineties: Introductory Readings.* ed. Johnnetta B. Cole, 182–210. New York: Free Press.

Taussig, Michael. 1980. *The Devil and Commodity Fetishism in South America.* Chapel Hill: University of North Carolina Press.

———. 1987. *Shamanism, Colonialism, and the Wild Man: A Study in Terror and Healing.* Chicago: University of Chicago Press.

———. 1989. History as Commodity in Some Recent American (Anthropological) Literature. *Critique of Anthropology* 9 (1): 7–23.

Trinh Minh-ha. 1989. *Woman, Native, Other: Writing Postcoloniality and Feminism.* Bloomington: Indiana University Press.

Trouillot, Michel-Rolph. 1991. Anthropology and the Savage Slot: The Poetics and Politics of Otherness. In *Recapturing Anthropology: Working in the Present,* ed. Richard G. Fox, 17–44. Sante Fe, NM: School of American Research Press.

Turner, Victor. 1987. *The Anthropology of Performance.* New York: PAJ.

Ulin, Robert. 1984. *Understanding Cultures: Perspectives in Anthropology and Social Theory.* Austin: University of Texas Press.

———. 1991. Critical Anthropology Twenty Years Later: Modernism and Postmodernism in Anthropology. *Critique of Anthropology* 11 (1): 63–89.

Valentine, Betty Lou. 1978. *Hustling and Other Hard Work: Life Styles in the Ghetto.* New York: Free Press.

Vincent, Joan. 1991. Engaging Historicism. In *Recapturing Anthropology,* ed. Richard Fox, 45–58. Santa Fe, NM: School of American Research Press.

Walker, Alice. 1973. The Revenge of Hannah Kemhuff. In *In Love and Trouble: Stories of Black Women,* 60–80. New York: Harcourt Brace Jovanovich.

———. 1982. *The Color Purple.* New York: Harcourt Brace Jovanovich.

———. 1983. *In Search of Our Mothers' Gardens.* San Diego: Harcourt Brace Jovanovich.

———. 1989. *The Temple of My Familiar.* New York: Pocket Books.

Wallace, Michelle. 1990. *Invisibility Blues: From Pop to Theory.* New York: Verso.

West, Cornel. 1988. Postmodernism and Black America. *Z Magazine,* June, 27–29.

———. 1991. *The Ethnical Dimensions of Marxist Thought.* New York: Monthly Review Press.

Willis, Paul. 1981. *Learning to Labour: How Working Class Kids Get Working Class Jobs.* New York: Columbia University Press.

Wilson, Lynn. 1988. Epistemology and Power: Rethinking Ethnography at Greenham. In *Anthropology for the Nineties: Introductory Readings,* ed. Johnnetta B. Cole, 42–58. New York: Free Press.

Wolf, Eric. 1982. *Europe and the People without History.* Berkeley and Los Angeles: University of California Press.

Zavella, Patricia. 1991a. *Mujeres* in Factories: Race and Class Perspectives on Women, Work, and Family. In *Gender at the Crossroads of Knowledge: Feminist Anthropology in the Postmodern Era,* ed. Micaela di Leonardo, 312–36. Berkeley and Los Angeles: University of California Press.

———. 1991b. Reflections on Diversity among Chicanas. *Frontiers: A Journal of Women Studies* 12 (2): 73–85.

Chapter 5: Probing the Legacy of Empire

NOTE

1. Gordon K. Lewis was a renowned scholar whose writings addressed the contemporary Caribbean's major dilemmas as a locus of neocolonial—and in some cases still very much colonial—power and economic control. Without apology or masking, his political analyses were written from "the ideological standpoint of European democratic socialism" (Lewis 1987, ix) and the experiential perspective of one who lived a life of intellectual and political engagement in the region. He was married to a black Barbadian woman, Sybil, with whom he raised a family. In other words, his intellectual production did not emerge from abstract, artificial debates about the Caribbean in colloquiums within metropolitan universities. Instead, it grew out of a more organic context.

In his first book, he situated Puerto Rico in the context of U.S. neocolonialism while at the same time interpreting the island's political reality in terms of a Pan-Caribbean framework. This enabled him to illuminate important parallels with and relationships between the Hispanic Caribbean and the English, French, and Dutch Antilles (Lewis 1963). In his second book, he shifted his focus to the English-speaking Caribbean (Lewis 1968). This was a seminal, foundational study of the social and political legacy of British colonialism in the modern, independence-era West Indies (which included the mainland countries of British Honduras/Belize and British Guiana/Guyana). Lewis's next two books (1978, 1983a) addressed the development of ideologies and public discourses on slavery, colonialism, and freedom from the vantage points of English and West Indian thinkers and activists. His last book was on Grenada: the rise and demise of the New Jewel Movement between 1979 and 1983 (Lewis 1987). It placed the demise of the Grenada revolution in the context of a long history of violence (4).

REFERENCES

Abrahams, Roger D. 1983. *The Man-of-Words in the West Indies: Performance and the Emergence of Creole Culture.* Baltimore: Johns Hopkins University Press.

Austin, Diane. 1984. *Urban Life in Kingston, Jamaica: The Culture and Class Ideology of Two Neighborhoods.* New York: Gordon and Breach Science.

Baron, Harold M. 1971. The Demand for Black Labor: Historical Notes on the Political Economy of Racism. Special issue, *Radical America* 5 (2): 1–46.

Barry, Tom, Beth Wood, and Deb Preusch. 1984. *The Other Side of Paradise: Foreign Control in the Caribbean.* New York: Grove.

Braithwaite, Edward. 1975. Caribbean Man in Space and Time. *Savacou* 11/12 (September): 1–11.

Calathes, William. 1988. Criminal Justice and Underdevelopment: A Case Study of the Jamaican Gun Court Act. *Journal of Caribbean Studies* 6 (3): 323–58.

Carnegie, Charles V. 1992. The Fate of Ethnography: Native Social Science in the English-Speaking Caribbean. *New West Indies Guide* 66 (1–2): 5–25.

Centre for Contemporary Cultural Studies. 1982. *The Empire Strikes Back: Race and Racism in '70s Britain.* London: Hutchinson in association with the Centre for Contemporary Cultural Studies, University of Birmingham.

Drake, St. Clair. 1954. Value Systems, Social Structure and Race Relations in the British Isles. PhD diss., Department of Anthropology, University of Chicago.

———. 1955. The "Colour Problem" in Britain: A Study in Social Definitions. *The Sociological Review* (New Series) 3 (2): 197–217.

———. 1987. *Black Folk Here and There: An Essay in History and Anthropology.* Vol. 1. Los Angeles: Center for Afro-American Studies, UCLA.

———. 1990. *Black Folk Here and There: An Essay in History and Anthropology.* Vol. 2. Los Angeles: Center for Afro-American Studies, UCLA.

Drake, St. Clair, and Horace Cayton. 1945. *Black Metropolis: A Study of Negro Life in a Northern City.* New York: Harcourt, Brace.

Edie, Carlene. 1991. *Democracy by Default: Dependency and Clientelism in Jamaica.* Boulder, CO: Lynne Rienner.

Fanon, Frantz. 1963. *The Wretched of the Earth.* New York: Grove.

Giddens, Anthony. 1979. *Central Problems in Social Theory: Action, Structure and Contradiction in Social Analysis.* Berkeley and Los Angeles: University of California Press.

Gray, Obika. 1991. *Radicalism and Social Change in Jamaica, 1960–1972.* Knoxville: University of Tennessee Press.

Hall, Stuart. 1999. Thinking the Diaspora: Home-Thoughts from Abroad. *Small Axe* 6: 1–18.

Hall, Stuart, Charles Critcher, Tony Jefferson, and John Clarke. 1978. *Policing the Crisis: Mugging, the State, and Law and Order.* New York: Holmes and Meier.

Harrison, Faye V. 1975. British Race Relations and Community Organization: A London Case Study. Unpublished manuscript.

———. 1976. Down Mean Brixton Streets: Youth, Community, and Conflict. Unpublished master's theses, Department of Anthropology, Stanford University.

———. 1982. Semiproletarianization and the Structure of Socioeconomic and Political Relations in a Jamaican Slum. PhD diss., Department of Anthropology, Stanford University.

———. 1987a. Crime, Class, and Politics in Jamaica. *TransAfrica Forum* 5 (1): 29–38.

———. 1987b. Gangs, Grassroots Politics, and the Crisis of Dependent Capitalism in Jamaica. In *Perspectives in U.S. Marxist Anthropology,* ed. David Hakken and Hanna Lessinger, 186–210. Boulder, CO: Westview.

———. 1988a. Democracy, Jamaican Style: The Politics of Repression. Paper presented at the African American Studies Program Colloquium, spring 1988, University of Illinois, Urbana.

———. 1988b. Dependent Capitalism and Clientelist Democracy in Crisis: A Perspective from Jamaica's Grassroots. Unpublished manuscript.

———. 1988c. The Politics of Social Outlawry in Urban Jamaica. *Urban Anthropology and Studies of Cultural Systems and World Economic Development* 17 (2–3): 259–77.

———. 1988d. Women in Jamaica's Urban Informal Economy: Insights from a Kingston Slum. *Nieuwe West-Indische Gids* 62 (3–4): 103–28.

———. 1989. Drug Trafficking in World Capitalism: A Perspective on Jamaican Posses in the U.S. *Social Justice: A Journal of Crime, Conflict, and World Order* 16 (4): 115–31.

———. 1991. Ethnography as Politics. In *Decolonizing Anthropology: Moving Further toward an Anthropology for Liberation,* ed. Faye V. Harrison, 88–109. Washington, DC: American Anthropological Association.

———. 1997. The Gendered Politics and Violence of Structural Violence: A View from

Jamaica. In *Situated Lives: Gender and Culture in Everyday Life,* ed. Louise Lamphere, Helana Ragoné, and Patricia Zavella, 451–68. New York: Routledge.

Henry, Paget. 1991. Political Accumulation and Authoritarianism in the Caribbean: The Case of Antigua. *Social and Economic Studies* 40 (1): 1–38.

Jordan, Glenn H. 1991. On Ethnography in an Intertextual Situation: Reading Narratives or Deconstructing Discourse? In *Decolonizing Anthropology: Moving Further toward an Anthropology for Liberation,* ed. Faye V. Harrison, 42–67. Washington, DC: American Anthropological Association.

Ledgister, F. S. J. 1998. *Class Alliances and the Liberal Authoritarian State: The Roots of Post-Colonial Democracy in Jamaica, Trinidad and Tobago, and Suriname.* Trenton, NJ: Africa World Press.

Lewis, Gordon K. 1963. *Puerto Rico: Freedom and Power in the Caribbean.* New York: Monthly Review Press.

———. 1968. *The Growth of the Modern West Indies.* New York: Monthly Review Press.

———. 1978. *Slavery, Imperialism, and Freedom: Studies in English Radical Thought.* New York: Monthly Review Press.

———. 1983a. *Main Currents in Caribbean Thought: The Historical Evolution of Caribbean Society in Its Ideological Aspects.* Baltimore: Johns Hopkins University Press.

———. 1983b. The Making of a Caribbeanist. Working Paper No. 10, Caribbean Institute and Study Center for Latin America. Inter-American University of Puerto Rico, San German Campus.

———. 1984. Graduation Ceremony Address. University of the West Indies, St. Augustine, Trinidad and Tobago, January 14.

———. 1985. The Contemporary Caribbean: A General Overview. In *Caribbean Contours,* ed. Sidney W. Mintz and Sally Price, 219–50. Baltimore: Johns Hopkins University Press.

———. 1987. *Grenada: The Jewel Despoiled.* Baltimore: Johns Hopkins University Press.

Lewis, Oscar. 1965. *La Vida: A Puerto Rican Family in the Culture of Poverty—San Juan and New York.* New York: Vintage Books.

Maingot, Anthony. 1991. The Passionate Advocate: Gordon K. Lewis and Caribbean Studies. The Gordon K. Lewis Memorial Lecture, University of Walwick, Center for Caribbean Studies, Coventry, England, November 26.

Mintz, Sidney W. 1960. *Worker in the Cane.* New Haven, CT: Yale University Press.

———. 1985. *Sweetness and Power: The Place of Sugar in Modem History.* New York: Viking.

Monroe, Trevor. 1986. Comments on Thomas. In *The State in Caribbean Society,* ed. Omar Davies, 84–89. Mona, Jamaica: University of the West Indies, Department of Economics.

Nader, Laura. 1969. Up the Anthropologist—Perspectives Gained from Studying Up. In *Reinventing Anthropology,* ed. Dell Hymes, 284–311. New York: Vintage Books.

Rodney, Walter. 1975. Contemporary Political Trends in the English-speaking Caribbean. *The Black Scholar* 7 (1): 15–21.

Scott, James. 1985. *Weapons of the Weak: Everyday Forms of Peasant Resistance.* New Haven, CT: Yale University Press.

Steward, Julian H., Robert A. Manners, Eric R. Wolf, Elena Padilla Seda, Sidney W. Mintz, and Raymon L. Scheele. 1956. *The People of Puerto Rico: A Study in Social Anthropology.* Urbana: University of Illinois Press.

Stone, Carl. 1980. *Democracy and Clientelism in Jamaica.* New Brunswick, NJ: Transaction Books.

———. 1985. A Political Profile of the Caribbean. In *Caribbean Contours,* ed. Sidney W. Mintz and Sally Price, 13–53. Baltimore: Johns Hopkins University Press.

Sutton, Constance. 1987. The Caribbeanization of New York City and the Emergence of a Transnational Socio-Cultural System. In *Caribbean Life in New York City: Sociocultural Dimensions,* ed. Constance R. Sutton and Elsa M. Chaney, 15–30. New York: Center for Migration Studies of New York.

Thomas, Clive Y. 1988. *The Poor and the Powerless: Economic Policy and Change in the Caribbean.* New York: Monthly Review Press.

Vélez-Ibáñez, Carlos. 1983. *Rituals of Marginality: Politics, Process, and Culture Change in Urban Central Mexico, 1969–74.* Berkeley and Los Angeles: University of California Press.

Wolf, Eric. 1982. *Europe and the People without History.* Berkeley and Los Angeles: University of California Press.

Chapter 6: Gangs, Politics, and Dilemmas of Global Restructuring in Jamaica

NOTE

1. The fieldwork on which this study was based was conducted in 1978 and 1979 and later during the summers of 1984, 1988, 1992, and 1996. During 1996, my research was seriously limited by local unrest, which made working in Oceanview nearly impossible. Nonetheless, I managed to do some interviewing and to follow the news coverage so that I could document how the violence was represented and explained within the mainstream. Over the years, my research, data analysis, and write-ups were funded by fellowships and grants from Stanford University, the Fulbright-Hays Program, the Wenner-Gren Foundation for Anthropological Research, the Dorothy Danforth Compton Fellowship Program, the Ford Foundation, and faculty professional development grants from the University of Louisville's Committee on Academic Excellence and the University of Tennessee's Professional Development Awards Program. Furthermore, fieldwork would not have been possible without the cooperation and support I received from those who consented to participate in my research, among them senior and junior members of Oceanview's two major gang networks, police officers, PNP and JLP activists, community organizers for government-sponsored urban redevelopment and social welfare agencies, and members of the local PTA. Correspondence and telephone conversations were important sources of data when travel to Jamaica was impossible. When travel to Jamaica was possible, support and guidance from the individuals to whom I have assigned the pseudonyms Ras John and Beulah Brown in my publications were key to my ability to maintain connections to Oceanview and its diaspora elsewhere in Kingston and in the United States. Comments on an earlier version of this chapter from David Hakken, Hanna Lessinger, and Merrill Singer were helpful and greatly appreciated, as was the chance to publish my work in

Perspectives in U.S. Marxist Anthropology (Hakken and Lessinger 1987). More recently, I must express my heartfelt thanks to Gina Ulysse and Deborah D'Amico for their comments on this piece as well as their warmly appreciated encouragement.

2. For a journalistic account of posses in Jamaica and the United States, see Gunst (1995). For an examination of the political and economic dynamics of Kingston's downtown neighborhoods in the late 1990s, see Price (2004). Gray (2004) offers a general analysis of the political culture of the urban poor. See Ulysse (1999, 2007) for an insightful analysis of the gender, class, and color dynamics involved in downtown economic life, particularly from the perspective of Informal Commercial Importers.

3. This combination of income strategies is often achieved within households if not by individuals.

4. Even small businesses were on the margins of solvency. Small proprietors and own-account tradesmen are often compelled to seek supplementary income from state/party contracts.

5. Thanks are due to Elliott Leib and Jake Homiak, who have done research on the Rastafari movement, for reminding me that Rastafarians, particularly the Twelve Tribes of Israel sect, encouraged rival gang leaders to join forces and organize a truce. See White (1983, 299–300).

6. Varying explanations exist regarding the Green Bay affair. According to PNP supporters, the Central Kingston gang was involved in the JLP's destabilization campaign. The police claim that the gang was involved in serious criminal offenses. White claims that the gang was reputed to be an intractable gang of PNP clients (1983, 299).

7. Girling (1983) pointed out that the CBI was also flawed in that it excludes many labor-intensive industries such as textiles, footwear, and leather goods from its concessions. Rum and sugar were still subject to quotas. Moreover, the lack of markets was not the crux of the balance-of-payments deficit problem. The real problem lay in the low prices received for export commodities. Since the CBI was put into effect in 1984, it has been amended several times. The Caribbean Basin Economic Recovery Expansion Act of 1990 (CBI II) made the program permanent and made provisions for improvements. For instance, "certain import-sensitive articles originally ineligible for duty-free treatment (handbags, luggage, flat goods, work gloves, and certain leather wearing apparel) have been accorded by the 1990 amendment preferential tariff treatment at reduced but still positive rates" (Congressional Research Service Issue Brief IB95050, "Caribbean Basin Interim Trade Program: CBI/NAFTA Parity," updated February 12, 2003, http://www .ncseonline.org/nle/crsreports/03Apr/IB95050.pdf). Ten years after CBI II, U.S. President Bill Clinton enacted the Caribbean Basin Trade Partnership Act to ensure export markets for U.S. goods and services. CBI amendments have authorized tariff and quota provisions that are identical with or very similar to those accorded Mexico under NAFTA.

8. As a result of local government elections held in July 1986, the PNP restored its control over the KSAC (*Weekly Gleaner* 1986).

9. Although this project was initiated and organized by a nonpartisan group of activists, the benefactors—among them service club members, major Jamaican businesses, banks, and the United States Agency for International Development—were not necessarily nonpartisan in their loyalties and agendas. Furthermore, such a private, nongovernmental program is compatible with current national policies, which limit government support

of social services and encourage private initiative in development. This approach was integral to neoliberalism.

10. I am alluding to the April 1978 One Love Peace Concert concert organized to support the Peace Movement. Bob Marley was the featured performer. After calling Manley and Seaga on stage, he sang "One Love" while locking hands with the two political leaders in a raised pyramid.

REFERENCES

African Mirror. 1978. Jamaica's Dilemma: Is it Manley's Fault? (October): 39–46.

Ambursley, Fitzroy. 1983. Jamaica: From Michael Manley to Edward Seaga. In *Crisis in the Caribbean,* ed. Fitzroy Ambursley and Robin Cohen, 72–104. Kingston, Jamaica: Heinemann.

Amnesty International. 2001a. Jamaica. *Amnesty International Report 2001.* http://web .amnesty.org/web/ar2001.nsf/webamrcountries/JAMAICA?OpenDocument.

———. 2001b. Jamaica: Police Killings—A Human Rights Emergency. Press release, April 10. AI-index AMR 38/010/2001, http://web.amnesty.org/library/Index/ENGAMR3801 02001?open&of=ENG-JAM.

———. 2001c. Killings and Violence by Police: How Many More Victims? Report, April 10. AI-index AMR 38/003/2001, http://web.amnesty.org/library/Index/ ENGAMR380032001?open&of=ENG-JAM.

Austin, Diane J. 1984. *Urban Life in Kingston, Jamaica: The Culture and Class Ideology of Two Neighborhoods.* New York: Gordon and Breach Science.

Barry, Tom, Beth Wood, and Deb Preusch. 1984. *The Other Side of Paradise: Foreign Control in the Caribbean.* New York: Grove Press.

Bonilla, Frank. 1962. The Favelas of Rio: The Rundown Barrio in the City. *Dissent* 9: 383–86.

Castells, Manuel. 1982. Squatters and Politics in Latin America: A Comparative Analysis of Urban Social Movements in Chile, Peru, and Mexico. In *Towards a Political Economy of Urbanization in Third World Countries,* ed. Helen Safa, 249–82. Delhi: Oxford University Press.

Clarke, Colin. 1971. This Changing World: The Development and Redevelopment of the Waterfront in Kingston, Jamaica. *Geography* 56 (252): 237–40.

Daily Gleaner. 1984. PNP Questions State's Ability to Cope with Economic Strains. July 3.

Department of Statistics, Jamaica. 1970. *Demographic Atlas of Urban Areas: The Kingston Metropolitan Area.* Vol. 6, part 1. Kingston, Jamaica: Division of Census and Surveys, Commonwealth Caribbean Population Census.

Espeut, Peter. 2001. Reaping the Whirlwind. *Weekly Gleaner,* July 19–25, 7.

Fagen, Richard. 1983. Theories of Development: The Question of Class Struggle. *Monthly Review* 35 (4): 13–24.

Girling, Robert. 1983. Pulling the Aid Plug. *South* (January): 63.

Girvan, Norman, and Richard Bernal. 1982. The IMF and the Foreclosure of Development Options: The Case of Jamaica. *Monthly Review* 33 (9): 34–48.

Gray, Obika. 2004. *Demeaned but Empowered: The Social Power of the Urban Poor in Jamaica.* Kingston, Jamaica: University of the West Indies Press.

Gunst, Laurie. 1995. *Born Fi' Dead: A Journey through the Jamaican Posse Underworld.* New York: Henry Holt.

Hakken, David, and Hanna Lessinger, eds. 1987. *Perspectives in U.S. Marxist Anthropology.* Boulder, CO: Westview Press.

Hall, Stuart, Charles Critcher, Tony Jefferson, and John Clarke. 1978. *Policing the Crisis: Mugging, the State, and Law and Order.* New York: Holmes and Meier.

Harrison, Faye V. 1982. Semiproletarianization and the Structure of Socioeconomic and Political Relations in a Jamaican Slum. PhD diss., Anthropology Department, Stanford University.

———. 1987. Crime, Class, and Politics in Jamaica. *TransAfrica Forum* 5 (1): 29–38.

———. 1989. Drug Trafficking in World Capitalism: A Perspective on Jamaican Posses in the U.S. *Social Justice* 16 (4): 115–31.

———. 1990. Jamaica and the International Drug Economy. *TransAfrica Forum* 7 (3): 49–57.

Headley, Bernard D. 1985. Mr. Seaga's Jamaica: An Inside Look. *Monthly Review* 37 (4): 35–42.

———. 1996. *The Jamaican Crime Scene: A Perspective.* Washington, DC: Howard University Press.

Keith, Sherry, and Robert Girling. 1978. Caribbean Conflict: Jamaica and the United States. *NACLA Report on the Americas* 12 (3): 3–36.

Lacey, Terry. 1977. *Violence and Politics in Jamaica, 1960–70.* Manchester, U.K.: Manchester University Press.

Laguerre, Michel. 1982. *Urban Life in the Caribbean: A Study of a Haitian Urban Community.* Cambridge, MA: Schenkman.

Leeds, Anthony. 1973. Locality Power in Relation to Supralocal Power Institutions. In *Urban Anthropology: Cross-Cultural Studies of Urbanization,* ed. Aidan Southall, 15–42. New York: Oxford University Press.

Lessinger, Johanna. 1985. Nobody Here to Yell at Me: Political Activism among Petty Retail Traders in an Indian City. In *Markets and Marketing,* ed. Stuart Plattner, 309–31. Lanham, MD: University Press of America.

National Planning Agency. 1978. *Five Year Development Plan, 1978–82.* Kingston, Jamaica: Ministry of Finance and Planning.

New York Times. 2001. Violence Subsides in Jamaica, but Wounds Still Fester. July 12, A3.

Patterson, Orlando. 2001. The Roots of Conflict in Jamaica. *The New York Times,* July 23, http://www.nytimes.com/2001/07/23/opinion/23PATT.html.

Portes, Alejandro, and John Walton. 1976. *Urban Latin America: The Political Condition from Above and Below.* Austin: University of Texas Press.

Price, Charles. 2004. What the Zeeks Uprising Reveals: Development Issues, Moral Economy, and the Urban Lumpenproletariat in Jamaica. *Urban Anthropology and Studies of Cultural Systems and World Economic Development* 33 (1): 73–113.

Roberts, Bryan. 1978. *Cities of Peasants: The Political Economy of Urbanization in the Third World.* Beverly Hills, CA: Sage.

Robotham, Don. 2001. The Cocaine Connection. *Weekly Gleaner (N. A.),* July 26–August 1, 8–9.

Schechter, Danny. 2001. Toward an "Overstanding" of Genoa and Jamaica. MediaChannel. http://www.mediachannel.org/views/dissector/overstanding.shtml.

Singer, Paul. 1982. Neighborhood Movements in Sao Paulo. In *Towards a Political Economy of Urbanization in Third World Countries,* ed. Helen Safa, 283–303. Delhi: Oxford University Press.

Stephens, Evelyne Huber, and John D. Stephens. 1986. *Democratic Socialism in Jamaica: The Political Movement and Social Transformation in Dependent Capitalism.* Princeton, NJ: Princeton University Press.

Stone, Carl. 1973. *Class, Race, and Political Behavior in Urban Jamaica.* Mona, Jamaica: Institute of Social and Economic Research, University of the West Indies.

———. 1980. *Democracy and Clientelism in Jamaica.* New Brunswick, NJ: Transaction Books.

Susser, Ida. 1982. *Norman Street: Poverty and Politics in an Urban Neighborhood.* New York: Oxford University Press.

Swartz, Marc. 1968. Introduction to *Local-Level Politics: Social and Cultural Perspectives,* 1–51. Chicago: Aldine.

Ulysse, Gina. 1999. Uptown Ladies and Downtown Women: Female Representations of Class Color in Jamaica. In *Representations of Blackness and the Performance of Identities,* ed. Jean M. Rahier, 147–72. Westport, CT: Greenwood.

———. 2007. *Downtown Ladies: Informal Commercial Importing, a Haitian Anthropologist and Self-Making in Jamaica.* Chicago: University of Chicago Press.

Urban Upgrading. n.d. *Introduction to Urban Upgrading.* Kingston, Jamaica: Ministry of Local Government.

USA Today. 2001. Jamaican Soldiers on Guard. July 11, 11A.

Vélez-Ibañez, Carlos G. 1983. *Rituals of Marginality: Politics, Process, and Culture Change in Urban Central Mexico, 1969–74.* Berkeley and Los Angeles: University of California Press.

Weekly Gleaner. 1983a. Church Council Calls For New Elections. December 12, 1.

———. 1983b. JLP Returned to Power. December 5, 1.

———. 1984a. Economic Hardships. Carl Stone column. December 22, 11.

———. 1984b. KSAC Council Dissolved. October 22, 1.

———. 1984c. Nation within a Nation. John Hearne column. May 28, 13.

———. 1985a. Alcoa Closing. February 11, 1.

———. 1985b. Mr. Seaga's Government. November 11, 11.

———. 1985c. The PNP's Problem. Stone column. October 7, 11.

———. 1986. PNP Sweeps Local Government Polls. August 4, 1, 3.

———. 2001a. Chaos Spreads. July 12–18, 2.

———. 2001b. JDF [Jamaica Defense Force] Empowered. July 12–18, 3.

———. 2001c. Politicians Are Dons' Prisoners, Golding Says. May 17–23, 3.

———. 2001d. Terror in the City. July 12–18, 1–3.

White, Timothy. 1983. *Catch a Fire: The Life of Bob Marley.* New York: Holt, Rinehart and Winston.

Worsley, Peter. 1972. Frantz Fanon and the Lumpenproletariat. In *The Socialist Register,* ed. Ralph Miliband and John Savile, 193–230. London: Merlin Press.

———. 1984. *The Three Worlds: Culture and World Development.* Chicago: University of Chicago Press.

Chapter 7: The Gendered Violence of Structural Adjustment

REFERENCES

Abrahams, Roger D. 1983. *The Man-of-Words in the West Indies: Performance and the Emergence of Creole Culture.* Baltimore: Johns Hopkins University Press.

Antrobus, Peggy. 1989. Crisis, Challenge and the Experiences of Caribbean Women. *Caribbean Quarterly* 35 (1–2): 17–28.

Barry, Tom, Beth Wood, and Deb Preusch. 1984. The *Other Side of Paradise: Foreign Control in the Caribbean.* New York: Grove.

Basch, Linda, Nina Glic Schiller, and Cristina Szanton Blanc. 1994. *Nations Unbound: Transnational Projects, Postcolonial Predicaments, and Deterritorialized Nation-States.* Langhorne, PA: Gordon and Breach Science.

Beckford, George. 1972. *Persistent Poverty: Underdevelopment in Plantation Economies of the Third World.* New York: Oxford University Press.

Bolles, A. Lynn. 1991. Surviving Manley and Seaga: Case Studies of Women's Responses to Structural Adjustment Policies. *Review of Radical Political Economy* 23 (3–4): 20–36.

———. 1992. Common Ground of Creativity. *Cultural Survival Quarterly,* Winter: 34–37.

Campbell, Mavis C. 1977. Marronage in Jamaica: Its Origins in the Seventeenth Century. In *Comparative Perspectives on Slavery in New World Plantation Societies,* ed. Vera Rubin and Arthur Tuden. *Annals of the New York Academy of Sciences* 292: 446–80.

Carnegie, Charles V. 1987. Is Family Land an Institution? In *Afro-Caribbean Villages in Historical Perspective. ACIJ Research Review* 2: 83–99.

D'Amico-Samuels, Deborah. 1991. Undoing Fieldwork: Personal, Political, Theoretical, and Methodological Implications. In *Decolonizing Anthropology: Moving Further toward an Anthropology for Liberation,* ed. Faye V. Harrison, 68–87. Washington, DC: American Anthropological Association.

Deere, Carmen Diana, Peggy Antrobus, Lynn Bolles, Edwin Melendez, Peter Phillips, Marcia River, and Helen Safa. 1990. *In the Shadows of the Sun: Caribbean Development Alternatives and U.S. Policy.* Boulder, CO: Westview.

Edie, Carlene. 1990. *Democracy by Default: Dependency and Clientelism in Jamaica.* Boulder, CO: Lynne Rienner.

Enloe, Cynthia. 1989. *Bananas, Beaches and Bases: Making Feminist Sense of International Politics.* Berkeley and Los Angeles: University of California Press.

Feldman, Allen. 1991. *Formations of Violence: The Narrative of the Body and Political Terror in Northern Ireland.* Chicago: University of Chicago Press.

Ferguson, James. 1992. Jamaica: Stories of Poverty. *Race and Class* 34 (1): 61–72.

Harrison, Faye V. 1987a. Crime, Class, and Politics in Jamaica. *TransAfrica Forum* 5 (1): 29–38.

———. 1987b. Gangs, Grassroots Politics, and the Crisis of Dependent Capitalism in Jamaica. In *Perspectives in U.S. Marxist Anthropology,* ed. David Hakken and Hanna Lessinger, 186–210. Boulder, CO: Westview.

———. 1988. The Politics of Social Outlawry in Urban Jamaica. *Urban Anthropology and Studies in Cultural Systems and World Economic Development* 17 (2–3): 259–77.

———. 1990. Jamaica and the International Drug Economy. *TransAfrica Forum* 7 (3): 49–57.

———. 1991a. Ethnography as Politics. In *Decolonizing Anthropology: Moving Further toward an Anthropology for Liberation,* ed. Faye V. Harrison, 88–109. Washington, DC: American Anthropological Association.

———. 1991b. Women in Jamaica's Urban Informal Economy: Insights from a Kingston Slum. In *Third World Women and the Politics of Feminism,* ed. Chandra T. Mohanty, Ann Russo, and Lourdes Torres, 173–96. Bloomington: Indiana University Press.

Haviland, William. 1990. *Cultural Anthropology.* 6th ed. Fort Worth, TX: Holt, Rinehart and Winston.

Ho, Christine G. T. 1993. The Internationalization of Kinship and the Feminization of Caribbean Migration: The Case of Afro-Trinidadian Immigrants in Los Angeles. *Human Organization* 52 (1): 32–40.

Köhler, Gernot. 1978. *Global Apartheid.* World Order Models Project Working Paper No. 7. New York: Institute for World Order.

Lacey, Terry. 1977. *Violence and Politics in Jamaica, 1960–70: Internal Security in a Developing Country.* Manchester, U.K.: Manchester University Press.

Le Franc, Elsie, ed. 1994. *Consequences of Structural Adjustment: A Review of the Jamaican Experience.* Kingston, Jamaica: Canoe Press.

Lewis, Gordon K. 1968. *The Growth of the Modern West Indies.* New York: Monthly Review Press.

McAfee, Kathy. 1991. *Storm Signals: Structural Adjustment and Development Alternatives in the Caribbean.* Boston: South End Press.

National Labor Committee. 1992. *Preliminary Report: Paying to Lose Our Jobs.* New York: National Labor Committee Education Fund in Support of Worker and Human Rights in Central America.

Pan American Health Organization/World Health Organization. 1992. *The Health of Women in the English Speaking Caribbean.* Bridgetown, Barbados: Pan American Health Organization, Offices of Caribbean Program Coordination.

Phillips, Daphene. 1994. The IMF, Structural Adjustment and Health in the Caribbean: Policy Change in Health Care in Trinidad and Tobago. *21st Century Policy Review* 2 (1–2): 129–49.

Race and Class. 1992. The New Conquistadors. Special issue, 34 (1): 1–114.

Sacks, Karen Brodkin. 1984. Computers, Ward Secretaries, and a Walkout in a Southern Hospital. In *My Troubles Are Going to Have Trouble with Me: Everyday Trials and Triumphs of Women Workers,* ed. Karen Brodkin Sacks and Dorothy Remy, 173–90. New Brunswick, NJ: Rutgers University Press.

Safa, Helen. 1995. *The Myth of the Male Breadwinner: Women and Industrialization in the Caribbean.* Boulder, CO: Westview.

Sparr, Pamela. 1992. How We Got into This Mess and Ways to Get Out. *Ms.,* March/April, 29–36.

———, ed. 1994. *Mortgaging Women's Lives: Feminist Critiques of Structural Adjustment.* London: Zed Books.

Statistical Institute of Jamaica. 1991. *Statistical Yearbook of Jamaica.* Kingston, Jamaica: Statistical Institute of Jamaica.

Thomas, Clive Y. 1988. *The Poor and the Powerless: Economic Policy and Change in the Caribbean.* New York: Monthly Review Press.

Vélez-Ibañez, Carlos. 1983. *Rituals of Marginality: Politics, Process, and Culture Change in Urban Central Mexico, 1969–74.* Berkeley and Los Angeles: University of California Press.

Weekly Gleaner. 1988a. Free Zone Operators 'Going Public' with Grouse. March 28, 5.

———. 1988b. JIC [Joint Industrial Council] for Free Zone Workers. March 14, 13.

———. 1988c. More Garment Workers Strike. March 21, 24.

———. 1988d. Textile Workers Strike to Get 'A Better Deal'. March 14, 28.

———. 1993a. Landslide Election Marred by Bungling, Violence. April 2, page 4.

———. 1993b. Nomination Day Violence. March 19, page 2.

———. 1993c. Peace Treaty Signed. February 26, page 3.

Whitehead, Tony Larry. 1986. Breakdown, Resolution, and Coherence: The Fieldwork Experiences of a Big, Brown, Pretty-Talking Man in a West Indian Community. In *Self, Sex, and Gender in Cross-Cultural Fieldwork,* ed. Tony Larry Whitehead and Mary Ellen Conaway, 213–39. Urbana: University of Illinois Press.

Wilson, Peter J. 1973. *Crab Antics: The Social Anthropology of English-Speaking Societies of the Caribbean.* Repr. 1995, Prospect Heights, IL: Waveland Press.

Wolf, Eric. 1990. Distinguished Lecture: Facing Power—Old Insights, New Questions. *American Anthropologist* 92 (3): 586–96.

Chapter 8: Everyday Neoliberalism in Cuba

NOTE

1. My understanding of this relationship is derived from two sources. First, I owe a great deal to Jorge's account of his neighbors, whom he considered friends. Second, I also am indebted to the Canadian who married Jorge's neighbor. Through Jorge's encouragement, I met his Canadian friend over the telephone and maintained intermittent communication with him for at least two or three years. Because he traveled regularly to Cuba, he agreed to deliver letters and gifts I wanted to send to Jorge's family. After talking with him on the phone and sending him packages for two years, I eventually met him face-to-face during a trip to Canada. At that meeting, I learned more about his experiences as a Canadian tourist who eventually became a member of an extended network of Cuban relatives and friends.

REFERENCES

Abu-Lughod, Lila. 1991. Writing against Culture. In *Recapturing Anthropology: Working in the Present,* ed. Richard G. Fox, 137–62. Santa Fe, NM: School of American Research Press.

Anderson, Patricia, and Michael Witter. 1994. Crisis, Adjustment and Social Change. In *Consequences of Structural Adjustment: A Review of the Jamaican Experience,* ed. Elsie Le Franc, 1–55. Kingston, Jamaica: Canoe Press.

Barriteau, V. Eudine. 1996. Structural Adjustment Policies in the Caribbean: A Feminist Perspective. *NWSA Journal* 8: 142–56.

Bengelsdorf, Carollee. 1997. [Re]Considering Cuban Women in a Time of Troubles. In *Daughters of Caliban: Caribbean Women in the Twentieth Century,* ed. Consuelo Lopez Springfield, 229–55. Bloomington: Indiana University Press.

Calderón, Mirta Rodriguez. 1995. Life in the Special Period: "Cuba Adapting to a Post-Soviet World." *NACLA Report on the Americas* 29 (2): 18–19.

Daniel, Yvonne. 1995. *Rumba: Dance and Social Change in Contemporary Cuba.* Bloomington: Indiana University Press.

Davidson, Julia O'Connell. 1996. Sex Tourism in Cuba. *Race and Class* 38 (1): 39–48.

Diaz, Elena, Esperanza Fernandez, and Tania Caram. 1996. *Turismo y Prostitucion en Cuba.* Havana, Cuba: Facultad Latinoamericana de Ciencias Sociales.

Encyclopedia of World Cultures. 1995. Cubans. 8: 86–90. New York: G. K. Hall.

Enloe, Cynthia. 1989. *Bananas, Beaches, and Bases: Making Feminist Sense of International Politics.* Berkeley and Los Angeles: University of California Press.

Fernandez, Nadine. 1999. Back to the Future? Women, Race, and Tourism in Cuba. In *Sun, Sex, and Gold: Tourism and Sex Work in the Caribbean,* ed. Kamala Kempadoo, 81–89. Lanham, MD: Rowman and Littlefield.

Fusco, Coco. 1996. Hustling for Dollars. *Ms.,* September/October, 62–70.

Harrison, Faye V. 1982. Semiproletarianism and the Structure of Socioeconomic and Political Relations in a Jamaican Slum. Unpublished PhD diss., Stanford University.

———. 1987. Gangs, Grassroots Politics, and the Crisis of Dependent Capitalism in Jamaica. In *Perspectives in U.S. Marxist Anthropology,* ed. David Hakken and Hanna Lessinger, 186–210. Boulder, CO: Westview.

———. 1988. The Politics of Social Outlawry in Urban Jamaica. *Urban Anthropology* 17 (2–3): 259–77.

———. 1990. Jamaica and the International Drug Economy. *TransAfrica Forum* 7 (3): 49–57.

———. 1991. Women in Jamaica's Urban Informal Economy: Insights from a Kingston Slum. In *Third World Women and the Politics of Feminism,* ed. Chandra T. Mohanty, Ann Russo, and Lourdes Torres, 173–96. Bloomington: Indiana University Press.

———. 1997. The Gendered Politics and Violence of Structural Adjustment: A View from Jamaica. In *Situated Lives: Gender and Culture in Everyday Life,* ed. Louise Lamphere, Helena Ragoné, and Patricia Zavella, 451–68. New York: Routledge.

———. 2002. Global Apartheid, Foreign Policy, and Human Rights. *Souls: A Critical Journal of Black Politics, Culture, and Society* 4 (3): 48–68.

Herrera, Georgina. 2000. Poetry, Prostitution, and Gender Esteem. In *Afro-Cuban Voices: On Race and Identity in Contemporary Cuba,* ed. Pedro Perez Sarduy and Jean Stubbs, 118–26. Gainesville: University Press of Florida.

Hoetink, H. 1985. "Race" and Color in the Caribbean. In *Caribbean Contours,* ed. Sidney W. Mintz and Sally Prices, 55–84. Baltimore: Johns Hopkins University Press.

McGarrity, Gayle. 1996. Cubans in Jamaica: A Previously Neglected Segment of the Cuban Diaspora. *Caribbean Quarterly* 42 (1): 55–83.

Mesh, Cynthia J. 1997. Empowering the Mother Tongue: The Creole Movement in Guadaloupe. In *Daughters of Caliban: Caribbean Women in the Twentieth Century,* ed. Consuelo Lopez Springfield, 18–38. Bloomington: Indiana University Press.

Momsen, Janet H., ed. 1993. *Women and Change in the Caribbean: A Pan-Caribbean Perspective.* Bloomington: Indiana University Press.

NACLA Report on the Americas. 1995. *Cuba: Adapting to a Post-Soviet World* 29 (2).

National Labor Committee. 1996. *Disney Goes to Haiti.* Video. New York: National Labor Committee.

Safa, Helen. 1995. *The Myth of the Male Breadwinner: Women and Industrialization in the Caribbean.* Boulder, CO: Westview.

Sawyer, Mark Q. 2006. *Racial Politics in Post-Revolutionary Cuba.* Cambridge: Cambridge University Press.

Senior, Olive. 1991. *Working Miracles: Women's Lives in the English-Speaking Caribbean.* Bloomington: Indiana University Press.

Smaldone, William. 1996. Observations on the Cuban Revolution. *Monthly Review* 47 (11): 20–32.

Sparr, Pamela. 1992. How We Got into This Mess and Ways to Get Out. *Ms.,* March/April, 29–36.

———, ed. 1994. *Mortgaging Women's Lives: Feminist Critiques of Structural Adjustment.* London: Zed Press.

Springfield, Consuelo Lopez, ed. 1997. *Daughters of Caliban: Caribbean Women in the Twentieth Century.* Bloomington: Indiana University Press.

Stout, Jan. 1995. Women, the Politics of Sexuality, and Cuba's Economic Crisis. *Socialist Review* 25 (1): 5–15.

Trouillot, Michel-Rolph. 1988. *Peasants and Capital: Dominica in the World Economy.* Baltimore: Johns Hopkins University Press.

———. 1992. The Caribbean Region: An Open Frontier in Anthropological Theory. *Annual Review of Anthropology* 21: 19–42.

Ulysse, Gina. 2007. *Downtown Ladies: Informal Commercial Importing, a Haitian Anthropologist and Self-Making in Jamaica.* Chicago: University of Chicago Press.

Wilson, David L. 1997. Do Maquiladoras Matter? *Monthly Review* 49 (5): 28–34.

Chapter 9: Global Apartheid at Home and Abroad

REFERENCES

Abu-Lughod, Lila. 1986. *Veiled Sentiments: Honor and Poetry in a Bedouin Society.* Berkeley and Los Angeles: University of California Press.

Alexander, M. Jacqui, and Chandra Talpade Mohanty. 1997. Introduction: Genealogies, Legacies, Movements. In *Feminist Genealogies, Colonial Legacies, Democratic Futures,* ed. M. Jacqui Alexander and Chandra Talpade Mohanty, xiii–xlii. New York: Routledge.

Ansley, Frances. 1992. U.S.-Mexico Free Trade from the Bottom: A Postcard from the Border. *Texas Journal of Women and the Law* 1 (2): 193–248.

Appadurai, Arjun. 1991. Global Ethnoscapes: Notes and Queries for a Transnational Anthropology. In *Recapturing Anthropology: Working in the Present,* ed. Richard G. Fox, 191–210. Santa Fe, NM: School of American Research Press.

Balibar, Etienne. 1991. Is There a "Neo-Racism"? In *Race, Nation, Class: Ambiguous Identities,* ed. Etienne Balibar and Immanuel Wallerstein, 15–28. New York: Verso.

Basch, Linda, Nina Glick Schiller, and Cristina Szanton Blanc. 1994. *Nations Unbound: Transnational Projects, Postcolonial Predicaments, and Deterritorialized Nation-States.* Langhorne, PA: Gordon and Breach Sciences.

Bourgois, Philippe. 1995. *In Search of Respect: Selling Crack in El Barrio.* New York: Cambridge University Press.

———. 1996. Confronting Anthropology, Education, and Inner-City Apartheid. *American Anthropologist* 98 (2): 249–58.

Buck, Pem Davidson. 2001. *Worked to the Bone: Race, Class, Power, and Privilege in Kentucky.* New York: Monthly Review Press.

Collins, Patricia Hill. 1991. *Black Feminist Thought: Knowledge, Consciousness, and the Politics of Empowerment.* New York: Routledge.

———. 1998. *Fighting Words: Black Women and the Search for Justice.* Minneapolis: University of Minnesota Press.

Collins, Sheila. 1995. *Let Them Eat Ketchup! The Politics of Poverty and Inequality.* New York: Cornerstone Books, Monthly Review Press.

Davis, Angela Y. 2003. *Are Prisons Obsolete?* New York: Seven Stories Press.

Enloe, Cynthia. 1989. *Bananas, Beaches and Bases: Making Feminist Sense of International Politics.* Berkeley and Los Angeles: University of California Press.

Fanon, Frantz. 2004 [1961]. *The Wretched of the Earth.* New York: Grove Press.

Ford-Smith, Honor. 1997. Ring Ding in a Tight Corner: Sistren, Collective Democracy, and the Organization of Cultural Production. In *Feminist Genealogies, Colonial Legacies, Democratic Futures,* ed. M. Jacqui Alexander and Chandra Talpade Mohanty, 213–58. New York: Routledge.

Gilroy, Paul. 1991. *"There Ain't No Black in the Union Jack": The Cultural Politics of Race and Nation.* Chicago: University of Chicago Press.

Gooding-Williams, Robert, ed. 1993. *Reading Rodney King, Reading Urban Uprising.* New York: Routledge.

Gupta, Akhil, and James Ferguson. 1992. Beyond "Culture": Space, Identity, and the Politics of Difference. *Cultural Anthropology* 7 (1): 6–23.

Hall, Stuart, Charles Critcher, Tony Jefferson, and John Clarke. 1978. *Policing the Crisis: Mugging, the State, and Law and Order.* New York: Holmes and Meier.

Harrison, Faye V. 1997a. Gender, Sexuality, and Health in a Turn-of-the-Century "Black Metropolis." *Medical Anthropology Quarterly* 11 (4): 448–53.

———. 1997b. The Gendered Politics and Violence of Structural Adjustment: A View from Jamaica. In *Situated Lives: Gender and Culture in Everyday Life,* ed. Louise Lamphere, Helena Ragoné, and Patricia Zavella, 451–68. New York: Routledge.

———. 2000. Facing Racism and the Moral Responsibility of Human Rights Knowledge. *New York Academy of Sciences* 925: 45–69.

———. 2001. Imagining a Global Community United against Global Racism. *Anthropology News* 42 (9): 22–23.

———. 2002. Subverting the Cultural Logics of Marked and Unmarked Racisms in the Global Era. In *Discrimination and Toleration: New Perspectives,* ed. Kirsten Hastrup and George Ulrich, 97–126. The Hague, Netherlands: Martinus Nijhoff/Kluwer Law International.

———. 2004. Global Apartheid, Environmental Degradation, and Women's Activism for Sustainable Well-Being: A Conceptual and Theoretical Overview. *Urban Anthropology and Studies of Cultural Systems and World Economic Development* 33 (1): 1–35.

———, ed. 2005. *Resisting Racism and Xenophobia: Global Perspectives on Race, Gender, and Human Rights.* Walnut Creek, CA: AltaMira.

Hartigan, John Jr. 1999. *Racial Situations: Class Predicaments of Whiteness in Detroit.* Princeton, NJ: Princeton University Press.

Kesić, Vesna. 1996. Never Again a War: Women's Bodies Are Battlefields. In *Look at the World through Women's Eyes: Plenary Speeches from the NGO Forum on Women, Beijing 95,* ed. Eva Friedlander, 51–53. New York: Women, Ink.

Köhler, Gernot. 1978 [1993]. Global Apartheid. Working Paper No. 7, World Order Models Project. New York: Institute for World Order. Reprinted in *Talking about People: Readings in Contemporary Cultural Anthropology,* ed. William A. Haviland and Robert J. Gordon, 262–68. Mountain View, CA: Mayfield.

Leeds, Anthony. 1994. Cities and Countryside in Anthropology. In *Cities, Classes, and the Social Order,* ed. Roger Sanjek, 51–69. Ithaca, NY: Cornell University Press.

Lynch, Owen M. 1994. Urban Anthropology, Postmodernist Cities, and Perspectives. *City and Society Annual Review,* 35–52.

Mies, Maria, Veronika Bennholdt-Thomsen, and Claudia von Werlhof. 1988. *Women and the Last Colony.* London: Zed Books.

Mohanty, Chandra Talpade. 1997. Women Workers and Capitalist Scripts: Ideologies of Domination, Common Interests, and the Politics of Solidarity. In *Feminist Genealogies, Colonial Legacies, Democratic Futures,* ed. M. Jacqui Alexander and Chandra T. Mohanty, 3–29. New York: Routledge.

Mullings, Leith. 1997. *On Our Own Terms: Race, Class, and Gender in the Lives of African American Women.* New York: Routledge.

Nash, June. 1994. Global Integration and Subsistence Insecurity. *American Anthropologist* 96 (1): 7–30.

National Labor Committee. 1996. *Disney Goes to Haiti.* Video. New York: National Labor Committee.

Newman, Katherine S. 1988. *Falling from Grace: The Experience of Downward Mobility in the American Middle Class.* New York: Vintage Books.

Ong, Aihwa. 1987. *Spirits of Resistance and Capitalist Discipline: Factory Women in Malaysia.* Albany: State University of New York.

———. 1991. The Gender and Labor Politics of Postmodernity. *Annual Review of Anthropology* 20: 279–309.

Ortner, Sherry. 1991. Reading America: Preliminary Notes on Class and Culture. In *Recapturing Anthropology: Working in the Present,* ed. Richard G. Fox, 163–89. Santa Fe, NM: School of American Research Press.

Page, Helán E. and R. Brooke Thomas. 1994. White Public Space and the Construction of White Privilege in U.S. Health Care: Fresh Concepts and a New Model of Analysis. *Medical Anthropology Quarterly,* New Series 8(1): 109–16.

Pierce, Paulette, and Brackette F. Williams. 1996. "And Your Prayers Shall Be Answered through the Womb of a Woman": Insurgent Masculine Redemption and the Nation of Islam. In *Women Out of Place: The Gender of Agency and the Race of Nationality,* ed. Brackette F. Williams, 186–215. New York: Routledge.

Price, Sally. 1993. *Co-wives and Calabashes.* 2nd ed. Ann Arbor: University of Michigan Press.

Ransby, Barbara. 1996. U.S.: The Black Poor and the Politics of Expendability. *Race and Class* 38 (2): 1–12.

Robinson, William. 1996. Globalization: Nine Theses on Our Epoch. *Race and Class* 38 (2): 13–31.

Sacks, Karen Brodkin. 1984. Computers, Ward Secretaries, and a Walkout in a Southern Hospital. In *My Troubles Are Going to Have Trouble with Me: Everyday Trials and Triumphs of Women Workers,* ed. Karen Brodkin Sacks and Dorothy Remy, 173–90. New Brunswick, NJ: Rutgers University Press.

Sen, Gita, and Caren Grown. 1987. *Development, Crises, and Alternative Vision: Third World Women's Perspectives.* New York: Monthly Review Press.

Sentencing Project. 2006. Factsheet: Women in Prison. http://www.sentencingproject .org/Admin%5CDocuments%5Cpublications%5Cwomen_factsheet_prison.pdf.

Sparr, Pamela. 1992. How We Got into This Mess and Ways to Get Out. *Ms.,* March/April, 29–35.

———, ed. 1994. *Mortgaging Women's Lives: Feminist Critiques of Structural Adjustment.* London: Zed Books.

UNICEF. 1989. *The Invisible Adjustment: Poor Women and the Economic Crisis.* Santiago, Chile: The Americas and the Caribbean Regional Office, Women in Development Regional Office.

Valentine, Bettylou. 1978. *Hustling and Other Hand Work: Life Styles in the Ghetto.* New York: Free Press.

Whitehead, Tony L. 1997. Urban Low-Income African American Males, HIV/AIDS, and Gender Identity. *Medical Anthropology Quarterly* 11 (4): 411–47.

Williams, Brackette F. 1996. Introduction: Mannish Women and Gender after the Act. In *Women Out of Place,* ed. Brackette F. Williams, 1–33. New York: Routledge.

Winant, Howard. 1994. Racial Formation and Hegemony: Global and Local Developments. In *Racial Conditions: Politics, Theory, Comparisons.* Minneapolis: University of Minnesota Press.

Chapter 10: Justice for All

REFERENCES

Edelman, Marc. 1999. *Peasants against Globalization: Rural Social Movements in Costa Rica.* Stanford, CA: Stanford University Press.

Harrison, Faye V. 1995. The Persistent Power of "Race" in the Cultural and Political Economy of Racism. *Annual Review of Anthropology* 24: 47–74.

———, ed. 1997. *Decolonizing Anthropology: Moving toward an Anthropology for Liberation.* 2nd ed. Arlington, VA: American Anthropological Association.

———. 1998. Introduction: Expanding the Discourse on "Race." *American Anthropologist* 102 (1): 609–31.

———. 2000. Facing Racism and the Moral Responsibility of Human Rights Knowledge. *Annals of the New York Academy of Sciences* 925 (December): 45–69.

———. 2002a. Global Apartheid, Foreign Policy, and Human Rights. *Souls* 4 (3): 48–68.

———. 2002b. Subverting the Cultural Logics of Marked and Unmarked Racisms in the

Global Era. In *Discrimination and Toleration: New Perspectives,* ed. Kirsten Hastrup and George Ulrich, 97–126. The Hague, Netherlands: Martinus Nijhoff/Kluwer Law International.

———. 2003. From the Chesapeake Bay to the Caribbean Sea and Back: Remapping Routes, Unburying Roots. Keynote address presented at the Southern Anthropology Society meeting, Baton Rouge, Louisiana, February 27–29.

———. 2005. What Democracy Looks Like: The Politics of a Women-Centered, Antiracist Human Rights Coalition. In *Resisting Racism and Xenophobia: Global Perspectives on Race, Gender, and Human Rights,* ed. Faye V. Harrison, 229–50. Walnut Creek, CA: AltaMira.

hooks, bell. 1989. *Talking Back: Thinking Feminist, Thinking Black.* Boston: South End Press.

Jones, Delmos. 1970. Towards a Native Anthropology. *Human Organization* 29: 251–59.

———. 1987. The Community and Organizations in the Community. In *Urban Anthropology in the United States,* ed. Leith Mullings, 115–36. New York: Columbia University Press.

———. 1993. The Culture of Achievement among the Poor: The Case of Mothers and Children in a Head Start Program. *Critique of Anthropology* 13 (3): 247–66.

———. 1995. Anthropology and the Oppressed: A Reflection on "Native" Anthropology. *NAPA Bulletin* 16: 58–70.

———. 1997. Epilogue. In *Decolonizing Anthropology: Toward an Anthropology for Liberation.* 2nd ed. Ed. Faye V. Harrison, 192–99. Arlington, VA: American Anthropological Association.

Knoxville News-Sentinel. 2003. Klan Rally Greeted with Protests in Greeneville. March 30, B5.

Leeds, Anthony. 1973. Locality Power in Relation to Supra-local Power Institutions. In *Urban Anthropology: Cross-Cultural Studies of Urbanization,* ed. Aidan Southall, 15–51. New York: Oxford University Press.

Nash, June. 1994. Global Integration and Subsistence Insecurity. *American Anthropologist* 96 (1): 7–30.

National Center for Human Rights Education. 2002. Southern Human Rights Network and Conference. http://www.nchre.org/about/shron.shtml (accessed March 14, 2002).

Project South: Institute for the Elimination of Poverty and Genocide. n.d. Global/Local Project. http://www.projectsouth.org/pages/Programs/Global/global_strategies_intro .htm.

Scheper-Hughes, Nancy. 2002. Min(d)ing the Body: On the Trail of Organ-Stealing Rumors. In *Exotic No More: Anthropology on the Front Lines,* ed. Jeremy MacClancy, 33–63. Chicago: University of Chicago Press.

Smith, Barbara Ellen. 1998. The Postmodern South: Racial Transformations and the Global Economy. In *Cultural Diversity in the South: Anthropological Contributions to a Region in Transition,* ed. Carole E. Hill and Patricia D. Beaver, 164–78. Athens: University of Georgia Press.

Stack, Carol. 1996. *Call to Home: African Americans Reclaim the Rural South.* New York: Basic Books.

Stoller, Paul. 2002. *Money Has No Smell: The Africanization of New York City.* Chicago: University of Chicago Press.

Susser, Ida. 2000. Obituary: Delmos Jones (1936–1999). *American Anthropologist* 102 (3): 581–83.

Wilson, Richard A. 1997. Representing Human Rights Violations: Social Contexts and Subjectivities. In *Human Rights, Culture, and Context,* ed. Richard A. Wilson, 134–60. London: Pluto Press.

Chapter 11: Teaching Philosophy

REFERENCES

Buck, Pem Davidson. 2001. *Worked to the Bone: Race, Class, Power and Privilege in Kentucky.* New York: Monthly Review Press.

Freire, Paulo. 1970. *Pedagogy of the Oppressed.* New York: Herder and Herder.

Harrison, Faye V. 1990. "Three Women, One Struggle": Anthropology, Performance, and Pedagogy. *Transforming Anthropology* 1 (1): 1–9.

hooks, bell. 1994. *Teaching to Transgress: Education as the Practice of Freedom.* New York: Routledge.

Chapter 12: Academia, the Free Market, and New Voices of Diversity

REFERENCES

Alvarez, Robert. 1994. Un Chilero en la Academia: Sifting, Shifting, and the Recruitment of Minorities in Anthropology. In *Race,* ed. Steven Gregory and Roger Sanjek, 257–69. New Brunswick, NJ: Rutgers University Press.

American Anthropological Association. 1995–96. *Guide: A Guide to Departments, a Directory of Members.* Arlington, VA: American Anthropological Association.

Anthropology Newsletter. 1995. Cancellation of the Anthropological Promise. Correspondence. November, 36 (8): 1, 6.

Baer, Hans. 1995. President's Column: Higher Education and the U.S. Political Economy. *Southern Anthropologist* 22 (2): 5–6.

Bolles, A. Lynn. 1995. Decolonizing Feminist Anthropology. Paper presented at the Association for Feminist Anthropology invited session, "From an Anthropology of Women to the Gendering of Anthropology." Annual meeting of the American Anthropological Association, Washington, DC, November 15–19.

Christian, Barbara. 1987. The Race for Theory. *Cultural Critique* 6 (11–19): 51–63.

Cruse, Harold. 1967. *The Crisis of the Negro Intellectual: From Its Origins to the Present.* New York: William Morrow.

Dominguez, Virginia. 1994. A Taste for "the Other": Intellectual Complicity in Racializing Practices. *Current Anthropology* 35 (4): 333–48.

duCille, Ann. 1994. The Occult of True Black Womanhood: Critical Demeanor and Black Feminist Studies. *Signs* 19 (3): 591–629.

Givens, David B., Patsy Evans, and Timothy Jablonski. 2000. 1997 Survey of Anthropology PhDs. American Anthropological Association, http://www.aaanet.org/surveys/97survey.htm.

Gregory, Steven, and Roger Sanjek, eds. 1994. *Race.* New Brunswick, NJ: Rutgers University Press.

Guinier, Lani. 1994. *The Tyranny of the Majority: Fundamental Fairness and Representative Democracy*. New York: Free Press.

———. 1998. *Lift Every Voice: Turning a Civil Rights Setback into a New Vision of Social Justice*. New York: Simon and Schuster.

Haraway, Donna. 1991. Situated Knowledges: The Science Question in Feminism and the Privilege of Partial Perspective. In *Simians, Cyborgs, and Women: The Reinvention of Nature*. New York: Routledge.

Harrison, Faye V. 1991a. Anthropology as an Agent of Transformation: Introductory Comments and Queries. In *Decolonizing Anthropology: Moving Further toward an Anthropology for Liberation,* ed. Faye V. Harrison, 1–14. Washington, DC: American Anthropological Association.

———, ed. 1991b. *Decolonizing Anthropology*. Washington, DC: American Anthropological Association.

———. 1993. Writing against the Grain: Cultural Politics of Difference in the Work of Alice Walker. *Critique of Anthropology* 13 (4): 401–27. Condensed version reprinted in *Women Writing Culture,* ed. Ruth Behar and Deborah Gordon, 233–45. Berkeley and Los Angeles: University of California Press, 1995.

———. 1995a. Auto-Ethnographic Reflections on Hierarchies in Anthropology. *Practicing Anthropology* 17 (1–2): 48–50.

———. 1995b. The Persistent Power of "Race" in the Cultural and Political Economy of Racism. *Annual Review of Anthropology* 24: 47–74.

Herrnstein, Richard J., and Charles Murray. 1994. *The Bell Curve: Intelligence and Class Structure in American Life*. New York: Free Press.

hooks, bell. 1995. Sisters of the Yam: Intellectual Life in and beyond the Academy. *Z Magazine,* November, 25–29.

Hsu, Francis. 1973. Prejudice and Its Intellectual Effect In American Anthropology: An Ethnographic Report. *American Anthropologist* 75: 1–19.

Hu De-Hart, Evelyn. 1995. The Undermining of Ethnic Studies. *The Chronicle of Higher Education,* October 20, B1–2.

Jackson, Eileen M. 1993. Whiting-Out Difference: Why U.S. Nursing Research Fails Black Families. *Medical Anthropology Quarterly* 7 (4): 363–84.

James, Joy, and Ruth Farmer, eds. 1993. *Spirit, Space, and Survival: African American Women in (White) Academe*. New York: Routledge.

Leatherman, Courtney. 1995. A Name for Herself: When Black Feminism Needed a Voice, bell hooks Was Born. *The Chronicle of Higher Education,* May 19, A22, 24.

Lutz, Catherine. 1990. The Erasure of Women's Writing in Sociocultural Anthropology. *American Ethnologist* 17 (4): 611–25.

———. 1995. The Gender of Theory. In *Women Writing Culture,* ed. Ruth Behar and Deborah A. Gordon, 249–66. Berkeley and Los Angeles: University of California Press.

Moses, Yolanda T. 1989. *Black Women in Academe: Issues and Strategies*. Washington, DC: Association of American Colleges, Project on the Status and Education of Women.

Obbo, Christine. 1990. Adventures with Fieldnotes. In *Fieldnotes: The Makings of Anthropology,* ed. Roger Sanjek, 290–302. Ithaca, NY: Cornell University Press.

Page, Helán E. 1993. Teaching Comparative Social Order and Caribbean Social Change. In *Spirit, Space and Survival: African American Women in (White) Academe,* ed. Joy James and Ruth Farmers, 63–82. New York: Routledge.

Sharff, Jagna, and Hanna Lessinger. 1994. The Academic Sweatshop: Changes in the Capitalist Infrastructure and the Part-Time Academic. *Anthropology Today* 10 (5): 12–15.

Snyder, William T. n.d. *Toward a Climate for Enhancing Diversity on the UTK Campus.*
Knoxville: University of Tennessee, Knoxville.

Vincent, Joan. 1991. Engaging Historicism. In *Recapturing Anthropology: Working in
the Present,* ed. Richard G. Fox, 45–58. Santa Fe, NM: School of American Research
Press.

Women's Review of Books. 1996. Gorilla in the Midst. 13 (5): 31–32.

Chapter 13: A Labor of Love

NOTES

1. In a June 21, 2002, e-mail message, Linton Freeman, a prominent sociologist who has
made a major contribution to the study of social networks, wrote that after serving in the
Navy during World War II he transferred from the University of Chicago to Roosevelt
College (later to become Roosevelt University) because he wanted to study with St. Clair
Drake, who had been a graduate student at Chicago when Freeman was an undergraduate.
Freeman wrote, "[A]fter all my years in academe, I remember Drake as the best lecturer
I ever heard. He would begin a fifty-minute lecture at, say, 9 A.M. The subject might be
something like the difference between Malinowski's and Radcliffe-Brown's conceptions of
function. There would be perhaps 35 students present at the beginning. At the end of the
50 minutes Drake would typically be so wound up that he would not hear the class bell;
he would lecture right on through it. One or two students might leave for other classes.
The rest of us would remain, spell-bound. The lecture would continue right through the
10:50 bell, but at that point another lecturer and a new bunch of students would demand
the classroom. So all but a few of us would get up and walk out into the hall. Drake stayed
with us and his lecture never missed a beat. The whole class would follow Drake very
slowly down the hall, up three flights of stairs, and as far as his office door. Most of us
would stand there in the hall for maybe another hour; no one was willing to miss any
part of Drake's extended lecture. It is no wonder that Ewart Thomas characterized him
as the 'preacher man' in his eulogy" (Baber 1999).

2. The ABA/Eleggua Project group was multiracial but predominantly African American. At the Havana hotel where we stayed, the service some of us received in the dining
room left a great deal to be desired, to put it politely. A white Cuban waiter treated a
number of us quite rudely as though he felt we did not belong there and should not be
treated as guests. I remember one incident in particular that was upsetting. A group of us
wanted to have dinner together, so we put two or three tables together. Then we asked the
waiter to clear the extra tables, which still had dirty dishes and napkins left from guests
who had left. The waiter had such a nasty attitude and told us that we were not supposed
to move the tables and that we would have to eat at the tables that were already cleaned in
other parts of the dining room. That meant that we would not be able to sit together in the
larger group. After that incident, we began comparing our experiences and realized that
the waiter resented having to serve us. Race and color were at issue, yet this was Cuba not
the United States, where Denny's has been sued for the discriminatory treatment meted
out to black customers. It was obvious that the hotel staff was not accustomed to serving

black folk in more than very small numbers, if that. For more on tourist apartheid, see Sawyer (2006, 108–10).

3. I say "rehearsed" here to refer to that first public performance of "Three Women, One Struggle" in 1988, because it gave me the confidence to undertake a more full-fledged dramatization, a one-woman show, without a hard copy of the script and with simple props, music, and body language choreographed to mark the character shifts at the Black Cultural Festival in Dayton, Ohio, during summer 1990. I would like to thank Marvin Haire, former Dayton community activist, Pan-African political scientist, and friend, for making that performance possible. I really appreciate his openness to blurring the boundaries between anthropology and political science and between academic social science and the real world of struggle, including the realm of cultural politics. That openness was expressed again in spring 2002 when he presided over the thirty-third meeting of the National Conference of Black Political Scientists (NCOBPS), whose theme was "Interdisciplinary Approaches to the Study of Black Politics."

4. My husband's surname is Conwill. Together with our three sons, we are the Harrison-Conwill family. Not uncommonly, I am called Faye Conwill, and people who know me as Faye Harrison call my husband William Harrison. We both prefer our own family names. At the time of my International Women's Day performance, William was working with a group of homeless people who were being assisted and settled by a municipal program. The program hired him, a counseling psychologist, to offer psychoeducational services.

5. For an excellent analysis of the Rainbow Coalition as a new social movement, see Collins (1986).

REFERENCES

Aschenbrenner, Joyce. 1999. Katherine Dunham: Anthropologist, Artist, Humanist. In *African-American Pioneers in Anthropology,* ed. Ira E. Harrison and Faye V. Harrison, 137–53. Urbana: University of Illinois Press.

Baber, Willie L. 1999. St. Clair Drake: Scholar and Activist. In *African-American Pioneers in Anthropology,* ed. Ira E. Harrison and Faye V. Harrison, 191–212. *Southern Anthropological Society Proceedings,* no. 28. Urbana: University of Illinois Press.

Buck, Pem Davidson. 2001. *Worked to the Bone: Race, Class, Power, and Privilege in Kentucky.* New York: Monthly Review Press.

Clifford, James. 1988. *The Predicament of Culture: Twentieth Century Ethnography, Literature, and Art.* Cambridge, MA: Harvard University Press.

Collins, Sheila D. 1986. *The Rainbow Challenge: The Jackson Campaign and the Future of U.S. Politics.* New York: Monthly Review Press.

Deloria, Ella Cara. 1988. *Waterlily.* Lincoln: University of Nebraska Press.

Dominguez, Virginia. 2000. For a Politics of Love and Rescue. *Cultural Anthropology* 15 (3): 361–93.

Drake, St. Clair. 1954. Value Systems, Social Structure and Race Relations in the British Isles. PhD diss., Department of Anthropology, University of Chicago.

Dunham, Katherine. 1969. *Island Possessed.* Chicago: University of Chicago Press.

Harding, Sandra, ed. 1993. *The "Racial" Economy of Science: Toward a Democratic Future.* Bloomington: Indiana University Press.

Harrison, Faye V. 1982. Semiproletarianization and the Structure of Socioeconomic and Political Relations in a Jamaican Slum. PhD diss., Stanford University.

———. 1990. Three Women, One Struggle. *Transforming Anthropology* 1 (1): 1–9.

———. 1993. Manet Fowler: Living, Surviving, and Celebrating Professional Commitment to Anthropological Practice. Unpublished manuscript.

———. 1995a. Auto-Ethnographic Reflections on Hierarchies in Anthropology. *Practicing Anthropology* 17 (1–2): 48–50.

———. 1995b. "Give Me That Old Time Religion": The Genealogy and Cultural Politics of an Afro-Christian Celebration in Halifax County, North Carolina. In *Religion in the Contemporary South: Diversity, Community, and Identity,* ed. O. Kendall White Jr. and Daryl White, 34–45. Athens: University of Georgia Press.

———, ed. 1997a [1991]. *Decolonizing Anthropology: Moving Further toward an Anthropology for Liberation.* 2nd ed. Arlington, VA: American Anthropological Association.

———. 1997b [1991]. Ethnography as Politics. In *Decolonizing Anthropology: Moving Further toward an Anthropology for Liberation.* 2nd ed. Ed. Faye V. Harrison, 88–109. Arlington, VA: American Anthropological Association.

———, ed. 2005. *Resisting Racism and Xenophobia: Global Perspectives on Race, Gender, and Human Rights.* Walnut Creek, CA: AltaMira Press.

Harrison, Faye V., and Ira E. Harrison. 1999. Introduction: Anthropology, African Americans, and the Emancipation of a Subjugated Knowledge. In *African-American Pioneers in Anthropology,* ed. Ira E. Harrison and Faye V. Harrison, 1–36. Urbana: University of Illinois Press.

Harrison, Ira E., and Faye V. Harrison, eds. 1999. *African-American Pioneers in Anthropology.* Urbana: University of Illinois Press.

Hurston, Zora Neale. 1935. *Mules and Men.* Philadelphia: Lippincott.

Sawyer, Mark Q. 2006. *Racial Politics in Post-Revolutionary Cuba.* Cambridge: Cambridge University Press.

Smith, Raymond T. 1987. Hierarchy and the Dual Marriage System in West Indian Society. In *Gender and Kinship: Essays toward a Unified Analysis,* ed. Jane Fishburne Collier and Sylvia Junko Yanagisako, 163–96. Stanford, CA: Stanford University Press.

Ulysse, Gina. 2001. A Poem about Why I Can't Wait. In *The Butterfly's Way: Voices from the Haitian Dyaspora in the United States,* ed. Edwidge Danticat, 209–20. New York: Soho.

———. 2005. My Country in Translation. In *Resisting Racism and Xenophobia: Global Perspectives on Race, Gender, and Human Rights,* ed. Faye V. Harrison, 209–11. Walnut Creek, CA: AltaMira.

Williams, Brackette. 1996. Skinfolk not Kinfolk: Comparative Reflections on the Identity of Participant-Observation in Two Field Situations. In *Feminist Dilemmas in Fieldwork,* ed. Diane L. Wolf, 72–95. Boulder, CO: Westview.

Index

ABA/Eleggua Project group, overview of, 289, 343–44n2
Abrahams, Roger, verbal performances, 190
Abu-Lughod, Lila: diversity in academia and, 34; writing against culture, 35
academia: academic plantations in, 127; advising the Social Science Research Council (SSRC), 267–68; affirmative action in, 274, 296; balancing career, family, and civic participation in, 295–99; bifurcated positioning, 275–77; black women's status in, 272, 276–77, 279; commodification of "stars," 275; conservative backlash within, 269; corporate capital, 270, 273–74; crisis of native/subaltern intellectuals, 268–69; desegregation court order in, 273; diversity climate in, 267–81; FIPSE program, 274; hostility in, 273, 276; labor markets, 270, 276; mixed messages about diversity, 274–75; peripheralization in, 277–79; proactive anthropology, 280–81; publish or perish in, 278; racial division of intellectual labor in, 276, 278; racialized and gendered politics of reception, 270; racism in, 272, 278; social justice in, 295; teaching as vocation and site of praxis in, 261–66
activism: community development work as, 32; participant-observation, 32; political organizing within the profession, 47; transnational strategies of, 232–33
advocacy research: changing regional political economy, 251–53; decolonization of

knowledge, 242–43; human rights struggles from local to global, 246–48; intensified abuse of human rights, 244–45; organizing in the postmodern South, 249–55; overview of, 238–40; political culture of achievement, 245–46; problems in coalition politics, 254–55; promoting a critical "Native Anthropology," 242–43; responsibility of social researchers in the age of recolonization, 243–44; transborder political projects, 253–54; vulnerabilities of regional and global coalitions, 248–49
African and African-American Studies (AAAS) Program, support of, 238
AIDS/HIV: incidence of, 96; risk-taking behaviors and illegal economic activities, 224
Alternative Women in Development (Alt-WID), feminist research, 233
Alvarez, Robert: anthropology's diversity, 275; demographics of race, 34; "Presidential Session" withdrawal, 268–69
American Anthropologist: Contemporary Issues Forum: Race and Racism, 41, 43; historical survey on cross-subfield collaboration and synthesis in, 40
Amnesty International: Jamaican government, 154; human rights violations, 253; state repression, 147
Angela, Frances, English photographer, 16
anthropological knowledge, peripheralization and decolonization of, 17
anthropological praxis: history of black

FAYE V. HARRISON is a professor of anthropology, director of African American Studies, and affiliate faculty member in the Center for Latin American Studies and the Center for Women's Studies and Gender Research at the University of Florida. She is editor of *Resisting Racism and Xenophobia: Global Perspectives on Race, Gender, and Human Rights* and coeditor of *African-American Pioneers in Anthropology.*

The University of Illinois Press
is a founding member of the
Association of American University Presses.

Composed in 10.5/13 Adobe Minion Pro
by Jim Proefrock
at the University of Illinois Press
Manufactured by Sheridan Books, Inc.

University of Illinois Press
1325 South Oak Street
Champaign, IL 61820-6903
www.press.uillinois.edu